MW01092495

BUILDING FOR WAR

BUILDING FOR WAR

*The Epic Saga
of the Civilian Contractors
and Marines of Wake Island
in World War II*

BONITA GILBERT

CASEMATE
Philadelphia & Oxford

Published in the United States of America and Great Britain in 2012 by
CASEMATE PUBLISHERS
908 Darby Road, Havertown, PA 19083
and
10 Hythe Bridge Street, Oxford, OX1 2EW

Copyright 2012 © Bonita Gilbert

ISBN 978-1-61200-129-6
Digital Edition: ISBN 978-1-61200-141-8

Cataloging-in-publication data is available from the Library of Congress and
the British Library.

10 9 8 7 6 5 4 3 2 1

Printed and bound in the United States of America.

For a complete list of Casemate titles please contact:

CASEMATE PUBLISHERS (US)
Telephone (610) 853-9131, Fax (610) 853-9146
E-mail: casemate@casematepublishing.com

CASEMATE PUBLISHERS (UK)
Telephone (01865) 241249, Fax (01865) 794449
E-mail: casemate-uk@casematepublishing.co.uk

Frontispiece: Only an inscription on a coral rock on Wilkes Island, etched by an unknown
American prisoner, or prisoners, before the October 1943 massacre—"98 U.S. PW
5-10-43"—remains to mark their presence on the atoll. *Author's collection*

CONTENTS

IN MEMORY OF MY FATHER, TED OLSON

PREFACE

I started looking for my family's Wake story a few years after my father died, beginning with a box of old papers. As many such searches go, I found little of what I sought, but a great deal more than I expected. As my family's story grew, so did my search. Many other families and survivors offered up letters written on onionskin paper, diaries smuggled through prison camps, and yellowed newspaper clippings pasted into disintegrating scrapbooks. My search expanded to archival collections and the records of Wake's primary contracting company in 1941, Morrison-Knudsen Company. Correspondence and documents revealed the complex calculations behind the projects, the challenges and frustrations of the economic moment, and the rewards and losses that resulted from risks taken. I also met and corresponded with a number of the survivors who shared their stories with me. Over the years, they have "agreed to disagree," on events, but the discrepancies proved too great for me. For this work, I elected to rely on contemporary primary sources. They allow me to tell an old story from a new perspective, free of the distortions of memory and the baggage of hindsight.

The dramatic elements of the Wake Island story have often overshadowed a key, underlying question: Why Wake? In seeking to answer that question, secondary sources (with the very valuable baggage of hindsight) proved essential. I chose to focus much of this book on the months preceding the U.S. entry into the Pacific war in order to provide that background and to tell a civilian story that was more than just a backdrop to military action. The narrative follows members of my family and their friends and fellows as momentous historic events unfold around them. I have reproduced their informal letters and diary entries, including errors and variant spellings, as they were written. These people are active participants: their choices have consequences and their letters and diaries mirror the moments.

ACKNOWLEDGMENTS

I AM MOST GRATEFUL TO THE MEN WHO WROTE THE LETTERS AND diaries before and during the war and to those who saved and secured the record. In my family I am indebted to the late Harry Olson, Ted Olson, and Katherine (Olson) Madison, as well as Donna Olson Barrigan and Dorothy Olson.

Thanks also to the many others who also wrote down their thoughts and experiences and to their family members for sharing those precious letters and diaries: Peter Russell, Stephanie Perssons, Mary-Anne Collins, Joe McDonald, Jim Bair, Artys Hoskins, and Arlene Smalley. For fleshing out my family's stories, I thank Donna Barrigan, the late Walter "Swede" Hokanson and Mae (Hokanson) Dukes, June (Hokanson) Hohner, and Bethene Schlicker, daughter of Eudelle (Russell) Olson. Ed Harvey and Pat McGee shared valuable photographs, Floyd Forsberg shared important trial transcripts and family documents, Dorothy Mitchell Irwin and Mary Berg offered firsthand Pearl Harbor recollections, and Pam McClary and Robert Rust generously granted me open access to Harry and Ann Morrison's personal papers. Thanks also to Leilani Magnino, Dee Leavitt, and the late Bob Ward and Bea Ludington.

While I used oral histories and memoirs only sparingly, my heartfelt gratitude goes to the Wake survivors who shared their stories with me, especially Lloyd Nelson, Leroy Myers, Joe Goicoechea, Joe Miller, Marshall Sturdevant, Gary Rogde, J. O. Young, Oral Nichols, Herb Brown, Jim Allen,

Gus Priebe, Mick Johnson, Russell Thomas, Glenn Newell, Frank Mace, Dar Dodds, Tony Serdar, Ed Doyle, and Suey "Eddie" Lee, through his daughter, Lana Lee. Sadly, some of the fellows have passed away during the writing of the book. These men and others whose stories I have read enriched this book immeasurably: I do not quote them, but they are right around the corner, on the next bunk, or just coming up the road on Wake.

Thanks to historian Greg Urwin of Temple University, author of *Facing Fearful Odds* and *Victory in Defeat*, for fielding my frequent queries, sharing sources, and for offering suggestions and continued support for my project; Bill Kauffman for sharing interviews and stills from his 2002 film, *Those Who Also Served*; Kurt Schweigert of TEC, for a copy of his 2008 inventory of the Wake Museum (with permission); the late Roger Mansell and Wes Injerd for their invaluable POW research and access to databases; Fumihiko Mori for translations; and Daniel Pope, Glenn May, Jeff Hanes, and Alan Kimball of University of Oregon for suggestions and support.

A key component of this project has been access to records. I am grateful to Alice Ingham and June Faubion for sharing records and contacts from the Survivors of Wake, Guam, and Cavite. Many thanks to Bruce Walters and Jerry Yantek of the Records Division of URS Corporation for locating and granting open access to the records of the Morrison-Knudsen Company in Boise, Idaho, over four years, and to URS Corporation for permission to use the records. Thanks also to Lara Godbille and Gina Nichols at the U.S. Navy Seabee Museum at Port Hueneme, California; Robert Glass at the National Archives, Pacific Region, San Francisco; Carolyn Bowler at the Idaho State Historical Society; and Paula Dasher at the Coeur d'Alene Public Library.

Thanks to the 611th Air Support Group under the command of Colonel Robyn Burk for inviting me to accompany their team to Wake in 2011 to support the COMPACAF tour, and to Chugach Federal Solutions, Inc. the present contractor on Wake. My "alter world" friend, Barbara Bowen, was my eyes and ears on Wake for years, and I am deeply grateful to her for generously sharing sources, contacts, and an abiding passion for Wake's history and future. Thanks to the Joint POW-MIA Accounting Command at Joint Base Pearl Harbor Hickam for its current mission on Wake and openness to sharing sources.

Finally, I am grateful to family and friends, including many in the "Wake Family" who shared my quest, and my personal family members, for their help and support. Last and most, thank you, Tom Gilbert, for your eagle eye, your frequent technical rescues, and your unwavering love and support.

BONITA GILBERT
September 2012

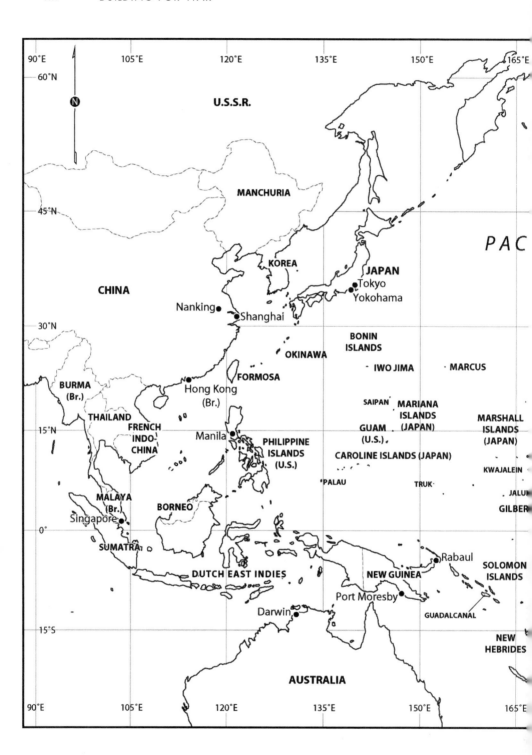

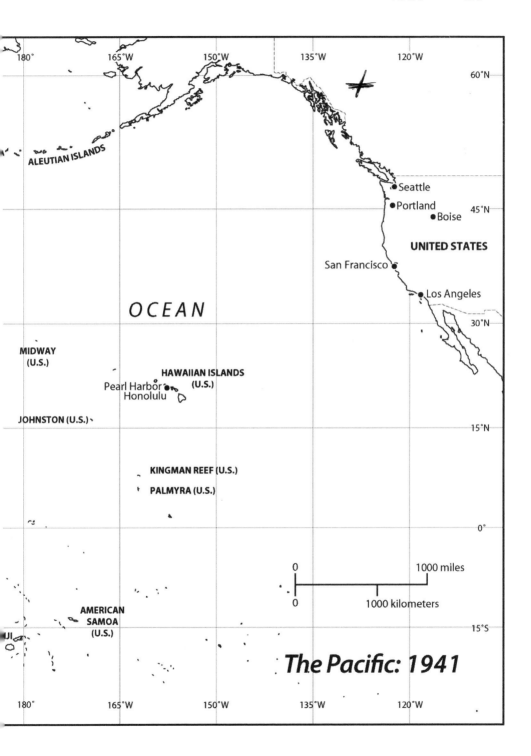

The Pacific: 1941

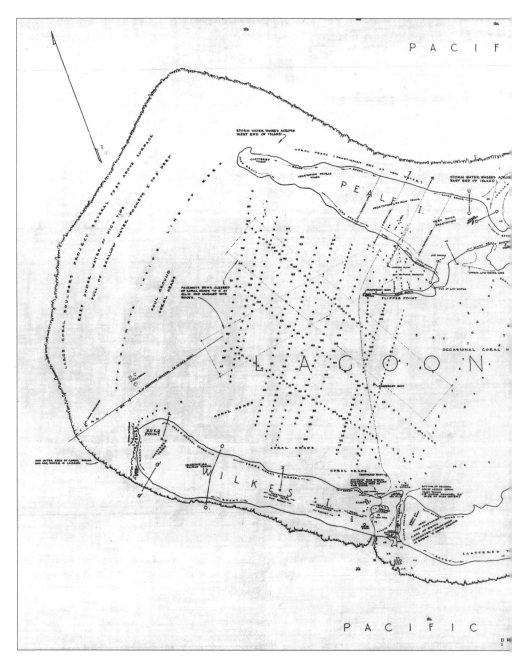

This detailed map shows Wake Island in 1935 prior to any human development. Drawn by Lt. C. W. Porter during a top-secret navy survey that took place under the cover of the first Pan American Airways visit, this map marks the beginning of military interest in the strategic potential of the atoll (see Ch. 2, page 29). The upper right legend shows detailed grade, elevation, coral strata, and vegetation for various locations. Little grew on

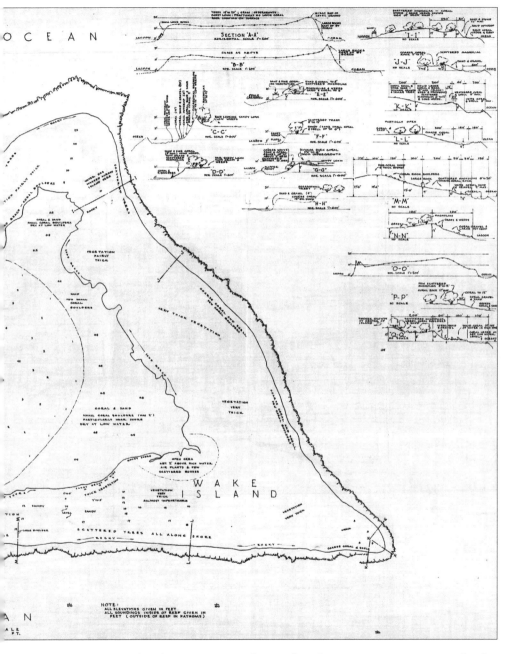

Wake but "weeds, tuft grass & scattered magnolias" but many areas were covered with thick vegetation, "almost impenetrable" where the E-W runway would eventually be built. Porter notes where storm water washes across the island and signs of inundation, as well as the coral heads, tough coral ledges, and "foul grounds" in the lagoon. A whale skeleton rests on the east end of Peale; a "Jap well" is marked on the east end of Wilkes.

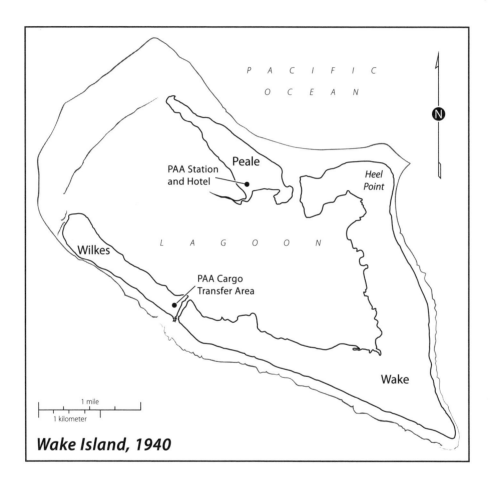

Wake Island, 1940

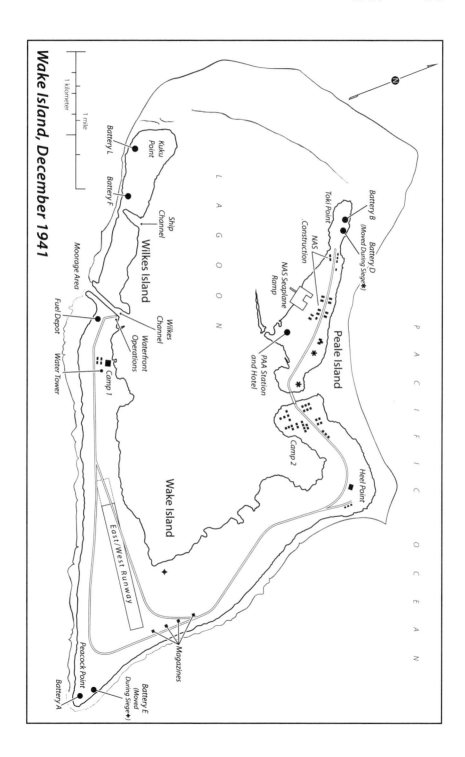

Wake Island, December 1941

1 kilometer
1 mile

Battery L
Kuku Point
Battery F

Ship Channel
Wilkes Island

Moorage Area
Fuel Depot
Water Tower

Wilkes Channel
Waterfront Operations
Camp 1

L A G O O N

Toki Point
Battery B
Battery D (Moved During Siege✱)
NAS Construction
NAS Seaplane Ramp
PAA Station and Hotel
Peale Island
Camp 2
Heel Point

Wake Island

East/West Runway

Magazines
Battery E (Moved During Siege◆)
Peacock Point
Battery A

P A C I F I C   O C E A N

N

This routine blueprint drawing of Wake shows construction progress to date, a date that would soon make this map historically significant. CPNAB engineer C. P. Schoeller created the map and accompanying graphs to depict the status of naval air station projects, airstrips, and dredging, on average about 65% complete on the eve of war (see Chapter 9, page 192). Note the extensive dredging and blasting in the lagoon, which created safe "runways" for seaplanes through the maze of coral heads, the top-priority ship channel being dug through the middle of Wilkes, and the four high explosives magazines dotting Wake's east shore that would be converted to command posts and hospitals during the coming siege.

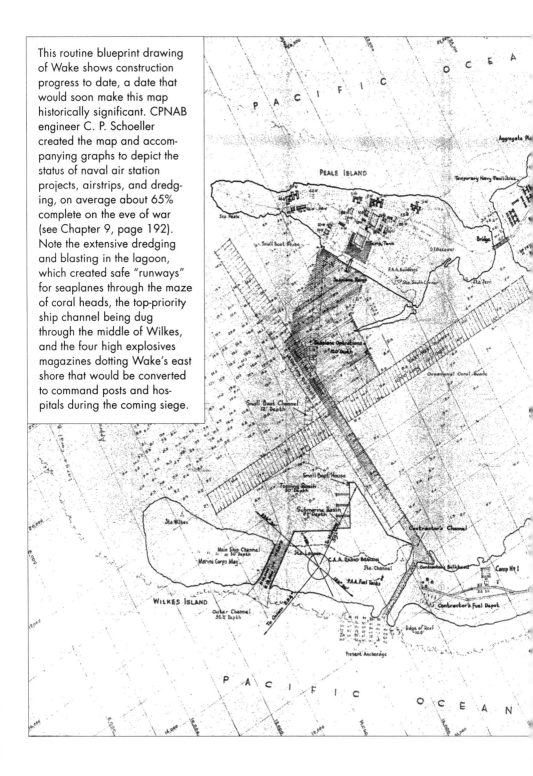

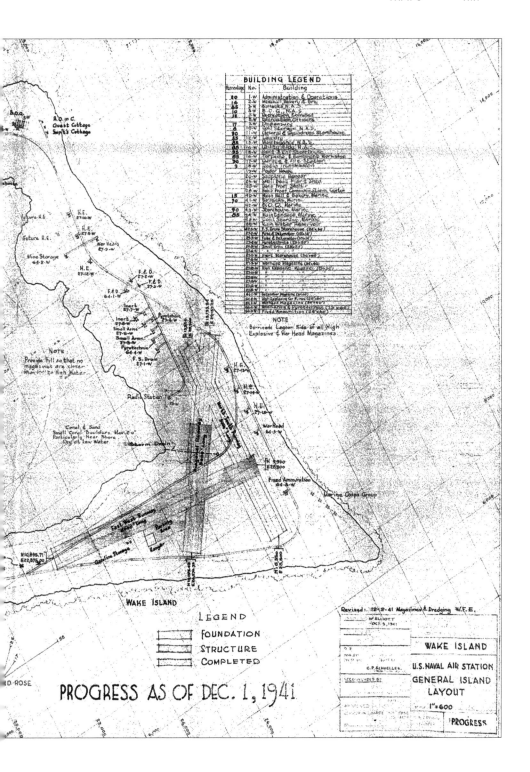

PROGRESS AS OF DEC. 1, 1941

INTRODUCTION

―――――――――――――

WAKE ISLAND TEEMED WITH ACTIVITY DURING THE FIRST WEEK OF December 1941. More than a thousand civilian contractors swarmed over the atoll, working around the clock to build barracks and storehouses, grade runways, dig channels, and dredge coral for a naval air base. Several hundred military personnel scrambled to set up communications, shore batteries, and antiaircraft guns along the V-shaped atoll. Ships rocked offshore, Pan American Clippers shared the lagoon with navy patrol planes, Flying Fortresses stopped just long enough to refuel on their way to the Philippines, and a squadron of Wildcat fighters flew in off the aircraft carrier USS *Enterprise*. Sitting two thousand miles west of Hawaii and just six hundred miles north of Japan's Marshall Islands, Wake was well on its way to becoming a fully-equipped forward base for the United States Navy as it prepared for eventual war with Japan. At the end of that busy week, the civilians and most of the military personnel enjoyed a rare day off. The next day, December 8, war came suddenly and without warning to Wake. Across the international date line, it was December 7, 1941, the day that would live in infamy. For the civilian contractors on Wake Island, it was the beginning of a long nightmare.

Dwarfed by the ever-expanding Pearl Harbor library, a modest shelf holds a growing collection of works on Wake Island and the fate of the Americans caught there. The Marine Corps-led defense of the atoll dominates the accounts of Wake. The surprise attack, sixteen-day siege, and bitter surrender to Japanese forces comprise a campaign small enough in geography, time,

1

and sources to recount in detail, yet large enough in drama and heroism to swell the hardest heart. The stories told by civilian survivors also dwell on those dramatic December days and the dark years of internment as prisoners of war. By all accounts, the months leading up to December 1941 serve as a mere preface to the main event. This book is the first to focus on the story of the civilian contractors who took a risk, came to Wake, and built a naval air base from scratch, only to see it (and themselves) snatched away by a grossly underestimated enemy. The story sheds new light on why the Americans were taken by such surprise the day the sky fell in.

The massive defense contracts funded by Congress at the end of the 1930s opened the door out of a decade of Depression, and American business and labor eagerly seized the new opportunities. War raged in Europe and Asia, close enough to warrant throwing off the cloak of isolationism, but far enough away for Americans to enjoy the fresh air of economic stimulation. The return of jobs and decent wages and the commitment to national military strength brought a flush of optimism to the nation. The mainland defense jobs quickly attracted mobs of men, but jobs in the Pacific demanded more careful consideration. The distance and dangers of the farthest Pacific island jobs meant greater risk for greater reward, but many workers from the Northwest and California took the plunge, confident that Uncle Sam would take care of the "danger" aspect. Distance and time were the chief concerns for many men and their families: homesickness made many a heart grow fonder, but the long separation strained some relationships to the breaking point.

In the decades following World War II, historians have reexamined the debacle of Pearl Harbor from many perspectives, but paid scant attention to the angle represented by "Contractors Pacific Naval Air Bases" (CPNAB). In 1939, the U.S. Navy contracted with a consortium of civilian construction companies to expand the fleet base at Pearl Harbor and build strategic outlying bases, including Midway and Wake, far out in the Pacific. From 1939 to 1943, the civilian organization grew from three companies to ten, from five projects to dozens, and from a handful of men to tens of thousands. The unprecedented no-bid construction contracts grew from $15.5 million to $332 million at their termination in December 1943, making CPNAB the largest defense contractor in history, up to that time.[1] ($332 million in 1943 is equivalent to about $4.43 billion in 2012.) The prewar interaction between the CPNAB defense contractors and the navy on one of those projects, Wake Island, reveals prevailing attitudes and inefficiencies that contributed to the lack of readiness for the coordinated Japanese strike in the Pacific in December 1941.

The only full-length treatment of the CPNAB history, now long out of print, was commissioned by the CPNAB executives in 1944: David O. Woodbury's *Builders for Battle: How the Pacific Naval Bases were Constructed* (E. P. Dutton and Co., 1946). Historians have regularly used Woodbury as a key source for the prewar defense contracts and projects, and his work provides many valuable details and a lively description of events. However, the contractors commissioned Woodbury to write their story, and his book lacks perspective and objectivity, particularly with respect to relations between the navy and contractors. The author was at once too close to principals and events, and too far from the inside stories. Writing in the final year of war, Woodbury was blocked from classified navy documents and correspondence, and unable or unwilling to seek out pertinent business details hidden in reams of company paperwork. Nearly all of the contractors had gone home by then; others, including the Wake prisoners, had yet to come home to tell their story. On a short leash, Woodbury related the joint efforts of navy officers and Pacific defense contractors as a string of heroic accomplishments. As for Wake, Woodbury blamed Congress for its inexcusably late start in appropriating base construction funds. "Because Capitol Hill dallied, the Japs stole from us an advance base with most of the heavy work done, fitted with much valuable equipment," wrote Woodbury. "Wake was the glory of the American fighting man but the shame of the sluggard country behind them."[2]

Congressional approvals and appropriations to fortify island bases in the western Pacific can only be considered "late" in hindsight. The capture of Wake was due to a far more complex set of circumstances, one that has its origins in the acquisition of an impossibly far-flung Pacific empire at the turn of the century and the obligation to protect it against an increasingly aggressive neighbor. Decades of underfunding and isolationism undercut American naval capabilities in the Pacific, but once Congress made the commitment to expansion of military defenses, the navy found itself swimming in a sea of red tape. Although time was of the essence, overlapping jurisdictions and interdepartmental frictions slowed the decision-making progress and complicated logistics. Then as now, defense contractors underwent careful scrutiny to ensure against shoddy construction or excessive profiteering at the public's expense. With the Nye Committee investigations of World War I munitions manufacturers fresh in the public memory, the CPNAB projects were subject to budgets and deadlines, strict government oversight, and layers of navy supervision that attended every plan and decision. In addition, the diplomatic and economic decisions of the Roosevelt administration heightened conflict with Japan rather than ameliorating it, and push came to shove before the Pacific bases were ready for battle.

The story of the Pacific defense contractors also reveals a prevailing national bias as it follows preparations for a war according to American strategy. New warships, planes bristling with hardware, and strategically located outlying bases were intended to intimidate Japan and protect U.S. interests in the Pacific. The nation and its military placed great faith in American technological superiority and its permanent lease on the moral high ground —dangerous preconceptions in an industrialized world. Racial bias blinded Americans to the possibility that the Japanese could develop and employ technology capable of besting their own. In *War without Mercy*, historian John Dower offers a compelling argument that Westerners shared this disparaging attitude toward the Japanese in the prewar period and consistently underestimated Japan's intentions and military capabilities. The fate of the men caught on Wake Island demonstrates the consequences of those dangerous preconceptions.[3]

While ostensibly built as defensive installations, the remote Pacific bases really had little in the way of practical defensive capabilities. On Wake frequent delays in approvals, altered sequence of the building program, and belated defensive measures demonstrate that the navy underestimated the potential for direct attack. In fact, Wake's primary role in the navy's secret offensive strategy was to serve as a base for the attack and seizure of bases in the nearby Japanese-held Marshall Islands once war began.[4] In theory, the base would be complete and the civilian contractors long gone by the time the fighting started. The navy had no contingency plans for the civilians in case of attack except to anticipate that some of them would volunteer to aid the defense. The possibility that Japan might capture the island was too remote to warrant consideration. The civilian contractors on Wake watched the marines arrive, heard the news on the radio, and worked at a feverish pace as the navy's demands multiplied during the fall of 1941, but they shrugged off distant dangers: Uncle Sam would take care of them.

The events that transpired in December 1941 were inconceivable to the band of contractors that first set foot on Wake Island nearly a year before and to the hundreds who followed as the months went by. Their job was to build an air base, and their battles were with the raging sea and the stubborn coral. Armed with dynamite, powerful machinery, and the can-do attitude that would carry over to the navy's seabees, the civilian contractors tackled the job they were hired to do during that year before enemy bombers dropped out of the clouds: carve out a military toehold in the middle of the vast Pacific.

PART I

Plans and Preparations

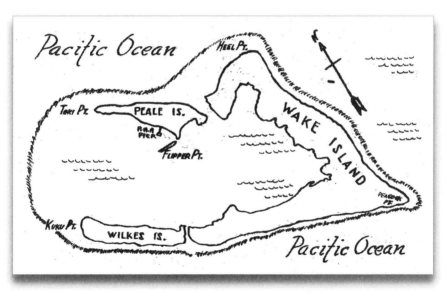

Wake Atoll, drawing in *Wake Wig Wag*, July 1941.—*McClary-Morrison Collection*

CHAPTER 1

ONE BIG OCEAN

―――――――――

WAKE ISLAND, OCTOBER 1940

THE TYPHOON CAME BOILING UP OUT OF THE WESTERN PACIFIC, A furious marriage of wind and water bearing down on the tiny toehold of land in its path. It pummeled Wake Island on October 19, 1940, with winds of nearly 140 mph and ten-foot waves. Welded by a thick coral limestone table to the top of a volcanic cone, the V-shaped atoll did not budge. Countless generations of experience had wired the feathered residents of Wake with early warning systems, and the frigate birds, boobies, and bosuns had long since flown out of harm's way. Hermit crabs scuttled off the beach in borrowed shells to ride out the storm, and the diverse reef residents sought their customary storm shelters in the lower shelves.

The only human residents of Wake in the fall of 1940 were two dozen Pan American Airways employees who feared for their lives as the second major storm in less than two weeks battered their little compound on Peale Island, the northern arm of the atoll. For them, the "gigantic toadstool on a slender stem" reaching twelve thousand feet to the ocean floor not only budged but also shook under the pounding. In 1935, the airline company had built a refueling and overnight base on Wake for its transpacific Clipper service, and in five years of weather data collection they had not clocked winds over 40 mph until this month. However, the large coral boulders thrown high up on the beach and a series of coral dikes indicated that severe weather had paid plenty of past visits to the atoll.[1] [In agreement with primary sources, the terms "Wake" and "Wake Island" will be used interchange-

9

ably for the entire atoll and the main islet and "Peale Island" and "Wilkes Island" will be used for the islet extensions, although they are not technically islands.]

The Pan American employees huddled in a concrete cold storage building as rain-lashed winds shredded scrubby trees, shattered windows, ripped roofs off buildings, toppled the station's direction finder and light beacon tower, and pushed structures off their foundations. Planks torn from the long seaplane pier tumbled out of the open end of the lagoon into the mouth of the storm. A fifteen-ton barge broke its mooring in the lagoon, crashed into the landing pier, and dropped a tractor overboard before the angry sea sucked the lighter out through the channel and threw it back onto the beach in a heap. A mile across the lagoon from Peale, the typhoon swept over the cargo transfer area on Wilkes Island with a violence that left the five-year-old operation utterly destroyed: broken boats and scows lay underwater and no pier remained standing.[2]

The ill-tempered glutton chewed up Wake, swallowed some, and spat out the rest, littering the narrow beaches with splintered wood, gasoline drums, and dead rats. As the surf burped and coughed and the birds returned to pick through the debris the next day, a shaken radio operator managed to contact the Pan American base at Midway Island to transmit the damage report to Honolulu. The airline's first priority was to repair this vital link in its Pacific chain and resume service, but Pan American's Honolulu office also was quick to notify Pearl Harbor and the operating base of Contractors Pacific Naval Air Bases (CPNAB), the navy's defense contractors. This was more than a courtesy: CPNAB was packing a big tool belt for its maiden voyage to Wake to build a naval air base, and the sooner the contractors arrived to help, the better for Pan American.[3] [As used herein "contractor(s)" may refer to contracting companies that are part of CPNAB or to individual employees working under contract for one of the companies.]

At the CPNAB operating base at Pearl Harbor, George Youmans relayed the news to the small knot of men who formed Wake's advance team. Youmans oversaw Morrison-Knudsen Company's share of the CPNAB defense projects, including Midway, Wake, and an underground fuel storage project on Oahu, the latter two of which were still in the planning stages. The three M-K projects were among more than a dozen in the Pacific Islands held by the five-company CPNAB consortium. Typhoon damage on Wake added another layer of problems to the contractors' plans. Less than two weeks earlier a gale had swept away every trace of a navy survey party's tent camp, which the contractors had planned to use for their initial base of operations on Wake. If there was any good news it was that the contractors themselves did not yet have anything on the island for the typhoon to destroy.[4]

Honolulu reporters and the Associated Press took note of Wake's typhoon, and the Hawaiian papers and a few on the West Coast carried the story, which was little more than a curiosity in the grand sweep of news in the fall of 1940. From Honolulu, Youmans wrote a detailed report of the damage to Harry Morrison, president of Morrison-Knudsen Company, in Boise, Idaho. Morrison-Knudsen had joined the CPNAB consortium just a few months earlier, and Morrison himself had just returned from a visit to assess M-K's share in the Pacific defense projects and the enormous challenges of the Wake job. From the start, two problems loomed large and they both emanated from the navy: delays in shipping and lack of firm plans for the facilities themselves. Typhoon damage on Wake was one more setback.[5]

PROJECT NO. 14

Naval Air Station, Wake Island, one of the main projects in a new, no-bid CPNAB defense contract signed in July 1940, took several months to get off paper and into action. That summer the Bureau of Yards and Docks had provided its chosen contractors with a short list of projected buildings and installations for Project No. 14 on Wake. The $7.6 million price tag approved and appropriated by Congress included $6 million for naval aviation shore facilities and $1.6 million for defense installations. With only this vague outline of the Wake project, a handful of men at the CPNAB operating base began to order equipment and supplies from the mainland for the voyage to the distant atoll, two thousand miles to the west. Meanwhile, the CPNAB operating committee, which included executives from each of the participating construction companies, prepared a plan of initial operations for Wake and prodded the navy for firm plans and drawings for the structural locations and layouts. Half a dozen other large-scale island projects were already underway and several new ones on the drawing boards. Back on the mainland, Harry Morrison tackled the personnel issue for Wake and M-K's other Pacific projects. A cadre of experienced, reliable key men was essential to organize and supervise the challenging Wake project, and time was of the essence.[6]

Much of Harry Morrison's success in the heavy construction business was due to his embrace of new technology, innovative approach to joint ventures, and commitment to hiring the best men for supervisory positions and holding on to them through thick and thin. The Morrison-Knudsen Company was formed in 1912 when Harry Morrison (with "no money, just guts") joined Morris Knudsen to expand Knudsen's small construction company. It did not take long for the young entrepreneur to make the transition from the hundred horses "broad of chest and stout of hoof" featured in the company's 1923 annual company photograph to the gas-powered machinery of the future. In the early 1930s, Morrison formed the Six Companies consortium that won the Boulder (Hoover) Dam contract with a bid of just under $50 million. Bidding with or against each other on the big government contracts of the Depression era, the Six Companies made money and employed thousands of men in tough economic times. M-K showed a profit every year except the "thin" years of 1932 and 1937. Throughout, Harry Morrison held on to seasoned, loyal M-K men who enjoyed a job security that was otherwise in short supply during the Great Depression. As the big dam contracts began to give way to defense contracts in 1940, M-K's growing share of the latter promised a steady stream of "thick" years ahead, "fed by the same inexhaustible springs of the national treasury," as a contemporary writer observed a few years later.[7]

For Project No. 14 and M-K's other Pacific island jobs, Morrison began to cull many of his own superintendents, foremen, and managers, and used his connections with powerful construction executives from the Six Companies to bring in more like them from outside the company. The untried conditions, remote locations, and long stretches of time away from the comforts of home demanded great fortitude and flexibility. High-quality supervisors ensured stability in the island workforce and the integrity required to complete the contracts on time and without overrunning costs. Although Morrison did not hire the outside men directly, his contacts and job offers built a strong basis for the process. One name high on Morrison's list of pending offers in October 1940 was Harry Olson, the rigging superintendent at Grand Coulee Dam in Washington state.[8]

HARRY B. OLSON

As a young man Harry Olson worked in the forests of the Pacific Northwest where his uncles ran a logging operation. In 1918 he left a young wife and son in Seaside, Oregon, to join the Marine Corps, serving with distinction as a corporal until his discharge in February 1919. After the war, Olson returned to the Northwest where he turned to work on the rivers, where there was "better pay than the woods" for a man with a growing family to support. He worked steadily, bought a house in Portland, Oregon, and the family moved to town so the children could attend good schools. Even during the lean years of the Depression, Olson always had a job and continued to expand his experience and skills.

In 1936 Olson traveled up the Columbia River from Portland to oversee a barge leased to the Bonneville Dam project and was hired on the spot to work on the dam. Harry and his wife, Katherine, moved to North Bonneville, bringing the second of their three children, Ted, to finish high school nearby, far from the distractions of the big city. Two years later, as the Bonneville project neared completion, the Six Companies joined with another group to win the contract for the main spillway dam at Grand Coulee, up the Columbia River in eastern Washington. The new consortium, Consolidated Builders Inc., brought many of the Bonneville men along, including Harry Olson.

Harry and Katherine moved upriver to Mason City (the "world's first all-electric city") at the base of Grand Coulee Dam in 1938. As she had at Bonneville, Katherine kept house for Harry in a tiny, one-bedroom, company bungalow where their stormy marriage often rattled the windows. During their long absences from home, family friends lived in the Portland house and cared for Donna, the youngest Olson, while she attended school. Jim, the eldest, attended Reed College, and took an apartment in town with his new wife. High school diploma in hand, Ted followed his parents to Mason City where he worked as an ironworker on the dam until enrolling at Washington State College in Pullman, Washington, in the fall of 1940 to study architectural engineering.

That fall, the towering Grand Coulee Dam was 98 percent complete, far ahead of its scheduled completion date of March 1942. In October Harry Olson received a surprising letter from Harry Morrison. Using his connections to come up with quality key men for the new Pacific Island jobs Harry Morrison had contacted the head of Consolidated Builders on Grand Coulee, Edgar Kaiser, son of the well-known entrepreneur Henry Kaiser. Kaiser recommended Olson on the basis of his supervisory experience and skills in cofferdam and crib construction in the swift waters of the Columbia River and released him to Morrison for the challenging work in the Pacific.

Harry Morrison quickly offered Olson an assistant superintendent's job on Wake Island. Olson would be "in charge of rigging, harbor work, boats and barges," the letter read, at better pay than he currently made. The offer included transportation, room, board, and laundry, and "a vacation with pay would be allowed and a bonus depending on how successfully his part of the work was done." Morrison projected the job would last for two years and Olson would have to report for work in Honolulu by November 15, just a few weeks away. "At present there is no place for the family."[9]

The offer was tailor-made for Harry Olson. The challenge, adventure, and long distance from his troubled marriage appealed to him. A second letter arrived from Pete Russell, another ex-Grand Coulee hand, now working for CPNAB in Honolulu: the job included a tax-free salary with all expenses paid, but Olson must make his decision quickly; time was of the essence. Katherine raised all manner of objections on the grounds of distance, danger, and family responsibilities, but Harry took closer counsel with one of his best riggers, Walter "Swede" Hokanson, whom he had hired a year and a half earlier. The men knew that Consolidated Builders would be ready to turn Grand Coulee over to the Bureau of Reclamation in less than a year. Hokanson had taken the civil service exam in anticipation of continuing on the dam with the Bureau, but both men suspected that the future now was in defense contracts. Harry made up his mind to take the Wake job and told Swede that as soon as the project opened up he would send for him. Hokanson later recalled Katherine's sharp retort: "Yes and the Japs will get you, sure as hell!"[10]

THE NEWS: FALL, 1940

In 1940, small towns got the big news from the radio and the nearest city newspaper. Residents of Mason City read the Spokesman-*Review,* delivered from Spokane, Washington, two hours to the southeast. In the fall of 1940, the impending presidential election between Franklin Roosevelt and Wendell Willkie and the war in Europe dominated the news. Headlines featured the German bombing of London, Britain's campaign in Iraq to thwart the Axis drive for the rich oil fields of Mosul, and the first peacetime draft in the United States. Over seventeen million American men aged twenty-one to thirty-five had registered with the Selective Service on October 16. At night, Edward R. Murrow, broadcasting from London on CBS, brought the fiery rain of German bombs right into American living rooms. While war reporting typically focused on bombs and battles, Murrow's London broadcasts offered harrowing accounts of London's "unsung heroes," caught in circumstances beyond their control. "Black-faced men with bloodshot eyes" fought the fires, and young women braved war-torn streets to drive ambulances carrying the wounded. Explosives "looked like some giant had thrown a huge basket of flaming golden oranges high in the air." However, when the radio was turned off and the paper was laid aside, Mason City, like most American towns, slept in peace and quiet that fall.[11]

News from East Asia seldom commanded the front pages, but most Americans knew that Japan had seized Manchuria in 1931 and had been at war with China since 1937. American sympathies generally lay with the Chinese and the American missionaries who wrote home with terrifying accounts of the war. As Japanese aggression escalated in the late 1930s Americans were aware of the transfer of U.S. naval forces to the Pacific and a growing embargo on strategic exports to Japan, but most remained indifferent to events the distant Far East. Headlines blazed, however, when Japan signed the Tripartite Pact with Germany and Italy in September 1940, an ominous development given the Axis defeat of virtually all of western Europe over the past six months.

In the few October weeks before Harry Olson was to leave the mainland for the Pacific islands, he and Katherine combed the Spokane *Spokesman-Review* to add some substance to their hazy visions of Pearl Buck's China and the South Seas isles of Robert Louis Stevenson. They found snippets: a photograph of a Japanese freighter loading scrap iron in Seattle to beat the embargo deadline, President Roosevelt vowing vaguely but vigorously that the United States would defend the hemisphere. An October 23 article "New Navy Bases in Pacific Plan" looked promising, but the statements of Frank Knox, the new secretary of the navy, evaporated into thin air: "We have Pacific bases . . . but need more—and we will have them. . . . How far flung these . . . must be awaits the outcome of events now in the making." The urgency surrounding Olson's new job did not allow for the luxury of time to explore the deep currents that underlay the Pacific situation, but they had a great deal to do with why he was going to Wake Island.[12]

RISING PACIFIC POWERS: 1898–1920

The United States needed defensive fortifications thousands of miles out into the Pacific because it had acquired possessions and interests there that required protection. Since the end of the nineteenth century both the U.S. and Japan had expanded their spheres of interest and influence in the region, and the escalation of Japanese expansion in the 1930s threatened the status quo in Asia and the western Pacific. For forty years, with varying degrees of effort and effectiveness, the United States had pursued a foreign policy that included maintaining the balance of power in Asia, protection of trade with China, and the recognition of the colonial claims of friendly European powers in the Orient. It was the American flags that flew over the Philippines and the Territory of Hawaii, however, that obligated the nation to take an armed stand in the Pacific.

The acquisition of such a distant colony as the Philippines, seven thousand miles from the West Coast, was less a product of objective intent than an opportunity that had come knocking in 1898. The decade of the 1890s was ripe with such opportunities for the United States as it claimed ownership of American Samoa and other island possessions and annexed the Hawaiian Islands in the summer of 1898. That year, the U.S. went to war with Spain in support of the Cuban revolution, beginning what Secretary of State John Hay termed a "splendid little war." In the course of the Spanish-American War, which ran from April to August 1898, the U.S. Navy sank the Spanish fleet in the Philippines as the navies of the European Great Powers jockeyed for position to watch. Elbowing aside the Filipino revolutionaries who had fought for years to topple their Spanish overlord, American forces presided over the capture of Manila, and the United States found itself the occupying power of the Philippines. The settlement of the Spanish-American War awarded Spain's former colonies of Puerto Rico and Guam to the victor, and, for the price of $20 million dollars, the entire Philippine archipelago. The treaty narrowly passed in the U.S. Senate, a vote that reflected the controversy over acquisition of foreign colonies. Despite the political division most Americans were imbued with a sense of manifest destiny and national unity after sharing the risks and now the rewards of the first war since their own divisive Civil War in the 1860s. The Philippines were the "pickets of the Pacific," declared one administration official, "standing guard at the entrances to trade with the millions in the Far East." A British admiral observed with unusual foresight, however, that by taking the islands America was "giving hostages to fortune, and taking a place in the world that will entail on her sacrifices and difficulties of which she has not yet dreamed . . . with outlying territories, especially islands, a comparatively weak power has facilities for wounding her without being wounded in return."[13]

With the members of the Great Powers club looking on to see how the new kid handled the ball, the United States had hoisted the Stars and Stripes over Manila, but encountered stubborn resistance from the Filipino population. The Filipinos had established a functioning government well before the treaty with Spain and expected independence with the expulsion of Spain from the Philippines, not just an exchange of colonial masters. Over the coming months, resistance and skirmishes, which were dismissed by some armchair American observers as "mere guerilla fighting," developed into full-blown war. Despite considerable public opposition back home, American reinforcements were shipped across the Pacific to secure the islands. After three years and a terrible toll in human lives the United States claimed victory in the Philippine-American War. Now in possession of a substantial foreign colony of its own the United States could claim status as a Great Power on the world scene, although the Philippines "could produce no logic of territorial proximity or military safety."[14]

While proving its imperialist prowess on the battlefield, the United States also earned its credentials at the diplomatic table. With European powers and Japan clamoring to piece-out a politically weak China, American diplomats engineered the Open Door policy that sought to protect equal access to trade while maintaining the territorial integrity of China. In 1900, when Chinese protesters rose up against Western influence, the United States joined with the other powers to put down the Boxer Rebellion and keep China's doors propped open to trade. America's stake in Asia and the western Pacific was cemented by its expansionist foreign policy and emergence as a Great Power at the very time that another emerging power, Japan, was asserting its presence in the region.

Japan's rapid embrace of Western technology and trade enabled it to rise as the dominant Asian power in the late nineteenth century. Japan had expanded its reach by asserting claims to nearby island groups in the 1870s, gone to war with China in the 1890s, and established its presence in Korea, yet its debut on the Great Power stage took the West by surprise. In competition with Russia over Manchuria, Japan went to war with the Russian Empire in 1904. The Russo-Japanese War ended in 1905 with Japan's defeat of the Russian Navy, and Japan staked its own claims to Manchuria and Korea. Japan's success at the expense of Russia upset the East Asian balance of power and established Japan as a military power of the first order.

President Theodore Roosevelt won the Nobel Peace Prize for his mediation of the Russo-Japanese conflict. The pattern was soon set for the United States to negotiate diplomatic deals that traded on the security of the Philippines, thousands of miles from home but virtually next door to Japan. Roosevelt acknowledged that, "from a military standpoint, the Philippines form our heel of Achilles." The adage often linked with his foreign policy—"Speak softly and carry a big stick"—would have a long shelf life in the Pacific, although the size of the stick varied over the coming decades. In effect, it said, take care to avoid provoking Japan, but make certain to show plenty of American muscle. When Roosevelt dispatched the U.S. Navy's Great White Fleet on a world tour in 1907, Japan took note of the display, as well as its departure. Japan, apparently not intimidated by a fleet that had no permanent presence in East Asia, went on to annex Korea in 1910.[15]

While keeping an eye on the Philippines and on China's nationalist revolution of 1911–12, the United States concentrated on expanding economic and political influence closer to home in Latin America. Japan also watched for opportunities to expand its sphere of influence in East Asia and the western Pacific. The United States assumed a neutral posture in European tensions and stayed aloof from the scaffolding of alliances that soon toppled and in August 1914 drove the European nations into war. Japan, however, joined the Allies in the Great War and was quick to take control of undefended German possessions in the Pacific, including a number of island groups north of the equator. The Marianas, Carolines, and Marshalls stood squarely in the path between the United States and the Philippines, with Wake just outside, and Guam, the largest of the Marianas, virtually surrounded. The United States entered the war in 1917, but focused its efforts on supporting the Allies in Europe and playing a key role in the postwar peace settlement. After the war, the League of Nations awarded the Pacific islands to Japan as mandates. Both nations were now firmly in the ranks of the Great Powers, but both had significant interests in the same Pacific neighborhood.

PACIFIC STRATEGY: 1905–1930

With its acquisition of the Philippines and Guam, the United States began to develop a Pacific strategy soon after the turn of the century. Strategists took note of Japan's victory over Russia in 1905, but anti-immigration riots in California in 1906–07 prompted the first war scare. The United States initiated strategic planning with the establishment of a joint board of the navy and army that frequently found themselves at loggerheads. The board anticipated that eventually Japan would attack the Philippines or other Western claims in order to expel foreigners from its sphere of influence. War Plan Orange, so named for the color code assigned to Japan, called for American forces (Blue) to make their way to the Philippines, reinforce and secure the territory, and then besiege, blockade, and bombard Japanese forces. The logistics of War Plan Orange remained topics of heated debate among strategists, but all agreed on the result: total victory, as befitted a Great Power. When Japan acquired the large Pacific island groups as mandates in the settlement of the war, the strategists had to take War Plan Orange back to the drawing boards. While Japan did not pose a direct danger to the United States, it could very well close off Western trade and access to China and Southeast Asia.[16]

In the aftermath of the horrors of the Great War, many nations held high hopes for international peace and placed great faith in the honorable intentions behind signatures. Most, including Japan, joined the League of Nations, but the United States did not for a number of reasons, including aversion to the league's principle of collective security. As an alternative to league membership, America sought world peace in the 1920s through disarmament agreements and pacts that renounced war. The Washington Naval Conference of 1922 limited naval construction among the five leading powers, including the United States and Japan, and many nations joined in postwar international commitments to peace such as the Kellogg-Briand Pact of 1928.

Japan's Pacific island mandates fell into a category that prohibited fortification, and the United States agreed to the same restriction for its western Pacific possessions by the terms of the Washington Naval Treaty. Behind closed doors, military strategists argued over the merits of a step-by-step approach or a "Through Ticket" rush to the Philippines for War Plan Orange. The Japanese-occupied islands compromised the "best line of approach" across the Pacific, and the prohibition against fortifying the Philippines and Guam made those American possessions virtually indefensible by any naval strategy. The Through Ticket strategy that dominated War Plan Orange into the early 1930s called for the fleet to speed to Manila when Japan attacked, even if it could not hope to get there in time to save the Philippines. To support either strategy the fleet required fueling bases en route as the navy had not yet perfected the technology of underway replenishment. Although the navy moved some of its fleet into the Pacific after the war, a substantial portion was retained in the Atlantic where traditional dangers had always dwelt. Until the late 1930s the United States Fleet was based in San Diego with a supply base at Pearl Harbor on Oahu. The independent and smaller U.S. Asiatic Fleet protected American nationals, property, and commerce in the Far East and Philippines, occasionally paying courtesy visits to Japan and other ports.[17]

"A MERE DOT"

In a footnote to the imperialist saga of 1898 little Wake Island also came into the possession of the United States. En route to join the fight in the Philippines in July 1898, Brig. Gen. F. V. Greene paused to claim the uninhabited atoll, which one contemporary writer described as "a mere dot on the waste of waters," for the United States. On January 17, 1899, Comdr. E. D. Taussig of the USS *Bennington* took formal possession of Wake Island by order of President William McKinley. Likely, ship crews took note of old shipwreck detritus on the beaches and breathed more easily when they were safely away. Thus Wake joined a short list of Pacific islands and harbors acquired by the United States in the late nineteenth century: Midway, Kingman Reef, American Samoa, Johnston and Sand Islands, and the Hawaiian Islands. "The little piece of American territory known as Wake Island will never cause any international trouble," wrote journalist M. A. Hamm in 1899. "Indeed, if the future is to be judged from past and present, it will never excite human interest." As America made plans for a transpacific cable to link the mainland with the Philippines officials briefly considered Wake for a cable station between Honolulu and Guam. However, an April 1899 report revealed that the coral reef was a "solid wall" surrounding the island and channel excavation would require up to two years and cost as much as three million dollars. The cable was eventually laid via Midway Island.18

Lonely Wake commanded little attention during the early decades of the twentieth century. Uninhabited, lacking fresh water and resources, and unapproachable by large ships because of the shallow reef that encircled it, the atoll was home only to birds, rats, and marine life. Seamen from the Marshall Islands visited to ravage the local bird population for feathers that found their way via Tokyo and London to New York hat-makers; Japanese fishermen occasionally came ashore to camp, likely consuming the cache of supplies left by General John J. Pershing in 1906 for "chance victims of shipwreck." The atoll's obscurity contributed to considerable name confusion on western charts. In 1568, Alvaro de Mendana of Spain had sighted and named it the Island of San Francisco, but the atoll acquired a variety of names over the ensuing centuries. Eventually it became known as Wake, named for a British captain who visited in 1796.[19]

A few ships called on Wake in the 1920s and sent sailors ashore in long-boats to run off steam or diligent scientists to take notes and collect specimens. The two islets appended to Wake's arms were named for American naval officer Charles Wilkes and naturalist Titian Peale, who had explored the atoll on a voyage in 1840. A field notebook from the 1923 *Tanager* visit, a joint Bishop Museum and U.S. Bureau of Biological Survey expedition, described the ruins of a substantial Japanese camp on Peale: two eighteen-by-twenty-foot, tin-roofed houses, two smaller buildings, and a tin-encased storehouse standing on poles. A tank, barrels, and clay jars suggested a rudimentary rainwater catchment system. Boxes, tin cans, metal kettles, bamboo trays, a pile of oakum, and a boat lay scattered in the vicinity. A Japanese inscription later translated stated that the camp had been abandoned in 1908. While naval observers surmised that the lagoon might serve as a protected refuge for flying boats, the shallow reef would bar the tenders that seaplanes depended upon. The Americans gave little thought to Wake as a potential pawn on a Pacific chessboard during these years: it "could have sunk beneath the water for all that war planners of the 1920s cared." Focused on the Through Ticket to the Philippines, war planners saw no role for Wake, and the navy dropped the atoll from its jurisdiction by the end of the decade. Wake fell under no departmental administration. The term "useless" was often used to describe the lonely possession.[20]

1930s: ISOLATIONISM AND WAR

Relations between the United States and Japan deteriorated in the early thirties as the global Great Depression spread economic distress and political upheaval throughout the industrial nations. With a burgeoning population, limited resources, and an increasingly militaristic government, Japan turned again to China in 1931 and within two years had seized Manchuria, where it set up a puppet state and extracted vast quantities of coal, iron, and timber. Japan embarked on a policy of expansive economic development and population resettlement in Manchuria and elsewhere within its sphere of control. Japan's policies effectively slammed closed the Open Door, but the U.S.

protest and moralistic policy of nonrecognition had no discernible effect on Japan. Rejecting the protests of fellow powers Japan withdrew from the League of Nations in 1933 (but kept the Pacific islands it held as League mandates), and dismissed other international treaty obligations including naval limitations. Japan sought economic growth and the security of a new pan-Asian order, but remained vulnerable because of its continued dependence on Western imports.[21]

Hard-hit by the Depression the United States turned inward and Americans became increasingly indifferent to world affairs. U.S. foreign policy lacked coherence and became increasingly reactive, responding to outside challenges as they arose. Isolationism and Depression-era budget cuts further limited naval expansion in the Pacific and the United States Fleet fell well below treaty strength. With diminished stick and dampened voice the United States tiptoed around confrontation in the Pacific. When Franklin Roosevelt took the helm in 1933, the domestic economy demanded his administration's full attention. While former Assistant Secretary of the Navy Roosevelt brought a firm commitment to isolationism he also supported building the navy up to treaty strength, both to revive the shipbuilding industry and to protect U.S. commerce on the high seas. In 1934, the president signed the Philippine Independence Act, which recognized the distant colony's independence to be effective July 4, 1946, after adoption of a constitution and establishment of a commonwealth government. In 1935, Roosevelt requested the largest peacetime defense budget in U.S. history.[22]

Still, Americans shrank further from foreign involvement in the mid-1930s. In 1934, the Senate's Nye Committee began investigation of munitions manufacturers ("merchants of death"), shipbuilders, and war profiteers during the Great War, and suggested unsavory collusion between business and government in drawing the country into the war against Germany. With the rise of fascist governments in Europe and the onset of the Spanish Civil War, Congress passed a series of neutrality acts in the second half of the decade. The neutrality legislation prohibited loans and shipment of arms to belligerent nations, that is, nations that the president recognized to be in a state of war. While the Nye Committee's findings had minimal effect on legislation, the press coverage of the congressional inquiry contributed to the isolationist mood that prevailed in the thirties. Most isolationists agreed on a fundamental aversion to U.S. involvement in foreign war and supported unilateralism, but most Americans were simply indifferent.[23]

Isolationists in Congress and the media called for the utmost caution in the Pacific, arguing that the best defense was to avoid provoking Japan. In a move to expand its Greater East Asia Co-Prosperity Sphere, Japan bombed Shanghai and Nanking in mid-1937, opening the Sino-Japanese War. The "China Incident" soon spread to Shanghai, the center of U.S. commercial interests in China. The United States protested, but maintained neutrality. In October 1937 President Roosevelt denounced the "epidemic of world lawlessness" that was threatening peace-loving nations. In a bold but vague speech Roosevelt suggested a quarantine to contain it, implying a radical change in U.S. foreign policy toward collective action, but his administration made no corresponding commitments. Indeed, by declining to give official recognition to the state of war between Japan and China the United States could continue to make loans and sell military hardware to China and still maintain trade with Japan. In an effort to deter escalating aggression, however, the Roosevelt administration began to employ economic sanctions against Japan starting with an embargo on export of aircraft in mid-1938. The embargo grew to encompass many materials vital to Japan's war effort: aircraft parts, various minerals and chemicals, aviation motor fuel and lube oil, and iron and steel scrap. In 1940 the United States Fleet moved into the Pacific for maneuvers and Roosevelt ordered the navy to transfer the fleet base to Pearl Harbor as another deterrent to Japanese aggression. Meanwhile, the navy and army urgently lobbied Congress to develop and expand the nation's defenses.[24]

The outbreak of war in Europe in September 1939 shocked Americans, but initially they felt secure with the insulation of distance from the conflict. Likewise they felt safely removed from ongoing Japanese aggression in the Far East. As the German war machine bore down on western Europe in 1940 Americans watched the collapse of the European order from across the Atlantic. Debates raged over the role of the United States in the growing conflagration and the measures required for adequate national defense. Congress passed appropriations for more ships, planes, and military bases, and passed the Selective Service Act, which would select draftees by lottery for twelve-month terms in defense of U.S. territories and possessions. The candidates in the presidential campaign of 1940 outdid each other to reassure voters that the United States was not going to war. "I will never send an American boy to fight in any European War," claimed the Republican challenger, Wendell Willkie. On October 30, 1940, Democratic incumbent

Franklin Roosevelt declared, "Your boys are not going to be sent into any foreign wars," and, three days before the election, "this country is not going to war."[25]

Although thousands of men had enlisted in the armed services, thousands more were still needed to man American defenses. Across the nation young men waited with mixed emotions for the initial Selective Service drawing on October 29, 1940. In the Sigma Alpha Epsilon fraternity at Washington State College, Harry Olson's son Ted breathed a sigh of relief when his number was not drawn, and he turned his attention to his father's new defense job somewhere out in the middle of the Pacific Ocean. A spin of the globe in the fireside room did not reveal Wake Island, but the broad expanse of blue looked inviting. With the European war dominating the news the Pacific seemed calm and quiet in comparison.

CHAPTER 2

OPPORTUNITY KNOCKS

THE PAN AMERICAN CONNECTION

THAT THE NAME WAKE ISLAND RANG ANY BELL FOR THE AVERAGE American in 1940 was due to publicity surrounding the new Pan American Airways seaplane service that connected mainland America with the Philippines. Pan American Clippers carried airmail, a few fortunate passengers, and the wistful daydreams of armchair travelers from San Francisco Bay to Manila and back, overnighting en route in Honolulu, Midway, Wake, and Guam. The route would extend to Singapore in 1941. The Pan American Clipper route traced a bright arc over a complex Pacific situation of which it was an integral part. It was not coincidence that the U.S. Navy slated the island pearls in the airline's Pacific necklace for future naval air bases.

When Pan American president Juan Trippe requested renewable, five-year leases on Wake and Midway from the secretary of the navy in October 1934 and inquired about obtaining a Pacific airmail contract, few in the government knew anything about either one of these dots on the map. Midway, the westernmost island of the Hawaiian chain, housed a small cable station; Wake, a further thousand miles southwest of Midway and on the far side of the international date line, housed nothing. However, Trippe's idea stirred some interest within the navy. Long restricted from strategic development in the Pacific, war planners chaffed at the difficulties posed by the long stretch of ocean strewn with Japanese possessions between the Hawaiian Islands and the Philippines: the Marshalls, Carolines, and Marianas, with Palau and Bonin islands completing the barrier. Given Japan's

25

abrupt withdrawal from the League of Nations and Washington Naval Treaty renegotiations, and the shroud of secrecy that hung over the mandates, many suspected that Japan was fortifying the islands, which would not bode well for War Plan Orange. The Pan American plan offered a back-door opportunity for the navy to gain toeholds in the mid-Pacific. In November 1934 the chief of naval operations (CNO) issued orders for the USS *Nitro* to visit Wake to conduct a preliminary survey in advance of the proposed Pan American project on its return voyage from Asia. The survey would address the "practicability of landing, anchoring, and servicing" naval aircraft in Wake's lagoon.[1]

The United States still officially held to the terms of the Washington Naval Treaty, which was scheduled to expire at the end of 1936. The treaty forbade military base development on U.S. possessions west of Hawaii, including Midway, Wake, and Guam, three islands now conveniently targeted for Pan American development of commercial seaplane runways and facilities. Commercial developments offered a head start on the remote islands, and the navy could quickly convert civilian facilities to military use if push came to shove in the Pacific. In the event of war with Japan, the navy's long-projected march across the Pacific required seizure or neutralization of Japanese possessions en route, and these island stepping-stones could provide the bases for support and attack. President Roosevelt placed Wake under the jurisdiction of the navy by executive order on December 29, 1934, and just as the *Nitro* survey wrapped up in early March 1935 the secretary of the navy issued Pan American Airlines formal permission to develop the island base.[2]

Confident of receiving the green light from the navy Pan American had been outfitting its supply ship since January 1935, and the SS *North Haven* departed San Francisco Bay on March 27 to set up initial bases on Midway, Wake, and Guam. The close connection between the commercial airline and the U.S. Navy continued with the voyage of the *North Haven*. The CNO and the chief of the Bureau of Yards and Docks issued orders to two naval engineers to join the Pan American expedition with the admonition that the navy was "particularly desirous of not giving any publicity whatever to there being any Navy Department representatives" on the trip to equip the islands for the commercial airline. Navy civil engineer corps (CEC) Lt. C. W. Porter boarded the *North Haven* in San Francisco to observe the unloading process at Midway and Wake, report on construction operations, and evaluate conditions on the remote atolls. Lieutenant W. E. Cleaves joined the expedition in Honolulu to study potential air operations at Midway and Wake. Both Pan American and the navy reaped benefits from the relationship: Pan American made use of the navy's preliminary *Nitro* study, the airline hosted the navy's secret passengers, and the confidential reports from the mission, including observations, maps, charts, photographs, and analyses added immeasurably to the navy's early knowledge of Midway and Wake.[3]

When the *North Haven* arrived at Wake in early May 1935 the impenetrable coral reef encircling the three-island atoll fiercely resisted its would-be human habitants. The shallow reef stretched out flat for several hundred feet offshore, dropped quickly to eighty feet, and then disappeared entirely, leaving no target for the supply ship's anchor. The Pan American scouting party found jagged coral boulders and thick, thorny brush covering the ocean-side shore on Wilkes Island, which offered the only break in the reef and feasible spot to land small craft. A mile across the lagoon, Peale Island boasted a twenty-foot elevation and more hospitable location for the fledgling air station. Short of a shipwreck, however, Peale was a challenge to reach with equipment and supplies, and so the captain held the *North Haven* off Wilkes as the men ferried equipment to Wilkes on small barges. Wake came as close to impossible as any piece of the Pan American plan, but impossible was not an option.[4]

Upon their arrival, the Pan American men threw up a radio shack to make contact via Midway and Honolulu with the PAA home base in Alameda, California, and with good weather, good luck, and ingenuity, the Wake station quickly took shape. Workers blasted a shallow channel between Wilkes and Wake to enable them to bring small boats and lighters inside the lagoon. They fashioned a short railway across Wilkes to roll cargo from the landing area over to the lagoon side, which they then floated over to Peale. Inside the lagoon divers planted dynamite to blast coral heads to allow unobstructed water for a seaplane runway. Finally, on August 17, 1935, a Pan American Clipper landed on the lagoon at Wake .[5]

By the end of 1935 Pan American Clippers were making the full round trip to Manila and back, and soon began to carry paying passengers in addition to the sacks of airmail that were the airline's bread and butter. A journalist and a photographer from National Broadcasting Company made the first round trip as nonairline passengers on board the *Philippine Clipper* in December 1935. Wedged between bulging mail sacks and crates of fresh produce, they sent radio broadcasts en route describing to an eager audience each adventurous leg of the journey and the local color at each stop. The public got its first glimpse of tiny Wake Island, a short hop of 1,182 miles from Midway, through these reports and a subsequent *National Geographic* article. The "model community" on previously uninhabited Wake surprised passengers and readers alike. William B. Miller wrote about the Chinese boy who offered a tray of cigarettes to disembarking passengers and stylish, personalized place cards at the dinner table in the recreation hall. Employees offered guests underwater goggles for viewing the colorful fish and corals in the clear lagoon water and air rifles for the nightly rat-shooting expeditions. A day tour of Wake revealed thousands of fearless terns resting and nesting, red-footed boobies preening and posing, and frigate and bosun birds soaring overhead. At sunset, the image of Old Glory coming down the flagpole and the Clipper afloat on the lagoon "caused a hot surge of pride as we realized that here, under the protection of that flag, an island, worthless to mankind until a short time ago," had been turned into a mid-ocean resting spot for travelers to "the Orient and beyond." By June 1936, guests enjoyed their overnight stay in a modern, prefabricated hotel with all the amenities.[6]

QUIET NAVY SURVEYS

Beginning in 1935 a number of naval and other government surveys of Wake underscored the important implications of the Pan American connection. With treaty restrictions officially remaining in force through 1936 the navy conducted the early surveys under utmost secrecy. After the treaty expired the expeditions received the navy's public seal of approval, but the data, interpretations, corresponding plans, and photographs remained strictly classified. The first of these surveys occurred with the *Nitro* visit from March 8–10, 1935. The party marked its visit by etching the ammunition ship's name and the date "3-9-35" into a sturdy rock on Wilkes Island. Lieutenant Jesse G. Johnson, a naval aviator temporarily attached to the *Nitro* expedition, carried out an airplane field investigation. Johnson made his observations aloft, flying over the atoll in a small aircraft brought along for that purpose. While seaplane operations were possible at Wake, conditions were far from optimal: the atoll lacked fresh water, and its sharp drop-off made it vulnerable to the close approach of deep-draft enemy ships. Johnson noted that Wilkes, lying nearest deep water, offered the best option for a channel into the lagoon.[7]

Lieutenant Porter, traveling with Pan American's *North Haven* expedition in the spring and summer of 1935, made the most thorough observations of Wake to date for the navy. His lengthy report, submitted in October 1935, included a daily log, maps, charts and data, lists of materials, drawings, and photographs. A large map to scale showed much of the atoll covered by "fairly thick vegetation," with "occasional magnolias," six to twelve feet tall, tuft grass, weeds, and thick undergrowth. The surface was entirely composed of coral, whether sand, gravel, boulders, ledges, outcroppings, weathered, white, coarse, or fine. Porter's observations and recommendations for dredging a channel into the lagoon particularly interested the Bureau of Yards and Docks. After charting depths, monitoring tides and winds, and estimating volume of removal, Porter concluded that dredging across the reef at the western opening into the lagoon would allow protection from prevailing northeast winds while leading directly to deep water in the lagoon. The extreme extent of the reef off Peale and strong winds that precluded ship approaches made the natural channel between Wake and Peale unusable. The channel between Wake and Wilkes offered a more favorable approach, but it was only six inches deep at low tide and led directly into a treacherous section of the lagoon. "In general," Porter wrote, "I believe that, as mentioned before, the islands lend themselves well to the development of an air base but the great amount of difficult dredging which would be required to provide a base for submarines, destroyers and similar ships, as well as the limited size of the lagoon, would not justify such development."[8]

Subsequent surveys added accurate soundings and borings to determine depths and characteristics of the substructure and methods for removal and concurred that a channel through the western opening was optimal. Pan American, continuing to blast coral heads in the lagoon with divers and dynamite, requested government-funded harbor developments at both Wake and Midway. (It is likely that this was a charade to cover navy-motivated development.) At the end of 1935 Rear Admiral William S. Pye, then director of the navy's War Plans Division, recommended building air bases on Wake and other U.S. atolls for use in War Plan Orange strategy: "We must get there first." Congress authorized surveys of the atolls in the River and Harbor Act of August 30, 1935, and when the U.S. Army Corps of Engineers conducted the survey of Wake in early 1936 they took into consideration navy suggestions for greater channel widths and lagoon depths. The chief of engineers argued that the "inherent benefits to the commercial interests of the Nation and the potential value . . . to the national defense" warranted construction of an entrance channel and turning basin at Wake Island. In the end, however, the Army Corps of Engineers approved Midway for dredging operations, but not Wake. Meanwhile, the navy sent Lieutenant W. L. Richards (CEC) to survey Wake in February and March 1936. Working alone, Richards accumulated more data and observations, adding to the volume of information on tiny Wake Island. In the revised War Plan Orange Wake would provide air cover for the navy's proposed thrust into the Marshall Islands to seize Japanese bases early in the war. The remote atoll was no longer "useless."[9]

U.S. NAVAL EXPANSION

At the end of 1936, with the expiration of treaty restrictions on expansion and island fortification, the navy more openly pursued development of the Pacific island bases. Naval officials, mindful of isolationists who objected to anything that smacked of warmongering, directed their lobbying effort at the defensive aspect where it stood the best chance of breaking the congressional logjam. Finally, in May 1938, Congress passed the Naval Expansion Act, which called for a 20 percent increase in the size of the fleet, the acquisition of three thousand scouting aircraft, and the establishment of a board to investigate expansion and new construction of bases in both the Atlantic and the Pacific. The secretary of the navy appointed Admiral Arthur J. Hepburn, outgoing commander in chief of the U.S. Fleet (CINCUS) and early proponent of naval development of Wake and other outlying Pacific islands, to chair the new investigative board.[10]

In June 1938, the Hepburn Board began its work. Over the next six months, board members pored over reports and traveled to the continental coasts to assess defenses, but relied on paper—charts, seaplane ranges, and environmental reports—to assemble the great Pacific puzzle. In December 1938, the board submitted its recommendations to the secretary of the navy for enlargement of existing bases and construction of new ones. Among those listed for earliest completion were air bases in Alaska and at Pearl Harbor and Kaneohe on Oahu, Midway, Wake, Johnston, Palmyra, and Guam. The board also recommended submarine bases for Midway, Wake, and Guam.[11]

Congress took up the Hepburn Board recommendations and the estimated price tag of $65 million to put them into effect, including $2 million for Wake Island. The item most likely to generate opposition was base development at Guam, which many considered to be too far inside the Japanese sphere to be anything but a dangerous provocation to Japan. Rear Admiral Ben Moreell, the chief of the Bureau of Yards and Docks, and other navy officials argued persuasively for the base construction and justified each cost. Moreell proposed using private contractors and cost-plus-fixed-fee (no-bid) contracts to expedite the work "in the interest of the national defense." After much debate in the House and Senate, Congress passed the bill in April 1939, and Public Law 43 authorized all of the bases excluding Guam. During the appropriations process, the House Appropriations Committee also excised the $2 million for aviation facilities at Wake, "without prejudice and pending the receipt of additional information." In May 1939, the Senate passed and President Roosevelt approved the $63 million appropriation for naval air bases on the mainland, Puerto Rico, Alaska, and the Pacific, except for Guam and Wake. Seaplane facilities for Wake Island dropped to priority number 730, "which means," Moreell lamented, "that in the ordinary course of events this development will not be reached for many years."[12]

Tasked with recommending facility development, the Hepburn Board did not study military emplacements or strategic developments for the Pacific islands. In early 1939 Chief of Naval Operations Admiral William D. Leahy initiated plans for defensive battalions to be sent to the outlying islands. By his directive Marine Corps Colonel Harry K. Pickett was dispatched to assess Wake, Midway, and Johnston Islands for "priorities, probabilities, positions, and personnel" for defensive installations with a specific allotment of weapons. Pickett's survey of Wake included assessment of Pan American Airways facilities and additional evaluation of tides, strata, and rainfall data (essential for drinking water supplies), as well as detailed recommendations for gun emplacements. These highly classified files built on the accumulation of data for War Plan Orange operations and remained securely out of the public eye.[13]

CONTRACTORS PACIFIC NAVAL AIR BASES

The navy split the defense contracts for the 1939 congressional appropriations into three regional groups: the mainland coasts, Alaska, and the Pacific. Congress authorized cost-plus-fixed-fee contracts for the outlying Pacific bases that Rear Admiral Moreel had requested "in the interest of speed." In contrast to the usual lump sum, competitive bidding process, these contracts did not require thorough plans and specifications prior to the commencement of work, a process that would take untold months in remote, untried locations. The navy would choose contractors based on their experience, reputation, and reliability, and on their ability to provide management, labor, materials, and equipment. Contractors and naval engineers would work out the details as the work proceeded, and the navy would reimburse the contractors' costs. The navy assumed the risk and guaranteed the contractors a reasonable profit, which became the fixed fee. The system placed trust in the contractors to conduct business in a prudent manner and to hire the kind of workers who would follow suit. The navy promised reasonably low costs and satisfactory construction by employing a process of plan approval and inspections by naval officers. Project budgets, time frames, navy approval channels, and oversight by the Bureau of the Budget, would preclude waste and profiteering.[14]

Construction companies from across the nation applied for the lucrative contracts. Admiral Moreell headed the newly formed Naval Air Base Construction Board, which whittled the list of applicants for the Pacific island contracts down to three groups of large-scale, experienced, financially sound firms and invited them to present their plans. The confident and competent Harry Morrison of Morrison-Knudsen Company headed the first group invited to interview with the board in July 1939, but he failed to win the opening round. Anticipating that the navy would piece out the projects, Morrison's team had prepared a detailed plan for Midway. The presentation impressed the board, but it lacked preparation on the other projects. The remaining contractor groups followed in the interview process, and, at the end of the month, the board chose the group that presented the most thorough, detailed, and solid plans for the Pacific projects: Hawaiian Dredging of Honolulu, and New York-based Turner Construction and Raymond Concrete and Pile. Harry Morrison tucked away the experience and went on to acquire other defense contracts on the mainland in addition to M-K's ongoing construction jobs. M-K remained at the top of Admiral Moreell's list for consideration when it came time to expand the consortium.[15]

The United States Navy awarded contract NOy-3550 to Contractors Pacific Naval Air Bases (initially the consortium of Raymond, Turner, and Hawaiian Dredging) on August 7, 1939. The initial three-year contract amounted to $13,809,500 with a fixed fee of $898,000, for a total of $14,707,500. Work began immediately on a supply base at Alameda, California. In the space of four weeks the contractors erected the CPNAB operating base, a two-story office building on Kuahua Peninsula in the filled-in marshes of Pearl Harbor. The contract covered five naval air stations: Ford Island, Kaneohe, and Johnston, Palmyra, and Midway islands. CPNAB started the Kaneohe seaplane base on Oahu's east shore in September 1939 and by November the first remote base, Johnston Island, was underway. The Palmyra project commenced within a few weeks. The three companies worked all of the projects jointly, pooling plans, resources, materials, and personnel.[16]

When war broke out in Europe in September 1939 the United States officially remained neutral. Public debate swelled over the war and the appropriate role of the nation, a debate fueled and fanned by radio and newspapers. At the same time, defense contractors were sweeping up hundreds, then thousands of workers off the streets, bringing bacon back to the breakfast tables of Depression-weary America. In Hawaii CPNAB quickly tapped the local labor market, and then turned to the mainland to feed its growing demands. In the spring of 1940 the contractors broke ground on Ford Island and at Midway, where in two years army engineers had managed to dredge only a shallow barge channel through its unyielding coral.

That spring and summer, as Germany bore down on Western Europe and Japan continued its unrelenting expansion at the expense of its neighbors, the president called on Congress to pass wave upon wave of defense appropriations. In the prevailing atmosphere of crisis, between May and September 1940 Congress approved over $7 billion for the national defense. The navy received approval and funds for the western Pacific bases, including Wake, Guam, and Cavite in the Philippines, as well as expansion of the Midway project and a new, top-secret, underground fuel storage system on Oahu. Already stretched thin, the three CPNAB contractors added two more firms to the consortium: Morrison-Knudsen Company of Boise, Idaho, and J. H. Pomeroy and Co., Inc., of San Francisco. The five companies signed Contract NOy-4173 for $30,870,000, including a fixed fee of $1,600,000, on July 1, 1940. Given the green light on Wake at last Admiral Moreell reflected that when naval strategists first urged him to seek a million dollars for a channel on Wake and Congress turned him down, his "strategic friends" advised, "the thing to do is to ask for $2,000,000 . . . and again [he] took it on the chin." However, when Moreell asked for $7.6 million, "to be perfectly frank about it, I was more surprised than any one else when I got it." Clearly, the mood of Congress and the nation had shifted in a year's time, and the wars raging in Europe and China had everything to do with it.[17]

With the expansion CPNAB abandoned its all-for-one approach for the new projects and operated the two contracts as one. The contracting companies centralized operations at Alameda and the operating base in Pearl Harbor for optimal efficiency and divided the new projects and add-ons among themselves. While it was generally not possible to staff a project solely with men from a single company, CPNAB hired as many key men as possible from or through the sponsoring company. (Regardless of the company affiliation or background, CPNAB was the employer of record for contractor personnel.) Due to the remote locations and difficulty of communication with the operating base, the contractors had to organize each project with key personnel capable of independently conducting a large-scale construction contract and making decisions "in the same manner as any executive in the parent companies." This required a large pool of capable executives and key men, and the CPNAB contractors agreed to share them as needed. Morrison-Knudsen took on the Wake project and the massive underground fuel storage project on Oahu. Harry Morrison chose his long-time vice president George Youmans to head the company's CPNAB operations, and Youmans headed for Honolulu in August 1940. At the same time, the four-month-old Midway project was floundering, its general superintendent had suddenly resigned, and the CPNAB Executive Committee asked M-K to take that project on as well. By the end of the month, George Youmans carried a full plate for Morrison-Knudsen in the Pacific, and Harry Morrison began funneling seasoned key men to the island projects.[18]

HARRY OLSON HEADS WEST

Harry Olson knew little of the background behind his new job in the Pacific, but he had made a good living for his family with government contract work for ten years without knowing all of the details that underlay the projects. A job was a job and this one promised interesting travel, independence, and two years of steady work. In early November 1940 Harry secured the clasps on his heavy trunk, loaded it and Katherine into the Ford, and put Grand Coulee Dam in the rearview mirror. He bade Katherine farewell at the train station in Spokane, Washington, and she returned to close up the house, arrange for movers, and then drive to Portland where somehow she would fit into the crowded house on Moore Street. Harry's train headed south from Portland and he joined fellow travelers in the club car to drink scotch and listen to the election results as snow fell on the Siskiyou Mountains. In Oakland Harry checked into the Hotel Leamington on the afternoon of November 6 and headed straight for the naval base at Alameda to begin his processing.[19]

The navy had commissioned the Alameda Naval Air Station on November 1, 1940, just a few days before Harry Olson arrived in California. Located next to Oakland on the east shore of San Francisco Bay, the Alameda base fell under the same funding that Congress had approved for the Pacific bases. Still under construction, Alameda Naval Air Station held one busy section: the "service of supply" base for Contractors Pacific Naval Air Bases. Here engineers from all of the contracting companies broke plans down into materials, purchasing agents ordered supplies and equipment, an expediting department obtained ship space, and packers and dockworkers loaded the ships for Honolulu to feed the swelling defense projects across the Pacific. As Harry signed his paperwork, heavy equipment and crates of supplies destined for Wake Island sat within a mile of the very man who two months later would direct their unloading in the raging swells of the mid-Pacific.[20]

While CPNAB earmarked few men for the Wake Island project at this early stage, hiring agents signed up hundreds of civilian workers at the new employment offices in San Francisco and Los Angeles for the other projects in the Pacific. Like Harry, they packed their trunks, said their goodbyes, and made their way to the forwarding station at Alameda. If a man passed his physical examination at the Navy Receiving Station on Treasure Island (an island made from bay dredging for the 1939 World's Fair), he received shots and a ticket for Honolulu on the next westbound ship. CPNAB officials negotiated with national union leaders on the mainland, promising skilled workers a full-year contract that included transportation, room and board, medical care, and protection under workmen's compensation laws. In return, the unions agreed to allow members to cross trade lines, which rankled many a seasoned carpenter and plumber ordered to unload a ship's cargo on a distant island. Handpicked by Harry Morrison for the Wake Island job, Harry Olson would be the man issuing orders like these to the union men on Wake. On November 8, 1940, Olson boarded the SS *President Cleveland* with a $125 first-class ticket, and settled in for the voyage to Honolulu. A few days into the trip, he sat down with a ship's pen and stationary to write a letter to his teenaged daughter, Donna, in Portland.[21]

At Sea, Sunday A.M., November 10, 1940
Dear Donna:
The poet who sang of life on the ocean wave should be here now. The
majority of the ship's company would be very well pleased with more
life and less wave. I find it exhilarating and suffer no ill effects. As I
write this the wind is blowing a mild gale from the south and . . . the
ship is inclined to wallow in the trough of the waves. All the sky is gray
and occasionally we drive through a gusty squall of fine misty rain.
About half of the passengers didn't make it for breakfast. We are about
800 miles from San Francisco and are due to arrive in Honolulu some
time Wednesday. About a third of the people are going to the Orient.
None of them seem to have any fear of trouble between Japan and the
U.S. Of course very few of them are American citizens. . . .

I share a cabin with bath with an Englishman going to the Straits
Settlements near Singapore where the British Govt. employs him. A
university man and well read, he has just returned from England and
a year's vacation. And what a vacation. He was in London and Liv-
erpool during all the bombing. You should hear the stories he can tell.
Believe me, the newspapers have not exaggerated their accounts any.
He is a true Briton however, and always speaks of his experiences objec-
tively and with amazing reserve. I can understand why England will
never be whipped for he says they (in spite of the bombing) will not
surrender and that the Germans will have to kill every man, woman
and child to take the Island. None of this was said in a spirit of
bravado, just a plain statement of fact that carries a lot of conviction.
We have some great discussions of world politics and problems and see
eye to eye on most questions. It is all a great pleasure to me to meet
someone that it is not necessary to explain what I am talking about.
There is a Frenchman aboard, traveling for a big jewelry house in the
Orient and we corralled him in the smoking room yesterday afternoon.
It all started peacefully enough but after a few scotch & sodas we all
took down our hair and it developed into a real argument. I am happy
to state that there is one Frenchman in the world that knows just
exactly how the English speaking peoples regard the French debacle
and their conduct since that time. We almost missed dinner but it was
very enjoyable.

My table in the dining salon seats four. Dinner is formal in all respects except dress. Eight and ten course affairs with about three times as much as I can eat. Besides myself there is a Dutchman who is the technical advisor to the Chinese customs service at Shanghai, his wife, an expatriate White Russian, and the wife of a naval officer traveling to Honolulu to meet her husband. . . . However all these people may differ in their own national problems, they are all in accord on one vital premise and that is that the United States is the hope of the world. They are all amazed at the spirit of unity that prevails there in spite of the election and I know that we have some volunteer ministers of good will preaching the American doctrine of freedom in the far corners of the earth.

Still at Sea, Wed:
Two days have elapsed since the last was written. The mild gale I spoke of lost all its mildness and it was a lot of fun. The wind howling through the rigging sounded just like it did in the picture "Hurricane,"—a high fierce note of implacable strength. The waves were huge and the wind blew the tops of them into a spiral of twisting spray. The bow of the ship would dive into an oncoming wave and tons of water would come rushing back against the superstructure. I was fascinated by it all and spent a good share of the time forward watching it. The wind was dead ahead and like an invisible wall in its intensity. One had to lean heavily into it in order to breast it. The marvel of it all is that I was not sick.

I think I kept my stomach so full there was no place for it to get started. There wasn't any room for it to slosh around. Breakfast at 8:30, Bouillon at 11:00, Drinks in the bar from 12:00 to 1:00, lunch at 1:15, tea at 4:00, cocktails at 6:00 to 7:00, Dinner at 7:15, Demitasse in the smoking lounge and the serious drinking usually from 10:00 until 2:00 A.M. I am beginning to get the well fed appearance of a Chinese Mandarin.

I have made many friends from all walks and stations, for this is a golden opportunity to acquire first hand information. I gather them up, get a table, get a few drinks into them and start them to talking. As soon as they get going I shut up and listen. Oddly enough they all appeal to me to settle their disputes. Truly, silence is golden, perhaps all reputations for wisdom are gained along these lines.

We are 1700 mi. from San Francisco and due to arrive at Honolulu in about 24 hours, from where I will mail this and write again.

Love, Dad

CHAPTER 3

HONOLULU HOTBED

TERRITORIAL HAWAII, NOVEMBER 1940

HONOLULU'S PIER 31-A, LEASED BY CONTRACTORS PACIFIC NAVAL AIR Bases in the spring of 1940, was running at full speed by the fall. Dockhands and stevedores unloaded crates, steel, timbers, and pipe off supply ships arriving from the mainland. Cranes and forklifts delivered mirror images of themselves from the decks to the docks, destined for construction of the remote Pacific naval air bases. The men at 31-A sweated and swore, oblivious to a similar delivery machine operating at the passenger liner dock under the shadow of the Aloha Tower. As luxury liners arrived, dockhands lashed thick ropes to piers and secured gangplanks with practiced precision, stewards escorted passengers, and crewmembers heaved trunks and suitcases onto carts. The band played as young men and boys knifed into the bay to retrieve coins tossed by the arriving passengers. Piles of fragrant leis draped dewy, brown-skinned arms, ready for the white necks of arriving workers and tourists. Along Honolulu Harbor, these patterns repeated weekly, often daily, and the future promised plenty more of the same. Honolulu rode the monster wave of commerce like a master.

The flood of defense appropriations in 1939 and 1940 powered that monster wave. During the first decades of the century, Territorial Hawaii's economy revolved around the sugar industry and the financial oligarchy that dominated it. The U.S. Army had built Wheeler Field and Schofield Barracks on Oahu in 1922, and the airfield had hosted historically significant Pacific flights of the 1920s and 30s, but Pearl Harbor had languished during

39

those years, a victim of sparse funding. However, by the end of the 1930s all branches of the U.S. military were benefiting from the heightened defense commitment. As the new headquarters of the Pacific Fleet in 1940, Pearl Harbor commanded a generous portion of the funds appropriated by Congress that year for defense. By the fall of 1940, the harbor was a human beehive of defense contractors and sailors.[1]

THE CPNAB PROJECTS

To the five planned naval air stations (Ford Island, Kaneohe, Johnston, Palmyra, and Midway) covered under the 1939 contract NOy-3550 with Contractors Pacific Naval Air Bases, effective July 1940 the CPNAB construction consortium added the new projects of contract NOy-4173:

Naval air stations on Maui, Molokai, and at Bishop's Point
Wahiawa radio station on central Oahu
Pearl Harbor submarine base
Ewa landplane base
Makapala housing project
Underground fuel storage tanks on Oahu
Naval air station on Wake Island
Naval base and fuel storage on Guam
Naval base and fuel storage on American Samoa

Principals of each of the five CPNAB companies (Raymond, Turner, Hawaiian Dredging, Morrison-Knudsen, and Pomeroy) formed the CPNAB Executive Committee, with W. V. McMenimen of Raymond Construction serving as chairman. Harry Morrison represented Morrison-Knudsen. Together, the companies had a minimum of $10 million dollars invested in the contracts at all times. Early in CPNAB operations the companies arranged with their banks to establish a credit of $3 million as an overdraft account. As the projects grew, so grew the overdraft accounts and additional financing. While the fixed fee amounts stipulated in the navy contracts seemed to promise a very profitable return on investment ($898,000 on the original NOy-3550 and $1,600,000 on NOy-4173, not including additional fees associated with subsequent change orders), they were not net payments to the contractors. Nonrecoverable items included travel expenses of executives, other transportation costs, and legal expenses in connection with the work, among other items. In order to retain and adequately compensate men going out to the islands for several years, "not only for the hardships they were undergoing but also for the risks that they were taking," the contractors set aside an amount not to exceed 10 percent of the net earnings for the year as a bonus fund. The members did not base division of the fee on any fixed formula, but according to what members could and did bring to the operation. It was a complex and changeable situation that occupied many meetings of the executive committee.[2]

The CPNAB Operating Committee, chaired by George F. Ferris of Turner Construction, supervised the entire organization from the operating base located near the fleet's submarine base in Pearl Harbor. George Youmans took a seat for M-K on the operating committee in July 1940, stood in for Ferris as chairman in his absence, and oversaw the three large projects assigned to Morrison-Knudsen: Wake, the underground fuel storage on Oahu, and Midway, the last shared with Raymond and Turner, its previous sponsors. The first two projects existed only on paper; Midway, which had grown to include a full submarine base, wallowed in dysfunction. The CPNAB operating base served as the headquarters for all of the projects and the centralized operation contributed to greater efficiency and cost control. Typical mainland projects could subcontract various aspects of the work, but there were no subcontractors on the remote islands, so CPNAB provided its own, stationing experts at the base to send out to the projects as needed. In addition to the chief executives, the base housed a full accounting department; engineering departments, including mechanical, electrical, structural, and waterfront design; and a planning department. The base also oversaw Pier 31-A, the transshipment of materials and men to the outlying islands, and supervised all of the CPNAB work on Oahu.[3]

Under the leadership of RAdm. Ben Moreell, the Bureau of Yards and Docks originated and administered the project recommendations and approved contractor plans and expenditures. Commandant of the 14th Naval District, RAdm. Claude C. Bloch, supervised the public works division in charge of construction of shore establishments under the defense contracts and provided navy transportation to and from the outlying islands. (14th Naval District was responsible for the Hawaiian Islands and the outlying islands to the west.) In addition, Bloch served as the base defense officer responsible for the Hawaiian Sea Frontier, which included the outlying islands of Johnston, Palmyra, Midway, and Wake. At Pearl Harbor Captain

Henry Bruns served as the officer in charge (OinC) of the CPNAB contracts and oversaw the resident officers in charge (RoinC) assigned to each outlying island project. Every decision had to pass the OinC before the contractors took action. Most of this process occurred at CPNAB's operating base and at the public works offices in Pearl Harbor.[4]

The operating base increased its scope and speed to meet the multiplying demands and dollars of the U.S. Navy in 1940. Necessity mothered invention repeatedly as engineers and contractors in the field stretched imagination and experience to meet untried conditions. As time went by the navy encouraged the use of plans drawn up for one location in others. However, despite common features of the coral atolls, each location had unique conditions. Adaptation was not an occasional challenge but a constant requirement in the Pacific.

THE WAKE TEAM

Shortly after the *President Cleveland* arrived in Honolulu on November 14, 1940, Harry Olson met the Wake Island contingent at the operating base. George Youmans introduced Olson to the group, which included Nathan "Dan" Teters, Wake's general superintendent. Teters, just turned forty, had grown up in Spokane and, after brief service in the war building airfields as a teenager, attended Gonzaga and Washington State College where he studied engineering. He had worked for Morrison-Knudsen for a number of years, interrupted by a five-year stint during which he tried a construction business of his own. In August 1940 Harry Morrison had tapped the tough, versatile, and experienced Teters as project superintendent for Wake. The handful of men comprising the early Wake team included L. H. "Pete" Russell, building superintendent for Wake, John Polak, office manager, and C. P. Schoeller, who would remain at the operating base as the Wake project engineer.[5]

Project No. 14, as the Wake job was officially titled, called for a long list of excavation and construction jobs that could not even begin until the contractors established a base camp and water distilling facilities on the remote atoll. Isolated Wake stood two thousand miles from its supply depot at Pier 31-A in Honolulu and a thousand miles from Midway. (Far closer stood Roi in the Japanese-held Marshalls, some six hundred miles south of Wake.) The navy would have to ship every item of equipment, all supplies, food, and workers to the atoll, and it would take months to establish a base of operations before they could even begin building the naval base. Naval Air Station, Wake Island, called for extensive dredging operations for a channel, turning basin, and bulkhead; a seaplane runway, ramp, and parking area; as well as an emergency landplane runway and construction of numerous shore facilities. Storage for 400 thousand gallons of gasoline, fresh water supply, and saltwater fire protection systems were essential to the operation. Barracks for military personnel, bachelor officer quarters, mess halls, recreation facilities, and dozens of other structures and facilities filled pages of lists. Some of the plans would be duplications of those used first at Midway because the two projects were similar in many ways and, as both jobs were under the direction of George Youmans, "they could and did profit from the lessons learned there," as Harry Olson later observed.[6]

When the first Wake contractors had arrived in Honolulu in late summer, they found that the navy's survey party was still on the atoll and only general sketches of the Wake plan existed. In anticipation of the new contract, Captain Bruns ordered a survey of the atoll in late June 1940. Lieutenant Harold W. Butzine (CEC) and a crew of twenty traveled to Wake on the USS *Chaumont*, arriving on July 9, 1940. They set up a main engineers' camp (the "Hawaiian boys," who had been hired as divers and laborers, pitched their tents several hundred feet away, Butzine noted in his report) and two field offices, including one in a leaky stone building that had been part of Pan American's first camp called "Coral Gables" on the northeast shore of Peale. The men made a thorough topographic survey, drilled core samples, and took dozens of photographs as they assessed the atoll for placement of facilities and the substructure for dredging. Shortly after his arrival in Honolulu in July, George Youmans paid a brief visit to Wake via Pan American Clipper and observed the survey party's slow progress. The challenges on Wake promised to be nothing if not daunting.[7]

Lieutenant Butzine's survey party returned in early October, bringing the long-awaited maps and data that would allow for concrete planning. As the CPNAB Operating Committee continued to request firm plans and authorizations from the navy, the Wake team worked on the "Master Program and Estimate," which supplemented the previous plan of August 21. Basing their projections on the list of approved facilities, the men utilized plans from other CPNAB projects already underway, their own experience, and a hefty dose of imagination. Meanwhile, at Pier 31-A in Honolulu three shifts worked round the clock to build shallow-draft cargo barges that would be used to carry an estimated seven thousand tons of materials and equipment per month from Honolulu to Wake. Captain Bruns finally released the first layout proposals and some building authorizations on the last day of October. It was guesswork, couched in terms of "proposal" and "modification," but at least the Wake team had a green light. All they needed now was a ship to take them there.[8]

The Wake team's most pressing problems in November 1940 were delays on plans and transportation and the recent typhoon damage on the atoll. Not only was the navy's decision-making process proceeding at a snail's pace, but the expectation of shipping out to Wake in November had evaporated as the navy informed CPNAB that a ship would not be available until December. Designated for the outlying Pacific island work, the USS *William Ward Burrows* was delayed in California. Meanwhile, supplies and equipment piled up at the waterfront and lists and estimates piled up at the operating base. The district commandant's office coordinated field surveys, public works supervision, and transportation of equipment and men to all of the outlying projects. Rapid expansion strained the system while red tape and overlapping jurisdictions of naval offices, bureaus, and commands added bottlenecks.

More men arrived in Honolulu to join Wake's pioneer party as it waited for transportation to the distant atoll and in the interim some received assignments on temporary jobs under the CPNAB umbrella. George Youmans wrote to Harry Morrison that Harry Olson "looks like just the man we want for the Wake job," and sent Olson to the Kaneohe Naval Air Station during the wait to work on the new, prefabricated seaplane ramps that CPNAB proposed to use on Wake. The remote Palmyra project had revealed that casting the massive concrete slabs used for the ramps was too expensive and time-consuming on site, so operating base engineers worked out a method to cast the slabs at Kaneohe and then tow them on steel barges to the outlying islands. The method to seat them was complex, but the engineers reasoned that trained supervisors could quickly perform the task with equipment and labor on the islands.[9]

Harry joined other CPNAB employees in residence at the MacDonald Hotel on the edge of the Manoa Valley for six weeks as preparations continued for the voyage to Wake. For the first two weeks he drove a Dodge pickup forty miles to his CPNAB assignment at Kaneohe Bay. In letters home to his wife and daughter he marveled at the scenery, weather, and Waikiki nightlife. Family friends from the Bonneville Dam days lived near Diamond Head and Harry's social circle quickly broadened to include many friends and frequent parties. By the end of November Harry had completed his work at the Kaneohe "laboratory," and he joined the Wake team at the operating base in Pearl Harbor as they prepared for the still-delayed voyage to the distant atoll. None of them had a firm idea about the future, but the plan called for two years from start to finish of the job on Wake Island.[10]

LABOR PROBLEMS

At first CPNAB had hired Honolulu men, including workers who left the sugar plantations by the hundreds and flocked to the "gold mines" of Oahu. The advantages of hiring locally included immediate availability, no transportation or housing costs, and workers already acclimatized to tropical conditions. A local man making two or three dollars a week diving for coins thrown from the passenger liners could make as much as twenty dollars a day as a Pearl Harbor diver. However, the contractors tapped the local market as they quickly bumped up against ethnic issues. Along with native Pacific Islanders (sometimes called "Kanakas," a labor term with a pejorative cast), there were residents of Chinese, Filipino, and Japanese ethnicity. The Japanese alone comprised a third of the population. In a rare nod to the underlying premise of the defense contracts, the navy forbade employment of Japanese Americans on the outlying island projects, but they made up a good portion of the CPNAB carpenters working on Oahu. The contractors hired Pacific Islanders chiefly as divers and coral-blasters, while Chinese Americans hired on as cooks, mess attendants, and domestic workers.[11]

As the months went by, CPNAB turned increasingly to the mainland for labor. The first large group of defense workers for the navy contracts arrived on November 5, 1940, just ahead of Harry Olson: 895 men for projects in Hawaii and another 100 for the outlying islands. Most of the skilled and unskilled construction workers on the island projects were and would continue to be whites from western states, a reflection of the segregated hiring practices of the times. However, no matter how many workers CPNAB hired, it was never enough to keep up with the to-and-fro nature of the turnover. Ships returning to Honolulu from supply runs to the outlying islands usually brought back a number of disgruntled workers, fed up with the no-booze, no-dames isolation of the lonely island outposts.[12]

"Accommodations are hard to find and getting worse due to the influx of Navy yard workers," Harry Olson observed in late November, "about 200 per week. The govt has just announced an $11 million housing project. They also have a very serious traffic problem on their hands. It takes an hour to get to Pearl Harbor or back, a distance of 10 miles. Cars are lined up six blocks at traffic lights, and every one mad except the Orientals. Speed limit in town is 30 mi. and they would rather you would do 40. It's the only way they can hope to get the cars over the streets. All main streets except King have native names and are not marked. Newcomers have a terrible time. I live on Punahou. In saying a native word always sound all the vowels which lead a full and abundant life here."[13]

Despite housing and traffic problems, Honolulu pulled out all the stops to welcome the influx of mainland workers and sailors and their dollars. Hastily constructed barracks housed enlisted men and workers, and laborers destined for the remote island projects found bunks in the "Naval Employees Hotel," a building in the Bishop Museum complex north of downtown Honolulu, as they awaited the next outbound navy ship. Busses loaded with boisterous young men crept along the teeming streets leading from docks to quarters. The newcomers dropped their jaws at the tropical paradise and their dollars at its amenities. Bartenders, prostitutes, and policemen kept busy around the clock and the local community struggled to adjust to the invasion of rowdy, often rude mainlanders. Local newspapers followed the labor riots in Los Angeles, navy blacklisting and union blackballing fights, and the ongoing controversy over the "local gravy train national defense boys." A December 1940 Honolulu newspaper article quoted Burton K. Wheeler, the isolationist senator from Montana, as he castigated defense contractors who "not only take their fixed fee commission, but spend Uncle Sam's money like the proverbial drunken sailor for materials and supplies."[14]

SERIOUS BUSINESS

Far from the proverbial drunken sailor, the Wake team soberly prepared for the challenges that awaited them at the atoll. The navy revised the sailing date to December 15, and then to December 23—"subject to change every 15 minutes." Harry Olson began meeting with the captain and executive officer of the *William Ward Burrows* in early December to discuss the enormous challenge ahead of them at Wake. "We have a serious problem getting our first shipload of equipment unloaded," he wrote to Katherine on December 9. "There is no dock and the ship can't get within a quarter mile of the

Island. We are taking a barge along and will unload at sea and try to move the barge in and beach it. At one load a day it will take us a couple weeks to do it if the weather is good. I know we will lose some of it and we will be lucky if we don't sink the barge. So wish us luck."[15]

Captain Ross A. Dierdorff, commander of the *Burrows*, later described the physical problem with the Pacific atolls: in "eons past, the industrious little [coral] polyp was not at all co-operative regarding the inclusion of natural harbors in the atolls which rose slowly above the waves to crown what were probably ancient volcanoes." While Pan American divers and powder men had blasted seaplane runways through the coral heads studding the lagoon for Clipper take-offs and landings, no progress had been made toward establishing a safe harbor at Wake or a channel into the safe waters of the lagoon. "Considerable rearranging of the topography," observed Dierdorff, was required to turn the atoll into a "full-fledged air base." Two and a half years of army dredging at Midway, with similar topography, had finally enabled contractors to bring a partially loaded navy cargo vessel into the lagoon in November 1940 "by carefully picking a route which we had sounded a few days before and saying many prayers."[16]

At Wake, Pan American had continued to use the small cove notched into the barrier reef near the southeast end of Wilkes, as it did when the *North Haven* first arrived in 1935. While a supply ship rocked fifty yards offshore, a motor launch maneuvered a small lighter to deliver cargo over the shallow, uneven bottom to shore. A flimsy looking narrow-gauge marine railway carried the cargo overland to the lagoon side where it was then floated across to the Pan American complex on Peale with equipment that had literally been dragged through the Wilkes channel at high tide. The dangerous, time-consuming process had changed little in five years, until the typhoon in October 1940 destroyed the airline's small cargo operation.[17]

The key to a viable naval operation on Wake was access to the lagoon and facilities for ship and seaplane operations and, despite the back-door opportunity that Pan American had provided, the CPNAB contractors would be the first to tackle Wake's most stubborn problem. They gave channel and lagoon dredging the longest completion target in Project 14 plans, projecting that dredging would reach into 1943. By the end of 1940, the $7.6 million Wake project under Contract NOy-4173 had increased by another $2 million to deepen the harbor and channel at Wake.[18]

The contractors fine-tuned their plans and lists as they awaited a firm departure date for the *Burrows*, and Harry Olson went aboard ship frequently to develop plans for barge towing and cargo unloading. Olson and Captain Dierdorff soon found that they shared connections in Portland, Dierdorff's hometown, and "from then on we were old friends. A Captain in the Navy really rates on his own ship," Harry observed. "He does not have the nebulous quality of God but otherwise there is not much difference."[19]

Writing to Katherine to report yet another delay in the departure, Harry expressed his hope that they would be gone by New Years. "I shudder when I contemplate the possibilities of a New Years' Eve! People are always speaking of the Hawaiians being equally at home on land as in water. I can testify that they are as much at home in liquor. I fear I haven't the will power to cope with that situation." His letter then turned to a practical solution for the family's crowded situation in Portland: after Christmas, Katherine and Donna should move to Pullman for Donna to enroll in college with Ted, and all three could share an apartment to save money. Ted might balk at deprivation of his fraternity activities, Harry wrote, but "he must develop enough self reliance to keep himself studying." Lest Katherine be "prone to criticize," Harry reminded her that he was "paying the freight. None of us out here are looking forward to the job at Wake with any degree of pleasure, for conditions out there won't permit any. We all feel that we are committed to the job and intend to see it through. It is by far the toughest of the current jobs and the only fun to it will be the pleasure of achievement."[20]

THE NEWS: DECEMBER 1940

News of the U.S. draft and the European war continued to dominate the front pages of American newspapers in December 1940. The Greek army, having expelled the Italians, pressed on against Axis forces in the Balkan Peninsula, and the British opened an offensive in Egypt against Italian forces. The Germans conducted "ethnic reconfiguration" in Poland as they directed Poles and Germans to trade farms, shuffled population groups in Poland and Warsaw, and established a Jewish ghetto. As these actions apparently did not involve headline-worthy troop movements, death, or destruction, news agencies devoted little newsprint to them.[21]

On the other side of the globe, U.S.-Japanese diplomatic relations continued to fester. The United States escalated the embargo on exports to Japan to underscore its opposition to Japan's ongoing war with China, expansion south, and membership in the Axis alliance. Japan protested the embargo, arguing that expansion southward enabled access to vital resources such as oil, rice, rubber, and tin, and each side accused the other of hostile intentions. At the beginning of 1940 the United States had abrogated the 1911 commercial treaty with Japan and trade continued only on a day-to-day basis, subject to manipulation for diplomatic purposes. Petroleum, however, continued to flow in great quantities to Japan.[22]

In early December, Yosuke Matsuoka, the Japanese foreign minister, declared, "We have no difference that cannot be surmounted if we keep our heads cool and mind our own business. . . . We do not pass judgment on what the United States does in the West, and we try to confine ourselves to this part of the world." Outsiders misunderstood Japan's actions in China, Matsuoka asserted. Japan had only economic interests in China, "no territorial ambitions." American journalists decried the Axis alliance as Japan's foreign policy keystone. A foreign correspondent in Tokyo reported that many Japanese "dreaded but expected war" because of American "meddling." Many Japanese wondered why the United States was so interested in the region if it was soon to withdraw its flag from the Philippines upon independence, leaving no large areas in the Far East under American domination. Meanwhile, American shipyards churned out one new ship for the fleet every twelve days, despite competition for skilled workers and cost overruns, and President Roosevelt voiced support for direct aid to Britain "from the selfish viewpoint of American defense."[23]

By the winter of 1940-41, the Japanese advance had stalled in China. To many observers in the United States it appeared that after occupying Chinese coastal areas in the late 1930s, Japan was simply bogged down, wreaking a lot of havoc, but unable to finish off a "lesser foe." The attitude reinforced American perceptions of Japanese military inferiority.[24]

WAKE ON THE HORIZON

As Christmas approached in Honolulu, the Wake pioneer party had grown to nearly eighty men and preparations for the impending voyage dominated their days and dreams. Dockworkers swarmed over the *Burrows* and the barge, packing holds and loading equipment into every square inch of space. At the CPNAB operating base in Pearl Harbor the offices buzzed with Wake-focused activity even as work continued on all of the other projects. At the MacDonald Hotel Harry Olson wrote letters to his family over the last days, fully aware that his world was about to change.

Honolulu T.H., Dec. 23, 1940
Dear Donna:
Two of your most welcome letters are at hand and now I owe you two as you owed me two a week ago. It reminds me of the time Joe and I were buying each other six beers at a time. . . .

We all have been struggling hard to get all our gear ready to take off for the great unknown the day after Xmas. We sail at 1:00 P.M. That will be at 3:30 your time. You can imagine trying to get enough stuff together to start a job like Bonneville and get it on the ship. If we have forgotten anything we will just do without. We expect one ship a month but doubt if the Navy keeps that schedule. The first six ships will have to be unloaded the hard way. That is unloaded on a barge at sea and brought to shore. Wake is really three islands thus . . .

It is about 8 miles long and about 1/3 mile wide. The permanent development will be on Peale as it is the highest—21 feet. There was a typhoon there last week and Wilkes and Wake were under water. I hope this don't happen while we are unloading as we would lose all our stuff. The channel between Peale and Wake is 15 ft. deep and infested with sharks. So in case of a storm we would have to get on the boat and go to sea to ride it out. The Navy really regards this job as the most difficult they have started. Opinion is about evenly divided as to whether it can be done. So far I have had my way in the preparations as to the tow and how to handle it. Of course if it don't work I am in a mess but they all agree it is O.K. and if we lose it we can call it an act of God. I think I would cry to see that beautiful barge load of nice new machinery going down. We lost two barges last week. One near Midway and one 600 miles out of San Francisco. I still think ours would weather a like storm but I may be mistaken. . . .

If you can, get a copy of the book "Skyway to Asia." I made a friend last week—Dave Richards. He is mentioned in the book and you can get more first hand information about Wake from reading it than I can give you. Dave is a Kahuna, which is native for witch doctor. For all their education and sophistication the Kanakas still believe in this stuff and Dave told me many amusing and mystifying illustrations of this credulity. . . .

The kids all shoot firecrackers here to celebrate Xmas. Funny isn't it? Japs and Chinese are nuts anyway. Everyone here speaks Pidgin Eng-

lish and that in itself is the principal deterrent to better speech. I still think it is half telepathy for I know no one can understand it. I find white men here that can speak nothing else from long practice. The unusual racial condition here is responsible for an exotic form of artistic expression that is above average but otherwise I find no pretense toward the development of any significant culture.

So Merry Christmas Friday, and thanks for the lift.

Robin

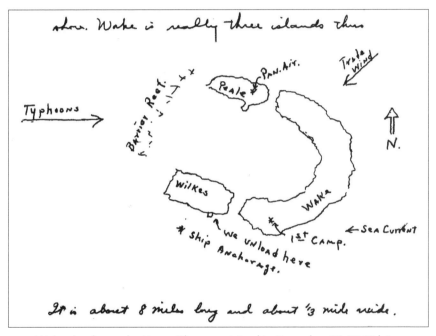

Wake sketch map by Harry Olson, contained in December 23 1940 letter to his daughter Donna.—*Olson Family Collection*

Harry closed his letter to his daughter with a long-shared private joke, playing on a Robinson Crusoe theme. As the pioneer party made its final preparations for an experience that was very similar to that of Pan American's *North Haven* five years earlier, Harry read *Skyway to Asia*, written in 1937 by expedition leader William S. Grooch, with great interest. Grooch described each adventurous leg of the journey, the vivid personalities (making no mention of the top-secret navy passengers), and the island destinations of the long round trip from San Francisco to Manila and back. When the ship arrived in Honolulu to take on additional workers and supplies Grooch purchased a ton of dynamite and shopped around for an experienced powder man to direct the extensive blasting for seaplane runways in the lagoons at Midway and Wake. He found one in Dave Richards, eager to go "shoot coral." Richards signed on with the *North Haven* party and took charge of the dynamite, chickens (provided at Midway and bound for Wake), and a good portion of the ship's entertainment. Diversions included the then-popular shipboard outlet of catching and maiming a shark, throwing it back in, and watching its brothers tear it to shreds.[25]

Photographs in *Skyway to Asia* showed workers clearing the shallow channel between Wake and Wilkes using pickaxes and foot power. Dave Richards, Bill Mullahey, and a gang of Hawaiian divers drilled holes underneath large rocks, packed them with dynamite, attached fuse caps, backed off, and fired, sending showers of water and shattered rock skyward. Soon Richards had cleared the channel down to bedrock and widened it just enough for all hands to push and pull a lighter through to the lagoon. This would enable them to move equipment into the lagoon to transport cargo from Wilkes across to Peale, where the Pan American station would stand. To Harry Olson, the Pan American process seemed almost primitive, given the powerful dragline and dredging equipment that the CPNAB contractors were bringing to Wake to battle the coral.[26]

In Honolulu, Christmas day 1940 dawned with the usual chatter of birds, breaking the "incessant din of firecrackers" that had gone on all night and continued through the day. Harry repacked his belongings at the Mac-Donald Hotel, opened his gifts from home: a billfold and a fruitcake, and wrote a last letter from Honolulu to his wife. "Well, we sail tomorrow at 1:00 P.M.," he wrote. "This trip should be quite an adventure as we are not at all sure that our purpose can be accomplished. We have had a Kona (south) wind for the last two weeks and stormy weather all around us. It is always nice here but the Kona makes the weather sticky and warm. It is beautiful here this morning. The sun shining brightly and at long last the trade wind is blowing again. Every thing is as green as Oregon in May and no fooling the trade wind really does something to you, it is so soft and seductive. . . . I'm 2 ½ hrs behind you now but soon will be 16 hrs ahead." He closed with "Merry Xmas and a Happy New Year to you all and pray for good weather," but did not acknowledge her birthday. That afternoon, Harry and a group of friends went for a swim at Waikiki Beach, and then drove out to the friends' house at Diamond Head for Christmas dinner. "Andy has a gallon of whiskey and a couple of quarts of scotch so we should do all right." Across Honolulu, dozens of other members of Wake's pioneer party polished off copious quantities of alcohol as they celebrated the holiday and their last night in civilization for a long time to come.[27]

CHAPTER 4

PIONEER PARTY

––––––––––––––––––––––––––––––

BON VOYAGE

ON DECEMBER 26, 1940, THE USS *WILLIAM WARD BURROWS* STOOD at Pier 31-A in Honolulu, loaded and ready for the contractors' voyage to Wake Island. Holds were crammed with everything from cement mixers to chewing gum and decks towered with lashed-down oil drums, boats, reefers, and steel pontoons. The contractors had given their all-important water distilling equipment a trial run and rechecked their lists to ensure that they had every piece of equipment and all essential supplies. They left nothing to chance, as it would be sixty days before a second supply ship came to Wake. Eighty contractors, "some laden with leis, some with hangovers and some with both," as Captain Dierdorff observed, boarded the ship throughout the day while a gang from the operating base gathered to send them off. Finally, in the late afternoon, the ship pulled away from the dock, the crowd cheered, and tearful wives and girlfriends waved farewell. Outside the harbor, the crew paid out eight hundred feet of towline to a heavily loaded barge, and another towline stretched to a fifty-five-foot tugboat, the *Pioneer,* with crew of four aboard. The *Burrows* set course for Wake Island, two thousand miles away, and the CPNAB Pioneer Party settled in for two long weeks at sea.[1]

Captain Dierdorff noted what a "fine crowd they were—each man an expert in his line." During the voyage, as Dan Teters, Harry Olson, Pete Russell, and the rest were "sitting around in the wardroom yarning, we often had to ask them to translate their rich and racy technical slang into comprehensible terms as they recounted their experiences in revising the topography of the United States. It soon became evident that we could count both upon their full cooperation and their warm friendship." Lieutenant Harold Butzine, who had led the survey party on Wake from July to October 1940, and now joined the party as the navy's RoinC for Wake, counted as the most experienced "Wake hand" in the group. His stories and observations added valuable information to the pioneer party on the westward voyage.[2]

The first week brought one hot, lazy day after another, and the contractors whiled away the time reading, sunbathing, and playing cards. Russell and Olson monitored the loads in the holds and on deck to ensure that they did not shift and they frequently went "overside" to check on the barge and to carry oranges to the seasick tug crew far out in tow. The supervisors enjoyed Captain Dierdorff's wardroom hospitality, camaraderie, and good food at mealtimes, and passengers and crew alike gathered to watch movies on the top deck under the stars each night.[3]

"The Pacific gets bluer and clearer each day and gleams at night from the phosphorous in the water," Harry Olson wrote to his wife. "We pass through many schools of flying fish. I believe some make as much as a hundred feet before they hit the water. Once in a while we see an albatross or a frigate bird but otherwise no signs of life. We are south of the ship lanes so we have the sea to ourselves. It is very beautiful but monotonous and I shall be glad to see Wake. Standard Honolulu joke. Guy says to gal: 'How would you like to go to wake with Harry?' 'O.K.,' says she, 'but I would rather go to sleep with him.' I had it pulled on me a dozen times. A low form of humor but stimulating to the imagination."[4]

A few days into the voyage, all rang in the New Year, 1941, with "lots of bull," sixteen bells—eight for the old year and eight for the new—and a cheery song written by the ship's chief engineer:

Heigh Ho! Heigh Ho! It's out to Wake we go.
Heigh Ho! Heigh Ho! With a tug and a barge in tow.
From Honolulu we took our start,
With the hope the towlines wouldn't part . . .

Just after New Year's Day luncheon, the door to the wardroom burst open, and a young bridge messenger announced "Sir! The barge's done busted loose!"[5]

The ship's anchor chain that served as part of the long towline had bro-

ken and now the barge, loaded with an eighty-ton crane, several heavy bulldozers, tractors, diesel hoists, and two six thousand-pound anchors, bowled
away in the rough seas. Olson took charge of the recovery operation, brought
the tug alongside the *Burrows* in thirty-foot swells, and led twelve men to
jump for it. "That ride on the tug was the wildest I have ever had," he wrote
to Katherine. "When we got alongside the barge it was worse yet but I
watched my chance and finally jumped aboard. The others followed when
the tug and barge would bounce together." It took four hours to pull the
500 feet of fifteen-inch manila rope and 180 feet of chain up out of the
water with hoists, "6 or 8 fathoms at a fleet," observed Captain Dierdorff.
"It was late in the afternoon ere the 'bitter end' came in view and we were
ready to couple up." Dierdorff backed up the *Burrows*, shot a line to the
barge, and gradually made up the tow, the work party returned to the ship
in the heaving seas, and they resumed the voyage by dusk. Pete Russell acknowledged that the rescue was "very good work on Olson's part." That
evening, the seas were still so heavy that the New Year's dinner of turkey and
all the trimmings skidded about on the wardroom table. Pete "had a bit of
John's pie as it went by."[6]

Three days later, on the west side of the 180th meridian that marked
the international date line and swallowed a day whole, the morning light
revealed that the towline had broken again during the night and the unruly
barge rode loose, two miles astern. The work party, this time including both
Olson and Russell, boarded the *Pioneer* and made for the barge, drenched
from the heavy swells that broke over the little tug. Again, they secured the
lines, the *Burrows* pulled the barge back to tow, and all hands returned safely
to deck. The ship's executive officer vowed that he would not again write
"Holiday Routine" in the orders as "the barge invariably misinterpreted these
instructions."[7]

174°E – 20°N, 6 Jan 1941
Dear Donna:
This is the eleventh day at sea and I hope they find an island pretty
quick. There has been a big storm up north and we are getting some
monstrous rollers from it broadside. I couldn't sleep last night as every
time I would doze off I would roll out of bed. We have had forty-eight
hours of it now and everyone is getting tired of it. This desk in my room
is bolted to the wall and I have to hang onto it with one hand to keep

my chair from sliding out from under me as I write. Otherwise the weather is marvelous.

Yesterday we broke the towline again and we had some fun getting it back up again. When you are out in the rough sea in a small boat the ship looks very comforting as you know it is the only thing above the water for a thousand miles. After we got the towline aboard and while we were connecting it again, some of the fellows caught a shark. It was about eight feet long and ran mostly to head. It provided a lot of excitement when they finally got it on deck as it thrashed around a lot. They finally cut its tail off and threw it back in the sea and its antics were very funny as it could not submerge or swim in a straight line. Of course it only lasted a couple minutes as the other sharks attacked it right away and ate it up. A rather grim sort of humor but the shark would do the same or worse to one of us if he could. Anyway it all provided a sort of break in the monotony. All we do is eat, sleep and go to the show. Of course there is endless talk of the job, particularly the unloading [at Wake]. We have landed this cargo so many times the boxes are practically worn out.

The movies are under the stars. It seems quite unusual to me. The screen is fastened to the stern mast up high and the speakers just below it. This is a pretty big ship and has six decks above the water line. The picture can be seen from the three upper decks aft and everyone picks out his own favorite spot. Most everyone sits in a steamer chair. The moon is at the first quarter and of course the sea is very beautiful with the moonlight on it. It is always just warm enough at night to sit out in shirt sleeves in comfort so it is a very enjoyable experience. Most of the pictures I would class as turkeys but once in a while we get a good one. . . .

We should reach Wake in about sixty hours and then the fun starts. I will be glad to step on land again but we will have to stay on the boat for the first two weeks.

Love, Robin

I have a spare day I could lend you if you should get behind in your business.

7:30 P.M. Wed. Jan 8: The lights of Wake just came into view. It is stormy and the sea is running high so I don't know if we can land in the morning.

ARRIVAL AT WAKE

The *Burrows* raised the outline of Wake Island early in the evening on January 8, 1941, but stood away during the stormy night. The morning light revealed a forbidding sight: a low, brushy, horseshoe-shaped atoll ringed by crashing surf. The afternoon of January 9 a landing party of ten, including Captain Dierdorff, Lieutenant Butzine, Dan Teters, Olson, and Russell, boarded a motor launch and aimed for the notch where Pan American unloaded freight. The view from up close silenced the party. Wake was a "sorry looking sight" that day, Dierdorff recalled. The floating pier, short marine railway, two small boats, and all of Pan American's unloading equipment still lay in a tangled mess of debris where the October typhoon had spat it out. The landing party made for the shore two at a time in a little skiff they had towed with them, jumping out on the coral-studded beach of Wilkes Island, Wake's left hand. Their first job was to clear the area of the "unholy alliance" of typhoon-tossed gasoline barrels and dynamite. The men gingerly carried the sticks of dynamite some distance down the beach to explode them safely.[8]

Pan American operators radioed the news of the *Burrows* arrival to their Midway station and on to the CPNAB operating base at Pearl Harbor. The rain, wind, and high seas had abated, and the Wake operator reported ideal weather for the landing of the CPNAB pioneer party. Until the contractors erected their own radio shack, "Pan Air" was their only means of contact with the outside world. The *Burrows* had been out of range for several days, so George Youmans was relieved to get word of the arrival. A few days later Youmans wrote a report to Harry Morrison in Boise, including a brief description of the ship's misadventures en route and stating that he was "glad to have Olson along with the expedition, as I think he is an exceptionally good man under the conditions we will encounter." The conditions the men encountered upon their arrival at Wake promised to test them all.[9]

"Wake is just as I had it pictured," Harry wrote home on January 10. "It is low and brushy, a sort of ironwood, quite dense with much evidence of high waves going over it. There is no soil or sand underneath solid coral. . . . The sea water is the wonderful part. It is warm, 80°, limpid, clear and incredibly blue. Each degree of sunlight gives it another shade of blue and it is so clear one can see bottom plainly at 60 ft. depth. And full of fish of all colors and shapes. The fellows dive and spear them. The fish are not afraid of a man under water and you can swim right up to them."[10]

The endless planning sessions in Honolulu and on the *Burrows* proved to be time well spent when it came time to unload the ship. The risks to ship and cargo (not to mention life and limb) were great, but the pioneer party attacked the job with confidence. The motor launch *Hopei* and tug *Pioneer* cast off from the *Burrows* to carry workers and blasting equipment across the swells and surf to the shore. Unable to anchor, the *Burrows* maneuvered offshore, altering course and speed to enable workers to unload supplies onto the lighter and to keep the unwieldy cargo barge under control.

In the small landing cove a crew went to work with an air compressor, dynamite, and jackhammers to drill and blast coral heads and boulders to widen and deepen the area for the heavy cargo barge. Meanwhile, the little lighter ferried supplies from the *Burrows* to Wilkes Island for a first camp. On the third day, the *Pioneer* towed the cargo barge to a position about three hundred feet off the cove and men attached it to cables anchored on the beach. The dynamite crew hurried to finish clearing the cove in time to land the barge at high tide that afternoon. Down to the wire, they had no time to verify depth by taking soundings in the murky water, so fifteen men lined up on the shore, linked hands, and strode into the water until it was up to their necks, checking the bottom for obstructions with their feet. They signaled the O.K.

Pulled by diesel hoists, the barge moved slowly toward the beach, then ground to a halt forty feet short of the landing. "This did not stop Harry Olsen who was directing the operation," Captain Dierdorff wrote. Olson changed the trim of the barge by moving the two heavy bulldozers on it, and nudged the barge into place with its bow eight feet above the beach. "Ensued then one of the prettiest displays of teamwork that I have ever witnessed," Dierdorff continued. As the crane operator dropped a ramp to the beach, cat skinners drove the bulldozers and other heavy equipment to the edge where they "teetered precariously on the brink," and then quickly scuttled off. The ramp was too steep for the crane itself, however, so bulldozer operators built up a coral ramp, and the crane laid it with timbers from the barge. Night had long since fallen by the time the ramp was ready for the crane. A full moon and headlights lit the scene as the crane operator inched the valuable piece of machinery off the barge and down the ramp. The pioneer party held its collective breath, and then let out a great cheer as the crane landed safely on the level shore. Now they were in business.[11]

A TOEHOLD

With the landing area established the pioneer party went to work unloading the *Burrows* the next day. Most of the workers moved off the ship to a rag camp on Wilkes, close to the unloading operation, but the supervisors stayed aboard the ship at night. Their day started when a mess boy woke them at 5:30, and they ate breakfast in the wardroom. Day after day the *Burrows* approached Wake from its overnight safety zone several miles off the atoll and then steamed in three-mile circles as Harry Olson directed the transfer of cargo from rolling ship to rocking barge to rugged shore. "This ocean is never calm," he wrote. "There is always a long rolling swell about ten feet high which makes the loads swing about crazily and hard to land as the barges and boats are bobbing around also." When a motor launch pulled a loaded barge to the small opening in the barrier reef, men attached lines from the anchored buoy to the deadman on shore, and slid the barge in close. "Of course this is done right in the surf and it's about as bad as riding a bucking horse." After a sixteen-hour day Olson returned to the ship by about eleven most nights and then went into a huddle with the captain and his executive officer for an hour, planning the next day's operations. However, ten days of hard work and short nights took their toll on the forty-six-year-old, and the ship's doctor ordered him to take a rest. "I have lived such a soft life in the last few years," Olson wrote his wife, "that it will take some time to accustom the heart muscles to the increased tempo."[12]

By January 18 the ship was half unloaded and all of the heavy equipment was ashore. Across the narrow channel on Wake, dozers cleared the site for a camp, and lumber piled up for the mess hall and tent frames that soon began to rise from the coral. Translating the plan from paper to action did not come easily. The sudden onset of heavy physical labor under a strong sun, abrasive personalities in close proximity, long hours, and poor chow taxed all of the men, but Wake offered no alternative to itself. There was no door to slam. Strong supervision kept the operation on a more or less even keel and the sight of the Pan American Clippers flying in and out of Wake's lagoon every few days lessened the feeling of utter isolation.[13]

The pioneer party brought two thousand tons of machinery, equipment, and supplies to Wake in January 1941, but one of its most powerful tools weighed less than a pound: the plan prepared by Dan Teters and the Wake team at the CPNAB operating base in Hawaii during the fall. The "Master Program and Estimate," completed December 23, 1940, and submitted to the navy, totaled more that $10 million based on then-known units of work for the project, a figure nearly $3 million more than the initial allocation. The schedule called for completion of all work except dredging by the end of 1942, and the dredging by the end of the following year. The pioneer party had packed every item in an order that would facilitate efficient unloading and establishment of a base of operations on Wake. The schedule projected the subsequent, sequenced arrival of equipment and men to accomplish the entire Wake project, as defined and approved by the navy at that time, by January 1, 1943. Despite many problems that threatened to undermine the plan during the coming months, the master schedule proved to be a durable and flexible foundation for an efficient operation that lasted from the moment the first contractor set foot on the atoll until work abruptly stopped eleven months later.[14]

ON THEIR OWN

When the now empty *Burrows* finally left Wake on January 29, 1941, Harry moved with Pete Russell into a screened tent in camp and began the adjustment to sleeping on "quiet" beds that did not roll with the swells through the night. In the evenings the men read and wrote letters. Pete tuned his radio to pick up distant stations, wrote in his diary, and kept up with a steady flow of correspondence from his second wife, Eudelle, his extended family, including two teenaged children, and dozens of men wanting work. The USS *Chaumont* arrived on February 1, bringing forty more men for the job and the first ships mail, including a "bar of candy from my darling, papers & magazines. No letters" for Pete. Like Harry Olson, Leal H. "Pete" Russell was an Oregon native and a veteran of Bonneville and Grand Coulee dams and other construction projects in the Northwest. One of the first Wake hires, Russell came equipped with an engineering degree from Oregon State College and years of construction experience, valuable attributes in the early months of the Wake project when his job entailed buying equipment and hiring men from the mainland for the pioneer party. Pete and Harry became friends on Wake where the job threw them together and similar interests and tastes drew them together.[15]

> *Wake Island, Feb. 2, 1941*
> *Dear Katherine:*
> *We finished unloading Wed. at 3:00 A.M. and from the time we*

arrived, I worked at least sixteen hours a day. I stayed aboard ship but the rest of the personnel moved ashore four days after we landed. Their camp was a very makeshift affair and like me everyone was working long hours. One mechanic made $560.00 with his overtime in January and spent half of the month traveling. It was some job. Imagine loading two thousand tons of cargo and foodstuffs into motor launches and small barges and running it ashore through the surf and unloading on a coral beach. No sand. By the way the beach is dazzling white in the sunlight and one cannot stand it without dark glasses. We had about a hundred tons of meat and perishable food that had to be kept frozen all the time. But we made it and now have our mess hall up and quarters finished. Our greatest worry is fresh water. For a long time we only had 3 gallons per day per man. In this climate one needs thirty and if left to their own devices the consumption will average forty. It did on the ship. Our kitchen has all of the latest and most modern equipment and our quarters are nicely furnished. I write this on a very modern metal desk that Donna would covet and sleep on beauty-rest spring and mattress. The nights are cool and we all use one blanket. The trades are blowing steady and Pete and I picked the tent farthest to windward. The tents, 16 X 20, are floored and the walls come up about three feet. The next four feet is screened and the wind blows through constantly. It comes off the lagoon and might as well come direct from the sea as you can stand in the middle of the Islands and almost throw a rock in the ocean on either side of you. It's only 800 feet at the widest and is the coral encrusted top of a volcano. A quarter mile offshore it is a mile and one half deep. I know I have said it before but the sea water is the most heavenly shade of blue you can imagine. I stand and gaze into it for hours enchanted by the shifting play of colors. I can't describe what it does to me. It's just out of this world. The climate is perfect. You could not imagine one any better. I expect it will get warmer as summer comes.

I can buy all the beer or liquor I wish but have not gone over to [Peale] island as yet. Only three of us have that privilege. Pan Air is located on [Peale]. The unloading was a complete success. No equipment damaged and I got many compliments (which I did not deserve) from the ship's people and Dan. . . .

I thought I might get some more Xmas mail on the Chaumont but did not. I am quite content with what I got. . . . I have had no word

*of or copy of Fortune. So henceforth I seek not good fortune. I myself
am good fortune. Henceforth I toil not, thirst not—sleep alone.*
                                                    W. Whitman Olson

Letters formed fragile lines of communication between the men on
Wake and their families and friends back home. Written by hand in quiet
moments and received with eager anticipation, they were tangible reminders
of civilization on this lonely toehold of land in the middle of the Pacific
Ocean. As the weeks went by, parcels, magazines, and newspapers arrived
by ships mail, books were shared, radios delivered news and music, and
before long open-air movies carried imaginations off the island, but the men
treasured personal letters above all. When a regular stamp cost three cents,
airmail traveled at the princely price of thirty-five cents a half-ounce—and
Pan American Airlines reaped princely profits on those airmail contracts—
but the speed was worth it to far-flung families and increasingly indispensa-
ble to business, military, and government. Navy transports also carried mail
for the outlying islands, and remained the only conduit for atolls like
Palmyra and Johnston, which were not on the Pan American Clipper route.
Contractors on Johnston had nearly rioted in December 1940 when a ship
that had picked up their mail returned with all of the letters because someone
had forgotten to mail them in Honolulu.

THE NEWS: JANUARY–FEBRUARY 1941

Isolated as the men on Wake were they kept up with news of the outside
world. Pete's radio picked up the *Richfield Reporter* most evenings, and the
men listened to updates on the European war that was spreading into the
Balkans and North Africa. The blitz continued in Britain, killing thousands
and injuring thousands more each month. In the closing days of December
1940, as the *Burrows* carried the pioneer party westward to Wake, President
Roosevelt had called the nation's attention to the Nazi menace and the grave
threat that it presented. "We must be the great arsenal of democracy," Roosevelt declared. A few weeks later, the president introduced Lend-Lease, a
new plan to extend arms credits and aid to Great Britain. In January and
February the halls of Congress rang with heated debates over the $7 billion
Lend-Lease proposal as well as Roosevelt's request for defense appropriations
in the then astronomical amount of nearly $11 billion for fiscal 1942.[16]

Along with generous economic aid to the British, who bore the full brunt of the German war machine, Roosevelt promised to "throw America's great industrial machine into battle against the Axis powers." Newspapers reported that a "cloak of secrecy" shrouded the U.S. acquisition of Atlantic naval bases from the British. In early 1941, it seemed clear that Hitler posed the greatest threat to the United States, yet many still strongly opposed "fighting another European war." Senator Burton Wheeler led the opposition, arguing that Lend-Lease would "plow under every fourth American child." President Roosevelt decried Wheeler's charge as the "rottenest and most dastardly untruth." Amidst the furor, volunteer enlistments in the U.S. military forces outnumbered the draft quota.[17]

Despite the strident opposition of numerous senators and headline-magnet Charles Lindbergh to Lend-Lease (the "surest road to war"), the rising tide of support for "self-protection" broke down isolationist arguments that spring. Rear Admiral Ben Moreell argued before Congress that bases in the far western Pacific and other bases acquired from England were "absolutely vital to the defense of the United States." As part of an enormous expansion of the defense program approved in the spring of 1941 the House funded development of naval bases—diplomatically called "harbor development"— at Guam and American Samoa. Admiral Harold R. Stark, CNO since August 1939, asserted that it was "inconceivable . . . that Japan could or would take offense at any such inoffensive measures." Japan, however, perceived each of these "inoffensive measures" as a potential obstacle in its quest to establish the Greater East Asia Co-Prosperity Sphere.[18]

Radio announcers and headlines also delivered the news that a significant reorganization of the United States Navy had taken place February 1, 1941. With the expanded defense budget the United States Fleet, based in Pearl Harbor since the previous spring, was growing rapidly. Now the navy formally split this organization into the Atlantic and Pacific Fleets while continuing the small U.S. Asiatic Fleet, which was based in the Philippines. Admiral Husband E. Kimmel took command of the new Pacific Fleet as commander in chief Pacific (CINCPAC), while retaining the senior title of commander in chief United States Fleet (CINCUS). Admiral Ernest J. King commanded the Atlantic Fleet, which was increasingly occupied with escorting merchant convoys to Britain. With German submarine attacks increasing in the Atlantic, the navy diverted a number of warships from the Pacific to the Atlantic to protect shipping. The changes reflected the growing priority of Europe in American strategy, but the navy did not let down its guard in the Pacific. The unbalanced Pacific Fleet resumed training exercises out of Pearl Harbor, and the navy stepped up its building programs. Far from the headlines, Executive Order 8682 designated Wake, Midway, Palmyra, and Johnston Island and Kingman Reef "Naval Defensive Sea Areas." The order restricted the atolls to public ships and aircraft of the United States, unless authorized by the secretary of the navy.[19]

The sudden flood of defense contracts on a Depression-level economy revealed inefficiencies, competition, and conflict. Harry S Truman, then senator from Missouri, called attention to wasteful spending and favoritism in the allocation of cost-plus-fixed-fee contracts on the mainland. Truman chaired the Senate Special Committee to Investigate the National Defense Program, established in March 1941. The Truman Committee focused on mainland defense contracts and targeted overlapping agencies, camp construction, labor problems in the coal industry, and aluminum production.[20]

That spring thousands of young American men seized the opportunities that the new defense contracts offered. Although newspapers reported strikes plaguing the mainland defense industries, the promise of good wages and automatic draft deferment appealed to many men. The Selective Service quickly authorized local draft boards to defer defense workers for six months, subject to renewal. The men who poured into the shipyards and mainland construction sites had little argument from family members, but jobs on the Pacific naval air base projects also brought the specter of long separation and danger to the table.[21]

LIFE ON WAKE

During the early months on Wake, the civilian contractors had time for the occasional book or game of cards in the evenings and Sundays. A CPNAB memorandum written in the summer of 1940 for employees headed for Palmyra, Midway, and Wake advised the men to take along fishing gear. Pete Russell liked to take a gun over to the lagoon side and shoot "spider crabs," and then shoot the big eels that came up to feed on them. In addition, there was always the old standby: bait a line for sharks, catch one and cut a fin off, then throw it back in and watch its fellows attack and tear it apart.[22]

Harry Olson was more inclined to spend his spare time picking up a book like Pierre van Paassen's 1939 anti-war memoir, *The Days of Our Years,* and wax philosophically about it to all who would listen. In long letters to his wife and daughter he also made frequent observations on his natural sur-

roundings. In early February, as the tent walls flapped loudly in the wind—
"a living wall of force ever present and a condition that influences every
action"—Harry wrote:

> *Life at Wake moves on apace. A snail's pace. Which is a poor simile, as*
> *we have no snails. Our nearest approach is hermit crabs, a preposterous*
> *little creature about the size of a small alarm clock. He literally obeys*
> *the biblical injunction to pick up his bed and walk: always going*
> *nowhere in reverse. . . . They are very sensitive to the approach of any*
> *moving thing but their only defense is to cuddle up as snugly and trust-*
> *ingly as possible in their combination bed and house that they carry*
> *on their back. . . . All of which serves as an introduction to a line of*
> *thought that engrosses me tremendously. That is an attempt on my part*
> *to correlate life as I see it on this island to life elsewhere in the light of*
> *the theory of evolution and along the line of philosophic thought. I*
> *think we may accept it as true that in a diminutive sense we may call*
> *this a continent. It is removed from any other land by a thousand miles*
> *of sea, an almost insuperable barrier to any forms of life except migra-*
> *tory fowls and it does not lie in any of their lanes of travel. So we may*
> *say that life as it exists is peculiar to this place, noting as irrelevant that*
> *the same condition exists on many other isolated Pacific Islands. The*
> *strongest argument for this idea is the fact that life that is native to this*
> *island could not exist if a single predatory influence were transplanted*
> *here. Of the birds, the majority are boobies (a well-named bird), next*
> *the frigates, a sort of benign buzzard, some snipe, the only ones with a*
> *chance of survival and—shades of a crossword puzzle—a species of rail*
> *bird. These last look somewhat like a quail but cannot fly. The boobies*
> *and frigates are very tame, or should I say have not sense enough to be*
> *afraid. They set up a plaintive sort of clamor in a scolding sort of fash-*
> *ion when approached but won't fly until you are about ten feet away.*
> *Then they usually get all tangled up in the limbs of the tree or bush*
> *they are roosting on and get mad at themselves, the bush, and you. They*
> *have no control of themselves and regurgitate about this time. On Peale*
> *Island there is also a species of moaning bird (their name) that live in*
> *the ground and make a sad sort of cry like a lost soul in torment. You*
> *can readily see that none of these would be able to cope with life as it*
> *has existed on any of the mainlands for the last million years. They*

would be exterminated almost overnight. The hermit crabs I spoke of and an abundance of rats that resemble an overgrown sort of field mouse are the only forms of ground life that exist in any numbers. There may have been others that these crude forms have succeeded in eliminating, a possibility that opens wide vistas of thought. On the whole I would say that the island does not support one half the life it is capable of. On the other hand the sea around us is literally alive with fish and all forms of marine life. That this abundance exists under the highest competitive system leads to the conclusion that this competition is a necessary corollary to the development of the higher orders or species. I know that the big fish eat the smaller ones but am puzzled as to what sustains the least of them.

The conclusion is inevitable that one must live dangerously and set his hand against his neighbors in order to achieve his strength and fulfill his destiny. Being a humanist at heart I find no comfort in all this and endlessly seek some other solution. Does all this sound screwy to you and do you think the islands are getting me?[23]

The *Burrows* left Wake supplied with six weeks' worth of food and fuel oil when it departed at the end of January. The *Chaumont* and several other navy ships stopped at Wake in the early weeks to look in on the operation and deliver parcels, but the contractors depended on regular shipments of food, fuel, equipment, and workers from their supply center in Alameda via Honolulu. Midway and the other remote CPNAB projects relied solely on food shipped from the mainland with fresh provisions riding in special refrigerated containers. With no source for fresh ground water on Wake, the contractors erected stills and pumps to distill seawater, large tanks on concrete footings for storage, and a Columbian tank to collect rainwater. Still, the regular cargo ships would carry thousands of gallons of fresh water from Honolulu to keep the contractors securely supplied on Wake.[24]

The contractors' camp expanded quickly during February as workers erected a full kitchen and mess hall, wired more tents for housing and offices, poured concrete slabs for storage and powerhouse foundations, and laid sewer lines out to sea. Cat skinners graded a five-mile road to carry the project around the base of Wake and up the other side of the V to the proposed location of the permanent camp, Camp 2. Among the men, tempers often flared, and personalities clashed, and at mid-month, some of the workers called for a meeting in the mess hall to air grievances. The workers elected a chairman and a committee, and discussed troubling issues arising from misrepresentations by the Los Angeles employment office. Pete Russell explained overtime policy to the group and noted later that it "ended up by everyone feeling a bit better about everything" and that they "decided to make it more or less a recreation body." This was the genesis of the Pioneer Club that held weekly meetings in the months to come.[25]

Harry Olson made good on his promise to send for several of his co-workers from Grand Coulee Dam when jobs opened up on Wake. In January, his friend, Swede Hokanson, made his way to California, leaving his young wife, Mae, and their eleven-year-old daughter to close up the little house and move on. Pete Russell found jobs for many fellows, including his cousin, Donald Rohan, a mechanic from La Grande, Oregon. In Boise, word spread that Morrison-Knudsen was looking for good men to take jobs on the company's contracts in the Pacific. On California construction sites, men like carpenter Peter Hansen heard about the jobs; if he could bear the separation from his wife and three children, a year in the Pacific would erase their crippling Depression debts and give his family a new lease on life.

LEARNING FROM EXPERIENCE

The outlying island projects shared the same navy supervision, CPNAB management, sources of supply, transportation, and similar contractual objectives and physical conditions, leading to a constant flow of information among them. A problem solved on one atoll could be a problem avoided on another. Palmyra's difficulties with on-site seaplane ramp construction in 1940 led to the prefabrication solution that carried over to subsequent projects. Project engineers often sent plans drawn up for structures on one island to another in the interest of saving time and money. Wake received quite a share of such hand-me-downs from Midway, but even with modifications, there were often problems translating them in the field.[26]

The Wake project got off on the right foot with its successful maiden voyage. While the *Burrows* suffered a few bumps and bruises, a punctured pontoon, a bent boom, and the hard-pressed motor launches sustained minor damage, given the adverse conditions the three-week unloading process had gone remarkably well. When the *Burrows* returned to Honolulu forty-two days later, its sides were "scarred, dented, and red with rust," but it bore no significant damage. Nearly a year before, Captain Swede Momeson had brought the first CPNAB contractors and four thousand tons of cargo to Midway aboard the *Sirius*, arriving March 27, 1940. At Midway, the sea had swallowed many costly items and the *Sirius* limped away with $40,000 damage. Careful planning and execution in equally challenging seas off Wake had resulted in no losses and minimal damage.[27]

The year-old CPNAB project at Midway offered many lessons in how and how not to build a remote island naval base. In the summer of 1940, when Morrison-Knudsen took over sponsorship of the operation, Midway was suffering from "severe starvation": too few men for too much work. The general superintendent had resigned abruptly, leaving the operation in disarray. M-K's George Youmans evaluated the situation and, with Harry Morrison's help, quickly found an experienced superintendent to step in at Midway at the same time they were lining up key men to begin the Wake project. Marlyn Sheik soon had the material and engineering challenges on Midway under better control, but the labor problem continued to bedevil the contractors. Despite more than doubling the workforce and trying all sorts of incentives to increase worker contentment, the turnover rate remained high on Midway. The average stay was just two months in the fall of 1940, and the time and cost of replacement crippled the operation. When the *Burrows* left the pioneer party on Wake at the end of January, Captain Dierdorff received orders to change course for Midway where he took on seventy-six disgruntled contractors and their baggage along with four sick men for Honolulu. In February 1941 the situation was so dire that Harry Morrison flew out on a Clipper from the mainland and with other CPNAB officials, accompanied by Captain Bruns, the OinC from Pearl Harbor, visited Midway for several days to study the problem. They came out with a commitment to open up additional hiring offices on the mainland, including Boise, in order to hire better quality workers than the thinned-out California halls were offering.[28]

A reasonably reliable workforce and strong supervision would help alleviate turnover on Midway, but CPNAB took care to structure the even more distant Wake operation to minimize labor discontent. Navy regulations remained firm on no women or liquor, although some supervisors enjoyed exceptions to the liquor rule, but the contractors offered excellent food, leisure-time activities, and plenty of work with overtime and bonuses for staying on: lessons that Midway learned the hard way, but that were integrated into Wake's plan from the start. The result did not inoculate Wake from the problem of turnover, but it was reduced.

Among the young men on the mainland who contemplated job opportunities in the Pacific that spring was Harry Olson's son, Ted. Festering in the crowded apartment in Pullman, Washington, that he shared with his mother and sister and worried that the draft board would draw his number next, Ted wrote to his father to test the waters. The days dragged by as he waited for Harry's response. Finally, the letter came, with Harry's list of reasons why it was not a good idea: it would "interfere seriously" with Ted's schooling, the travel to and from Wake would take too much time (and he "wouldn't have enough money to do that properly"), and, in the long run, it would be better for him to work for someone else. "I wasted about ten years of my life working for my folks and I know whereof I speak," Harry wrote. "Personally I would like to have you here with me a lot. It would mean much to me but for your sake I advise against it." Despite the negative response, Ted detected a tiny window of opportunity, and bided his time.[29]

Wake Island, Feb. 20, 1941
Dear Katherine:
I guess we are having what could be called a storm here tonite as the wind is howling a gale and the wind and salt spray is coming in the horizontal plane instead of falling. It isn't the least bit cold for I am sitting writing this in my shirt sleeves and we haven't anything but a screen door in our tent. Luckily it faces away from the wind. The temperature dropped to 75° last night and we all felt a little chilly. Usually it won't move 3° from eighty for months at a stretch. Practically perfect. This rain will help some as we will catch 15 or 20 thousand gallons of water. Maybe I can get a real bath tomorrow. The lagoon is only a couple hundred feet from my tent and the water clear as crystal, but did you ever try to bathe in salt water? The doctors advise at least two fresh water baths a week but so far ours has been of the sponge variety. Tomorrow our shower room should be finished and I suppose one will have to stand in line to get to one. The rainwater collection system was partially completed today. I have just finished erection of a steel tower [50] ft. high with a 2000 gal. tank atop. This is for salt water for the stills and fire protection. I have no riggers as yet so practically built it myself. . . .
After the Chaumont *came we had a case of scarlet fever in camp*

and were quarantined. That was not difficult. Then a sort of dysentery broke out and is still going on. (The quarantine is lifted.) It seems that the soil and even the air of these islands seems to be full of a type of colon bacilli and newcomers must become acclimated to it. The Pan Air people experienced the same difficulty when they first arrived. Some are immune and I am one of the fortunate few. You may tell Ted that this raises a problem of collaboration between the medical and engineering staffs in planning a camp so that the toilets are placed the proper distance from the quarters. Actual experience and observation has proven that ours are located a little too far away. In one case this was less than ten feet with the victim putting on a burst of speed as the immanence of disaster dawned on him. In case his engineering class should care to experiment on this problem, may I advise that the prospective victim or guinea pig be divested of his trousers as they are not only a deterrent to his ultimate speed but apt to prove a serious hindrance in his moment of trial.

Yesterday's Clipper that brought your letter had as passengers Ernest Hemingway and his wife. Dan, the lucky stiff, was over and had dinner with them. I could have gone also had I known. I was so disgusted this morning that I quit working and went over to Pan Air and spent the morning visiting Jack Bonamy (the Supt.). We had a couple bottles of beer. It sure tasted good and it felt good also to sit at a table in a comfortable chair and have some one standing over you saying, "What will it be?" This was the first relaxation I have had since we arrived. The hotel is nicely appointed and the grounds around it show evidence of their attempts to landscape though they still show strong evidence of this winter's typhoons. Jack showed me a lot of pictures taken immediately afterwards and it was a mess. That morning they received a standard Pan Air weather report. Wind N.E.—15 mi. Sky overcast occasional rain. Four hours later the wind was 135 mi. S.W. The second typhoon was not so severe (wind 110 mi.) but the day afterwards the seas were so high they were breaking over the Island where we are camped. Pan Air lost a thousand barrels of 100 octane gasoline—barrels and all. Another two thousand were scattered from hell to breakfast and are not all recovered yet.

We received a surprise message last night that some Navy ships (probably a light cruiser) would arrive in a week with 75 more men and 100 tons of food. We will have to hustle to provide accommodations for them. The Burrows *will be back Mar. 15—the* Sirius *Mar. 25—and the* Regulus *Apr. 5. This will keep me going as it means 6000 tons. We also have 12 1000-ton barges that will be put on this hauling. We expect to unload about 8000 tons per month for the next 16 months. We are digging a channel from the sea into the lagoon and unloading will be much easier from now on. I got a letter of thanks and commendation from H. W. Morrison on unloading the* Burrows *the first trip and believe it or not a raise of $50.00 per month. Also a promise of another raise and a better job or a bigger one. For the life of me, I cannot see why. As far as toughness goes I have done dozens on the mainland that were more difficult. I had no doubts in my own mind at any time about this one but felt that it would not be smart to say so. Of course we always have the risk of bad weather but this can be discounted to a certain extent as we are in the belt of the most equable and stable weather in the world.*

Since the above was written Dan has advised me that he has recommended my promotion to Asst. Gen. Supt. at a further raise in salary of $75.00. This will bring me to $475.00 per month which is not bad for a country boy far out to sea. This last raise is contingent on approval of the Operating Base at Pearl Harbor. If it goes through I will be in direct charge of all field work and the entire job when Dan is gone. I will have 12 Asst. Supts. under me and some of them are going to feel a little bad over it as they have been with Dan a long time. I saw the letter he sent in and it was very flattering. I don't think you realized all these years what a paragon of all the virtues and abilities you have lived with. At least the portrait as he drew it was unrecognizable to me and I thought that in event I should make some mistake, his opinion would swing into reverse with the same wholehearted conviction. . . .

It is trying to be warm here today but the trade wind is on the job so it is not having much success. I will be spoiled for extremes of weather the rest of my life. It is impossible for anyone who has not been here to imagine how nice this is. And what will get the newcomers goat is that the nights are the same as the days. I have been out here almost four months and it still seems odd to me.

Harry

A TOUCH OF CIVILIZATION

The Pan American Airways complex on Peale, across the channel from the proposed location of the contractors' Camp 2 on Wake, was only accessible by boat. Well-established after five years in operation, Pan Air had whisked hundreds of Clippers in and out of the Wake lagoon and hosted many guests in the stylish and well-appointed hotel and lounge. Repaired from the storm damage, the red-roofed Pan Air buildings, the "goal posts" of its direction finder, and the long dock with a covered pergola on the shore represented welcome reminders of civilization to weary Clipper passengers. Crushed coral and concrete paths led to tennis courts, an outdoor movie screen made of silver-painted boards, and to the hotel itself, where a large, rusty anchor from the 1866 shipwreck, *Libelle*, stood guard. Travel writer and Clipper passenger Dorothy Kaucher vividly described the prewar ambiance and unexpected charms of Wake during her visit in the summer of 1937. Stepping past the tall square columns on the portico and through the wide screen door, one entered another world: soft lamp light, French doors, drapes, and wicker furniture interspersed with art deco features in a blue and steel motif. A globe of the world sat atop a radio. White-clad Chamorro (Guamanian) employees served cocktails with clinking ice; dinner might include watermelon, lobster salad, and lamb chops on fine china.[30]

Shortly after the pioneer party arrived in January, the Pan American employees had invited the *Burrows* officers and contractor supervisors to their compound on Peale for a steak barbeque, where the main attraction was a case of scotch. The gathering softened the brittle edge of Wake, but, according to Harry, who was too busy handling cargo to attend, the liquor encouraged some to vent "things that were better left unsaid." In short order, however, Harry acquired special privileges to visit the Pan American hotel and lounge, even though it remained officially off limits to the navy's civilian contractors. In early March, Harry and Pete spent a Sunday over at Pan Air, got a "pleasant snootful of scotch," and ate both lunch and dinner there. That evening under the stars, the Chamorro employees entertained the party with an orchestra and a master of ceremonies. "They are quite musical," Harry wrote. "They are quite shy and I enjoyed it a lot." One of the added benefits of special access to Pan Air was the occasional company of women. In addition to overnight Clipper passengers, the hotel steward's wife lived at the complex and often joined the party. Still, "the absence of women out here is the source of many jokes," Harry lamented. "The latest is that on retiring we all look under the beds to see if any old maids are hidden there."[31]

Later, Harry sent Katherine a mimeographed transcription of a January 1941 U. S. Naval Institute *Proceedings* article by Homer C. Votaw entitled "Wake Island," which was widely circulated on the island. In the margin near Votaw's description of Pan American's "almost self-sustaining" features, including farm animals furnishing milk, meat, and eggs; hydroponic gardens; and wind and solar energy; Harry jotted "This is a lot of bull: there are no cows, chickens, gardens, windmills."

By early March, the contractors had equipped their camp for three to four hundred men and blasted a shallow barge channel nearly to the lagoon. A road, nicknamed "Wilshire Boulevard," stretched from the first camp to the location for Camp 2, on the opposite end of Wake. There the contractors cleared the site for the permanent camp, calculating that it would take three to four months to build the facilities, after which they would finally be able to start the naval air base itself. The smoke-belching machinery and dynamite blasting altered the Wake ambiance for Pan Air passengers and staff, but their ocean-crossing Clippers and nightly news broadcasts on the radio in the elegant lounge reminded them that war was not so far distant.

Wake Islands, Sat. Eve: Mar. 8, 1941
Dear Katherine:
All your letters came in this afternoon and I will try to answer some of the questions right away as there is a Clipper for the mainland Monday a.m. One of your letters was dated Feb. 15—one 22, one 28, so they cover quite a lot of ground. The Clippers have been all balled up. One came through from the coast with only enough mail to hold the contract. Bad weather over there. The radio is full of plane wrecks on the mainland. After the Clippers get to Honolulu they have good sailing but the last two have had mechanical trouble at Hong Kong and Manila. The area from Honolulu to Guam has the best and most even weather of any in the whole world according to the U.S. Geodetic survey. Wake is in the center of this. We have a small shower most every day. It lasts about 5 min. The rest is mostly sunshine and wind. It would get very hot if it wasn't for the wind. It usually blows about 10 to 15 mi. per hr.

Pan Air has a ship due tomorrow. The "Halstead," a regular cargo ship. As they lost most of their unloading facilities they will use ours.

This will mean a little work for me and I will get my pay in scotch. They have about 300 tons of freight and should be done in four days.

I have just finished overhauling all the boats and barges which took quite a beating unloading that first boat in the surf. We have quite a flotilla and will get another big barge and tug on the next ship which is due the 16th. From that time on we will have a ship at least every two weeks and probably oftener. To do this job in the scheduled time we need about 8000 tons of freight per month and that means at least 3 ships. I will have a crew unloading and hauling cargo around the clock seven days a week for the next 16 months. I plan on 3 cranes and 10 trucks for this job alone. And about 125 men. This is the biggest problem we have. We have to anticipate our wants for months ahead and fight all along the line to ensure its getting here. . . . There is no running down to the corner store out here. We try to keep 3 months ahead on all essentials like food, clothing, fuel oil, commissary stores, etc., in event of adverse weather or war. The only way we can be sure we have everything is to go through the most comprehensive catalogues we have and check each item we may need and ladies' clothing is about the only exception.

Our regular Doctor came in on the Clipper today. Seems to be a nice guy. We have needed him badly for we have some men who take advantage of the fact that they get paid whether they work or not. I take some pride in the fact that my department is the only one not affected that way. I have a different approach to my men than most of the fellows. Closer to them and it pays.

It really wrings my heart on Clipper day to see the eagerness with which the men await the mail. I have sat in the office and watched each man's reaction to his luck in the matter and it made one downright mad when some of them I know were downright anxious drew a dud. Being men they have no outlets for their disappointments and just grin and bear it. It is ten weeks since we left Honolulu and I am really surprised at the small amount of dissatisfaction manifested so far. Of course the biggest problem is the absence of women which affects some much worse than others. We have no diversions at all. This is something we will have to correct quickly or we are going to lose some men. I have harped on this subject continuously since I arrived at Honolulu and at long last everyone is beginning to agree with me. However it may be that it has been neglected too long as it will take as long to get action on this as anything else. We have a complete movie outfit at Honolulu and if we could get this it would help. Personally I keep pretty busy and have had no trouble. Then too I can go over to Pan Air any time I want to. No one else can go without my permission so in fairness to all I must use a lot of discretion.

Thursday, Mar. 13.
The Clipper didn't materialize after all but is supposed to arrive today. I have my doubts as the wind is howling a gale. The sea is very rough and we have squalls of rain. Tuesday afternoon Jack Bonamy (Pan Air Supt.), Slim Huston (Esco Supt.) and I went out to the Halstead *and the Captain, a red-headed Swede name of Johnson, broke out some scotch. Perhaps you can guess the rest. We wound up at the Pan Air hotel for dinner and had a wonderful time. I got home at midnite and found a dispatch awaiting me from the [Sepulga], a Navy tanker from San Francisco, saying she would arrive at daylight with eight tons of freight. So up I got in the morning and went out with the tug and a small lighter. The sea was rough and the wind freshening. The Sepulga came up into the wind and hove to and we secured the lighter on the lee side. The ship's people were inexperienced and just let her drift out to sea. We were ten miles out when we finally got our stuff and the waves were rolling thirty feet high. The tug would rise higher than the ship when on the crest of the swells and I stepped aboard it from the deck without using a Jacob's ladder. We had to tow the lighter back directly into the wind and it was really something. The waves would go clean over the tug at times. It took us two hours. I thought I would be sick as my stomach wasn't any too secure but came through O.K. It was really a lot of fun but I was mad as it was all unnecessary. My desk is fastened to the wall of the tent and the wind shakes it badly.*

Dan has not returned from Honolulu but should be here Saturday. So I don't know about my job as yet. The Burrows *will be in Sunday with eighty men and 2500 tons of cargo. This will mean a lot of work. We have this first camp completed now and a good start on the second one which is five miles away at the other end of this (Wake) island. This job has grown from eight to twelve millions since I came out and the end is not in sight. The navy sees this as the westward spearhead of*

American defense and are much concerned over its rapid completion. The burden is on them as our progress depends on delivery of materials.

Red Johnson of the Halstead *has offered to take me along with him on one of his westward jaunts. He goes to Guam, Manila and a flock of lesser Philippine ports. This is a real opportunity and I must admit I am tempted. Of course I don't know if I could get away but a guy could wish. It would take a couple months, one of which would be spent at sea. About six thousand miles round trip. The trip would cost me nothing but I would probably spend plenty at Apia and Manila as Red says there are some swell night spots there at one third the cost on the mainland.*

Well I have a lot of work to do to get ready for the Burrows *so will close.*

Harry

PART II
Building the Base

—National Archives

CHAPTER 5

SECOND GEAR

NEW BLOOD

THE *WILLIAM WARD BURROWS* RETURNED TO WAKE ON MARCH 16 AND the pioneer party welcomed the ship and its crew like long-lost friends. Among the seventy-six new faces were many friends and stateside coworkers, including Swede Hokanson, Harry's friend from Grand Coulee, and Pete's cousin Donald Rohan. *Burrows* Captain Ross Dierdorff and his executive officer, E. I. McQuiston, toured the waterfront and camp and were impressed by the progress on Wake in their absence. In addition to the new workers the ship carried nearly forty thousand gallons of fresh water and towed twenty-five hundred tons of cargo on the barge *Wake No. 2.* A tanker had brought "a dime's worth of pipe" a few days earlier and the Wake contractors were as glad to see the cargo as they were the new faces.[1]

Harry directed the tug *Pioneer* as it took the barge from its tow and brought it in to shore and then put Swede and the arriving workers right to work unloading cargo. The newcomers moved into the tent camp and began their adjustment to life and work on Wake. Some made the transition easier than others: Harry sweetened Swede Hokanson's adjustment by promptly promoting him and giving him a raise. However, when the *Burrows* departed on March 26 it carried twenty workers away from Wake, including the excavation superintendent and steward, who had been personally fired by Harry. Of those who quit on their own accord, "most of them have the same trouble which I will leave to your imagination," Harry wrote to Katherine. Shortly before the *Burrows* departed the *Cuyama* brought another thirteen new men to Wake. Pete Hansen, one of the *Cuyama* passengers, noted the workers heading in the opposite direction and wrote home: "Some quit, some got fired, and some were sent home because they had misrepresented themselves as being something they are not." Hansen also noted that his fellow incoming passengers included Herman Echols, who would be Harry Olson's counterpart as the assistant general superintendent for administration, and another supervisor: "Their salaries are enormous."[2]

Dan Teters returned to Wake on the Pan American Clipper in mid-March and made Olson's promotion to assistant general superintendent official. Two months into the project the contractors had two hundred men at work and a budget of $12 million, but were still far from starting work on the permanent navy facilities for the air base. Olson estimated that 75 percent of their effort that spring went to getting materials ashore and preparing to house more men. Interdepartmental rivalry raged over overtime claims, with some of the eight departments pulling down excessive amounts and others resenting them for it. In his new position Harry took immediate steps to control that imbalance and keep the peace. To supervise fieldwork during the day via Wake's five miles of road Olson received a shiny new light green G.M.C. pickup. The 1941 pickup came equipped with very fat, super-balloon tires, a Midway innovation that was superfluous on Wake, where the surface was hard finger coral instead of sand. Nevertheless, of the five pickups and station wagon that served as Wake's fleet, Harry's green truck was the top of the line: "Number one. I finally got to the head of the class," he boasted to Katherine. After six weeks and considerable wear, he would turn "number one" over to Pete Russell in favor of a brand new Ford, light gray with a "bright coral stripe around it. It is a honey."[3]

Among the March arrivals was the forty-year-old carpenter from Inglewood, California, Peter W. Hansen. Like many of the skilled workers who came to Wake, Hansen had a family to support during the long months apart. Anticipating a full year away, Hansen was delighted to learn that the Wake job came with a nine-month contract. With overtime, potential raises, and a rumored bonus, Hansen figured he could easily erase the couple's debts and build up their bank account. It was a long time to be without the comforts of wife and family, but Hansen wrote home frequently, meticulously counting the dollars earned and the days remaining to the end of his contract. "Darling, I'm going to be the most lonesome person in the world, but when I get this job done, we're all going to be the happiest in the world." By his count, he would be heading home just before Christmas.[4]

One CPNAB man did not have to yearn for his wife. Dan Teters received special permission from the operating committee and the navy to bring his wife to Wake, and Florence accompanied him on the Clipper from Honolulu in mid-March. CPNAB footed Florence's $300 Clipper fare, and she would live at the Pan American hotel on Wake (four dollars a night versus the going rate of ten), pending construction of their cottage. The cottage would be located on Heel Point, "about halfway around the island in an isolated spot facing the ocean," as Harry Olson observed to Katherine without a trace of yearning. "It is very lovely there. The sea too beautiful for words. It is on the windward side and will be pleasant as far as weather is concerned but I think she will be lonely."[5]

THE BOISE CONNECTION

In March 1941, the Boise newspaper ran a big spread on Morrison-Knudsen Company's widespread construction contracts, including the first public details of the company's participation in the PNAB joint venture. Thanks to M-K, Boise had become the hub of the wheel from which extended many spokes of huge national defense projects that would employ thousands upon thousands of men. In the first few months of 1941 Harry Morrison had added half a dozen new projects to the twenty-four defense and commercial construction contracts that the company had acquired, either individually or jointly, by 1940. In addition to the CPNAB projects, in early 1941 M-K's contracts included dam construction, flood control, harbor improvement, an army cantonment, and shipbuilding. The local paper named a dozen key men, engineers, and draftsmen from the Boise area who had already gone out to the islands for M-K's defense jobs, and that was just the beginning. In true booster fashion the *Idaho Daily Statesman* proudly touted Boise's own Morrison-Knudsen Company as a key to the region's future prosperity.[6]

In the winter of 1940–41 the island jobs were a hard sell in a West Coast market suddenly flush with mainland defense jobs. So many experienced, skilled men were snapping up good-paying jobs close to home that CPNAB had to keep widening its net to meet its needs. The higher the qualifications, the harder it was to make the hire. In November 1940 CPNAB had appealed to Morrison-Knudsen to assist in hiring architectural engineers and the company had quickly located six. In response to the turnover crisis on Midway and anticipating large labor orders with the new projects, Harry Morrison promised his fellow CPNAB executives to open an employment office in Boise and he did so March 1941. The Boise office promptly filled an order for 140 laborers, impressing CPNAB with the quantity and quality of reliable workers from the Inland Northwest.[7]

Several other CPNAB hiring offices opened in the Midwest and all promised to augment the California hiring office with a new crop of high-quality workers. The Boise office, located directly across the street from M-K headquarters, took scores of applications from local and regional men to build up a register of available workers. As orders for specific craftsmen and laborers came in from the various CPNAB projects to the central Alameda office, the call then went out to the branch offices that could most readily hire and forward qualified men to Alameda and then to the islands.[8]

The men hired through the Boise employment office might end up in any of a number of projects under the CPNAB umbrella. Still, M-K managed to ensure that the cream of the crop went to one of its three sponsored projects: Midway, Wake, or the Red Hill underground fuel storage project on Oahu. Harry Morrison, "always on the go" traveling to his far-flung projects and conferring with officials and executives, was doing right by Boise, the local newspaper reported. By the end of March, the first large group hired through the new employment office departed Boise in two rowdy busloads headed for Alameda.[9]

A JOB FOR TED

At Washington State College in Pullman, Ted Olson remained determined to come up with a plan to be one of those Inland Northwest men headed for Wake Island, but so far his father's responses had been discouraging. "I find on investigation that it is strictly against Navy policy to hire the son or close relative of a boss. In my case, it would be very difficult to get Ted on here," Harry wrote to Katherine in late March. "He could perhaps make one of the other island jobs. I might be able to give him a little boost on it but he could do as well for himself. The moral conditions are not so good at Midway from what I hear and the job is nearing completion. Some of the others are just starting. All the hiring is done at Morrison Knudsen offices on the mainland. I don't quite know just what to advise him to do. I have not listened to the news for a week or ten days. I do hope that come what may Ted will continue his studies. I survived a year in the service without any mishap so he hasn't anything really to worry about. He is of age and should really solve this problem himself."[10]

Schooled in the isolationist climate of the 1930s and utterly disinclined to take up a gun even for sport, Ted felt the draft shadowing him. Like many college-aged men, he reasoned that a short hiatus for a defense job—with the accompanying draft deferment—made sense. When Grand Coulee Dam officially opened that spring a New York paper noted that in time of stress and arrogant dictatorships, this "great, peacefully intended creation of free men is an inspiration." Like Grand Coulee, Wake Island offered Ted the opportunity to do right by his nation outside of a uniform. However, as the weeks went by his Wake plan seemed more elusive than ever.[11]

Wake Island, April 17, 1941
Dear Ted:
I guess I have owed you a letter for some time. My only excuse is lack of time not an unwillingness to write. Writing in itself is difficult down here. There is so little of interest to anyone in our every day lives. And I do not seem to be able to capture any of the South Sea spirit of romance or glamour. In truth the great legend of charm that has been built up around these islands stems in a great part from the charm of the natives' personality. This is in turn a product of thousands of years of living prosaic and utterly uninteresting lives which has made them the simple unspoiled children of nature they are. There is no chance of my getting that way from my short sojourn here as I am too thoroughly conditioned to a harsher more virile civilization. . . .

The Clipper came in today but I fared poorly, not a letter. I have been writing so steadily I guess everyone thinks it's not necessary to answer. I know you all have more time than I so I suppose it's another ball up in the mail. The Clipper had as passengers Mr. Geo. Ferris, chairman of the Operating Committee, and a party on their way out to Manila to start the Cavite job. A Mr. Cullum is to be the job supt. and he turned out to be an old friend from Bonneville. Mr. Ferris said they were also starting the Samoa job. Bob Dunlap is to be supt. down there and he sent his regards to me by Mr. Ferris. I was greatly tempted to try and arrange a transfer to either place. You know people live there and each or either would be a vast improvement on this place. But I didn't for I know they would not like it. Mr. Ferris was very pleased with the progress we have made and invited me over to Pan Air to visit a while after dinner tonight. So I will stop for now and continue tomorrow.

This is getting to be rather long drawn out and I have lost the sense of continuity of the letter. Anyway I went across to Pan Air and had a pleasant evening. The Clipper passengers have to retire early to get up early but during the course of the evening the Pan Air Doctor and I got into a deep discussion on philosophy. Aided and abetted by a few scotches and chartreuses. I enjoyed it a lot. The Doc is a student and a humanist and we have a very definite date to continue the discussion at his quarters some evening. To be honest I expect we bored everyone else to tears but we had a lot of fun so that's their hard luck.

We will finish this boat in a couple days. I'll be glad as we have cargo all over the place. We got over a million feet of lumber alone and it is scattered over about 40 acres. Our lumber hoister broke down right in the middle of the job. We have to haul all the cargo about five miles and of course the road grader broke down the day before the boat arrived. We left it right in the middle of the road and drove around it. One of the Woolridge scrapers conked out night before last and they're still welding on it. The universal on one of the trucks went out also so we radioed for a new one to come out on the Clipper and now we find we paid a hundred dollar postage bill for nothing as they sent out the wrong parts. One particular fitting we need very badly for each sewer connection at Camp 2 was not sent so I have to make those also. Also I can't find any pumps for the distillation unit at Camp 2 so life is not very pleasant. I am not happy. A guy came in a while ago with some complaint and I just fired him to relieve my mind. He had only worked 3 days and won't draw any travel pay. He will have to pay his way back to the mainland also. We have fifteen men in the hospital from accidents on a par with the one your mother had when she broke her nose. The doctor X-rayed one and while he was in the dark room developing the print he struck his eye on the corner of a shelf and we thought for a couple days he was going to lose his eye. One of our tugs is down for a month. Head cracked. They let a row boat get away last night. It went out to sea and came back on the rocks. We salvaged it but it will cost a hundred dollars to fix it up. Guess I had better close before I break my pen.

As ever, Dad

Less than two weeks after he wrote with no encouragement for Ted, Harry sent out a requisition for him as a rigger's helper on Wake at $165 a month. With overtime and bonus, Harry calculated, Ted would make "about $250 clean each month." The job started July 1, giving Ted time to finish the school year. "The only reason I am doing this is to protect him from the draft," Harry wrote Katherine. "I still don't think it is a good thing for him to work for me. If he wishes to come out I will expect him to disregard that situation and hold the job through his own efforts. I also hate to see him miss a year of school, but I hate more to see him go to war. I want it clearly understood that I desire him to continue his education as soon as possible. I have thought much about this problem and this is the only answer I can find."[12]

"SO MUCH DOING"

Not long into the Wake project, there were hints that navy transportation might become a problem. Despite the atoll's role in war plans, the process of bringing it to the level of viability was plagued with logistical problems. As the contractors worked through their initial shipment of supplies on Wake, they anticipated a sequenced delivery of cargo. However, as the pioneer party had experienced in Honolulu in the fall of 1940, navy transportation operated on a schedule in which delay was the rule rather than the exception. Nevertheless, the contractors sped through the preliminary construction of their own camps and facilities, items that were outside the contract for the naval air station.

Camp 1 was soon bursting at its seams and preparation of the new and larger camp on the north side of Wake Island became a priority. Graders worked steadily on the much-used Wilshire Boulevard connecting the two camps, and the contractors began building the steel structure for a bridge from Wake to Peale, where the permanent naval air base structures were to be located. Before long, Pete would no longer have to wade or drive equipment across the Peale channel, knee-deep at low tide, and hope he could get back across in time. "Too many sharks, eels and octopus in there to suit me." Camp 2 rapidly took shape as the first eighty-man barracks, mess hall, kitchen, warehouses, cold storage, and powerhouse rose from their foundations. Russell noted that the "dormitories are pretty good looking buildings when they're finished." Pete and Harry waded out on the reef one afternoon at low tide to lay out the route for a six-inch sewer line from Camp 2: waste disposal at sea was taken for granted.[13]

The Teters cottage and a guesthouse soon perched on the northeast beach of Heel Point, a comfortable distance away from the noisy camp under construction. Lieutenant Butzine, the RoinC for Wake, occupied the guesthouse as the contractors continued to work on the third cottage for naval officers. Harry noted that Florence had been "fooling around there for 2 or 3 weeks," decorating the cottages with a "conservative beach motif. Lord knows it has cost us plenty." He expressed doubts that Florence would stay more than a few months as her activities were very limited. "She cannot leave the house unless Dan or I take her. And she don't dare stay alone at night. She can't come into the camp areas as lots of the fellows run around naked and above all we don't want her to be involved in anything along the lines of rape, which could happen. For a while she can have a little freedom at the Pan Air compound but we are moving in there shortly and her activities will be limited there also."[14]

At the waterfront, dragline operators worked steadily to widen the shallow pilot channel between Wake and Wilkes in order to bring cargo barges into quiet water. High tides and swift currents in the channel wreaked havoc with the operation. On one occasion the outboard motor broke down on a skiff carrying the dragline operator, his oiler, two mechanics, and Pete Russell, who was straining under double-duty as both building and excavation superintendent. "Motor canned, current drifted us into and under catamaran—all went in the drink." When the pilot channel was finished at the end of March (fifteen feet deep and seventy feet wide at the base) it carried a relentless, eight-knot current seaward from the lagoon, but promised safer and quicker unloading operations than the open sea.[15]

A turning basin and bulkhead in the lagoon were essential components of the harbor, but the barge channel between Wake and Wilkes led directly to shallow, fiercely resistant coral. The men built a dike and stored large boulders for future use as riprap against the current, and draglines chewed at the turning basin site itself. Unable to put a dent in the hard coral with the smaller draglines, operators worked the two largest draglines two shifts a day in the basin. Dump trucks hauled muck out for roadbeds and operators pulled and piled boulders for the bulkhead just east of the channel entrance in the lagoon. When the draglines hit a hard spot, they called in a blasting crew to dive, drill holes, plant caseloads of dynamite, and shoot it off. Geysers of water, shattered coral and rock, and dead fish burst the surface of the lagoon with increasing frequency. Russell noted that a hard spot under dragline No. 1 "held six cases and nearly caused a tidal wave. Rowboat came bouncing over the island on top of a big wave." Sharks and birds quickly learned the "dinner bell" and swept in for an easy meal.[16]

By April ships approaching Wake were using the contractors' fifty-foot water tower as the new landmark to sight the island, as the USS *Regulus* did late in the afternoon on April 12, 1941. Harry was glad to see each incoming ship loaded with cargo and workers, but unloading materials and men onto barges and getting them safely into harbor remained a constant challenge. "The sea is sometimes kind but always relentless. It never lets up and if we do, we are just sunk. In more ways than one," Harry wrote to Katherine. "So far we have a very good record. The Operating Base has frequently complimented us on this. In my own feeble way I take some of the credit for this, and in so doing must accept the blame if an accident occurs."[17]

The waterfront crew used radiophones to coordinate moorage and unloading with incoming ships. Officially, the contractors were licensed to use the radio as a sea phone on their tugs for contact with ships, but they used three different sets of call letters under varying conditions and had a land station as well. "We know the Japs are laying down over the horizon listening to every word and we put out some amazing misinformation to confuse them. We have to be very careful to avoid using ships' names and itinerary." By June, Harry had a shortwave radiophone installed in his office. "This is a fulfillment of a life long ambition, to be able to talk back," he wrote Katherine. If conditions permitted, the Wake contractors could even talk directly to their Midway counterparts over a thousand miles away, "just like using a phone," or pick up amateur radio signals from far away.[18]

On the morning of April 13 the *Regulus*, assisted by Wake's tug, *Pioneer,* moored to several buoys positioned just off Wilkes. "Well, my ship came in," Harry wrote. "This isn't as good as it sounds, and reminds me of the guy who said he had had lots of luck—all bad. This boat has a barge on the deck big enough to reach across the ship and we have to launch it overboard at sea." Olson and Swede Hokanson planned and supervised the operation, positioning barges alongside the ship for unloading men and cargo. Some of the ninety-eight passengers gladly jumped to the barge for the last leg of their long journey, but many newcomers had to assist with the cargo unloading, a common task on Wake where there was no separate stevedore workforce. Don K. Miller, a young relation of Pete's wife from eastern Oregon, was one who stayed aboard to work the cargo. Nearly daily someone suffered a sprain, laceration, or contusion and had to pay a visit to sickbay or Dr. Barrett on shore. The *Pioneer* worked the barges carrying cargo from ship to the waterfront through the newly-widened channel. It took one week to unload the *Regulus*, during which time the executive officer took a series of official photographs of construction progress on shore. Pete lamented that in all the thousands of tons of cargo there was "nothing on the *Regulus* that we can use . . . so many things needed badly that we didn't get." As the weeks went by, the situation did not markedly improve. "I never saw a place that took so much doing to get a little done," Harry wrote a month later.[19]

LABOR AND MANAGEMENT ON WAKE

The Wake project shifted into higher gear in April. Gone were the eight-hour days and leisurely Sundays of the pioneer party: now the men who worked directly on construction put in nine or ten-hour days with only every other Sunday off. Camp 1 could house 260 in frame tents and more men squeezed in as the weeks went by. The tent camp offered a full array of services including a large mess hall and a canteen where the workers could buy toiletries, fishing tackle, light clothing, and cigarettes (at sixty cents a carton) with script drawn from their salary. Nights were comfortable, but the daytime sun burned. Essential items included dark glasses and work shoes with composition soles that could stand up to Wake's sharp coral. Many of the new men, wrote a recent arrival, were "ready to give it up and get the hell out" after the first day, but most quickly adjusted to the conditions and came to appreciate the comfortable beds and excellent food. For the most part, the men got along well "if they feel you are trying to carry your part of the job." In a sixteen-point bulletin issued to prospective employees that spring, Teters stated that opportunities for promotion "are excellent in so much as the job is in a formative period." Promotion would be based on a man's "camp and living conduct," as well as on his general working qualifications. Teters clearly forewarned the men that "there is noo [*sic*] beer sold on Wake Island, nor does the management expect to sell beer at any future time in this camp."[20]

From the CPNAB operating base in Honolulu, the calls for labor escalated with expanding projects and the constant, bedeviling trickle of attrition. Mainland offices scoured the market for skilled workers, especially men who had experience living in camps or were accustomed to separation from their families for work. Labor halls and employment offices scrambled to fill the rising demand and disreputable practices arose in the process. A glazier wrote to Dan Teters, informing him that an employment agency in Denver demanded a fee of $200 and 10 percent of his future earnings to secure him a job on Wake. Other agencies knowingly sent unfit or inexperienced workers for skilled jobs with predictable results. Unskilled workers were often hired at the lowest rate possible, creating considerable confusion when a hundred arrived all at once. It was left to the Wake superintendents to "find their capabilities and raise them to their proper level."[21]

Still, the CPNAB jobs attracted many men. Pay rates were comparable to mainland pay scales, with the added incentives of free transportation (provided the man stayed at least sixty days), other paid expenses, and tax-exempt wages. Contract wages on Wake ranged from $100 a month for mess men and janitors, $120 for unskilled laborers, and $145 for truck drivers, to $200 for a carpenter, an assistant engineer, or a crane oiler, to $400 and up for assistant superintendents and the doctor. For the remote islands the contracts covered room, board, and medical care for the duration of employment to the employee's return to the mainland. While workers on the closer islands contracted for a full year, labor contracts for Wake were for nine months, and, beginning in March, included a bonus system as incentive to workers to complete their contracts. After the worker's third month, he received a thirty-dollar bonus, and each month thereafter the bonus increased by another ten dollars to the end of the contract. Overtime and bonuses were credited to the worker's account, but held by the navy. Contractors Pacific Naval Air Bases was the employer, not the individual companies that made up the consortium, and CPNAB carried workmen's compensation insurance through the Liberty Mutual Life Insurance Company.[22]

Nothing could haul, plant, chew, or shoot without capable supervision and careful organization. As the general superintendent, Dan Teters worked directly with Lieutenant Butzine, kept in close touch with George Youmans and the engineers at the operating base in Hawaii, and provided overall supervision of the project itself. Harry Olson, the number-two man, oversaw all fieldwork and stood in for Teters in his absence. Privately, Harry noted that "Dan takes it pretty easy. He told one of the fellows the other day that he was going to let that big Swede [meaning Harry] build this one: that he was going to take it easy and attend to the political end of the project. Looks sort of tough for this Swede, eh?" Herman E. Echols supervised the office, engineering department, and camp facilities, and an able stable of a dozen assistant superintendents managed various departments. Their foremen led crews of steel workers, carpenters, electricians, plumbers, and laborers on the job. Olson remarked that some of the men, including a few department heads, had not worked on many big jobs, resulting in "some bad puzzles on time and cost accounting," but he hoped that they would grow into it.[23]

In addition to the construction workers, Wake had engineers and surveyors, clerks, secretaries, and timekeepers, laundry helpers and mess men, a blacksmith, cooks, a butcher, and a baker, all of whom filled essential roles that kept the operation in perpetual motion. Dr. Tom Barrett took care of all illnesses, injuries, and occasional shipboard mishaps until additional medical staff was brought on late in the project. The key to the operation was the timely flow of materials and supplies and an inflow—and not too much outflow—of good men to match. "Progress is necessarily limited by arrival of materials and men and curiously enough therein lies another of our major worries. How to maintain a proper balance between the two," Harry reflected in April. "If we get too much material we haven't the men to handle and use it up, and if we get too many men we haven't sufficient material to make a place to house and feed them. We have to build up like a stairway. We raise up on materials and men and then of necessity level off for a while as we prepare to build up again. Whenever we get big enough to care for the people it will take to do the job, we will be at the top of the stairs."[24]

Overwhelmingly, the supervisors and workers wielding the tools were white men from the mainland, most of them from the western states. Preferential hiring, ethnic biases, and segregation of workers were common practices in the defense industries, but the U.S. Navy specifically forbade workers of Japanese ethnicity from employment on the outlying islands. When prominent African American labor leader A. Philip Randolph was organizing a big march on Washington, D.C., to protest the exclusion of black workers from defense jobs, President Roosevelt issued Executive Order 8802 in June 1941. It affirmed a policy of full access to and participation in the defense program by all persons regardless of "race, creed, color, or national origin." (This resulted in Randolph and his associates canceling the march.) Nevertheless, selective hiring practices throughout the year brought no black workers to Wake. The workers in the kitchen, mess, and laundry were nearly all Chinese Americans from Hawaii or San Francisco and they bunked in segregated housing. Few African Americans came within the vicinity of the atoll during 1941, with the exception of several on the *Regulus* crew. Captain

"Jimmie" Doyle, Harry noted with disdain, "makes his officers wear whites at all times and has four Negroes to wait on himself."[25]

While the remote atolls were virtually uninhabited prior to the contractors' arrival the new CPNAB projects on Guam and Cavite in the Philippines were able to utilize local labor. Pan American brought natives of Guam to Wake as employees, but CPNAB did not follow suit. In April 1941, Harry Morrison floated a proposal with his fellow executives to bring several hundred Filipino workers to Wake. He speculated that they would "work cheap," although there would be the "problem of mixing with whites." Another CPNAB executive noted additional advantages to importing Filipino labor: minimal sickness, simple native housing, cheap food, openness to unskilled labor, and, most important, low hourly wages. Morrison continued to press his idea well into the fall, but in the end the CPNAB hiring offices on the mainland, including the one sponsored by Morrison-Knudsen in Boise, fed a steady supply of white construction workers and dozens of Chinese American domestics to Wake and the other island jobs.[26]

DIVERSIONS

Efforts to keep the workers content on Wake included amenities that may have appeared costly and frivolous, but they were implemented to minimize turnover. Some diversions were enjoyed by all; others were the special privileges of upper management, a core group whose stability was vital to the operation. In late March the Wake contractors installed an outdoor movie theater with a three-story tall screen, state of the art equipment, and a steady supply of recent movies brought in through the navy's film exchange, at a cost of $8,500. "There is no larger or better equipment in any theater anywhere," Harry wrote to Katherine on the eve of the April 1 gala premier. The contractors invited the Pan Air people for the grand opening and sixty-five came en masse. "After the show we served everyone a lunch in the mess hall—255 men and two women. So you see the social season was opened with considerable éclat." With twenty feature movies per month and four more on loan from Pan Air (which had a similar, but smaller, outdoor projection system), the men could enjoy entertainment under the stars nearly every night. Orders were for musical comedies and light fare. "The blood and thunder sort don't go over so good," Harry observed.[27]

In a letter home carpenter Peter Hansen described his typical daily routine on Wake in the spring of 1941: rise at 5:15, breakfast at 5:30, a ride to the job site, and work until 4:00 with a break for dinner around noon. With the work day finished, it was "another ride back to our camp and off with my clothes, except my shorts and shoes." He generally joined three others for a game of horseshoes in the sun until 5:10, and then stripped down for a swim. "The other boys in my tent don't swim—I guess they are afraid of the water or EELS." Hansen's daily swim-bath—rain or shine, hot or cold—involved taking a wash cloth and bar of soap, diving off the spring board in the lagoon, and swimming about twenty yards out to a raft where he gave himself a good scrubbing, dropped the soap in the water, and dove down nine feet to retrieve it and rinse off. After a fast swim a hundred yards out, he returned slowly on his back to "breathe the good fresh air." Back on shore, he dressed in clean clothes and joined the crowd for supper at 5:30. "Six o'clock we're out & usually read the news and bulletin board & gab around until 7, then usually go to the tent, and the six of us gab or fool around until eight & then the movie. The pictures are not the best, but not bad and it is entertainment until 10 & then to bed. (Now darling don't you think this is being good?)"[28]

In their spare time, the men gravitated to others who shared similar interests: some played music or pursued hobbies, others read the Bible together, and others gambled. Private radios on the island continued to bring in music and news when conditions were right. Many clustered around a set to listen to Paul Carson and his *Bridge to Dreamland* on Monday evenings and the *Richfield Reporter* nightly over KGEI, broadcasting from Treasure Island in San Francisco Bay. Secretaries in the office took the news from KGEI and British and Australian newscasts, edited it, and printed up a little newspaper known as the *Wake Wig Wag* for distribution around camp. The *Wake Wig Wag* also carried important announcements and grew to include local gossip and goings-on. Beneath the tropical isle banner the editor usually listed the upcoming Clipper mail schedule and movie showings, as well as evening meetings of the various clubs that took hold on Wake.

While workers made do with the camaraderie of the tent camp, upper management found more venues and occasions for entertainment, often at the Pan American hotel where notable Clipper passengers spent the night. The Heel Point guesthouse with four bedrooms, a saltwater bath, small kitchen, bar, and a glass-enclosed lanai for a living room, altogether a "very swanky place," according to Harry, housed CPNAB's special visitors. In anticipation of upcoming occasions, Harry and Pete ordered suits, dinner jackets, hats, and shoes from Manila through the Pan American pilots and stewards who bypassed what would have been a steep air express bill. A white or gray sharkskin suit (tailored to fit if one sent along another suit for a model, as Harry did), ran thirteen dollars; a white dinner jacket or tuxedo sold for eight. Evening cocktails, however, required no special dress code. CPNAB had experimented with alcohol in the camps on other, earlier island projects and determined that it was counterproductive. Wake, by regulation, was a dry camp, but management there and elsewhere enjoyed exceptions to the rule. Harry received regular gifts of scotch and "Oak," which he described as "Hawaiian moon made from taro root," from ship officers who frequented Wake. "I'm a pretty popular guy right after the ship leaves." A mechanic at Pan Air promised Harry two cases of San Miguel beer for moving the PAA direction finder for him. "I have my trunk half full now and am losing ground. Guess I will have to go into the liquor business," he wrote Katherine in May. By June, Harry had apparently done so as the captain of the *Halstead*, who had become a personal friend of Harry's and offered to take him to Manila with him—"Red travels strictly first class and has entrée to all the good clubs out there."—diverted to Wake to deliver two cases of Haig and Haig scotch whisky and a case of rum for him. "It will cost me about a third of what I would pay on the mainland and I can sell one case for enough to pay for all three."[29]

Famous visitors were a highlight on Wake, and top management met and socialized with many of them. Geographically, there were few places as isolated as Wake Island on the planet, but its visitors kept the world and the war within close reach. In early May Harry joined a pair of renowned aviators, Bernt Balchen and Clyde Pangborn, for breakfast. The pilots were ferrying one of several Consolidated Catalina 1 PBY flying boats from San Diego, California, to Manila for transport to the British in Singapore. "They are a pair of swell guys—as common as an old shoe." Balchen, a celebrated Norwegian American aviator, had flown on historic polar expeditions and made the first experimental transatlantic mail transport from the United States to Europe with Richard Byrd in 1927. In bad weather and out of fuel, Balchen took the stick and safely set the wheeled plane down in the surf off the coast of France. Pangborn, an American pilot, had made the first nonstop transpacific flight in 1931. Harry retold their stories and anecdotes in a richly detailed letter to his daughter. Balchen's "face grew grave and his voice husky as he told of finding the remains of Captain Scott's Antarctic expedition," he wrote Donna. Relating the story of Scott's historic trip to the South Pole, the disastrous return, and Scott's noble but futile sacrifice on behalf of his men, Harry said "It was not a pleasant story, but thinking of it gives me comfort when I recall what is going on in Europe. It is this same indomitable courage that sustains England in her hour of trial."[30]

The Pan American Clippers brought many high-profile guests to Wake that spring. Ernest Hemingway—"a guy after my own heart," Harry wrote— and his new wife, journalist Martha Gellhorn, stayed over in late February. Jimmy Roosevelt, the president's eldest son, came through Wake en route to China in April. Roosevelt told Harry, "I'm going to wire the old man about the marvelous fishing and I'll bet you all have him out here before long." Harry commented to Katherine that, the way things were going in Washington, he doubted that the "old man" would come. With Wake's designation as a national defense area in February, Pan American had to curtail extended vacation layovers for Clipper passengers and restrict visitors—officially—to the Pan American compound, but there were many opportunities for entertaining evenings for the big fish in the little pond.[31]

DETERRENCE AND PROVOCATION

The specter of Nazi aggression magnified through the lens of the Lend-Lease debate and news of the German offensive in the Balkans in the spring of 1941. In her weekly letters to her husband, Katherine Olson became increasingly upset over the European war situation. In early April Harry tried to reassure her by venturing a prediction: "Hitler has reached his peak and is on the downhill road at last. I doubt that he will be whipped, but I don't look for him to make many more conquests." Few shared Harry Olson's optimism. After weeks of debate in Congress the Lend-Lease Act had passed on March 11, 1941. Lend-Lease would funnel $7 billion in economic aid to Allied nations, overriding long-standing neutrality legislation that prohibited trade with or loans to belligerent countries.[32]

Secret meetings between American and British officials beginning in January culminated in the ABC-1 Staff Agreement of March 27, 1941, in which the United States committed to close cooperation with Britain and a Europe-first strategy when the nation entered the war. As attacks on Atlantic shipping dominated the naval agenda, Admiral Kimmel's unbalanced Pacific forces were further drained to protect shipments to Britain. Ships from the Pacific Fleet steamed through the Panama Canal to bolster escort duties for merchant convoys in the North Atlantic and in defense of naval bases in Greenland and Iceland. The ABC-1 talks led to the adoption of the Rainbow 5 war plan: when the United States entered the global war the first priority would be the defeat of Germany. If diplomacy and economic sanctions failed to restrain Japan, the Pacific Fleet would defend the security of the Western Hemisphere from Alaska to Pearl Harbor to the Panama Canal. Possessions outside that perimeter were, by necessity, expendable. Rainbow 5 additionally called on the United States to support associated powers in the Far East and thereby opened a window for limited offensive naval action in the Pacific. WPL-46, as the new war plan was coded, called for diversion of enemy strength from allied targets in the Far East by U.S. attacks on the Japanese Mandates, including the Marshall Islands due south of Wake.[33]

By the spring of 1941 Japan was down to just two years of fuel oil reserves and committed to expand into Southeast Asia in order to reduce its dependence on Western imports, particularly American oil. By the end of March Japan had acquired full use of the Saigon airport and controlled rice production in French Indochina. With the European war dominating their attentions, Americans could dismiss Japan's rising aggression as mere bluster by bolstering their own sense of racial and technological superiority. The long-standing isolationist fear of provoking Japan increasingly gave way to popular confidence in the ability to deter Japan with strategic displays of American military technology. The shift in the public attitude was encouraged by navy lobbyists in Congress, editorial cartoonists, and lecturers. The journalist Harrison Forman, a veteran of eleven years in the Far East, predicted that while the Japanese navy matched the American navy in size and equipment, it was doomed to lose. "I still ask the question: Who can shoot the straightest? I watched Japanese gunners try for weeks on end to hit something—anything—in Shanghai. They made perfect fools of themselves!" A showdown in the Pacific seemed quite remote to most Americans.[34]

Officially, it was everything short of war in the Atlantic and strictly defense in the Pacific. The Rainbow series of war plans, developed by army and navy strategists during 1939 and 1940, projected various scenarios for the United States with or without allies to pursue offensive and defensive operations in the event of war. Rainbow 5, promulgated in May 1941, called for joint allied offensive operations in Europe and Africa while maintaining a defense of the Western Hemisphere in the Pacific. Amendments to Rainbow 5 featured expanded air operations in the Pacific that enhanced the strategic value of Wake. Even as the United States committed to a Europe-first strategy, the Pacific Fleet remained "geared for the offensive." Behind closed doors, the Pacific offensive strategy took on new momentum with the explosion of funding, new construction, and bold new ideas. In February General Douglas MacArthur, military advisor to the Philippine government, offered new plans for the expansion of Philippine defenses and Congress funded base facilities in the far western Pacific. In addition, in the spring of 1941 naval intelligence cracked Japanese diplomatic codes (MAGIC), adding another "weapon" to the American arsenal. As the Philippines shifted from liability to asset, the long-standing line between provocation and deterrence in the Pacific began to crack.[35]

In January 1941 the navy's Greenslade Board had issued "Fundamental Requirements for the Naval Shore Establishment," a report that studied the outlying islands under CPNAB construction. The board specified land garrisons, submarines, air squadrons, and short-term supplies for each base, but the plans awaited approval from the CNO. As the bases at Midway, Palmyra, and Johnston neared completion in the spring, Admiral Kimmel ordered marine garrisons posted to the three CPNAB projects on Hawaii's flanks and then turned his attention to Wake. In 1939 Colonel Harry Pickett had conducted a survey of Wake for gun placements and troop dispositions. Pickett's report had noted Wake's strategic value to the U.S. as an advance base and as an essential link in the line of communication westward, as well as the physical limitations that made it vulnerable to enemy attack. Kimmel knew that with a depleted Pacific Fleet, he needed to strengthen the outlying bases. A marine garrison on Wake could defend the naval air base under construction and preclude Japanese seizure of the island where "Blue" improvements might well "benefit Orange."[36]

An armed Wake represented a considerable risk for the navy as Wake's proximity to the Marshall Islands might provoke aggressive action from Japan before the island was prepared for battle. The argument that a fortified American presence in the Pacific represented not provocation but deterrence to Japanese aggression had many backers, all the way up to the president, who had justified moving the fleet base to Honolulu for that reason a year earlier. Either way, provocation or deterrence was part of the defensive argument and the navy had far more in the works than "strictly defense."

During April 1941, as the Roosevelt administration and military planners turned their attention to anticipated hostilities with Germany and the need to beef up the American naval presence in the Atlantic, Admiral Kimmel and CNO Stark exchanged confidential correspondence about Pacific strategy. The administration, Admiral Stark noted with frustration, had naively suggested that that the navy should ensure that its ships continue "popping up here and there" in the South Pacific to "keep the Japs guessing." In a letter to Stark on April 18 Kimmel outlined Wake's advantages in the Pacific strategy and crippling disadvantages should Japan seize it early in a conflict. Then he introduced a bold idea: "If Wake be defended, then for the Japanese to reduce it would require extended operations of their naval force in an area where we might be able to get at them; thus affording us opportunity to get at naval forces with naval forces. We should try, by every possible means, to get the Japanese to expose naval units. In order to do this, we must provide objectives that require such exposure." Kimmel recommended continuation of the construction project and the progressive establishment of defense forces as soon as possible, "as facilities there permit."[37]

The completed facilities and a squadron of patrol planes on Wake would certainly provide "objectives" in Kimmel's argument. Adding a marine garrison, batteries of shore guns, and antiaircraft weapons would take Wake to yet another level. Bait aside, the new base warranted defensive facilities as a matter of practical necessity and Rear Admiral Bloch, Commandant of the 14th Naval District, reluctantly concurred with Kimmel. In May 1941 Secretary of the Navy Frank Knox approved the Greenslade Board's recommendations for development of island defenses at Wake. These included the project underway for a full air base for twelve patrol planes, emergency aviation facilities for thirty-six fighters, anchorage for seaplane tenders and light naval forces, accommodations and hospital for one defense battalion, three months storage of food and fuel, and a base for six submarines. On Wake, however, the contractors were just establishing water stores and accommodations for their own growing numbers, and had not even started the naval base structures and marine facilities.[38]

"THE VERY BRINK"

While developments in the Atlantic commanded the most attention the Pacific churned with activity. In late May Admiral Kimmel sent the Pacific Fleet to sea for war games. Most ships were out of Pearl Harbor and seaplane tenders and squadrons of PBY patrol bombers headed for the outlying islands. Several of the seaplanes came through Wake en route to the Philippines and the Wake contractors rushed to set anchor buoys in the lagoon for a larger, incoming squadron that would stay for a week. A seaplane tender and the squadron of Catalina PBY flying boats arrived at Wake on the afternoon of May 22 and the contractors gave the officers a tour of the project the next day. A few days later, the pilots reciprocated and gave four of the civilians, including Dan Teters, Harry, and Pete, their own tour of Wake—from the air. For the men on Wake, the week with the squadron in residence reinforced their faith in the superiority of American naval forces in the Pacific and the safety of Wake Island.[39]

> *Wake Island, May 30, 1941*
> *Dear Katherine:*
> *I didn't get a letter to any of you on the last Clipper, but by making an earlier start will try to do a little better. I got your two letters mostly about Ted last Sunday and was glad to hear he was on his way. Also in the same mail I got a routine letter granting him permission to finish his school term. I imagine you have got something along the same line by now. It's too bad this misunderstanding came up about it but happy to find he had missed the draft which was the main purpose of the whole affair. I doubt if Ted likes it very well down here. It's alright for a while but must be very monotonous for a working man. Also it's warming up a little.*
> *We had three ships last week. One was a sea plane tender (not a carrier). He came in the early morning and got word that his planes would be along at 1:00 P.M. Inasmuch as he had to put out moorings for them to tie to, he was up against it. So I came to the rescue and put them out for him, thus earning his undying gratitude. When the planes came in I met all the flyers through him and the commander of the squadron, Capt. Hughes invited me for a ride. Boy that was somepin'. We flew all morning. Part of the time I rode in the Bomb pit and was much tempted to drop a few on some of the spots of the job that have annoyed me. Then I got in the copilot's seat and he let me fly a while. These navy bombers are very good, dependable ships and it is easier to fly one than drive a car. It was a thrill for me and I could use pages telling about it. The flyers all got away Tuesday morning and peace descended on Wake again. Friday we got another barge from San*

Francisco and today (Sunday) I get a wire that the Sirius will arrive at sundown with 91 men and 3000 tons of cargo. We have Friday's barge unloaded so will attack the ship upon arrival. All this relating to ships and plans are more or less naval secrets so don't spread any of it unduly. The dredge you sent the clipping about will arrive in a couple days. I have her crew here now and am working them on the project.

May I inform you again that no copies of the magazine Fortune *have ever arrived here for me. As before, may I advise you to cancel this and get your money back. At this date I am not interested in any back issues of it should they arrive. Belle gave me a present of* Readers Digest *and it also has not come so I advised her likewise. I cannot understand why I should have this trouble as each ship brings us tons of magazines and we have somewhat of a problem to get rid of them. I haven't read a magazine or cracked a book since I came here. We have a thousand-book library, about half of which are recent best sellers along Book of the Month lines. I would like to get into some of them but don't have the time.*

We will have another ship around the middle of the month and Ted will probably be on it. Naval transportation is no fun for the working man so I imagine he will be very glad to get here. I had written to Belle to send me some hats but the boat I told her to send them on has gone to Midway, so she may send them out by Ted if he looks her up as I suppose he will. I have a good hat and white shoes coming from Manila but haven't heard anything from them for a month.

Pete Russell and I went over to the Hotel last night and inhaled a few scotches with Betty Tiers. She is the steward's wife. They have Pete and I over for cocktails and dinner occasionally. You would be amazed if you could see the typical Clipper passengers. A very weird and exotic lot. Every nationality in the world and some real oriental natives. The most interesting one last night was an ex-British flyer. He didn't like the way the British were running the war so he quit. He is an Australian and had been flying Bombers from Newfoundland to England. None of the fliers coming through have any use for the British altho they all want England to win. Martha Gellhorn was down in Dutch East Indies and Australia and she said that all those people were critical of the United States for staying out of the war. I think their attitude was and is based on self-interest more than reason or a practical point of view. She felt the same way. By and large the Navy has no fear of Japan.

Love, Harry

On the other side of the world, the escalation of the war prompted President Roosevelt to proclaim a state of "unlimited national emergency." In a long and sober Fireside Chat on May 27 the president declared that the Nazis were expanding the European war into a war for world domination and warned that "war is approaching the very brink of the Western Hemisphere itself." Roosevelt did not mention Japan or the Pacific directly, but alluded to a looming Axis drive for control of the seas. The danger to the United States and its neighbors was clear and imminent, and the president called for heightened commitment to the nation's defense program and aid to Britain. Any voices still calling for peace at any price should heed the stark reality of war at the nation's doorstep. All citizens were expected to contribute to the "common work of our common defense." A civil defense program had begun and a new draft was set for July 1.[40]

Hearing the dire warnings in the president's speech forty of the contractors on Wake promptly quit and prepared to sail for home on the next available transportation. Among those who remained on Wake, many were more concerned for their loved ones at home than for their own safety. Pete Hansen wrote home, "The world position is very serious dear, I am afraid. We must watch the conditions very closely, also our feelings. I think we will *feel* the crisis before we will hear about it, and when we feel as though I should, I will come home immediately, because I want to be right with you in any crisis." Elected chairman of the Pioneer Club on Wake in early June, the first thing that Hansen did was to get the office to post the news every day, although he noted to his wife that "they are very slick about handling the news here." Hansen regularly monitored the news they received, asked his wife to keep him posted on news from the mainland, and filtered the constant rumors on Wake. "I have more fear for you fellows than myself on account of the trickery of the Japs and Nazi and I have a feeling that they are plotting a surprise. I don't want to be silly, but I don't want to be late and I never have had such a love for money that it meant more to me than the comfort of my loved ones. . . . In case of war or crisis I want to be right alongside of you."[41]

When rumors circulated on Wake that if war was declared the navy had the power to keep the civilian contractors on the island for the duration or until the job was completed, Hansen wrote that "all of the boys became alarmed. Naturally we were excited about this, so one of the boys went to the naval lieutenant and asked him about this." Lieutenant Butzine reassured the men that anyone who desired to leave in the case of war could do so immediately. "Of course I feel much better about the whole thing. He also said that we have destroyers at all times within 36 hours of the island and sometimes nearer. They are on constant patrol." Whether the lieutenant exaggerated to calm the workers or his reply was altered in the retelling, there is no evidence that the navy maintained such proximity to or protection of Wake.[42]

GEARING UP

On its second trip to Wake the *Regulus* carried 217 fresh faces for the island, sacks of mail and parcels, a full load of cargo, 14,000 gallons of diesel oil, and towed the *Justine Foss*, a sturdy tug joining Wake's waterfront fleet. Among the new arrivals on May 18 was Bill Ray, an expert equipment operator and excavation specialist. Pete Russell spent a few days showing Ray the ropes and gladly turned over the excavation superintendent's hat to the capable new man. Now able to turn his full attention to the building department Russell lamented the ongoing problems of supply: "No pumps, no 8" pipe fittings or valves; no this, no that! . . . Glanced at the reinforcing details. Looks like something a 6 year old kid had dreamed up. More fun!"[43]

The most essential item for the men on Wake, however, was fresh water. The contractors depended on their saltwater stills and rainwater collection, and cargo shipments frequently included quantities of fresh water. An occasional mishap with the stills or a stretch of dry weather prompted serious concern. "You can't imagine how it feels to be out where there just isn't any water," Harry wrote Katherine in late April after "the bottom dropped out of the ocean and our pumps ran out of water, shutting down the stills," leaving them four thousand gallons behind. "I often think what people who were shipwrecked here in the early days must have suffered before they finally died. With what I know, I could get by and probably keep 10 or 12 people in like circumstances, but the average person would be helpless. This island is very much different than the ones you read about or see in the movies." Water stores ran low again in mid-June, and Harry looked forward to the start of the "rainy season" to build them back up.[44]

On June 6, 1941, the 326-foot hydraulic pipeline dredge *Columbia* came lumbering up to Wake after a two-month tow from Oregon. Portland newspapers had covered the April 25 departure of the dredge, flanked with double three-inch planking for the sea voyage. Under tow by the tug *Seminole*, the *Columbia* crossed its namesake bar at Astoria and headed west into the Pacific carrying a skeleton crew of twelve: the chief, engineers, firemen, and deck hands. "Here we were out in the ocean bouncing around like a cork," wrote forty-seven-year-old fireman Claude Howes. All hands suffered bouts of seasickness and were glad to lay up in Honolulu for nine days before embarking on May 21 for the even more difficult leg to Wake. Howes recalled the dispiriting first sight of their destination. "If there ever was a deserted place, Wake was it—nothing there but birds, rats, and hermit crabs."[45]

Purchased from the Port of Portland for $590,000 and completely refitted for its journey and new mission, the *Columbia* was the most costly piece of equipment in the entire CPNAB arsenal. The contractors placed high hopes in its ability to carve a ship channel into the lagoon, a turning basin, and seaplane runways. With a capacity rated at three hundred thousand cubic yards a month, the contractors expected the dredge to accomplish these tasks in a little over a year. As the men gathered to watch the mighty dredge wedge through the barge channel into the safety of the lagoon, they felt a surge of pride. Now the big guns had arrived. Underscoring the importance of the occasion, the next day George Youmans, Honolulu-based head of M-K operations in the Pacific, flew in to Wake on the Clipper and Harry showed him around the operation. "George professed himself as very pleased with the job. I guess it would impress a stranger more than one of us who have been here and watched it grow step by step." The arrival of the dredge, however, brought the long-standing debate over location of the new navy ship channel to the forefront.[46]

As the contractors stripped the dredge of its planking and readied it for work Youmans raised the issue of the proposed navy channel. The ship channel and corresponding turning basin were the most vital aspects of the CPNAB project on Wake as they would enable seaplane tenders, cargo ships, and submarines to enter and maneuver in the protected waters of Wake's lagoon. Without the channel Wake was virtually useless in the Pacific strategy. The pilot channel that the contractors had widened between Wilkes and Wake had been eliminated from consideration for the main channel due to its shallowness and the fact that it led straight to a coral head studded area of the lagoon. Since 1935 surveys and studies had convinced the navy that the optimal location for the main channel was across the northwest reef at the open mouth into the lagoon, leading to a turning basin south of Peale. Boring samples had also revealed exceptionally hard strata across the reef, which had justified the acquisition of the costly dredge. Youmans and the contractors had long argued that a shorter channel could be more efficiently cut through Wilkes Island to the lagoon and a turning basin, but naval officials demurred. Awaiting the *Columbia* the contractors had punched and pummeled the stubborn lagoon coral with dynamite and draglines for months with minimal effect, confirming their opinion. Six months into the Wake project the channel still awaited final approval and the contractors were poised to go head-to-head with the navy over its location.[47]

The majority of Wake workers knew nothing of the heated debate over the channel as they struggled with their own tasks, often frustrated by the tempo of fits and starts. By mid-June Camp 2 was well on its way to completion. The carpenters assigned to building the camp barracks and structures were the first to move into them in mid-May, with forty men assigned to a building versus six to an airy tent. "Our tents were a paradise compared to the Barracks," carpenter Peter Hansen groused. The camp was in an uproar over the abrupt order and a sudden curtailment of overtime. "I want the overtime, and without it I don't feel as the job is worth the sacrifice," Hansen wrote his wife. The general unsettledness continued as the weeks went by. "The whole island is in a turmoil at present," Hansen wrote again on June 21. "First of all, we are out of everything and don't know when we will get any more material." Despite their sequenced plans and orders for materials, the contractors often received no manifest from naval ships en route and had no knowledge of what supplies were coming until they arrived. Lack of materials translated into reduced work and overtime. Secondly, according to Hansen, the war had the entire island in an uproar. Lieutenant Butzine had admitted to a few men that he thought they might even have to evacuate. Butzine ordered a rush job on the just-started airplane landing strips, intended to be 500 feet wide and paved, but now changed to a 150-foot width: "finish them off with beach sand and call it good." Tractors worked twenty-four hours a day and workers were diverted from the permanent barracks to start a concrete hangar prompting Hansen to speculate that the navy intended the Camp 2 barracks to be used for the marines "if they ever get here." Construction of a large dock was abandoned and orders came down to move the "five acres of steel" back to the boat landing, "so we really have reasons to become alarmed now." Hansen told his wife that he would watch the Suez and Panama Canals, and if something happened to either, he would grab the first boat possible.[48]

THE NEWS: JUNE 1941

On June 22, 1941, Germany attacked the Soviet Union in a surprise invasion of unprecedented size and force. More than three million German soldiers and auxiliaries, with thousands of tanks and aircraft, poured in from the west along a broad front from the Baltic Sea in the north to the Black Sea in the south, overwhelming the Soviet armies they encountered. News of the invasion spread across the globe in bold headlines and broadcasts. U.S. officials intensified their commitment to the Europe-first strategy, but stood clear of formally entering the war.

The United States Navy stepped up its formal escorts of both American and other merchant ships bearing American-manufactured munitions across the submarine-infested North Atlantic to Britain. The Atlantic Fleet priority continued to undermine Admiral Kimmel's attempts to shape the Pacific Fleet for eventual combat with Japan. Those problems trickled down to the island contractors working to build the bases on which the Pacific Fleet's strategy depended. The navy expanded the Pacific construction program with the addition of the Guam, Cavite, and Samoa projects, and three more companies were brought into the CPNAB consortium: J. H. Pomeroy for Guam, W. A. Bechtel for Cavite (near Manila in the Philippines), and Utah Construction for American Samoa. Meanwhile, projects on Wake and the other outlying islands were increasing in size and scope and the commandant's office was hard pressed to match transportation to CPNAB's ravenous appetite. During June 1941 the influx of defense materials so clogged piers and warehouses that night and weekend shifts were added to alleviate congestion. Ships were turned as quickly as they were loaded with cargo and busloads of waiting contractor personnel. [49]

"Our news down here is that a declaration of war is imminent," Harry wrote to Katherine in late June 1941:

"Life seems, for most of us, to flow on so evenly that it is hard to realize that these are the most momentous days since the Renaissance. From

that time to now, man was concerned about getting and keeping his personal liberty or freedom. That epoch or age is ended and a new concept of social and political life has dawned. We are distrustful of it and rightly so. There is nothing alluring about it for the common man. Should it triumph it would mean the utter consolidation of power and wealth in the hands of an ambitious few backed by all the authority of the state in which the common man had lost his voice. I freely predict the ultimate failure of this new order for this primal reason. It will perhaps take some time to right this maladjustment and perhaps it is well that this is so, that men will better realize the basic truth or values of the social, political and economic questions involved. Therein lays our only hope for permanence of the eventual solution."[50]

CHAPTER 6

HIGH CENTER

THE RIDE TO WAKE

WHILE THE FLOW OF VITAL SUPPLIES AND EQUIPMENT TO WAKE ISLAND hit bottlenecks during the summer of 1941, a steady flow of labor continued to fill the bunks and benches of Wake's camps. However, once material cargo arrived, it stayed on Wake. Not so the human cargo. Some inbound workers took one look at the tiny, flat atoll, shook their heads, and stayed on the ship for the return trip to civilization. Others managed a few weeks before they quit, and dozens of others were fired and sent packing. The superintendents kept busy requisitioning workers by trade, depending on the project's needs, status of camp facilities, and the turnover. It often seemed that they would never reach the "top of the stairway" that Harry Olson envisioned: the perfect balance of materials, facilities, and men.

Newly-hired employees who had applied for and received draft deferments from their local draft boards, passed a physical, got their shots, and signed a CPNAB contract, awaited the first available transportation from Los Angeles or San Francisco to Honolulu. For many it was the first time they had seen the Pacific Ocean; for most, it was their first trip in an ocean-going vessel. Luck of the draw determined what type of ship: it could be a navy transport, a company freighter, or one of the luxury liners that plied the Pacific. At the San Francisco docks on March 28, the first large group of workers hired by the Boise employment office had stood in the pouring rain staring at the looming shape of the USS *Regulus* before them. With a total of eighteen hundred civilians and sailors aboard the navy cargo ship, then embarking westward to service the CPNAB projects, "everybody had to stand in line for everything," as one of the Boise boys wrote home.[1]

Some employees drew a ticket on one of the company ships that carried the endless stream of cargo and reefers of food to the islands. Jack Hoskins, an engineering student at the University of Idaho, completed his final exams before rushing to Alameda for processing in early June. His ride to Honolulu turned out to be the company ship *Permanente,* which he boarded on June 15, 1941. Loaded with fifteen thousand tons of cargo including ten new Mack trucks lined up on deck, the ship ran aground before it even got out of San Francisco harbor, and a tug and navy ship had to pull it out before it could set course for Hawaii. Dinner jackets and dancing were out, but the contractors were free to lounge around with "nothing to do but sit, sleep, and get fat." Even with the dubious companionship of seasickness and Mack trucks, the men could marvel at their experience as Hoskins did when "at night the water just glows where the boat goes through."[2]

However, those who showed up on a day when one of the Matson or Presidential Line ships was scheduled to depart were in for the trip of a lifetime. With its cost-plus-fixed-fee contracts, CPNAB treated most workers to first-class sea transportation in the first half of 1941. The men ate well and often, played games, watched shows, danced with the ladies, and found numerous opportunities to rub elbows with the upper crust. Many brought along dinner jackets, but every first-class dinner found a mix of eveningwear. "You should see how the people dress for dinner, very swank" wrote Joe McDonald of Reno, en route on a Matson ship in early June, "and then some clown in overalls walks in behind them. No wonder we are considered the rabble, but we probably have more fun than anyone. . . . This life is really good and these boat types are just what they're cracked up to be."[3]

Harry Olson's son Ted also drew a voyage aboard a luxury ship that made the trip to Honolulu in late May 1941. Unwilling to wait until the end of the semester, Ted enjoyed a royal send-off by his fraternity brothers in Pullman, as well as a farewell party in Portland where family and friends gave him a new fountain pen as a going away gift. Katherine drove her son to Alameda for processing and waved a tearful goodbye at the dock. "The trip over was perfect," Ted wrote his mother from Honolulu. "I met a beautiful gal on the boat which made the trip more interesting. She is a professional model from Los Angeles and really a nice girl. We danced and swam, and altogether had a very enjoyable trip. I had to work part of the time keeping tab on 150 men, but it wasn't so bad." The ship docked near the Aloha Tower at 7:00 on a Sunday morning "amid the playing of bands and cheering of many people, both white and native," and another fresh batch of defense workers poured off the ship into the welcoming arms of the Honolulu streets.[4]

Whether greeted with bands and leis at the Aloha Tower or surly scowls at Pier 31-A, all of the men bound for remote island jobs ended up at the Naval Employees Hotel, a dormitory equipped to house five hundred men, while they awaited transportation. "Things are always a kind of jumbled up mess with this outfit, and we don't know from one day to the other what the score is," Ted wrote after arriving. "The fellows in my outfit for Pearl Harbor started to work this morning, so they don't seem to waste too much time." A few days later, Ted moved out of the employees' quarters to the home of the Olsons' friends in Honolulu, touring the island in their 1937 Packard, learning to play the ukulele, and swimming every day. He sprinkled his lighthearted letters home with phrases (apropos of nothing) such as "not to mention mashed potatoes" or "brother can you spare some poi," and pidgin or Hawaiian words that he was adding to his vocabulary. Like many newcomers experiencing a hiatus in Honolulu in 1941, Ted was having the time of his life.[5]

Joe McDonald, stuck in the Naval Employees Hotel, wrote his parents in Reno that the "joint looks like the Calif. State home for aged and decrepit with a side show from Alcatraz. It's called 'Boy's Town,' 'Dead End,' and Honolulu home for Wayward boys, but looks like the poor house." Lights-out was at ten, but the men filled the days swimming and sunburning at Waikiki beach and wandering the busy streets of Honolulu. Each new employee received twenty dollars every Saturday which he spent on hula shows, tours of the Dole pineapple factory and King Kamehameha's Palace, and all manner of less reputable distractions. When word came to report to the docks for the ride to Wake it was often with just a few hours' notice to pack up and send a quick cable home before boarding ship.[6]

While most Wake-bound workers happily waited in Honolulu for the next leg of the journey, the contractors occasionally flew in a high-priority worker by Clipper if space was available. In early June the Wake staff brought a labor foreman in by air, but the expensive alternative was wasted. The man "promptly went crazy as a bedbug" shortly after he arrived on Wake. "We finally had to get the Doctor to give him an intravenous shot and he went out like a light," Harry wrote. "Now it takes six men to guard him for a couple weeks till a ship comes in." Harry immediately laid out plans for a jail—one structure that the contractors had not anticipated needing.[7]

In Honolulu on June 16, 1941, the *Regulus* took on cargo, a handful of marines and navy personnel, and one hundred contractor employees, including Ted Olson and Joe McDonald. "They told me at 2:00 p.m., Monday, June 16, that I was supposed to sail at 4:00 p.m. the same day. I just barely had time to get to the boat," Ted wrote home. The ship cast off for the first leg to Midway in the late afternoon, towing a loaded barge. McDonald swore he could "swim twice as fast as it goes and probably be more comfortable." The civilians were assigned to three-decker bunks, ate beans for breakfast, and worked at jobs from peeling spuds to scraping paint. Unlike the posh accommodations and entertainments of the first leg, the workers found the second leg uncomfortable and dull.[8]

> *Aboard ship, USS* Regulus
> *Oh White Girl* [Ted's older sister Donna]:
> *Please, oh please, oh please forgive me for not writing sooner. For two weeks, I have done absolutely nothing, but it wouldn't have done any good to write as the Clipper does not pick up mail off the ships at sea, I don't think. Even if it did which it doesn't, I wouldn't cause I couldn't so it didn't. (The beat got me.)*
>
> *In all seriouslyness, tomorrow we get to Wake, and it is going to be quite a thrill to step off this ship and shake hands with* our *dad. We've been at sea for two weeks. We are towing a barge and had to go to Midway before Wake, I was kinda glad as I wanted to see the other islands too. The men were not allowed off the ship at Midway, but they have a pretty tough time stopping your kid brother.*[9]

Six days out of Honolulu, the *Regulus* reached Midway where the marines and two dozen contractors disembarked. Ted Olson received an invitation to dinner ashore with the Midway waterfront superintendent, an Olson family friend. The following morning, the *Regulus* set course for Wake Island and on Sunday, June 29, Wake's water tower came in sight. Harry rode out on the tug to board the incoming ship, as usual, and greeted his son. "You should have seen him grin when I first saw him on the ship," Ted wrote home. "I think he was glad to see me" The Wake tugs took the barge in first, moored the *Regulus*, and then carried the seventy-nine contractors ashore. Joe McDonald's first impression was that Wake looked "very similar to the Nevada desert—the ground is the same and the bushes look like grease wood, so I feel right at home." After the two-week trip from Honolulu, the passengers were glad to turn their backs on the *Regulus*, unaware that they were being spared the usual, onerous duty of unloading the ship before being allowed to disembark. "The trip was lousy," Ted wrote, echoing a sentiment shared by many. "It is about the worst ship I've ever seen."[10]

Once on dry ground the new arrivals received numbered badges to be worn "at all times," bed linens and towels, and assignments to quarters and crews. Most newcomers got little more than a quick look around, a saltwater shower and shave, a good dinner in the mess, and a restless first night's sleep before plunging right in to work the next morning. "I worked both yesterday and today, and at the present time, I'm almost dead. I've never worked so hard in my life," wrote Ted. "I eat breakfast at 5:45 A.M., catch a truck to work and start at 7:00 A.M. We get an hour off for lunch and a truck takes us up to the Camp 1 mess hall. Then I go back and work till 6:00 P.M. for a total of ten hours, two of which are overtime. It's pretty tough, but I'm really putting out, and I think I'll get along alright. . . . Ten hours a day after laying around for 8 months is no cinch and I 'ain't foolin'.'" The greenhorns crossed paths with disenchanted veterans who just shook their heads at them as they turned in their badges and packed their suitcases for a ride back to civilization. Over the course of five days, the *Regulus* was divested of its cargo and endured a string of mishaps including pipe lost overboard, broken winches, mooring lines carried away, and barge damage. Still, the contractors broke all records unloading the *Regulus* on this trip. Each day a few more fired or fed-up civilians reported aboard for transportation back to Honolulu until the ship departed July 4 with thirty-eight returning passengers.[11]

Harry found his newly arrived son "full of vim, vigor, and vitality and a vast enthusiasm that has abated somewhat in the face of the tropic sun and some real work. [Ted] thought that he had a good tan but found as everyone else that the sun at Wake Island has a wallop of greater intensity than elsewhere. This is due to the reflection from the coral sand. We tell them all but they all know better so we always have one or two sunburn cases in the hospital. I am the exception for I have had no trouble and it's so simple that I have to laugh. All I do is wear a shirt and pair of pants and my skin is just as white as when I left the mainland. Ted isn't in bad shape and I think he will be O.K. He had a wonderful time in Honolulu and he will appreciate it more the longer he stays here."[12]

THE PERMANENT WORK

With most of the preliminary camp and basic infrastructure work complete by early summer, the Wake contractors turned their full efforts to the projects defined in the contract, or the "permanent work." Just as they did so, the navy began to alter and supplement the work in the original CPNAB contracts, a practice that escalated during the second half of 1941. New projects included expanded fuel storage at Guam and American Samoa, the naval air base at Cavite, and full submarine bases at Wake and Midway, which came in the form of supplemental agreements to existing contracts. The three new CPNAB companies (Utah Construction, W. A. Bechtel Co., and Byrne Organization) joined the other five to sign Supplemental No. 1 on July 9, 1941. In an intercompany agreement signed earlier in April the companies agreed that all CPNAB management, resources, and facilities would be available to the new partners. Each of the eight companies made a commitment to the earliest completion of the new work, promising to turn down any outside opportunities that might interfere, and they also agreed on how to divide the work and the corresponding fee. For Supplemental No. 1, Morrison-Knudsen, Turner, and Raymond carried the largest shares at 18 percent each. At the signing, the agreement included $63,613,600 in costs and $2,800,000 in fees, for a total of $66,413,600. It would more than double over the coming months.[13]

On Wake the permanent naval air station construction projects included navy barracks, marine barracks, large storehouses, torpedo and bombsight workshops, a fire station, and other storage buildings that were all underway in early July. Harry pointed out that the chronic lack of essential materials would hinder the permanent work. "In building our own camp we could take some liberties with the plans but on the permanent Naval Air Base we cannot. I am afraid this will be a regular thing and do not see how we can hope to accomplish anything outstanding under those circumstances." How they would incorporate a full submarine base into the project was anyone's guess. The navy, as usual, had not included any plans. Even to carpenter Pete Hansen, the notion of adding such a major revision to the project in July seemed irrational. "To me it would seem foolish to carry on the work of building the submarine base; the job is too big and would take too long.

The bottom of the Lagoon is solid rock and very shallow. This would have to be dredged out to a depth of 40 ft. at least. The equipment we have here at present is for soft bottom and practically useless for the job. They have to blast every foot so far to loosen it up." From his perspective, it was even foolish to go ahead with the permanent buildings on Peale as it would take a full year for the carpenter work in the main warehouse alone. In all, seventy-five concrete-walled, bombproof buildings were planned for the navy base. "I think they are starting the job 5 years too late," Hansen wrote his wife.[14]

Meanwhile, in mid-July 1941 at Pier 31-A in Honolulu two heavily laden barges from Alameda waited over two weeks for a tow to Wake. By July 19 a total of six Wake-bound barges lined the pier in Honolulu. Admiral Bloch ordered transportation to be made available for Wake before July 25 and each cargo vessel to tow two barges simultaneously. He noted that the contractors' tug *Arthur Foss* had already accomplished this and was now en route from Wake to Honolulu with two empty barges. Unless the navy ships followed suit, "there does not appear to be any prospect of keeping up with the expeditious movement of essential supplies to Wake Island."[15]

The supply problems that plagued Wake had many sources, including, but not limited to, navy transportation. A nation-wide steel crisis, brought on by the doubling of defense production over the previous year, affected all types of steel and steel alloy products. The crisis hampered production in shipyards and munitions factories, as well as delivery to construction sites on the mainland and the offshore projects. Supply delays stretched into months for some customers at the peak of the crisis in mid-1941. Government controls and financial assistance to the steel industry brought additional supply on line in the coming months.[16] On Wake the contractors had laid out orders for materials and timed delivery months earlier in their master schedule, but the demands of the burgeoning defense industry affected procurement of all manner of supplies. The addition of new projects and corresponding material orders further bogged down the system at the service-of-supply in Alameda and in the overloaded transportation network, particularly at Honolulu where the 14th Naval District assigned the ships and barges for delivery to the outlying islands.

In addition, delays brought about by the engineers and nit-picking inspectors frustrated the contractors. Unimpeded by such detail-oriented delays the preliminary work had sped along, but the permanent work had to be completed exactly according to navy-approved plans and meticulously inspected. Dozens of civilian engineers, designers, draftsmen, and a complex chain of naval engineers and officers in charge at each step of the way had their hands in every plan that made its way to Wake and even then, it was subject to local adjustment and a long approval process. There was "plenty pilakea"—trouble—in the engineering department, Pete Russell groused in his diary, chaffing at the delays.[17]

"THE POOR OLD DREDGE"

The eagerly anticipated dredge *Columbia* fell into a category all by itself: plenty of potential and plenty pilakea. Captain W. A. Hanscom and his crew ate and slept on the dredge in the lagoon, which eased the pressure on camp facilities, although Hanscom's high salary demands (including a service bonus) and his crew's inflated bonus expectations raised additional problems. However, far more serious troubles attended the debut of the dredge. The first of these was the obstinate nature of Wake's coral; the second was a rush of changes and disagreements between navy and contractors over where, exactly, to dredge. "We are in more or less of a mess with the dredge you Portlanders sent down," Harry wrote Katherine after the dredge had been at work on Wake for all of one week, "for it won't dig this coral." Claude Howes, the young fireman who had ridden the dredge to Wake, described the frustrating process. "Our job was to dredge out this lagoon for seaplanes. This lagoon was very shallow and full of coral, and it was really very hard on the old tub. The *Columbia* was not built for this kind of material. They had to use tons of powder on this coral in order for the dredge to suck it up. The blasting loosened several tubes in the boiler."[18]

Contract NOy-4173 included $3 million for dredging at Wake: the ship channel, turning basin, and seaplane runways for a squadron of PBY patrol planes in the lagoon. From the start, the navy's plans had called for the ship channel to cross the long, shallow reef at the open mouth of the lagoon. Plans had gone forward to obtain a suction dredge to cut the cross-reef channel three hundred feet wide and thirty feet deep, with a thirty-foot turning basin inside the lagoon.[19]

Planners vacillated on disposal of the drilled material, now approaching an estimated 4,500,000 cubic yards. Meanwhile, the contractors had purchased the expensive dredge *Columbia* from the Port of Portland and overhauled it for the Pacific voyage. Just days after the *Columbia* arrived at Wake in early June to take up the task Captain Bruns ordered a new study of alternate locations for the ship channel. However, under pressure from RAdm. Patrick N. L. Bellinger, commander of Patrol Wing 2 in Honolulu, who wanted moorage for his seaplane tenders as soon as possible, Bruns quickly cancelled the study and ordered the contractors to begin enlarging their existing pilot channel immediately. The new orders called for the pilot channel between Wilkes and Wake to become the navy's ship channel with the turning basin and seaplane tender pier just inside the lagoon. Jaws dropped on Wake. Not only would the new plan disrupt the flow of cargo and put the dredge at great risk in the heavy current, but the toughest coral in the lagoon lay just inside that channel and low water stood at barely a foot, so the entire depth of channel and basin would have to be blasted and dredged. Captain Bruns cited "military advantage," which trumped any objections the contractors might raise, but he did acknowledge that the new scheme would "probably be detrimental to construction operations." The navy was not of one mind about Wake matters: Rear Admiral Bloch, 14th Naval District commandant, criticized the suggested channel change because he had not been consulted before the recommendation went to Washington, D.C.[20]

The contractors objected and, by early July, convinced Lieutenant Butzine to support their proposal for a channel dug straight through the sandy soil of Wilkes Island, as George Youmans had suggested a year earlier. The contractors' plan would save the dredge from a prolonged pounding on the reef and allow most of the excavation to occur on land with dragline equipment, as well as in the protected lagoon. At Pearl Harbor, Captain Bruns agreed to consider the contractors' plan, but reiterated that time was of the essence: the target to "allow protected anchorage" was no later than December 1941. Bruns ordered reports to compare yardage, time, and cost of each of the three schemes: over-reef, enlarged pilot channel, and Wilkes bisect. Meanwhile, the contractors put the *Columbia* to work dredging a fifteen-foot channel across the lagoon to allow the thousand-ton cargo barges to cross the lagoon for unloading at the naval facilities under construction on Peale. Then, on July 11, after struggling to dredge thirty thousand cubic yards of coral and rock, the *Columbia's* cutter engine suddenly exploded. The dredge was under repair until the end of the month, the first of many such frustrating occasions. It soon became fodder for the poets on Wake:

> The poor old Dredge broke down
> And made the durndest sound;

The bearings ran hot but the boilers would not,
And the cutter gears went Dong! Bang!
Bang! Dong! Bang! Bang![21]

A VACATION

By early July, Harry Olson needed a break from Wake Island, and he wrote to Katherine that he hoped to be able to get away for a short vacation by mid-July—the first staff vacation from the atoll:

> I think the trip will do me good as I am getting too irritable to live with. . . . I find myself as empty of news as a drum. For the past week I have had a curious sense of detachment—as tho I were sitting some place watching myself with a wry sort of dissatisfaction. Something that Henry Bergson would describe as the elan vital seems to have left me and everything seems flat.

Harry despaired over a life "empty of any achievement worthy of the name," and suspected that what he felt was a symptom of growing older:

> It is possible that I am not alone in this feeling: that men as a whole feel this futility and are willing to surrender the direction of the lives they are too tired to direct themselves. This might explain the rise of the dictators. It is easy to say that we need a resurgence of the faith of our fathers, but what does it avail a man if he shifts his faith from a dictator to a deity, or vice versa. In either case he is not the captain of his soul that Whitman sang of lustily, or his destiny. And if he should deny both and assert his inherent right to freedom what does it avail him if he finds no comfort or ease in it?"[22]

Katherine read her husband's lament in the hot, crowded Portland house where she and Donna were spending the summer. She immediately fired off a reproachful letter that accused Harry of delaying notice of his vacation until it was too late for her to join him in Honolulu. For good measure, she demanded an increase in the allotment he was sending her. Harry responded immediately with a harsh rebuttal, reminding Katherine of the uncertainties of his situation and calculating the exorbitant cost of getting Katherine to Honolulu on short notice, if she could even manage to get passage on a ship or Clipper. Less than a week later, Harry and a fellow staff member, John Polak, boarded the eastbound Clipper in the early morning of July 10, while Pete and Swede rode in Pan American's crash launch down the lagoon to wave a final farewell. At home, Katherine packed up her wounded pride and set off with family members for a road trip into the Canadian Rockies.

Honolulu T. H., Moana Hotel, July 17, 1941
Dear Katherine:
I have been here a week now and having a very nice time. In some respects it's the nicest vacation I've ever had. This is a lovely hotel but quite expensive judging by my purse. Just paid my first week's bill, 76.86. But it's fun and I don't regret it a bit. I made up my mind I would not care for once—just relax and do as I please. Bought me a flock of nice sport clothes and another suit. One of the fellows came up with me and we share a room altho I rarely see him. Our room costs us 18.00 per day which includes meals. I like this place better than the Royal [Hawaiian] altho it is a bit more expensive.

Anyhow it has done me a lot of good. I was getting pretty low down at Wake and a little worried about my physical condition. I haven't taken any great care of myself up here and drank a lot. Also have only had one good night's rest, but I feel so much better it's amazing. That dull, tired feeling I had is gone as is the pain I had in my lower legs. I didn't believe that the tropics could do that to you for I did not put out any physical effort, but I was slowed down to almost a stop. This week has done wonders for me and this morning I found myself running down stairs and feeling like doing things again.

My window looks out on Waikiki Beach and Diamond Head. The beach and surf is always full of people. I can see at least a hundred surf riders as I write this. I am not intrigued as it all looks like work to me. I saw Loretta Young down at the Royal yesterday. She doesn't look very glamorous in a bathing suit laying in the sand. I could pick a dozen any time of day that would appeal to me more.

Some friends just called and made a date for "Trader Vic's" tonite so I must stop and dress for dinner. Lord, how I enjoy being able to bathe again. I take at least two each day and sometimes more. I suppose I have some mail from you waiting down at Wake. I shall be down there a week from tomorrow and answer it then.

Love, Harry

During their vacation Harry and his roommate, Wake office manager John Polak, also managed to put in some time at the Pearl Harbor CPNAB operating base. George Youmans wrote to Harry Morrison, "Both men are excellent in their positions, and I am certainly glad that you were able to employ Harry Olson, for he has been a big help to Dan on his job at Wake." With M-K's three projects in full swing—Wake, Midway, and the Red Hill underground fuel storage, Youmans and Morrison discussed the necessity of having a number-two man trained to step in for the general superintendents on the projects. This was particularly vital on Midway where there were problems with the general superintendent, Marlyn Sheik, and on Wake because of its extreme remoteness. As for Wake, Youmans wrote, "Harry Olson has developed into a good man, and [Herman] Echols is a good 'foil' for him in taking care of administrative details."[23]

Midway Islands, July 24, 1941
Dear Katherine:
Well here I am on my way back and the vacation is over or will be tomorrow. It was a lulu and I had a marvelous time. It seems as though I am completely numb. You know how it is trying to adjust yourself to the everyday humdrum life. It will take a couple days.

I don't like Midway nearly as well as Wake. It is all sand and birds. The project here is much farther along than ours but is also much more of a mess. It is so crowded. Of course they started a year ahead of us but I still think we will make a better showing. Each of our jobs has a sub base tacked on it now and that will mean more work.

I suppose you will have returned from your vacation by the time you get this. Hope you had as much fun as I. Mine came up so quick that I was not prepared and I think that is one reason I enjoyed it so much. I was really a very tired man and the trip did me a world of good. I feel like a man again and have a bit of confidence again.

Riding the Clippers is a tiresome business. We climb up to 10,000 ft. and all we can see is clouds. When we can see the ocean below it has a hard metallic appearance, much the same as pictures you have seen of the moon. The motors drone along steadily until you are not con-

scious of them. They have a wonderful buffet lunch and everyone eats most of the time. Eat, read and doze. I am always glad when we come down and everybody is tired. One more day and I will be home.

All the Honolulu people, I mean the contractors, are very much pleased with our work down there. The job has been slowed up a lot the last two weeks but we are going to get a lot of materials now so I am going to have to go to work on my return.

The Japanese situation looks bad tonight but no one down here is worrying and we all feel that the next two weeks will tell the tale.

Harry

While Harry made his way back to Wake and Katherine made her way back to Portland, Harry's friends Pete Russell and Swede Hokanson made arrangements for their wives to join them in Honolulu for their upcoming vacations. Pete's wife, Eudelle, had just undergone surgery in California, but she would book passage on the *Lurline* for September; Swede's wife and daughter would make similar plans for the early fall. Apparently, where there was a will, there was a way to share vacation time with a loved one.

THE NEWS: JULY 1941

While the world's attention was riveted on the Axis war machine and the horrific casualties mounting in the Soviet Union, the potential for war in the Pacific notched up dramatically in late July. The German invasion of the U.S.S.R. in June had put Japan in a hot spot. Unprepared to join the attack on Russia and with dwindling oil reserves, Japan turned first to a southern target in an attempt to reduce dependence on Western resources. Japan gambled that an attack on Southeast Asia would likely irritate the United States, but would not by itself provoke war. In fact, the move triggered a chain reaction that made war between Japan and the United States inevitable, given the aversion of both countries to conciliation or compromise.[24]

The invasion of Indochina (Vietnam, Laos, and Cambodia), which lies directly across the South China Sea from the Philippines, began with the Japanese occupation of French military bases in late July 1941. The pro-German French Vichy government quickly acquiesced, "permitting Japan temporarily to occupy" the bases in the French colony. The Japanese ambassador in Washington assured diplomats that the move was meant to secure the flow of raw materials and food exports from the region to Japan, but the

United States suspended talks with Japan, calling the occupation a "policy of force and of conquest." Banking on Japan's vulnerability to economic pressure due to its lack of resources, U.S. officials tightened the screws, freezing Japanese assets of $138 million. Britain, and the Netherlands government in exile, quickly followed suit and Japan retaliated by freezing the Japanese-based assets of all three countries. Japanese troops landed in Indochina on July 28. On August 1 the United States imposed an oil embargo by revoking all export licenses for petroleum shipments to Japan. The Dutch East Indies quickly followed suit. As Japan depended on American exports for 80 percent of its oil the embargo packed a serious punch. The U.S. intended the embargo as a protest to Japanese expansion into Indochina; still, it was a risky move that might well provoke further Japanese expansion into the oil-rich Dutch East Indies to obtain vitally needed supplies. Chief of Naval Operations Harold Stark sent a "well-wrapped" war warning to Admiral Kimmel in Pearl Harbor on July 25 advising him of the impending economic sanctions. While Stark did not anticipate an overt, hostile reaction from Japan, he advised Kimmel to "take appropriate precautionary measures against possible eventualities."[25]

Amidst the flurry of asset freezes and oil embargos in accordance with provisions in the Philippine Independence Act President Roosevelt called the Philippine Army to active service and appointed General MacArthur as commander of U.S. Army Forces in the Far East. With stunning speed the Philippines went from a lost cause to a golden opportunity in U.S. Army strategy. MacArthur's optimistic and enthusiastic plans for a heavily fortified base promised to provide a deterrent to Japanese aggression and a viable defense for the Philippines. While the army quickly adopted the new plans, no corresponding plans for naval buildup emerged. Within weeks, MacArthur's command received top priority for new weapons, authorization for hundreds of B-17s as soon as they rolled out of U.S. factories, and a commitment to double U.S. Army forces in the islands. Rows of shiny new B-17 heavy bombers, aptly named Flying Fortresses, would surely make the Japanese think twice about expanding their sphere at the expense of their neighbors. The strengthened U.S. commitment in the Far East also included coordination of Pacific military strategies with Britain, the Netherlands, and China, Lend-Lease assistance to China, and the establishment of the Flying Tigers, a volunteer air corps, to train Chinese pilots with U.S. and British-made aircraft. At the Atlantic Conference in August, U.S. President Franklin

Roosevelt and British Prime Minister Winston Churchill met in Newfoundland and agreed to a far-reaching joint strategy against the Axis powers and principles for post-war international peace in the eight-point Atlantic Charter. As the summer passed tensions were tightening in the Pacific and the men on Wake could smell the change.[26]

CAMP WAKE

Through the late spring and summer the contractors gradually vacated Camp 1 for Camp 2, depending on the location of their work. The carpenters building the barracks were the first to move in May; by early July, they had completed the first ten eighty-man barracks, staff quarters and offices, and a mess hall that could serve eleven hundred in one seating, and a steady stream of workers and staff moved into the new camp in early summer. The camp continued to grow to accommodate the influx of men. Nearly nine hundred civilian workers were at work in early July and Camp 2 was designed to house fifteen hundred when complete. Among the last groups to leave Camp 1 was Joe McDonald's crew of surveyors in early August. Like Peter Hansen, McDonald lamented that the change was "very lousy as it was mighty fine there compared to the crowded noisy barracks." Now nearly vacant, Camp 1 stood equipped with tent housing, mess hall and kitchen facilities, water storage, sewer lines, and electricity, ready for whatever future use the navy deemed necessary. On July 18, Marine Corps officers arrived to inspect Camp 1, spurring rumors that a contingent of Leathernecks would soon be joining the Wake population. [27]

For Ted Olson, the first weeks flew by. "We work practically all the time we aren't asleep." With fourteen structures to build the new steel crews kept busy working ten-hour days, six to seven days a week. As the only steelworker on his crew who knew how to read a blueprint Ted became the "layout man," with no raise in pay, but the promise of valuable experience. He wrote to his sister:

> *There is a swell bunch of fellows my age out here. There is only one man in our crew that is over 30 years old, and do we have the fun. . . . Yesterday there wasn't much work to do so we spent about two hours pushing each other off the dock into the canal with clothes on. At least we got cooled off a bit. The weather is quite warm, but there is always a cool breeze blowing. We don't work quite as hard here as we did on*

the mainland because the humidity is so low that a person gets sick to his stomach if he works too hard. I've got the most beautiful sun-tan that you ever saw. No kidding, in another two weeks I'll be practically black. Ah, life, it's wonderful! [28]

For others the monotony of repetitive work and long hours was unbearably tiresome, even when the work was easy. By late July the lack of materials meant many workers got "all tired out trying to kill time and make a little job last until noon or quitting time," as Pete Hansen wrote. "This stalling around is getting us all down." Still, he figured that "75% are always happy, laugh a lot, enjoy everything and try to be happy under the circumstances. The other 25% are regular sourpusses, selfish, want the lights out early, always beefing about everything; they make life miserable for others and they hate themselves." A good sense of humor helped. Jack Hoskins wrote, "The birds are very thick and peculiar, the rats are our best companions being with us constantly in bed or out. Our cockroaches are magnificent specimens of manhood—two of them being able to carry an orange—they prefer candy." Hoskins admitted that he was "usually happy, but out here with little to do I often get disgusted."[29]

The lack of women on Wake was a frequent source of complaint and drove many a man to give up on his contract and take the next ship out. Among the stories that made the rounds was one from the Pan American pioneers on Wake. In the first year of Pan American's remote, island-based operations the company gave the isolated and homesick men on Wake permission to have a special thirty-pound baggage allowance for items to be sent from Honolulu. Four of the men wired the boss stating that they had decided to pool their allowance and were requesting a 120-pound blond. In another story from the early CPNAB days on Midway someone hung a sign stating that there would be a barge full of women coming in and any man who wanted to visit the barge was to report to the doctor's office the next morning. When the doctor came in to work he found a line stretching out the door and down the road, and it took considerable effort to get the men to stand down. The CPNAB contractors considered every possibility for the remote islands, but in the end, there was simply no acceptable alternative to "no dames."[30]

The men on Wake Island followed the news through their radios and the *Wake Wig Wag* reports, but the war seemed comfortably remote to many.

Those who disagreed opted for the next ship out; others, like family man Peter Hansen, kept close watch on the pulse of the war news. Those who stayed on worked hard, ate well ("the food is excellent—all you want and a huge variety, but I'd give $5 for a quart of fresh milk," wrote Joe McDonald), and calculated their earnings and time remaining on their contracts as the weeks went by. With room and board included, most of the contractors' wages went straight home or into bank accounts. The construction crews and heavy equipment operators on Wake earned overtime when the project was running well, but their foremen and the men who worked in the office or as timekeepers and in other camp support jobs were kept strictly to straight time. Engineers and surveyors working on the drill barge in the lagoon to map out the pending submarine base often worked well over eight hours a day, but were not eligible for overtime, even though their job was essential to the progress of the project. Nor, of course, did the big money go into the pockets of the scores of men who served the food, washed the dishes, sold the ice cream sodas on movie nights, did the laundry, and swept the barracks. Despite the bottleneck in materials and the turnover in workforce, the complicated project on the remote atoll continued to advance, and every man who remained stood to make a bundle.[31]

> *Wake Island, July 31, 1941*
> *Dear Mother,*
> *The time has come when I should once again take my trusty pen in hand and in my most inimitable style, scribble, and I do mean scribble, a few lines to you. I received your most welcome letter and am glad to hear you had such a pleasant trip. Dad got back on the same Clipper none the worse for wear. It was too bad that you couldn't meet him in Honolulu, but I guess it couldn't be helped.*
>
> *I am having quite a time getting comfortable to write this letter. It seems as though this morning we had a bit of a pile driving job on our hands. It was necessary for one man to take off all his clothes and do a little swimming. I'll give you one guess as to who was picked. At any rate, it seems that I have a beautiful coat of tan down as far as my belt and up as far as my trunks. At the present time I have a beautiful coat of sunburn right where I do my sitting down. It isn't very serious, but it is very uncomfortable. Such is the case of a Wacky Wakean.*
>
> *There isn't a heck of a lot to write about on Wake Island, which*

makes it very tough on a past master at the art of letter writing. We are getting a softball league organized at the present time. Swede came up to me a couple days ago and asked what I thought of the chances for the riggers to get a good team together. I told him we could but that we didn't have a pitcher. It seems that there is a fellow here from La Grande, Oregon, who won the Oregon State Tournament three years in a row. Plans are now under way to transfer him to the rigging dept. Swede says that he has seen the hiring of ball-players on other jobs so he'll try his hand at it. It's quite a joke among the people who understand what it is all about.

Well, I am a couple of days into my second month on the Island, and I have no regrets up to the present. There are a few people who I would like to see including my family and my favorite girl friend. By the way, I get a letter from Dee Dee every Clipper. What a gal. I think maybe she likes me a little bit. At any rate the feeling is mutual.

Roger Smalley moved up from Camp 1 a couple of weeks ago. We are now bunkmates. It is pretty nice to be able to talk over old times with someone you know. We have a lot of fun together. Well, it's getting along towards show-time so I'll close for now. Tell everyone hello . . . and if they happen to get in a letter writing mood, that I'm just the guy who likes to receive lots of mail. Again I must say Aloha.

Love, Ted

Everyone agreed that evenings on Wake brought pleasant respite from the hot days. Close to the equator, night dropped suddenly and the contractors, weary from a long day of work and full of good chow, enjoyed a cool night breeze and a few hours of relaxation before hitting the hay. The library had grown to hundreds of books and many workers had brought musical instruments from home. There was even a piano and some men took lessons. Fellows shared letters and photographs, talked about home, listened to radios, gathered for jam sessions and poker games, and wrote letters. Before the nightly picture show at eight (six nights a week, often in the open rain), an hour of amplified record or radio music played throughout the camp. Candy and cigarettes sold for a nickel at the canteen, payable by chit, and the soda jerks churned out ice cream sodas by the hundreds in the evenings. O. G. Skirvin, the forty-three-year-old "Ice Cream Maker," did not earn any overtime, nor was it clear how his job qualified as essential defense work, but his product kept many Wake workers content after a hot day on the job and ready to start all over again the next morning.

Patterned after Midway's successful *Gooney Gazette*, the *Wake Wig Wag* informed the CPNAB workers of global news and local events, reminded them of job policies and safety tips, and built camaraderie with entertaining local gossip and amusing tidbits. Edited, compiled, and mimeographed "almost daily" by Louis M. Cormier, the *Wig Wag* offered a tangible touch of civilization on the remote atoll. The July 15, 1941, issue, dedicated to "the folks back home," found its way into dozens of mailboxes on the mainland. Under the *Wake Wig Wag* banner, with its tongue-in-cheek drawing of palm trees leaning in the wind, the front page listed the evening's picture show and opened with a note of appreciation to the workers from Dan Teters.

The special issue included a brief description of the atoll and camp facilities built to date, as well as the glamorous Pan American Airways operation and famous visitors. Describing the workers' living quarters and conditions the editor remarked that in addition to steel lockers provided for their belongings, the men had cobbled together various shelves, tables, and dressers that "would give a real cabinet maker a case of the galloping heebie jeebies." The recreation center and sport courts and fields were still under construction, but the men enjoyed a soda fountain, canteen, shoe repair, and barbershop all under one roof. The special issue continued with a selection of poems, "The Spyglass" gossip section, and a compilation of radio news and sports scores. Finally, the editor appended a copy of an informative article on Wake's history by Homer C. Votaw that had been published in the U.S. Naval Institute *Proceedings* in January 1941.

The *Wig Wag*'s gossip section both reflected and encouraged a vital bonding among the contractors. The Wake workers comprised a group small enough to know who most everyone was, but big enough to spread the banter around. "Herb Brown over at #1 Warehouse will remember this July 4th for a long time. Seems someone with a sense of humor sent bottles of root beer out from Honolulu in boxes marked "Miller's High Life Beer" and the rumor spread like wild-fire that each of us would get two bottles of beer on the 4th! Herb almost went nuts when the gang swooped down on him and insisted on ransacking almost every case on the chance a stray bottle of honest to goodness beer had been put in by mistake!" Such stories had limited, local appeal, but in mid-July, Joe McDonald, the surveyor from Reno, became an official correspondent for the United Press at Wake Island. "I wish a Clipper would pile up so I could have something to write about," he wrote his parents. "That's about all that could happen out here that the navy wouldn't censor first."[32]

While a few workers were fortunate enough to have a radio within earshot in the evenings, most relied on the *Wig Wag* for news of the outside world, the war, politics, and sports. Cormier compiled the news from broadcasts picked up from San Francisco, Melbourne, and Tokyo between the hours of 5:00 and 8:00 p.m., and reminded newcomers to curtail their use of electric razors and drills during those hours as they interfered with reception. On July 15 the paper carried updates on the front lines in the Soviet Union and other hot spots in the war. In Washington debates loomed over expansion of the draft and use of American troops. Civilian defense director Fiorello LaGuardia pushed a plan to train the populations of Atlantic seaboard cities in air raid procedures and safe handling of bombs and poisonous gasses. Baseball league scores and Joe DiMaggio's latest record-breaking feats completed the day's news. (The Yankee Clipper's fifty-six game hitting streak, a record that still stands, started in May and ended on July 17, 1941.)

In the special July issue of the *Wig Wag*, Cormier also described the wide variety of reef and lagoon life on Wake including "Old Pappy Shark" who snatches the prize of many a fisherman "too long in bringing his fish to gaff." He noted that the Hawaiians excelled at spear fishing and were thrilling to watch as they dove into the shark-infested waters of the atoll. Recently the Hawaiian workers had brought in "four Japanese bluefish, ranging from 75 to 150 lbs each and a turtle tipping the scales at 150 lbs!" Many of the men wrote home about the unusual pleasures and perils of fishing on Wake. They would take a small boat or wade a mile out onto the reef with their spears and water glasses, watchful for the sharks, eels and octopus that called the reef home. On one July fishing expedition Joe McDonald marveled at the "millions of fish—all sizes, shapes & colors—it looked like an aquarium on the loose." Another day Jack Hoskins speared an octopus that retaliated by grabbing his arm with one tentacle and a rock on the bottom with another, pulling him under the water. In the end, man won over beast and Hoskins sent the dried beak of the octopus home along with dozens of shells and a polished chunk of ironwood on which he had engraved "Wake 1941."[33]

By the last week of July the news that Japanese forces had occupied Indochina abruptly dispelled the cheerful atmosphere conveyed by the mid-month *Wig Wag*. Over several days Pete Hansen wrote to his wife:

Things are reaching a crisis and I really think we will be shipped home real soon. A rumor came from the office today saying that arrangements are being made to take us off the island, and that transfers would be made for every good man. This is not authentic, though, just a rumor. In the meantime they are continuing to discharge men at the rate of from five to fifteen a day. As many are quitting each day and waiting for that boat that has not yet appeared.

Hansen noted that the day before, a Matson liner had steamed by in sight of Wake, the deck loaded with cars and trucks indicating an evacuation from some point to the west. The ship, steaming 120 miles off the regular shipping lanes from Guam and the Philippines, did not even answer the navy's signals from Wake.

Everyone seems to be concerned with the news now, and the few radios we have in camp are kept busy. . . . The best we could get tonite was that Japan is sending troops to French Indo China, which means the U.S. will be compelled to make good her agreement with Great Britain by retaining the status quo in the Pacific. Should Japan land these troops which are being escorted by 40 warships, it means war. *We also heard that the U.S. and Britain are already taking steps to completely blockade Japan.*

Two days later, he continued:

They must either get some guns and Marines here immediately or get us off the island. The Japanese owned Marshall Islands are only 300 to 500 miles south of us, it is only 1900 miles to Tokyo, and if this little island is as strategic as they claim it is they better get some guns on it right now, because if it's valuable to the U.S. it is just as valuable to Japan."[34]

BREAKING THE BOTTLENECK

Harry and John Polak flew from Honolulu via Midway by Clipper and arrived on Wake July 26, just in time to hear the latest orders from the navy: begin immediate construction of new landplane runways on Wake "on an emergency basis." The contractors began grading and laying a coral base. This project did not have to wait for the sluggish supply line, but it required use of the same heavy equipment as other key projects then underway. The navy had included emergency runways in the program from the start, complete with plans, estimates, and preliminary sketches, and the contractors had presumed that they would start the project soon after their arrival in January. Despite the contractors' arguments that building the runways in the early months would allow them to utilize the excavation equipment before it was required elsewhere, the navy deferred the project for months. As spring turned to summer the contractors had repeatedly requested firm plans, location, and authorization for the runways. In late May, preliminary approval came through for construction of a 3,000-foot, prevailing-wind landing strip with a rolled coral surface to a width of 150 feet. The last week of July the contractors received orders to "proceed immediately" on the east-west runway, now extended to 5,000 feet long and 200 feet wide. The orders conveyed such urgency that the contractors set right to work and completed the emergency runway and a parking area with mooring blocks by the first week of September. On September 6 the navy advised the contractors that U.S. Army Air Force funds had been authorized for full landplane runways. A fleet of Flying Fortresses was earmarked for the Philippines to bolster General MacArthur's strategy of deterrence to Japanese aggression in the Far East, and Wake Island was an essential fuel stop for the B-17s as they ferried from the mainland to Clark Field, outside Manila.[35]

The July bottleneck on cargo that had crippled progress for weeks on Wake broke in early August. The *Burrows* arrived on August 2 towing a very welcome cargo barge and carrying 132 new employees, fresh water, food supplies, and 122 thousand gallons of diesel fuel oil. The *Burrows*, freshly painted in "war color," held blackout drills every night en route to Wake. The sailors told contractors on the island that they had heard reports of a German raider in the waters and that Captain Dierdorff had requested an escort on all following trips. The newcomers, many hired from the Boise area, were put to work unloading the boat and barge. Orval Kelso, a powerhouse operator from Idaho, took time to make his initial observations for the folks back home: Wake is a "queer place," he wrote, "rocks float; wood sinks, fish fly and we have a bird here that runs but can't fly . . . and man-eating eels." The *Burrows* was emptied in short order and departed carrying sixty-four contractors back to Honolulu, as well as a little parcel containing a handmade necklace with over fifty shells, tenderly wrapped and mailed by Pete Hansen to his youngest child, Mary-Anne, for her seventh birthday.[36]

As soon as the *Burrows* departed the navy tug *Seminole* pulled up towing not one, but two barges loaded with cargo: Admiral Bloch had made his point in Honolulu. Within three days another tug the *Navajo* arrived with two more barges. However, despite the influx of supplies and the rush job on runway construction, the bottlenecks had disrupted the order and momentum of construction. Progress continued to lag on Wake and building was almost at a standstill on the naval air base structures. Hundreds of bundles of corrugated metal sheeting arrived ungalvanized, so Pete Russell had to organize a crew to paint it immediately to prevent it from rusting. "Tempo of the whole job is low," he wrote in his diary on August 6. "Too much stalling when we didn't have the material."[37]

Meanwhile, out in the lagoon the dredge *Columbia* was back on the job after an eighteen-day shutdown for repairs. On August 6 Captain Bruns notified the contractors that he accepted their plan to cut the ship channel through Wilkes Island into the lagoon and that he would recommend it to the Bureau of Yards and Docks. Bruns repeated that the contractors must give the project their highest priority, to which they replied that they could finish it in a minimum of six months. However, deadlines melted away as the plan went back into the navy approval process and the contractors awaited the green light to begin the channel. The dredge continued to chew and grind a barge channel across the lagoon toward Peale, breaking down with appalling frequency.[38]

The contractors also received a priority dispatch in early August to begin immediate construction of two temporary storage magazines for guns and ammunition and one detonator magazine for the marines. Permanent magazines had been in the general plan for months, but, again, lack of approved plans and authorization had held them up. Overall, the twenty-item list of marine facilities, including a two-story administration and operations building and three 150-foot radio towers, was firmer on paper than it was on the ground. The contractors went into high gear in mid-August: the new orders coupled with the deteriorating Pacific situation suggested that the navy needed its base on Wake in the shortest possible time. As if to underscore the rush, Mother Nature pushed the Pacific weather into high gear, stirring up typhoons in the western Pacific and sending high winds, rains, and seas into Wake's neighborhood.[39]

Wake Island, August 13, 1941
Dear Katherine:
We haven't had an eastbound Clipper for three weeks. The one I came back on is still at Guam. It has been there three times and had to fly back to Manila twice to escape typhoons. The weather has been more or less bad for the last two weeks. We even had a mild sort of typhoon ourselves yesterday but suffered no harm to speak of. The wind got up to 65 miles per hour and I never saw it rain so hard. We got four inches in less than two hours and have stored 60,000 gallons during the last two days. This is a big help for water is precious down here. It would cost us $10,000.00 to produce that much. It isn't all gravy however as production slumped badly. We also got some heavy seas that wrecked our jetties and bulkheads. We had a Navy tug standing offshore for two days waiting for a couple barges but we couldn't take them out and he finally went back to town without them. . . .

Tonight's war news is not very encouraging. Of course that depends on one's point of view, for surprising enough, a lot of these naval people would welcome war on the theory I suppose that it would justify the preparation they have made for it. As for myself, I have given up think-ing about it and let nature take its course. You will perhaps think it odd, but there is no apprehension among the people down here and we are the most vulnerable of any of the U.S.A. outposts. Most of the fel-lows are like me. Just don't pay any attention to it. I don't know what good it would do if we did.

The job is perking up a bit after a lull for want of materials. We are pretty well into permanent construction. Most of the foundations are poured and we are putting up the structural steel now. Of course it isn't all here and we may come to another stopping place on that account. I had many conferences with the Operating Committee about this when I was in town and they assured me that we would get at least

10,000 tons a month which would keep us going nicely, but I have my doubts. By the way, Mr. Youmans wrote down here that he was afraid I didn't get much of a vacation because he had me in the office so much. He used to come by the hotel and pick me up in the morning and take me out to Pearl Harbor until noon. I didn't mind it for I felt I could do some good for most of those people were not at all familiar with the project or our problems and they were avid for information. . . .

August 15:

I feel a little better tonight. To tell the truth I had been low for a few days. Late this afternoon I went over to the hotel and woke Betty up and demanded a beer. She felt that way too so we consumed a few. Hence the lift in spirits. She is leaving for San Francisco in two weeks and glad to get away. I hate to see she and Irv leave for they are the only social contacts I have here. Irv is going on flight duty. Betty and I have a hard and fast date to paint San Francisco red when I come back. This will probably go the way of all dates for it looks like a long time away. They have been very good to me. There has been a lot of trouble here lately over the liquor question and I am the only one that can buy it at the hotel. Even Dan can't which makes him mad. But I did right all along, hence the concession on my part. Let me give you a tip. Stand in good with the stewards and to hell with the rest on boats and planes.

We have a tanker coming in the morning with fuel gas and 16 men. The sea is still rough but I am going to try and get out to her in the morning. We also have two other ships and a tug towing a barge that are near so I hope it calms down. Keep this dark, but one of them has 150 Marines and 500 tons of guns and ammunition. I don't like this for now the Japs can start shooting at us instead of just coming and taking us. Well, if you don't worry over this any more than I do, you will sleep very well at night. I'll write more in a couple days.

Harry

STORMY WEATHER

The storms at mid-month wreaked havoc on Wake. High winds battered the island for days, and fifteen-foot waves washed off the end of the levee that the contractors had built to protect the entrance to the pilot channel. Again, sand and coral rock washed into the channel, closing the entrance, as the army engineers had predicted several years before. Storms from the southwest tended to pile up water in the lagoon, which then ran out the two natural channels, carrying sand from the islands out onto the reef. Reverse storms pushed the sand back onto the islands and through the channels into the lagoon. Any alteration to the natural channels promised to interfere with the natural storm flows. Blasted and deepened by the contractors, the pilot channel carried more material on the storm outflow and blocked the entrance. High waves pounding the outside made it impossible to get a rig out to the entrance to clear the channel.[40]

On shore, sheet iron roofs popped with the deluge and surveyors on a barge in the middle of the lagoon found that "there wasn't anything we could do but to duck down in the water to keep from getting blown away and our ears beat off by the driving rain." Wake emerged nearly unscathed: a few buildings sustained minor damage and the flagpole bent in half. Joe McDonald wrote his first article for the United Press about the storms, received approval for dispatch via navy radio to Honolulu, and was surprised to hear a truncated version of it the next night on the *Richfield Reporter*. The editing resulted in an overly dramatic effect that prompted several ships at sea to radio the storm-ravaged island and offer assistance. However, the contractors managed to reopen the channel, raise the flagpole, and repair the damage between storms on their own, and "the roving reporter" enjoyed a brief moment of fame. Despite all of the urgent activity, Harry and Pete found time after supper on August 14 to ride out to the end of Peale where they sat and watched the clouds.[41]

A few days later a navy tanker brought fuel to Wake and another ship delivered two thousand tons of food. While the sailors engaged the contractors in a softball game, the two ships were moored alongside each other for unloading and refueling, despite Harry's warning of unstable weather. "One might as well talk to the Rock of Gibraltar as to Naval Stupidity," Harry wrote Donna. "The wind was inshore and the weather bum. We have had a steady diet of thunder and lightning for a week but one of those squalls came up in earnest at midnite. We had to bring our barges in so the ships could get out and I'm telling you I think it was my prayers that did the job." Captain Bruns arrived the following day to inspect progress, surveyed the waterfront situation, and placed Harry in sole charge of all ship and barge movements at Wake. "Now I can tell those Navy captains what and how we propose to do this work. It just happened that my arch enemy Capt. John

Doyle [James Doyle, of the USS *Regulus*] came in this morning and I had the pleasure of telling him off first. So I am practically steeped in a rosy glow of satisfaction." The *Regulus* brought an important load to Wake Island on this trip: U.S. Marines and guns.[42]

CHAPTER 7

BAITING THE HOOK

━━━━━━━━━━━━━

MARINES ON DECK

On August 19, 1941, the *Regulus* approached Wake carrying 5 officers and 170 men of the 1st Defense Battalion under the command of Major Lewis A. Hohn, as well as 47 additional contractors for Wake. The defense battalion personnel comprised the initial component of shore defenses recommended by the Greenslade Board and implemented by Admiral Kimmel for the atoll. One new arrival of the battalion's Pioneer Platoon observed that Wake looked like a "flat pancake without any foliage," and the marine despaired that he had arrived at the "utter absolute end of the world." Half the servicemen stayed aboard for three days to discharge cargo onto flat lighters that then ferried the gear to shore as the *Regulus* steamed "on various courses and at various speeds to maintain position." The heaving seas snapped lines and high waves sent the lighters crashing into dangling crates and the sides of the ship. The operation soon came under control, however, as the marines glumly unloaded their supplies, guns, and ammunition while civilians clustered at the waterfront to watch.[1] Describing their arrival Harry wrote home:

> *The Marines have landed but the situation has gone to hell for they are all tangled up unloading their big guns. . . . There's 175 of them and their proud boast was that they were self sufficient. I guess they are if we give them time. They are working hard but don't know how. Here's a joke. They lost the Major's trunk overboard and everyone*

135

thought the scotch supply was in it. So all the boats put out to sea and an elaborate shore patrol was inaugurated until it was found that the liquor was in a wooden case and safe. The search was promptly abandoned. No one was interested in mere clothes except the Major. This station is getting more and more important. Hawaii may be the cross roads of the Pacific but Wake is the crossroads of Pacific defenses. It's a natural, and every important military man realizes it when he sees our setup. Strangely enough they all like us. They say our job is the best organized of all of them and run the most efficiently.[2]

As soon as the marines had erected their six-man tents on the outskirts of Camp 1 they turned to the laborious process of setting up heavy-gun emplacements. The detachment brought six five-inch guns, twelve three-inch antiaircraft guns, eighteen .50-caliber antiaircraft machine guns and thirty of the smaller .30-calibers, as well as six searchlights with accompanying generators. The shore guns would anchor the seacoast batteries at the three points of the atoll: Toki Point on Peale, Peacock Point on Wake, and Kuku Point on Wilkes. The navy ordered strict segregation of military and civilian work. Rear Admiral Bloch ordered Major Hohn to set up the marine camp and defenses "without interference with the construction work going on. . . . Our principle effort should be to complete the facilities at the earliest possible date," Bloch wrote, so there should be "no friction in any way, nor should construction personnel be called off their jobs" except in dire emergency. The sooner the contractors completed the facilities the sooner they could depart and make way for a full garrison to defend the strategic atoll.[3]

Most of the marines and contractors were given a rare day off on Labor Day, September 1, 1941, and fielded opposing baseball teams for a much-anticipated contest. Ted Olson, not long out of the hospital for a bad cold, wrote home, "We had a ball game with them today. Of course, I was the star (brag, brag). They were leading 1 to 0. I got a 2 base hit and scored to tie it up. Then I got a hit later to bat in the winning run. It sure felt good to be playing again." Over the coming weeks, the marines and civilians found similar areas of common ground when it came to sports and they occasionally shared food or drink—the civilians had the superior mess; the marines had the beer—but, as ordered, they kept their work segregated.[4]

To a couple of surveyors who spent weeks on barges in the lagoon taking soundings for seaplane runways, by mid-September it seemed as if the marines had taken over Wake Island. Despite admonitions to keep military activities and gun emplacements secret, Darwin Meiners wrote to his family in Oregon describing guns mounted at strategic spots and ammunition stored in newly-built, temporary magazines. Joe McDonald wrote his folks that the marines were "sure cluttering up the place" with their "whole boat load of five-inch guns, anti-aircraft equipment, ammunition and all kinds of other stuff to defend us with. I don't know what they will defend us against cause I can't understand why any country in their right mind would want this God-forsaken place, no matter how strategic it is supposed to be." As Peter Hansen noted, with a touch of sarcasm, the sight of the big guns and "enough powder to blow up the whole island . . . makes us feel better."[5]

The presence of the marine garrison reminded all of the civilians, in one way or another, of the other side of the Wake coin. The cold, metallic reality of guns and ammunition gave pause to all. Harry Olson and other war veterans recognized equipment that they had used more than twenty years before: vintage 1913 Springfield rifles, old helmets, and five-inch guns to be used as seacoast defense guns that were cast-offs from old navy battleships. The older civilian contractors, who had experienced a generation of technological advancement in construction, and now worked with some of the most modern equipment available, were taken aback to see that there was no corresponding military modernization available for Wake Island.

Many of the draft-age contractors found frequent occasion to ponder the choices they had made. If they had not previously secured deferments, draft boards found them on Wake, inquired of their status, and requested information from CPNAB before issuing deferments. Watching the servicemen and thinking about their brothers and friends back home the civilians had little doubt that the pay, the chow, and the work were better on the civilian side, but some had second thoughts. When the call came in early September for volunteers to train on the guns, dozens stepped up. Most, however, dismissed any immediate danger. "If it comes to war I think I will stay out here till they get damn tired of fighting," wrote McDonald. "At least there is no one shooting at you out here." Radio reports might be raising the specter of war, but he was glad to be "out here with about half the fleet within a couple of days sailing time in case anything happens." Still, he was one who volunteered to train on the antiaircraft guns: "it will be a lot of fun to learn how one of them works anyway."[6]

Stormy weather returned to Wake at the end of August. On August 28

Pan American radio operators received warnings that Wake should expect winds of 100 mph within twelve hours. All across Wake men scrambled to secure loose ends. Chet Ratekin, a surveyor from Nampa, Idaho, reported that they tied down all the lumber, braced and boarded up buildings. Truck drivers parked vehicles in front of each bunk house in Camp 2 to evacuate the workers to a new concrete and steel-frame building on Peale when the storm hit. "Half the men were scared to death," Peter Hansen wrote. "About 8 o'clock in the evening they notified us to pack all our belongings and fasten them, or make secure to the barracks, be ready to board the trucks and go to Peale" if the warning whistle blew. Hansen gathered all of his wife's letters and stowed them in his steel locker, and put her ring and his wrist watch in his pocket, and huddled with the others in the barracks as the wind howled. The next thing he knew, it was morning. "The storm got to within 80 miles of us and then veered off to the west," Harry wrote to Katherine afterwards. "We got a 50 mile wind and torrential rains, but suffered no damage. So now I'm in the fix of the guy who dug a tunnel only to have the mountain wash away. It all really did me some good and pepped me up. I can't tell you the whole story for it involves some hush hush (Navy). I did succeed in proving a theory I have long held," Harry said cryptically. "That is that there are two ways to do a thing. The right way and the Navy way." By September 1 peace had returned to the atoll. "There is a fitful moon gleaming wanly through scudding clouds on the lagoon tonight and it is beautiful beyond words," wrote Harry, quite possibly with a glass of scotch at hand. "Each little wavelet in turn catches its portion of the light and sends it back to the watcher. It's positively immoral."[7]

WAKE IN NAVAL STRATEGY

As RAdm. Ben Moreell (Yards and Docks bureau chief), naval engineers, and civilian contractors worked on plans and construction of Naval Air Station, Wake Island, through 1940 and 1941, navy strategists plotted the function of the atoll in evolving war plans. During the congressional debates over approval and funding the navy had promoted the defensive role of the outlying islands as vital for defense patrols at the outbreak of war. However, given the vast distances between the atolls and the Hawaiian Islands and the limited range of patrol planes, the strategic value of Wake actually lay in offensive war plans. War Plan Orange remained in force behind Rainbow 5. With a declaration of war the U.S. Navy, supported by the army, would initiate offensive action against the Marshalls to capture and control Japanese bases in the march across the Pacific. Wake alone stood close enough to the Marshalls to provide a base of operations and air cover for an early strike against the Japanese base at Eniwetok. U.S. planners acknowledged that Japan would likewise try to seize Wake quickly to establish a defensive outpost on the perimeter of the Marshalls, but they deemed the offensive value of the atoll worth the risk. A detachment of marines would fend off any aggressive moves and protect the project under construction.

Getting that detachment to Wake had turned out to be more complicated in fact than it had been in planning. Admiral Kimmel had requested garrisons for the outlying islands in the spring, but the number of marines available for the remote outposts was limited by the higher priority defense of the Hawaiian Coastal Frontier. The responsibility for local Hawaiian defense lay jointly with Lt. Gen. Walter C. Short, who commanded army land and air forces in Hawaii, and RAdm. Claude C. Bloch, Commandant, 14th Naval District. However, Navy Department orders had transferred the majority of trained and equipped Marine Corps defense units from the West Coast to the Atlantic and Cuba in the early summer, and the navy's resources were thinly spread in the Pacific. Interdepartmental rivalries, debates over priorities, and transportation logistics further complicated the process. Additionally, Wake Island could support only a limited number of men until facilities and fresh-water stores were in place. Any large influx of military personnel would necessitate a corresponding displacement of contractors and thus slow progress on base construction. By Marine Corps standards of the day, to fully man the guns on Wake required a garrison of 43 officers and 939 enlisted men. The 175 marines who arrived in August represented less than a tenth of that number, but it was a start.[8]

With its close proximity to Japanese bases in the Marshalls, Wake required protection, but the new defenses also served Admiral Kimmel's "bait" strategy. In early September, he reiterated his April speculation that an armed Wake might lure Japan to expose their forces even before the base and defenses were complete. "While by no means 'impregnable,'" Kimmel wrote to CNO Stark, "[Wake's] present defensive strength is considerable and will require the exposure of quite a force to capture it. . . . Should its capture be an early objective of Japan, such an effort might be supported by a substantial portion of their Combined Fleet, which would create for us, a golden opportunity *if we have the strength to meet it.*"[9]

By early fall, 1941, Admiral Kimmel was wrapping up his comprehensive, top-secret study of the defenses for Wake, Midway, Johnston, and Palmyra—the first such study since the 1939 Pickett surveys. The Greenslade recommendations and additional congressional funding that allowed expanded facilities, including submarine bases on Wake and Midway and a landing field at Johnston, warranted updated defense assessments for the outlying bases. The successive changes, plans, and increased appropriations had resulted in some "piecemeal" development; "the expression 'growing like Topsy' has been aptly applied to the situation," Kimmel observed. His study proposed to assess those construction developments, the navy's ultimate objectives, and what was required to attain those objectives.[10]

Kimmel evaluated the islands based on their eventual use as both defensive and offensive bases and, potentially, as offensive enemy bases operating against Hawaii and the eastern Pacific. Wake held both the highest probability of enemy attack and the highest priority for offensive U.S. naval operations. Kimmel speculated that "a raid on Wake would be in such force as to permit, in the event of quick and easy success, the capture and garrisoning of the island." Reviewing Kimmel's study in October, Rear Admiral Bloch wrote that he concurred with most of the report, but would argue that an enemy raid on Wake might rather have "the complete destruction of forces and facilities thereon" as its objective. Kimmel proceeded to enumerate the armaments, equipment, facilities, and personnel necessary to keep such an enemy "success" story from occurring. Significantly, CINCPAC recommended additional radar installations at the bases, including three more than the already-approved (but so far undelivered) two units for Wake.[11]

With the arrival of the marines on Wake in August, Admiral Bloch had ordered Major Hohn to consider completion of facilities the highest priority on Wake. However, because the current detachment was inadequate to man defenses in case of hostilities, Bloch suggested that Hohn make quiet inquiries and organize a group of civilian volunteers to train on the guns and other duties "in order that, in case of an emergency, each and every civilian would know where he is to go and what he is to do." Bloch cautioned that Hohn must maintain great discretion and that the civilians "must be kept in a pepped up frame of mind by jokes and their willing cooperation rather than being scared into it by fear of an outside enemy." Do nothing, he warned, that might "give the men the jitters and make them fearsome that something is about to happen" lest it cause the "chicken-hearted to quit working." Bloch firmly believed that when "something" did happen, it would occur in the Far East.[12]

In his "Study on Defenses," Admiral Kimmel also observed that some civilian employees could be expected to aid the defense, based on the facts that "many are ex-servicemen and on the results expected when the instinct of self-preservation asserts itself." Like Bloch, Kimmel warned against "open expression of the intention," which might cause civilians to realize that they were in a "hot spot" and rush to leave, "thereby delaying progress." By the time that Kimmel's report was ready for internal navy distribution and discussion in late November 1941, over a hundred of Wake's contractors had been training for weeks with the marines on guns and searchlights.[13]

WAKE IN ARMY STRATEGY

The shift toward reinforcement of the Philippines and recognition of the strategic importance of Southeast Asia in U.S. war plans favored the army. The change in strategy reflected rising support for defense of American possessions and interests in the face of Japanese aggression: a show of force in the region would convince the Japanese to stand down in Asia. British and American leaders alike assumed that if the Japanese did mount an attack, it would be against a European colony in Asia, such as Singapore or the Dutch East Indies, and that in any case, the Japanese would not prove to be a "formidable foe." In case of war strategists envisioned utilizing the Philippines as the base for offensive air operations against Japan, and B-17 bombers and P-40 pursuit planes were vital to the new strategy. Applying Teddy Roosevelt's adage from decades earlier, Henry Stimson, the secretary of war, claimed that the B-17 was the nation's "big stick" in the Pacific. General George Marshall vowed that if war came "we'll fight mercilessly. Flying Fortresses will be dispatched immediately to set the paper cities of Japan on fire." Delivering the B-17s to the Philippines, however, required careful planning. After considering various alternatives, advisors settled on the route from the West Coast to Hawaii, Midway, Wake, Port Moresby, Darwin, and finally to Clark Field on Luzon. Officers immediately investigated landing conditions and fuel supplies at each of the stops, including Wake.[14]

On September 7 the first nine westbound U.S. Army Air Force B-17s, under the command of Major General Frederick L. Martin, landed on Wake's new crushed-coral, east-west runway for refueling. Although many U.S. Navy and British amphibious bombers had lit on Wake's lagoon in previous months, this was the first the men had seen of the army's new, long-range strategic bomber, aptly nicknamed the Flying Fortress, and they were impressed. With no army ground crews on Wake to service the B-17s, and orders to keep the civilian contractors strictly on project-related work, "filling station" duties fell to the marines. Tankers pumped fuel to storage tanks on shore by leaky pipelines held afloat by barrels. With only one fuel truck, the marines had to transfer gasoline to the airfield in fifty-gallon drums and refuel the B-17s with hand pumps, each plane swallowing three thousand gallons "at a drink." Few men on Wake could keep their eyes off the massive bombers. Word passed across the atoll like wildfire: the B-17s were headed for Clark Field in the Philippines to serve as a powerful deterrent to Japanese aggression. The navy issued strict orders to keep the ultimate destination of the bombers secret and most did so in their letters. Pete Russell even drew a blank line in his diary in place of the name. The pioneer B-17 flight departed Wake that night, overflew the eastern Caroline Islands (Japanese mandates) in the hop to Port Moresby in southeastern New Guinea, pressed on to Darwin in Australia, and arrived at Clark Field near Manila on September 12, 1941. The adrenalin-boosting first visit would soon give way to a grueling repetition of B-17 fuel stops, and the time-consuming refueling job increasingly took the Wake marines from their primary task of erecting gun emplacements on the atoll.[15]

On September 11 Harry wrote Katherine:

Sunday we had a visit of nine Flying Fortresses. It was the initial test of our new land plane runways. They are beautiful planes somewhat as a tiger is beautiful for of course their purpose is destruction. The truth is that we had rushed for 3 weeks preparing so they could come. It was done for the benefit of the little brown brothers. I shall always remember their take-off that night at midnight. The moon was full and directly overhead. Our runway is a mile long and to outline it we had made flares and placed them at fifty foot intervals around the field. The flying fortresses look like flying Christmas trees at night for they have red, white, blue, and green lights on their wings and tail assemblies. They roared off into the night in groups of three on a flight that is a thousand miles farther than from Newfoundland to England. Most people don't realize how big the Pacific Ocean is. I can't tell you their destination but it was not any place you would think of. We have sent many planes there already. These fellows were fully armed and loaded and spoiling for a fight. One of them had to return an hour after he took off and we fixed him up. The rest of the flight went on but he didn't get away the second time until 3:00 A.M. A Gen. Martin who commands the Hawaiian Air Force was down a couple weeks ago. He said the Japs did not worry him in the least for the ships flew so high the Japs could not stop them. They could bomb Tokyo into submission with safety for the Japs have no plane that can fly above 20,000 ft. and these will go up to 40. I think the little brown brothers are beginning to see the light for there has been a noticeable about-face the last few days. Poor devils never did have a chance but they played their hand for all it was worth.[16]

As quickly as factories on the mainland churned out the Flying Fortresses and army air force bases churned out pilots, they island-hopped westward to the Philippines for General MacArthur's show of force. Of the 180 B-17s allocated for Hawaiian defense, Admiral Kimmel noted that only 12 remained by December, and only half of those in flying condition. The army deterrent in the Philippines remained the Pacific priority through the fall of 1941, with the en route Wake Island fuel stop an essential component in the strategy. With uncharacteristic alacrity, the navy quickly authorized construction of the main landplane runways that fall. The plans, duplicating those used on Midway, called for three paved runways totaling sixteen thousand feet in length, each five hundred feet wide with asphalt paving of three hundred feet. Midway's large asphalt plant would be dismantled and shipped to Wake as soon as their runways were surfaced, and Midway and Wake would split the "asphalt organization" between the two projects for future road and runway paving work. A $1,472,000 allotment from army funds would pay for runway construction on Wake, as the navy had limited funding to the temporary emergency airstrip. The contractors immediately commenced preparatory work on the permanent runways which would include both diagonal and crosswind (north-south) airstrips. The delayed start meant that heavy equipment would have to be shared between the airfield and the channel project when the contractors finally received the green light to start digging.[17]

THE NEWS: SEPTEMBER–OCTOBER 1941

As summer turned to fall American newspaper headlines focused on the relentless Nazi drive across the Soviet front and, closer to home, massive labor strikes across the nation affecting steel mills and shipyards. A German U-boat attack on the USS *Greer*, an American destroyer, and continued attacks on Atlantic shipping captured the attention of Americans and President Roosevelt denounced the aggression in early September. "It is the Nazi design to abolish the freedom of the seas," the president warned, "and to acquire absolute control and domination of these seas for themselves." Roosevelt ordered armed escorts for Lend-Lease convoys in the Atlantic and authorized them to "shoot Axis raiders" on sight. Many Americans feared that the president was leading the country onto a slippery slope to war. Famed aviator and strident isolationist Charles Lindbergh declared before a crowd of thousands in Des Moines that three groups were pressing the nation to war: "the British, the Jewish, and the Roosevelt administration."

While the national debate raged over war, few gave much thought to its possible emergence in the Pacific. "Japan's air industry is woefully weak and her air force is of low offensive strength," wrote an aeronautics authority in the September issue of *Aviation* magazine, as reported widely in the press. Even in peacetime, the writer asserted, Japanese pilots have the highest accident rate in the world and most of their military aircraft types are "obsolete or obsolescent." He judged Soviet air contingents superior in the Far East and Dutch-British air power greater than that of the Japanese navy in the Pacific. Such pronouncements, political cartoons demeaning the Japanese, and a lack of substantive news from the Far East allowed the public to stay focused on Europe.[18]

Katherine Olson followed the news, her sensors primed for anything that might indicate increased danger for her husband and son as she continued her regular correspondence with both of them. Carefully, she stored their letters from Wake as the weeks and months went by. In her letters to them Katherine expressed her worries, but focused on keeping the family ties stitched tight. Deftly, she used information received from one to fine-tune her responses to the other. Following a suggestion from Harry she prodded Ted to make a decision on what to do with his accumulating wages, and she took her son's advice to drop the vacation argument with Harry. Katherine sent her letters by airmail and boxes by ship's mail, responding promptly to any question asked or request made by them. She asked Ted what his father might like for a birthday gift, bought a seltzer bottle and some cartridges at his suggestion, and sent them for the occasion on September 11. When Katherine and Donna moved back to Pullman, Washington, for the start of the school year, Katherine approached the college to revise Ted's incomplete grades from the previous spring.

By mid-September German armies surrounded Leningrad in the Soviet Union, and Kiev had fallen to the Nazis. In Asia, Japanese forces drove deep into China's Hunan Province where they met fierce resistance. The United States continued to press Japan for cessation of aggression in China and Indochina, and Japan continued to oppose its punishment by trade embargo. Most Americans figured that as long as the diplomats were still talking and U.S. shipyards and factories were churning out ships and planes they had little reason for concern. The pattern of diplomatic parrying between the United States and Japan had kept the lid on the pot for years and Americans remained confident in their military superiority if that lid should happen to slip off the pot.

By the fall of 1941 the effects of the U.S. embargo brought Japan to a critical juncture. Repeatedly that fall Japanese diplomats requested a summit meeting between Prince Fumimaro Konoye, the Japanese prime minister, and President Roosevelt to discuss their unresolved differences, but the business of summit meetings was fraught with diplomatic difficulties. Preconditions, presumptions, and public expectations all figured into a decision to accept a meeting at the highest level where "peace with honor" was the primary objective. On the advice of Secretary of State Hull, on October 2, 1941 President Roosevelt turned down Japan's fourth request for a summit meeting. This had been the last hope of the moderate Konoye government, which by now operated as window dressing for the militarists. Two weeks later Prince Konoye resigned and the hardline war minister, General Hideki Tojo, took over the government. While negotiations continued in Washington, behind the scenes relations between the Japanese and American governments began to unravel with increasing speed.[19]

The resignation of the Konoye cabinet immediately raised the strong possibility of hostilities in the Pacific. Admiral Kimmel received orders to "take due precautions," but to do so quietly, so as to avoid provoking Japan. Kimmel dispatched submarines and patrol planes to Midway and Wake for regular patrols, continued the process of reinforcement of the outlying islands with marines and munitions, and ordered "alert status" on the islands.[20]

OBSTACLES TO PROGRESS

Oblivious to military strategy and diplomatic maneuvers the Wake contractors poured their full efforts into finishing the runways, fire station, squadron storehouse, and dozens of other projects. Plans for the ship channel and submarine base remained on the drawing board. During the last week of September 1941 authorization finally came through for both projects and the contractors began work on the ship channel through Wilkes Island. Three and a half months had passed since the contractors made the first report on modifying the channel and seven weeks had elapsed since the OinC had pressed for completion of the channel by December. Clearly December 1941 was no longer a feasible deadline for completion of the channel, so a new target was set for April 1942, a tight six months from the start of the project. Crews surveyed the location on Wilkes for the 350-foot-wide and 30-foot-deep channel and excavation commenced on September 25 with all available land excavation equipment. The contractors diverted machinery from the landplane runways for continuous work on the channel except when ordered to develop the crosswind runway. The atoll could not be adequately defended until the deep channel was complete. Until then, as Admiral Bloch had graphically noted the previous spring, navy ships outside the protective water of the lagoon would be nothing more than meat for a "submarine picnic."[21]

That same week in late September the navy also issued permission for the contractors to begin ordering materials for the new submarine base facilities. The Wake submarine base fell under the provisions of the First Supplemental National Defense Appropriation Act, 1942, signed on August 25, 1941, but the navy had yet to make a firm decision on its location. War plans experts had recommended construction at Wilkes, separate from the naval air station facilities being built on Peale Island. The contractors accordingly projected a turning basin to adjoin the lagoon side of Wilkes with a bulkhead. A fifteen-foot-deep channel across the lagoon would connect the new ship channel to Peale. Dredged material would provide the foundation for the submarine base at Wilkes. However, the navy now proposed to position the submarine base alongside the naval air station at Peale, which would necessitate major changes in dredging and building components. Under the new plan, the contractors would have to dig the deep turning basin in the lagoon near Peale and dredge a channel twice as deep across the lagoon to connect it with the ship channel. The new plan also required a steel-reinforced tanker pier instead of a bulkhead. Despite the go-ahead to begin ordering materials for the submarine base, the variables and unknowns hindered the ordering process. Whatever the eventual disposition of the submarine base the ship channel would be dug through Wilkes and now, at last, they could pour all available effort to that task.[22]

In addition to channels and base locations, seaplane runways and facilities for navy patrol bombers were key components of the naval air base. Survey crews had been busy for months on barges in the lagoon taking soundings for seaplane runways. Chainman Chet Ratekin wrote to a friend that he had worked eighty-three hours of overtime on preparations for the seaplane ramp, but would have to take the time back off when they were not busy. "I would much rather have taken the time off of the end of my contract or been paid for it, but they say they can't do that," he wrote in October. The surveyors and others in the engineering department often expressed their unhappiness with a system that rewarded common laborers, who could accrue overtime, with a better payday than trained surveyors could hope to make.[23]

With delivery of the precast sections for the seaplane ramp Swede Hokanson's crew began work on installation of the 270-foot ramp on Peale. The project got off to a rough start when the barge carrying the sections was tossed up on the rocks at the mouth of the channel in stormy weather. Another wave promptly pulled the punctured barge back into the water. Swede quickly towed the barge to the dock, and as it began to sink, ordered one crew to unload it on the double, while another crew set to patching the gaping hole. With contents and barge safe Swede resumed ferrying the sections to Peale and then oversaw the installation of the ramp itself. The job required constant improvisation and demonstrated why plans designed for one location were not so easily translated to another. The men drove 60-foot steel pilings deep into the coral, seated the precast ramp sections (the technique that Harry had helped develop at Kaneohe), and then poured concrete in five-inch holes underwater at the lower end of the ramp. Despite many challenges the seaplane ramp was installed in thirty days. The men who worked on or in the water fought what Joe McDonald called the "Chinese rot" from the salt and coral. Every scratch was an open door for infection, and boils and blisters burst from many dark-tanned limbs. Still, the men enjoyed the opportunity to cool off and "swim and work at the same time."[24]

Not long after the seaplane ramp was complete Harry wrote that "a plane hit a coral head and sank out here the other day. We loaded a crane on a barge and picked it up. We will bill Pan Air for this job. Pan Air will bill Consolidated Air Craft. They will bill the British Govt. The British will bill the Dutch Govt who will dip into the lend-lease money to pay it and you will pay your share the next time you drink a scotch. The moral of it all is to drink a lot of scotch and beat Hitler."[25]

Even during the calm between storms during the fall of 1941 the sea could still turn the most routine jobs into life-threatening events. In mid-September Harry described taking a tug out to meet arriving ships. "In our eagerness to get started working them we ventured out to sea a little quicker than we should have. As we passed the channel entrance we met a big sea face to face. It swallowed us. The ship's people were watching us and said we went completely out of sight. I was in the wheel house. The windows were open and the first I knew a wall of water hit me in the face. It washed me backwards and down an open companion way into the engine room. Of course we drove right on through the wave but we were a sorry looking mess. Two of the men on deck were swept the full length of the boat and just managed to catch a cleat at the stern. One of them was hurt. I was bruised up some and as usual managed to lose a good share of the skin from my shins. You may be sure that I have listened to a lot of loose talk about winding up in the basement." Nothing could be taken for granted on Wake Island.[26]

Inside the calmer waters of the lagoon, the dredge *Columbia* had struggled mightily with is task of carving the fifteen-foot-deep channel from the pilot channel entrance across the lagoon to Peale. When it encountered large boulders and masses of limestone-like coral, the dredge's ladder shook so severely that it loosened the boiler tubes, which began to leak in early September. The stress of the newly installed ten-inch cutter shaft and the stronger 500-horsepower engine proved too much for the ladder. The dredge needed a major overhaul, and so it sat in late September, a sorry sight in the lagoon, awaiting a solution while experts studied the problem from afar and the dredge crew festered over lost wages.[27]

The submarine base project remained stalled for weeks. Concerned with stretching its allotments the navy insisted that the Wake contractors use existing plans for most of the sub base projects and that orders for needed building materials be placed as soon as possible due to strains in the mainland markets. Eleven of the twenty-two projects for Wake were to use Midway plans and six others were "to be developed," including piers, quay walls, and berthing facilities, when navy determined the actual location of the submarine base. The contractors repeatedly requested that the decision be finalized in order to coordinate labor and equipment with the air base project. Between September 27 and November 26 the navy allowed the contractors to submit materials purchases for only twelve of the submarine base building projects and over half of those orders were subsequently cancelled, deferred, or modified by the OinC. The Wake Island Submarine Base was going nowhere fast.[28]

Construction of magazines for the storage of ammunition and warheads was also subject to long delays. Drawings and revisions had gone back and forth through the spring of 1941 with no sense of urgency and it was not until June 17 that Captain Bruns finally gave the specific order indicating the actual number, types, and sizes of bunkers to be built. The magazines suddenly took on high priority with the arrival of the marines, but the contractors did not yet have the required materials. Requisition of materials from Alameda was contingent on navy approval of a project, and delays in procurement in the strained mainland markets, compounded by delays in cargo transportation, meant weeks and even months between order and delivery. Lacking reinforcing steel and other key materials, in August the contractors only could build temporary magazines for the marines. The blizzard of project changes and additions in September and October resulted in orders to defer construction of the permanent magazines pending relocation and revised layouts from the navy. By the end of October all materials, except reinforcing steel, were in Honolulu awaiting transshipment to Wake. By the first week of December a few permanent magazines had been completed, a few more were under construction, and the rest still awaited the navy's determination of definite location.[29]

The CPNAB Operating Committee also received long-delayed approval from the OinC on September 24, 1941, for another important project: construction of a four-hundred person bombproof shelter on Wake. More than two months earlier the navy had assured the CPNAB Executive Committee that plans would be released for such shelters on Wake, Midway, and at Kaneohe on Oahu "within a few days." With the approval finally in hand the contractors immediately dispatched orders to Alameda for materials and equipment required to construct the bomb shelter. By early December only a small portion of the materials had arrived in Honolulu. The four-hundred person bombproof shelter on Wake was never even started.[30]

THE BUSINESS SIDE

At the end of August 1941 Morrison-Knudsen and its Six-Companies partners had expended or committed $9.5 million of the originally estimated $10,343,000 on the Wake project, which represented an average of over $1 million a month since the pioneer party had arrived in January. Harry Morrison pointed to the advance planning developed for Wake in the months prior to the departure of the pioneer party as a "substantially contributing factor to the rapid progress" despite the delays in navy plans and delivery of materials that plagued the job. Each change or additional project came wrapped in a tangle of red tape requiring new plans or adaptations, new approvals, and more materials. The problems were multiplied by similar changes on all of the other outlying projects as well as the navy's deployment of defense forces throughout the islands, increased air patrols, and the movement of the army's B-17 bombers westward. Rising demands seriously strained the system, but the contractors continued to make progress on all of their projects. In mid-October Morrison reported to the chairman of the executive committee that revised estimates of total costs, including landplane runways, had more than doubled the cost of the Wake project to $21.5 million. In addition the navy estimated costs of the newly added submarine base program to be just under $5 million, "which amount we are unable to check or re-estimate as we have no layout or detail plans available on which to base an estimate." At approximately $26.5 million, the Wake project amounted to about 12 percent of the total work authorized under contracts NOy-3550 and NOy-4173. Morrison pointed out that M-K's two other CPNAB projects, Midway and Red Hill, showed similar expenditures and project percentages.[31]

By late September George Youmans reported to Harry Morrison that the work on Wake, with the exception of dredging, was "progressing well and in accordance with the schedule, except that crews could be considerably increased, provided materials had arrived by the date requested." The process of stair-stepping materials and men, as Harry Olson had described it earlier, remained problematic. The contractors continued to consider use of non-U.S. citizens, specifically Filipinos, for work on Wake. While Admiral Moreell had authorized hiring local workers for CPNAB projects at Cavite in the Philippines and Guam, he would not commit to hiring Filipinos for Wake. CPNAB accountants meticulously calculated labor wages, staff salaries, general overhead, and camp operation costs on Wake and all of the other outlying island projects, and the CPNAB partners kept close tabs on their accruing shares of the profits.[32]

While few workers were aware that staff members received paid vacations, management considered them well worth the cost for maintaining a stable, reasonably contented supervisory staff. The Wake staff rotated through a vacation schedule that had begun with Harry's trip to Honolulu in July. Pete Russell had voluntarily deferred his vacation to September so that his wife, Eudelle, could join him in Honolulu for their "second honeymoon." Advised that Eudelle had booked passage on a Matson liner sailing September 5 from Los Angeles to Honolulu, Pete requested his three-week vacation to commence on September 13, but the eastbound Clipper was delayed by weather. On September 18, Pete finally boarded the Clipper as Harry, Swede, and two other supervisors gave him a grand, early-morning send-off. Two weeks later Swede also left for his vacation to Honolulu where his wife and daughter joined him. Apartments had been rented for the vacationing families and both men enjoyed prolonged vacations due to bad weather in the Pacific that delayed the Clippers. Meanwhile on Wake, workers pined for home and counted the months and days left on their contracts.[33]

Wake Island, September 26, 1941
Dear Mother and Sis,
I don't remember how long it has been since I wrote to you, but I know that I have been quite neglectful, and I shall try to mend my ways and write a few letters. As you have probably heard, there isn't a great deal to write about here so I will not promise one every Clipper, but I will try to keep you posted as to the life of the Olson family on this Eve-less Eden, as my dear father so aptly puts it.

Day after tomorrow my third month will be completed here. That is a third of my time on the island. If time keeps going as fast as it has up to now, I'm going to be home in no time. I may have to sign a second contract to stay out of the army, but whether or no, I am going to be home sometime during the month of April. I can take a month from the day I land at Frisco and still not lose my bonus. I am hoping and praying that I will not have to sign the second contract, but if I do I guess it will be better than the army.

Well, mother, I am not going to say that I'm homesick, but I do miss you and Donna very much. I miss Dee Dee a lot too. I think she means more to me than I realized before I left. Maybe I'm in love, ma. After listening to all these guys talk around here, I'm beginning to wonder if I know as many of the facts of life as I thought I did. You can imagine how a bunch of construction stiffs talk when they are five or six thousand miles from their women. But after listening to all this talk, I think my love for Dee Dee is still purely platonic. It is quite disgusting to hear some of the things which I have to listen to here. I feel very safe in saying that the Olson family is a long way above these people, and as God is my witness, I'll do all in my power to keep them there.

I guess maybe I got off on a bit of a tangent, but you can't imagine the thoughts which run through my mind as I lie in bed, late at night thinking "what fools we mortals be." I guess I can't condemn a person for his thoughts or for the things he says, but for the life of me, I can't see how a person can be anywhere near happiness and peace when he speaks, thinks and acts like some of these men do. Please forgive me for the rambling, but I got pretty well steamed-up and had to let it go some place. If this doesn't make sense, don't blame me. I know what my thoughts are, but as usual, I don't know a great deal about the art of expounding my views to anyone else.

Well, I guess school is well under way again. I sure miss it. I'd give just about anything I have to be back there this year. I do think that this trip and job has been quite educational to me, but I sure hate to have to lay out of college for another year. If you hear of any way that I can get out of the draft, let me know and I'll get back in time for second semester. I guess that is what one calls wishful thinking, but like I've said before, I can dream, can't I?

I don't get a great deal of time to talk to dad, but we have had a few nice talks anyway. I work most of the time and he works all the time so between us we don't have a great deal of time to visit. Dan is in Honolulu now for a couple of weeks so Dad is the big boss. I have never been able to find out exactly how he feels about this place. I know that he misses home a great deal, but I think he is quite interested in this job. The Clipper came in yesterday with Pomeroy and English, the agents for two of the five companies aboard. I saw dad driving them around in a station wagon showing them the job. Believe me, he looked like a six year old boy showing off his new wagon.

I believe that dad is a great man. He is very well liked by the men on the job. At times he has to be a little tough with some of the men, but he never beats around the bush. He leads straight from the shoulder and tells them just what the score is. I don't believe that there is a man on the job who would not give his right arm to help dad if he needed any help. As a matter of fact, I don't believe this job would go nearly as smooth as it does if it weren't for him.

Well, I guess I'd better get some sleep. We haven't had a day off since labor day, and I can't see the prospects of any in the near future. It looks good on the pay check but it sure gets tiresome.

Love, Ted

Twelve days later, Ted added a postscript to the letter: the weather had kept the Clippers down and no mail had gone out. He thanked Katherine and Donna for the photo album and candy they had sent by ship ("Roger and I finished the candy in nothing flat and it sure tasted good.") and Ted asked his sister for a favor: "Send me all the pictures you can find. Then take a bunch more of all the kids I know or don't know and send them to me. I know there are a lot of beautiful Tri-Delts and Alpha Gam's up there so how about some pictures. Oh, yes, how about a letter once in a while?"

THE MORRISON VISIT

The president of Morrison-Knudsen, Harry Morrison, and his wife, Ann, flew to Honolulu on the Pan American Clipper in early October to visit the CPNAB operating base and to tour the three navy projects under M-K sponsorship: the Red Hill underground fuel storage on Oahu and the Midway and Wake bases. The top-secret Red Hill program had grown dramatically in the past year, and the unprecedented design and scope of the vertical vaults and tunnels tested CPNAB's best engineers and miners. After Morrison toured Red Hill and other projects and his wife enjoyed sightseeing in Honolulu, George Youmans and the Morrisons boarded the westbound Clipper for Midway. Storms in the Pacific had interfered with the Clipper schedule, and the party was fortunate to find a window of good weather for the trip. Naval Air Station Midway had been officially established August 1, 1941, and fifteen hundred contractors remained to finish dredging, runways, and submarine base facilities. Ann Morrison, who often accompanied her husband on his travels to job sites around the world, was especially eager to see her nephew, Owen Daly, the excavation superintendent on Midway, and other "Boise boys" on both Midway and Wake.[34]

The Clipper carrying the Morrisons and George Youmans arrived on Wake—by now shades were drawn on all Clipper landings and take-offs for security reasons—on October 14 after an overnight stop on Midway. The three settled into the guest lodge, a cozy four-bedroom, three-bath house furnished with wicker furniture and grass rugs that reflected Florence Teters's decorating tastes. The guest house stood between two other east-facing cottages on Heel Point, a comfortable distance from the bustling Camp 2. On one side perched the Teters's own well-appointed cottage, "arranged with comfortable rattan furniture and decorated with mats and hangings from the Philippines . . . a miracle of civilization on the island," and fitted with an "elaborate radio aerial so they could enjoy something more than the Japanese broadcasts." The third bungalow on Heel Point was occupied by Lieutenant Butzine who was just then preparing to vacate his post. Lieutenant Commander Elmer B. Greey arrived October 10 to relieve Butzine as RoinC and Major James P. S. Devereux arrived on the same ship to relieve Major Hohn as the ranking officer on Wake. There were, however, no bungalows, well-appointed or otherwise, for the Marine Corps officers.[35]

Over two hundred men had been hired for the Wake job from in and around Boise, Idaho, and the Morrisons had personal connections with many of their families and friends from whom they brought messages. Joe McDonald of Reno had noted in mid-July that Morrison-Knudsen had surely "taken care of the Idaho natives—they even have signs 'Boise City Limits' posted around the island." While it seemed to some on the island that Wake was overrun with men from Idaho, in fact about 20 percent of the workers hailed from the Boise area; the rest had come from the West Coast and scattered states to the east. But when the big boss came to town, the Boise boys took front stage.[36]

The Morrisons, who had planned a week-long stay on Wake, dined in the mess hall where they were treated to a "more or less impromptu 'Idaho Night'" featuring songs by the Wake Island Glee Club in their "first public appearance." Masters of Ceremony Dar Dodds and Lloyd Lendewig interviewed Mrs. Morrison as well as two Idaho workers Pete Ingham and Bly Wilcox. Harry Morrison concluded the program with a short address praising the Wake Island men who were "out here doing their bit for Defense."

Of all of M-K's jobs, Morrison avowed that he knew of no place "where we have such a fine group of men or signs of accomplishment having been made as we find here on Wake Island. . . . We want to make your stay here as pleasant and profitable as we possibly know how, and we want each and every one of you to know that the latchstring is out and the door is open when you get back to the States if we can be of any help to you." Peter Hansen, counting sixty-nine days left on his contract, was thrilled to hear Morrison's assurance that any man who fulfilled his contract on Wake would be given "great preference" and M-K would place him in "desirable places with desirable jobs" as long as Morrison had work to do. After resounding applause, the entire company of eleven hundred men and Mrs. Morrison moved outdoors for the evening movie: *New Moon* starring Jeanette MacDonald and Nelson Eddy. "A beautiful setting: the heavens dotted with twinkling stars for a roof, a gorgeous moon, with a few scattered clouds," Ann Morrison wrote in her diary that night, also noting that the "oh's and ah's and comments of the various boys amused me greatly" during the show. Over the course of their visit many of the Boise boys took her up on her invitation to come visit them at the "Lodge," where she shared news from home and they shared their plans and dreams for the future.[37]

One Morrison family friend was Wake's postmaster, Frank Crowe, nephew of the renowned Boulder Dam builder of the same name, who told the Morrisons of his uncle's futile attempts to persuade him not to come to Wake: "You damn fool, the Japs will get you if you go over there." But young Frank and Mrs. Morrison agreed that they were "more worried about typhoons than we are about the Japs," echoing the prevailing attitude on Wake in late October 1941. Ann Morrison whiled away stormy afternoons in the cottage with her needlepoint, trying to pick up Japanese broadcasts from the Marshall Islands, just a few hundred miles south. She noted in her travel diary that "Tommy, the Chinese houseboy," turned the radio off every time her back was turned, telling her that the Japanese were poor fighters. He insisted that "he, with the aid of Henry, the laundryman, and the Chinese helpers at the mess could keep the Japs off the island if provided with guns and plenty of ammunition."[38]

Harry Morrison and George Youmans visited the job sites daily with Dan Teters and Harry Olson with little regard to the weather. They observed with special interest the action on Wilkes, where draglines and scrapers chewed away at the new ship channel, and the non-action in the lagoon where the ill-fated dredge languished. The *Columbia* broke down twice more during October, working a total of twenty-three days during the month as it sucked up material behind a drill barge that blasted coral ledges with dynamite. Crew problems compounded the *Columbia's* mechanical problems: dredge superintendent W. A. Hanscom, suffered a heart attack and had to return to the mainland and the dredge crew demanded promised bonuses and overtime. A new dredge captain, Roland A. Andre of Pendleton, Oregon, arrived to replace Hanscom.[39]

The October storms raged as the days went by, with towering waves, deluges of rain, and high winds, interspersed with occasional periods of sticky, beastly hot, calm weather. Ships piled up in the heaving waters surrounding Wake, waiting for opportunity to unload, and great excitement attended the successful landings of army bombers. Eastbound Clippers remained grounded far to the west and the westbound Clipper was not able to return to Wake until October 23, this one bearing thirty-one passengers, including Pete Russell, returning from his extended vacation, and a load of eagerly-anticipated sacks of airmail. "What an empty feeling!" Pete later wrote of his return to Wake. Harry and John Polak, as well as the Morrisons and George Youmans met the *California Clipper* upon its arrival, and Pete wrote that he was "glad to see the boys but would just as soon they had been on the mainland." Pete desperately missed Eudelle, who decided to remain in Honolulu in the little apartment on Uluniu St. Just across the street, the Hokansons had taken an apartment, and Swede was winding up his own vacation with Mae and their daughter June, who would also stay on in Honolulu to await his return.[40]

Wake Island, October 21, 1941
Dear Katherine:
This won't leave for 3 or 4 days as the Clipper is hung up at Manila. We are typhooning again. This is the fifth straight day of it and I am getting a trifle weary of it all. The wind just howls and howls and it rains in sheets and the waves breaking over the reef are higher than the island. I heard over the radio that they were having some high tides and waves along the Oregon coast and I don't doubt it from the size of some I have seen going by here. I had some fun trying to set a bomber in the water yesterday [after repairs]. When I lifted it, it started sailing like a kite and I thot for a while it was going to pull the crane in the

water. But my usual luck held and everything came out O.K. It's rain-
ing so hard right now that I can't see 200 feet.

I suppose you are wondering how all this war business seems out
here. We are not worrying much. We are fairly well prepared to defend
ourselves from any sort of an assault and the U.S. is not ready to relin-
quish this part of the Pacific as yet to any foreign power. The Navy has
ordered the women evacuated from Wake and Guam. We had 3. Two
Pan Air and one Contractors. All three are glad of the excuse to get
away and intend to make a little hay in Honolulu while their men
can't do anything about it. At least that's what they told me. I can't say
that I blame them much for it is very monotonous down here. There
are so many men that the women don't dare circulate around without
someone with them and of course there is no place to go. Mr. and Mrs.
Morrison are here on a visit. They are both very democratic and remind
me of mother and dad. Just common western folks. He told Ted he had
long been an admirer of mine and told me that he had heard a lot
about me from the time Bonneville was started and what had surprised
him was that all the reports were good. This surprised me for I knew
some of them should have been "not so good." He professed himself as
pleased with what had been done down here.

It's evening now and I have just returned from the Marine camp
where we were signaling to a Navy tug that just showed up with two
barges. It's too rough for us to go out tonight so I made a radio schedule
with him for 7:00 A.M. tomorrow. The wind seems to be moderating
some tonight and I hope we can get the barges in for we need the mate-
rials and the work. We have more men than we can use. . . .

Ted seems to be doing O.K. I doubt if he will stay past his nine
months tho. It's a shame for him to go in then, for if he would stay 20
or 24 months he would have enough to finish school with some left
over. He makes better than 300.00 per month and it's just too much.
Some of his friends are staying past their contract in order to get enough
to finish their schooling and I hope he will profit by their example. A
little emphasis on the enjoyment of school life in the letters you and
Donna write to him might help a little. Of course he can come in for
a month and then return but he would lose his month's salary plus
$60.00 per month bonus for 3 months and add what he would spend
and you have from 750.00 to 1000.00 his vacation would cost him.

As young as he is, the vacation isn't worth that much to him but he has no sense of value especially since he makes so much so easily. I will try my best to talk him into staying and I am really going to bear down on him to execute a transfer of funds to you so that he won't have so much money when he gets to town. He is . . . wild to spend some of that money. Ted is a good boy and just needs to find himself. . . . Another squall is blowing up and you should hear the wind howl.

Oct. 25: Since then have had a long talk with Ted which I think did some good.

We haven't got those barges in yet. We have 3 ships outside now and I doubt if we can get them in for a few days. The aftermath of all that wind was some tremendous seas that washed over the other end of the island and filled up the channel. I worked most of the nite last nite but the sea is moderating some now so I am going to sleep tonite. It is ten o'clock and nine Army bombers just roared away into the night, one for Honolulu and eight for Australia. Hope they make it. The last group have 3000 miles to fly. It's 2500 to Honolulu . . .

Harry

A week into the Morrisons' visit, Admiral Bloch ordered all American civilian women and children to evacuate from the outlying islands on the first available Clipper to Honolulu. Major Devereux conveyed the order on Wake reporting that the decision was based on the potential dangers associated with "increasing international tensions." Two of the resident women on Wake, wives of the station manager and steward of Pan Air, and Ann Morrison made preparations to leave immediately, but Dan Teters requested a special exception to allow Florence to remain on Wake. Harry Morrison appealed to Admiral Bloch on behalf of Teters, but Bloch "refused to bend." Meanwhile, stormy weather continued to hold up the eastbound Clippers and no one, regardless of gender, would be leaving soon.[41]

STICKING IT OUT

The stormy weather on Wake did not dampen enthusiasm for recreational pursuits among the workers. In addition to movies, sports, and other after-work activities, many of the men found ways to make a little more dough on the side. While some took up cottage industries, such as jewelry-making with wire and clasps sent from home—$15.00 for a lovely shell necklace for the lady back home—others were drawn into gambling. Some, like Joe McDonald, did both. While many of the men shied away from anything that might threaten their growing nest eggs, with every dollar made going to pay off the family's crippling Depression debt, as was the case for Peter Hansen, others were eager to risk their money in games of chance.

On Wake a man could bet on just about anything. There were the nightly poker and dice games and it was common to bet on favorite sports teams, with winning teams announced over the evening radio news broadcasts or in the next day's *Wig Wag*. Serious, and lucky, gamblers could make more on the games than their wages. McDonald endeavored to get an edge on the sports bets by having his parents send the football pool information and game schedules from the local Reno paper: his father was the editor. If the Clippers were running on schedule and they sent the "dope" airmail by Monday, he would have it in time to make his picks and a bundle to boot: "fifty seeds" here, "twelve and a half fish" there. The Wake men bet on the weather, on arrivals and departures, on food, on . . . Winners might spend their take on a sharkskin purse or Philippine hat from the store to send home as a gift or, more likely, place another bet. However, wages were protected by the system that sent them straight to the mainland, and winners and losers alike still ate well and kept their jobs. The workers never saw their checks and most did not even know who made them out or how the money arrived at home.[42]

Through the fall of 1941 many workers quit their jobs on Wake long before their contracts were up, but management applied increasing pressure with both carrot and stick to induce them to stay. On the mainland returning workers reported that it was impossible to get another defense job if a man broke his contract and the worker was required to show his clearance from his last job. During Morrison's extended stay on Wake he repeated his promise that a man who completed his contract would be assured a good job from M-K. Morrison made it known that he had instructed Dan Teters to make a list of all the men who finished their contracts and note their home addresses and information. "He said they never need worry about a job again," wrote Pete Hansen.[43]

Still, fired and disgruntled workers and war-worriers often opted to leave Wake on the next available eastbound ship and some even ponied up the $400 fare to Honolulu via the Pan American Clipper. Others, however, departed under different circumstances. One worker by the name of Thomas

P. Hamill, a veteran of the Great War, suffered a mental breakdown on Wake, convinced that the uniformed marines were there to shoot him. When the *Regulus* pulled away from Wake on October 1 it carried forty-three contract employees, including Hamill, who was put in sickbay under guard. Not an hour underway, Hamill managed to elude his guard and leaped overboard. Despite valiant efforts by the ship's crew to save him, the unfortunate man swam away and soon sank below the surface. Divers were unable to locate the body. The story circulated quickly through the civilian camp, providing "a bit of rather tragic excitement."[44]

October 9 marked the completion of the first nine-month contracts on Wake for those nonsupervisory contractors who remained from the January 9 arrival, the "real Pioneers." Coincidentally the pioneer party's ship, the *William Ward Burrows,* arrived at Wake October 9 with a load of supplies and men and the captain joined the celebration on shore. Dan Teters distributed commemorative pins bearing a raised outline of the Wake atoll flanked by the words "Pioneer Club, Wake Island," and a tiny chain connecting to a secondary tack "41," to each of the remaining pioneers, including an honorary pin for Captain Dierdorff. Most of the pioneers with completed contracts departed Wake on the *Burrows* on October 14. On Wake the workers anticipated the next group to reach the nine-month mark, each in turn taking over the title of "real Pioneer" or "short-timer." In the waning days of their contracts workers found themselves treated better, with good work assignments and little pressure. "The bosses are very good to the old timers," wrote Pete Hansen. "They really do not expect us to put out the work like you ordinarily would. I do just as I please about all the time anyway."[45]

On Wake the civilian workers stayed busy and suppressed thoughts of war as best they could. For some it was easy. "It's funny how little time does mean out here except in terms of how much of the contract is finished. No one ever seems to hurry or worry about anything. They've all got the attitude of there is always tomorrow," Joe McDonald wrote to his parents. For others, keeping thoughts of war at bay remained a daily challenge. "Looks like we're getting closer to war every day," Pete Hansen wrote to his wife. "I'm not afraid as long as the Japs remain quiet, but when they get tough I don't feel so comfortable here. We have a lot of guns here now & of course we have the feeling we could put up a fight so we don't worry."[46]

CHAPTER **8**

RUSH HOUR

─────────────────────────

TRAFFIC JAM

Ships, cargo barges, and the stream of Philippine-bound B-17s all ran into stormy weather at Wake during the last two weeks of October 1941. At the height of the traffic jam, there were ten ships and six barges maneuvering offshore, as well as twenty planes landing, fueling, and taking off. The navy tug *Seminole* with 22 civilian employees aboard and two cargo barges in tow was the first to arrive on October 21 followed by the seaplane tender *Curtiss* carrying 160 civilians, several dozen servicemen, and a load of fuel and ammunition. Major Devereux and Lieutenant Commander Greey, the new military officers on Wake, managed to reach the *Curtiss* by tug, but remained marooned there for several days. Advised that the channel was too rough for unloading the ships rode offshore in heavy swells and rain-squalls waiting for opportunity to disembark passengers, cargo, and fuel. High winds and waves continued to batter the atoll day after day.[1]

On October 24, when a Pan American radio operator reported another typhoon heading towards Wake, drivers again parked trucks and station wagons near the barracks and the guest cottage to carry the civilians to a designated shelter. The large, unfinished reinforced concrete structure had a floor and walls, but no roof. "If the water overflowed the island, that building would be a death trap," the visiting Ann Morrison wrote in her diary that night as the wind shook the guest cottage. "We even laid off work for two days because the weather was so bad," wrote Joe McDonald, "and if we lay off the weather has to be super bad." The typhoon eventually skirted Wake,

161

but high waves and winds continued for several more days. Two bright yellow Wooldridge scrapers bobbed in and out of sight on a barge offshore.[2]

The troubled waters around Wake were soon so full of ships that were unable to unload that "the place looked like Pearl Harbor," McDonald wrote. "It really looked odd to see so many boats as usually we only see about one every three weeks." The tug *Storm King* arrived with two barges in tow; the *Castor*, a stores issue ship that had convoyed with two destroyers, carried over two hundred more marines for Wake. Two submarines, the *Narwhal* and *Dolphin*, arrived to initiate the patrol of Wake's waters in accordance with Admiral Kimmel's heightened alert in response to the abrupt changes in the Japanese government in mid-October. Briefed by Devereux on the alert, Dan Teters discussed general procedures with him in case of an attack, the first such realistic discussions up to that time.[3]

On the *Curtiss* Comdr. S. P. Ginder established that he was the senior officer afloat, issued orders to the subordinate ships and vessels in the vicinity, and was "in constant communication with the shore and directed the methods to be followed." Harry Olson and Swede Hokanson had their hands full with the roiling seas, the haughty Commander Ginder, a cluster of ships with multiple needs, hundreds of by-now disgruntled or seasick (or both) passengers to unload, and a storm-wrecked channel to clear before anyone or anything from any ship or barge could make landfall.[4]

In spite of the daunting weather an unusual number of airplanes landed at Wake to refuel that week. The place was getting "as infested with airplanes as the Oakland airport," wrote Joe McDonald: Flying Fortresses bound for the Philippines, patrol bombers for the Dutch East Indies, and, of course, the Clippers. At one point, both eastbound and westbound Clippers shared Wake's lagoon. On October 24 several navy planes arrived on a routine mission, one carrying Lt. Comdr. W. L. Richards, who in 1936 had conducted the solo survey of Wake for the navy and now oversaw the outlying island operations from Pearl Harbor. Richards expressed his admiration for the rate of progress made by the contractors since his last visit in May, praised the "trim appearance" of their camp and facilities, and commended the contractors for their high morale, "astounded," as the *Wig Wag* editor put it, "at the very slight inroad the 'Languor of the Tropics' has made in our ranks." Richards later noted with some amusement that Commander Greey, the new RoinC who was stuck on the *Curtiss* in the stormy sea, was getting "some initiation" to Wake.[5]

October 24 also brought seven B-17s and one important B-24 to Wake. The large, eastbound Consolidated bomber carried diplomats on a globe-circling trip back to Washington D.C. from a goodwill conference in Moscow. The camp buzzed over the presence of the dignitaries, and the *Wake Wig Wag* editor wrote that the historic flight would cause "Jules Verne to turn over in his grave." The important mission injected a new note of optimism into the global struggle, and the close brush with history invigorated the men on Wake. The October 26 *Wig Wag* noted diplomatic reports of renewed Russian strength in the war against the Nazis. "Listening to them one could not help but feel that Uncle Sam and his many nephews and nieces and their many cousins in other lands are firmly resolved to see that Democratic ideals and principles shall not perish!"[6]

On the night of October 25 the B-24 departed to the east and the B-17s took off toward the west. As they had since the first Flying Fortresses passed through in early September the contractors lit the runway with oil barrels spaced five feet apart with ropes for wicks. On the *Curtiss* radar operators followed the aircraft departures. Mrs. Morrison watched the Flying Fortresses roar off into the night with a "tear in my eye and an ache in my heart for those young men flying into the unknown." One pilot lost his way and was contacted by Pan American's radio and urged to return. The following day ten more bombers arrived from Honolulu and two navy PBYs landed in the lagoon.[7]

Plane crews crowded the dorms and mess halls as the rough seas continued to hold ship passengers offshore. Pete Russell ordered his carpenters to work two ten-hour shifts a day on the navy barracks. At the storm-damaged channel three shifts worked around the clock with all available equipment to open it up and concrete crews poured blocks to use as riprap for a breakwater before the next predicted typhoon was expected to hit. Bucking high seas and raging winds Harry managed to get a harbor tug out to the *Seminole* on October 28 and brought the passengers back: a "motley-looking bunch— all happy to get to shore," according to Mrs. Morrison. Soon, Devereux and Greey were able to return to shore, and thirty-three men from the *Curtiss* rode a launch in through the channel. The new arrivals swore that they never wanted to see a ship again. The launch pilot refused to go back for more passengers until the seas calmed.[8]

On October 30 Harry brought the first of the barges in with one tug towing, another tug pushing, and two caterpillar tractors on either side of the channel pulling, along with a great deal of shouted advice from on-shore "experts." Pete Russell noted that Harry was "having a hell of a time trying to carry out a lot of fool orders from a bunch of nit-wits who never saw the channel before. They sure got things in a fine mess." A towline snapped on the second barge just as it was entering the channel, and a crewmember stripped, dove off the barge, swam through the churning waters to shore, grabbed another line, and swam back to the barge with it. Throughout the day, batches of seasick passengers staggered ashore. Harry brought the rest of the barges in the following day and the *Curtiss* discharged its aviation fuel into shore tanks. When the *Curtiss* departed on November 1, so did a vital piece of technology: radar that could detect planes at a distance. Despite Admiral Kimmel's recommendations for five radar units on the strategic atoll, Wake still had none.[9]

LEAVING WAKE

As the new batch of workers arrived to begin their nine-month contracts another group celebrated the completion of their contracts on November 1, nine months to the day from their arrival on February 1. Of the original group of thirty-nine, fifteen had remained through their contracts and again the *Wake Wig Wag* bestowed high praise: "Many of us fall by the wayside for various reasons and leave—some to return to more prosaic duties we had hoped to escape from for a while; others to continue that endless trek in search of Elysian Fields; and many in answer to the Call of Country. A goodly percentage of those completing the contract period remain, and some, with an undefinable feeling later to be classified as nostalgia for our Island, board ships for the return to the Mainland." The *Wig Wag* spoke for all when it congratulated those men who had "attained that sublime state of having completed our contract period—with a touch of envy in our voices," wrote the editor. Of the fifteen men listed for that accomplishment on November 1, 1941, six renewed their contracts and remained on Wake.[10]

"Also having 'completed their contracts,'" the *Wig Wag* reported, were Harry and Ann Morrison and George Youmans, now finally able to depart Wake by the long-delayed eastbound Clipper. Morrison professed that he was "extremely well pleased and more than satisfied with the progress made." He expressed his thanks to all for making possible an "extremely favorable report" to the CPNAB operating base, and assured some of the young work-ers, including Lloyd Nelson of Oregon, that if the U.S. and Japan went to war, "the Navy would be out to take us off the island." Morrison's parting words to the Wake superintendents were to build as quickly and with as few changes as was commensurate with a decent job. "The thing now is to get out of here as quickly as possible."[11]

Although the navy had ordered evacuation of all civilian women from the outlying islands the Clipper left Wake without the resident females. Major Devereux insisted that they leave the island on the next plane in accordance with the navy's orders. On Midway, where a fair number of families lived, the naval commander ordered the immediate evacuation of women and children, despite protests that the evacuation was an unnecessary precaution. The eastbound Clipper took them all aboard for the trip to Honolulu. Florence Teters departed Wake on the November 18 Clipper and took up residence at the Halekulani Hotel in Honolulu to await her husband; the last woman, the Pan American station manager's wife, Peggy Frei, left Wake the following week.[12]

Upon the Morrisons' return to the mainland the Boise newspaper carried a report of their long trip and their experiences on Wake. "Work is progressing rapidly," Morrison said, although he noted that there was "no prospect of completing the job before the end of 1942." The Idaho boys formed the "nucleus of activity for all 1200 men on the island," the paper claimed, and had erected a stone in the natural shape of Idaho on the main road. Signs at a busy intersection in camp noted the distance to Honolulu, Manila, New York City . . . and Boise. A sign over the main office building read, "Morrison-Knudsen Co., Inc., Farthest East Office." Despite "many delays in transporting men and materials under emergency conditions," work was proceeding according to schedule on Wake, where camp facilities were "splendid" and health of the boys "excellent."[13]

In late October, the navy ordered all employees to complete detailed "Personal History Declaration" forms regarding themselves and their extended families. Only a handful filled the forms out correctly the first time; the other 95 percent received the forms back for completion. The November 1 *Wake Wig Wag* announced: "IF YOU INTEND TO CONTINUE WORKING ON WAKE ISLAND, YOU MUST COMPLY WITH THIS REQUEST AT ONCE." These orders might have suggested that the navy anticipated action soon in the Pacific, but the bulk of *Wig Wag* news and scuttlebutt continued to focus on the European war with only sparse and vague pronouncements about Japan.[14]

THE NEWS: NOVEMBER 1941

As U.S.-Japanese diplomatic relations simmered behind the scenes and the American public was lulled into a no-news-is-good-news complacency about the Pacific, events of war on the other side of the planet escalated dramatically. In late October Soviet troops and the Russian rain and mud stalled the Axis advance on Moscow but soon the Germans were within fifty miles of the capital. Each month thousands of Soviet citizens were dying of starvation in besieged Leningrad. On October 30 President Roosevelt offered the Soviet Union $1 billion in Lend-Lease funds with generous terms. That day German submarines torpedoed an American oiler in the Atlantic and the next day sank the destroyer USS *Reuben James* off Iceland, killing 115 Americans. The escalating emergency prompted the U.S. Congress to vote on November 5 to stay in session indefinitely.

While events in East Asia rarely commanded bold headlines in the fall of 1941, newspapers continued to follow developments. In Japan, General Hideki Tojo's cabinet reflected a "strong military flavor" and gave no indication of abandoning Japan's expansionist policies. Newspapers carried photographs of the new leaders under the banner "Japan's Firebrands: Watch Them as Far East Crisis Grows." Several weeks after Tojo assumed power Secretary Knox declared that Japan's continued policy of expansion put that nation on a collision course with the United States. At the same time navy press releases that fall praised the CPNAB program as contributing to the U.S. Navy expansion program to build up the American two-ocean navy into the "greatest array of sea power the world has ever seen." The collision course was a two-way street. However, Japanese diplomat Saburo Kurusu traveled to Washington, D.C., in early November—his transpacific Clipper flight stopped at Wake—and joined Ambassador Kichisaburo Nomura to present Japan's proposals for compromises on the trade embargo, China, and expansion. Many Americans reasoned that as long as the diplomats were still talking war in the Pacific remained remote.[15]

Wake Island, November 8, 1941
Dear Mother,
By the time you receive this letter I will be over the hump and on the down hill grade. Five more days and I will pass the half-way mark on my contract. At times it seems like a very long time. At others it doesn't seem so long. At any rate, I only have four and a half months to go.

Dad and I finally got together a couple weeks ago. We had a very long talk about life and all its various by-ways. I think it was about the most interesting and constructive evening I've spent in years.

At the present time, I'm not positive of coming home when my contract is up. Of course it depends a great deal on world conditions. If I plan to sign another contract, I will come home first. If things look fair, I might stay over for a while. By staying over I will get a $90 bonus every month. That is quite a bit of money when you think about it. Dad and I both feel that I would be foolish to leave for good without $5,000. Do you realize what that amount of money could mean to me? I am very anxious to come home for a while. That is probably what I will do, but I can't tell for sure as yet. From next month on I'll be making a little better than $400 per month. That is a lot of money and a chance which probably will not present itself again for some time to come. I've got myself about half stupefied trying to figure out what to do. Maybe I'll be a little more definite in about 4 months.

I got your letter today. It was the first in three weeks because of no Clippers. My letter to you must have sounded a little different than I meant it to. I speak of the part about Dee Dee and I. Dee Dee is a very nice girl and a very good friend. My reference to "love" was merely in the line of conversation. Anyway Mother, don't worry your pretty head about your youngest son taking a jump that might not prove the wisest. You see, Deed and I had an understanding before I left that we were very good friends and would remain so for some time to come. There is to be nothing serious until such time as a few minor incidents have taken place. Said incidents being my travels around the globe and a couple of much-needed college educations. At such time as these minor incidents are finished, and if at such time we feel that there is any stronger feeling between us than just friendship, we will proceed to develop that friendship in the usual manner. . . .

Here is something I want you to do without fail. Take however much of my money is necessary and buy Donna a new formal as an initiation present from me. Have her write and tell me what it is like. If I don't get a letter to that effect inside of one month, I shall draw some money from Honolulu and take care of this matter through an agent of mine on the campus. I want this to be something exactly like she wants. Hang the expense. She only gets initiated to Tri Delta once,

and it's very seldom that I get to buy her anything. One more thing. Take a picture of her in the dress and send it to me right away. I guess this is about enough chatter for this week. Aloha No Ka Oi (far away).
All my love to you both, Ted

In the Hillside Apartments near the Washington State College campus, Katherine fretted over the sporadic letters from Wake. She worried constantly, unsure if it was weather, war, or waning affections that kept them from writing. Harry had been gone from home a full year now. She wrote to her son and her husband faithfully every Friday evening sharing Donna's activities and the general gossip as well as her concerns for their safety. An article by Clare Boothe in the November issue of *Life* magazine gave Katherine a glimpse of her husband's world when the famous writer related her recent adventure by Clipper across the Pacific. Photographs featured Boothe, slim and smart, in exotic locations including Wake. Harry might have even seen her take a dip in the "mermaids' lagoon" on Wake or play bridge in her bathing suit in the hotel lobby where he often went for drinks. Katherine sent her husband a lovely card for their twenty-seventh anniversary, but he made no mention of it or the occasion. It could have been the weather, the war, or waning affections: Katherine feared the last the most.[16]

Wake Island, Nov. 9, 1941
Dear Katherine:
I missed getting a letter off on the last Clipper and I suppose you are thinking we are all killed off as Ted said he missed it also. I was just too busy to write. We had 7 ships, 4 barges, 26 planes and a typhoon all at once and it was hell around here for about 10 days. It has all calmed down now tho and we have returned somewhat to normal.
The job is right at its peak now. We have 1200 men and are engaged in every phase of the construction at once. We are really spread out too thin and we would be better off to concentrate a little more and finish some of it before starting more. The people at headquarters have different views however and they want it all right now. This tiny island may prove to be one of the most strategic spots in the world. I am not at liberty to tell you much about it but if we can function successfully for the next two months the U. S. A. will not need to worry much about aggression from out this direction. So that's why I am busy

and for the first time in my life can say that I am of some importance. Please do not let any of all this out and someday I will explain further. In the meantime you may rest assured that we are well guarded and have no fears along that line. By the way, the special Japanese envoy to the U.S. will be on the plane that carries this letter. It is due here in a few minutes. . . .

The sun is setting as I write this and the western sky is a blaze of glory. For some reason it troubles me to think how many countless times this has happened with no one to see it out here. Or if some one was shipwrecked here and lived despairingly for years, what must his thoughts have been as he viewed this gorgeous display. It is such a tiny place and is so far from any other land. . . . As usual I have written a lot about nothing so will close. We have no twilight and it's pitch dark now. Our time does not square with solar time as it is six and shouldn't be dark so early. It's daylight at 5:30 in the morning. The dinner gong is ringing but it don't hold much promise on Sunday nite. I usually go over to Pan Air and eat dinner with Peggy and Godfrey Free on Sunday night but it's too late now.

Harry

PRESSURES AND PROBLEMS

By early November the Wake contractors were again working at full speed. Under increasing pressure to complete the base in the shortest possible time the contractors worked on the Wilkes ship channel and other key jobs around the clock. However, the Wake project demonstrated how the navy's internal decision-making hampered the very progress it was so eager to attain in preparation for war in the Pacific. Just as their indecision had delayed excavation of the ship channel for months, other vital components of the program crowded the navy's back burners. Revised estimates had more than doubled the original contract amount, but did not even include the proposed submarine base, the plans for which were still being debated. By the end of November, the navy had modified the plans for all ammunition and ordnance magazines and approved only four of the eleven buildings for the submarine facilities. Despite repeated requests from the contractors the navy could not produce a decision on location and design of the quay wall and submarine piers. With authorization the contractors could have started work immediately on a number of these projects. "I just can't imagine what the

Admiral can be thinking about, to allow this progress to lag the way it does," George Youmans wrote to Harry Morrison on November 20. In the end, orders for the layout of the Wake submarine base never arrived.[17]

In addition to delays in authorization, transportation problems continued to plague the projects in the late fall of 1941. Shipments of glass and reinforcing and structural steel were badly behind, holding up several projects. On November 20 two loaded, thousand-ton barges stood at Pier 31-A in Honolulu ready for the tow to Wake, but the navy could not spare a ship. The *Sirius* was out for overhaul leaving only the *Burrows* and *Regulus* and the contracted civilian tug *Arthur Foss* for transport to Midway and Wake. Surveying the situation from Honolulu, George Youmans noted that navy tugs were "conspicuous by their absence."[18]

The increased airfield traffic in late October had brought the issue of Wake's runway lighting system to the forefront, and the usual barrage of plans, estimates, and revisions attended the process. B-17s continued to refuel at Wake en route to the Philippines as the days of November turned into weeks, and Captain Bruns mulled over ways to reduce the cost of the light control plans or charge the costs off to the army. By early December, no work had begun on the runway lighting system, and the westbound B-17s still took off into the night sky by the light of rope wicks burning in the old oil barrels lining Wake's one completed runway.[19]

Another obstacle arose over the matter of housing and the plans for marine barracks camp facilities. Major Harry Pickett, the district marine officer at Pearl Harbor, insisted that satellite camps be located near the big gun emplacements on the three points of the atoll, but balked at orders for the "cheapest kind of construction" to stay within budget. Pickett, who had conducted the 1939 survey of Wake to determine optimal defense installations, argued that it would be "destructive to morale" if the smaller outposts were inferior to the main station projected for Peale. Each must have equal-quality barracks, officer quarters, and mess, storage, and recreation facilities, Pickett insisted. Such interdepartmental disagreements and time-consuming arguments lay behind many of the navy's delays and deferrals that frustrated the contractors.[20]

Despite the millions of dollars, months of work, and thousands of tons of supplies, defending Wake might very well boil down to one basic requirement: drinking water. Every survey of Wake had raised the fresh water issue. In his "Study on Defenses," Admiral Kimmel estimated that the projected naval air station distilling capacity of twenty thousand gallons per day and a like amount from proposed submarine base facilities should be sufficient to sustain military and civilian numbers anticipated for Wake, a total of 2,611 military personnel and an estimated 1,252 civilians until construction was completed. However, the existing saltwater distilling facilities in November 1941 restricted Wake to a maximum of three hundred additional men. Camp 1 had a stilling production capacity of four thousand gallons and Camp 2, eight thousand gallons per day, with storage facilities for more, but current stores already required careful rationing in the civilian camp. Recent storms had filled the contractor's rainwater catchment tanks, but the United States Navy could not depend on the whims of Mother Nature.[21]

Wake Island, Nov. 15, 1941
Dear Katherine:
Here I am faced by the same quandary: the necessity of writing a letter and not one thing to say. Nothing has or ever happens. Even our typhoon apparently has ceased. The weather is back to normal. I tried to rent a swell typhoon from Pan Air for a couple hours until I could catch a little rainwater but the man said he was fresh out. We are using about 30,000 gallons per day and only produce about 8000 so we are losing ground. We have a million gallons in storage and just completed the tanks that will hold that much more so I could use a little rain. If we don't catch some soon we will have to start hauling from town.

Our forces continue to grow. We have 1200 men now and another hundred waiting in Honolulu. The men are staying much better than they did earlier. Our turnover is only half what it is at Midway. Living conditions and work conditions are much better here. Our payroll was $280,000.00 last month. To be honest I don't think over $180,000.00 was really earned. Men can't work down here like they can in a cooler climate. It's still above eighty night and day. I am so acclimated I do not notice the heat at all. What I do notice is that it's impossible to go a day without bathing. One gets so sticky he cannot stand it.

All the women are gone from the island except one and she is employed at Pan Air. This was by Navy orders. The same is true at Midway. Personally I can't see any reason for it, for if Japan is able to attack us successfully we are woefully weak and should not let this question come to war. And I fail to see where Florence is any more valuable than

Dan. She certainly is not any help to him at Honolulu and someone has to stay out here and do this job . . .

Ted made 360.00 clear last month. That's a joke. These boys are going to be ruined unless they can be persuaded to put this money by for an education. Despite his assertions to the contrary, I think Ted is getting restless and I'm willing to bet he would quit if it were not for the draft. If he don't make a transfer of funds pretty soon, I'm going to get real rugged with him. It's so silly to pay him all that money and as far as I am concerned if he proposes to blow it on a good time I would just as soon he would be in the army.

This is all I can find to say of any interest so I'll stop. Personally I don't think it's thirty-five cents worth. I've written more letters since I came down here than all the rest of my life together. I don't know why.

Harry

By the end of October 1941, Harry Morrison confidently predicted that with Wake's high-quality workers, CPNAB would be ready to turn the base over to the navy by July 1, 1942. Morrison acknowledged that the turnover rate of 5 percent per month was "plenty high," but it was less that some of the other island jobs. He attributed the relatively high morale and stability of the Wake workforce to several factors, among them the steady core of men recruited from the Inland Northwest, including more than 25 percent from Idaho. He also noted the value of patient and understanding supervisors, excellent food and quarters on Wake, the absence of "labor agitators and union leaders," and the advance planning and vigorous supervision that contributed to the "spirit of accomplishment." While Morrison still advocated bringing in two hundred Filipinos for menial labor, "thus releasing American labor for the performance of those items of work which require greater skill and ability," he was certain that the Boise employment office would "in some manner or other obtain the men" necessary to keep the crews at full strength.[22]

During the month of October, 223 contractors had arrived and 92 departed from Wake, bringing the total to 1,171. Of the total, 933 were journeymen, 151 helpers or apprentices, and 87 foremen. Camp support and medical operations accounted for 164 men, while the rest worked on construction aspects of the project. The contractors occupied Camp 2 where barracks would soon be able to hold 1,500. Temporary housing had also

Harry B. Olson, Mason City, Washington, 1940. *Olson Family Collection*

Olson Family, left to right: Donna, Katherine, Jim, and Ted, Mason City, Washington, 1940. *Olson Family Collection*

Pan American
complex on Peale.
National Archives

Pan American Clipper
dock on Peale Island.
National Archives

Left: China Clipper
at Pearl Harbor.
National Park Service

Below: Martin
model 130 China
Clipper over San
Francisco Bay.
NASA

Camp 1, Wake Island—*National Archives*

Camp 1, Wake Island—*National Archives*

New contractor personnel disembarking at Wake. —*National Archives*

Harry W. Morrison
URS Corp.

George L. Youmans
URS Corp.

Nathan "Dan" Teters
URS Corp.

L. H. "Pete" Russell
URS Corp.

W. N. "Swede"
Hokanson—*URS Corp.*

Peter Hansen
URS Corp.

Joseph F. McDonald
URS Corp.

Jack Hoskins
URS Corp.

Frank Miller
URS Corp.

Top: Wake contractors at Camp 2 on Wake, Spring 1941.
National Archives

Center: Ted Olson, 1938.
Olson Family Collection

Below: Harry Olson, 1940.
Olson Family Collection

Wake-Wilkes barge channel between Wake and Wilkes, 1941.
National Archives

Wake Waterfront operations, on Wake, 1941.—*National Archives*

USS *Regulus* unloading oil outside the reef off Wake, 1941.—*National Archives*

Moored ship, tugs, and lighters off Wake, 1941.—*National Archives*

Right: Interior of a Camp 2 barracks room. The contractors generally preferred the airy tents of Camp 1 to the Camp 2 barracks. *National Archives*

Below: Hospital at Camp 2 under construction. *National Archives*

Camp 2 under construction. Note mess hall in the background on far right.—*National Archives*

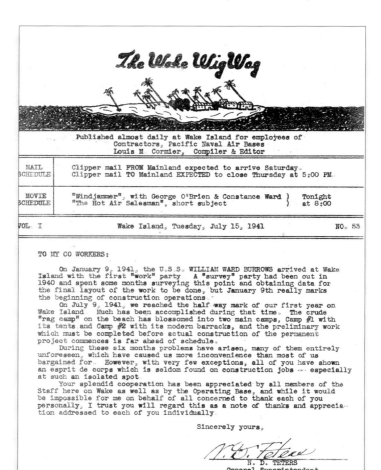

Front page of July 15, 1941, *Wake Wig Wag*, the contractors' more or less daily newspaper.—*McClary-Morrison Collection*

Above and below: Bridge between Wake and Peale under construction.—*National Archives*

Camp 2, bridge, and Peale Island, 1941. *Burdette Harvey Family Collection*

The dredge *Columbia*.
Burdette Harvey Family Collection

Wake workers
in 1941, left to
right: Jack Ward,
Kid Harvey,
Guy McGee,
Skippy Rivers,
Chet Ratekin.
*Guy McGee
Family Collection*

Hokanson family in Honolulu, October 1941, left to right: June, Swede, and Mae. *Dukes-Hohner Collection.*

Pete Russell's wife Eudelle Russell, January 1942, Honolulu. Following the war, and after obtaining divorces from their respective spouses, Harry Olson and Eudelle were married. *Dukes-Hohner Collection*

Harry Olson, January 1942, Honolulu. *Dukes-Hohner Collection*

Captured Wake contractors departing the island, January 1942.—*National Archives*

One of four cards from Ted Olson who was interned in Fukuoka-3 POW camp. *Olson Family Collection*

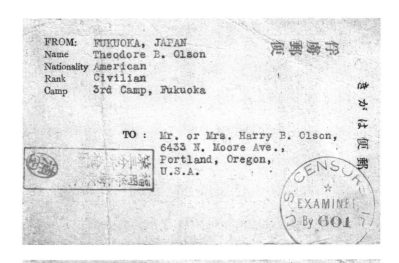

FROM: FUKUOKA, JAPAN
Name   Theodore B. Olson
Nationality American
Rank   Civilian
Camp   3rd Camp, Fukuoka

TO : Mr. or Mrs. Harry B. Olson,
       6433 N. Moore Ave.,
       Portland, Oregon,
       U.S.A.

CENSOR
EXAMINED
By 601

福岡俘虜收容所俘虜郵便   IMPERIAL JAPANESE ARMY

Dear Folks,
     I am interned in Fukuoka Camp.
My health is pretty good. I am working every
day. My love to you all.

          Theodore B. Olson

Theodore B. Olson

A U.S. Navy Douglas SBD-5 Dauntless dive bomber of bombing squadron VB-5 from the USS *Yorktown* (CV-10) over Wake Island, 5 or 6 October 1943.—*National Archives*

One of the four bunkers used in December 1941 as hospitals and command posts, 2011.—*Author's collection*

Japanese coastal defense gun on Peale Island, 2011.—*Author's collection*

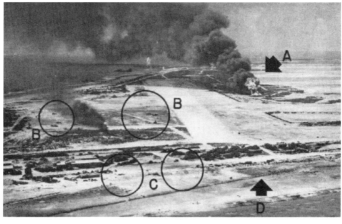

Aerial photograph of the attack on Wake Island by aircraft from Carrier Air Group Five (CVG-5) from the U.S. aircraft carrier USS *Yorktown* (CV-10) on 5 October 1943. (Legend: A: burning fuel dumps, B: Mitsubishi A6M2 and A6M3 Zero fighters, C: gun positions, D: trenches and barbed wire positions)—*Wikimedia*

Pete Russell, reunited with family in La Grande OR, Winter 1945.—*Peter Russell, Ogden, Utah*

Ted Olson and group of ex-POWs, December 1945, Boise, Idaho.—*Olson Family Collection*

been built for navy personnel in Camp 2 pending completion of permanent navy facilities on Peale and the marines occupied Camp 1, five miles away and "providing desirable isolation between the groups of men." Wake churned with the comings, goings, and work of sixteen hundred civilian contractors and military personnel.[23]

GIVING THANKS

"Be Fire-Conscious! Fire is our most dangerous potential enemy! Typhoons, Tokio, and Hitler are secondary!" So ran the headline of the November 6, 1941, *Wake Wig Wag*. Buried on page three, behind mainland election news, an update on the fate of the torpedoed destroyer *Reuben James*, and war news, was a report from Washington announcing that "all civilians not essential for defense have been ordered home from bases between Hawaii and the far east" and that women and children were being evacuated from Wake, Guam, and Midway. This may have been the first that many of the workers had heard of the orders, but they were reassured to read that the "Navy Department has stated there is nothing significant in the move and it is merely in keeping with general policy." Three days later, on its front page the *Wig Wag* printed "Blackout Bill" orders from Major Devereux dated November 6. The order described signals for blackout and detailed instructions for compliance.[24]

"The radio news tonite did not sound so good," Peter Hansen wrote his wife on November 10:

> *The Japs seem persistent about war, and may be too soon to suit us. But even though war is declared there won't likely be much action for some time (let's hope). Haven't seen any more of the Navy since the last ships sailed away. The planes have discontinued also. But in event of war I am positive they will station planes and ships both here. For some reason we don't hear much from the men about being alarmed, since the Marines have been stationed here, and since the guns have been set up. The Marines have called for civilian volunteers to take lessons to help handle the guns. There are about 300 Marines here now and equipment for 800 or more. They are even teaching the boys how to use rifles. So far I haven't taken part in any of it. I have been hoping that I would be out of here before the shooting begins. We might make it yet though. No one seems to be worried about it, such as they were*

the first time we had the war scare. I didn't feel too comfortable myself until they got some defense here."[25]

The contractors worked through Armistice Day, November 11, pulling double time. That day the *Burrows* pulled up to Wake with another fifty civilian workers and a dozen military personnel including the new doctor, Lieutenant (junior grade) G. Mason Kahn, USNR, and a U.S. Army Signal Corps crew of six, as well as a load of dynamite and the requisite barge of cargo. That evening Pete Russell and Harry joined the *Burrows* executive officer for beers after supper and talked over times old and new. Captain Dierdorff, who had orders to transfer to another ship after this trip, came ashore to say his final farewell to his pioneer friends. Other farewells were taking place that evening as a number of men having completed their contracts were taking leave of their friends and promising to look up family members on the mainland. Peter Hansen looked longingly at the packed suitcases and calculated that, at thirty to forty days for ship turnaround, it was likely that the *Burrows* would be back at just the right time to take him home in late December. "The *Burroughs* [sic] is the best boat that comes here," he wrote, but if he missed it on the next trip, he vowed he would take the "first tug or scow" that came available.[26]

As Thanksgiving Day approached—celebrated a week early in the White House, thirty-two mainland states, and the islands on November 20, 1941—only a handful of officers and civilian supervisors were aware of the elevated war crisis, and it did not seem serious enough to warrant working through the holiday. A visiting army chaplain spoke to the men the night before the holiday urging them to work with all their might and not to count the days. He assured the men that "God will bless us all for our sacrifice," as Pete Hansen told his wife. "I don't care about the hero stuff, I'm glad I have done something though, in the line of defense. I'm glad we have made *some* sacrifice, I think everyone should, but I will also be glad when it is all over. . . . The news today did not sound good, we have only 34 days to go, we must make it. They can't possibly become dangerous in that time. No work tomorrow," he noted. "The day will seem so long. We have lots of material, I don't see why we don't work, especially when the work is so slow. This type of work is so slow. The cost must be enormous. We work hours and days on the simplest things. . . . It would be impossible to estimate that kind of work. The report is that the project is costing 4 times as much as the original estimate."[27]

The civilians spent most of Thanksgiving playing games, shell hunting, fishing, and letter writing. Camp 2 now boasted a recreation hall large enough for three hundred, with a meeting hall, library, reading room, pool tables, ping-pong, card tables, and a post office. In addition to the excellent mess hall, outdoor theater, and recreation hall, there was a "modern laundry," canteen, store, shoe shop, barber shop, tennis court and horseshoe courts, the ball field, and a swimming area in the lagoon, netted to keep the sharks out. They missed fresh milk, liquor, and women (not necessarily in that order), but many availed themselves of Wake's amenities on the holiday. Swede Hokanson took groups of men by tugboat out to a large barge anchored offshore for deep-sea fishing. Thanksgiving dinner for twelve hundred, an impressive spread colorfully described by Joe McDonald in a letter home and carried in the Reno newspaper, left everyone more than sated. The fine dinner, carried thousands of miles to Wake in refrigerated containers, included "turkey with all the fixin's, roast beef, vegetable salad with fresh tomatoes, fruit cup, shrimp cocktail, celery, olives and other appetizers, mince pie, ice cream and coffee." The Boise paper also carried an account of the holiday drawn from a letter received by Raymond Forsythe's family: "Today is a day of feasting and rest on Wake island. This is the first day some of the boys have had to themselves since they arrived." The men ended the day with an outdoor picture show, *The Hurricane*.[28]

The *Wake Wig Wag* reported that the contractors were looking forward to their first big play, *The Wake Island Revue*, to be held at the open-air theater where a several-hundred dollar stage had recently been built "for the boys." Management was "really going to town" for the show, bringing in costumes, spotlights, and other equipment and supplies for the entertainment. Talented workers had been meeting and rehearsing since early October, and the cast of sixty was putting the final touches on the show. Prop men, stagehands, soundmen, electricians, spotlight operators, and prompters joined actors, singers, and other performers, including a harmonica orchestra accompanied by accordions and trumpets. The organizers of *The Wake Island Revue*—"a show for the men on Wake Island, by the men on Wake Island"— boasted that their performance would far eclipse those staged at Midway, Johnston, and Palmyra.[29]

Late November also saw many taking spare time to engage in an "all-out poetry blitzkrieg. The boys wore pencils down to the eraser and their fingers to a nub and wallowed for days in iambic pentameter, blank and free verse." The result was a twenty-five page poetry supplement to the *Wig Wag* featuring original poems by Wake civilians and marines. The Wake poetry ranged from the humorous to the serious, from "The Wake Island Wacky-Woo," by Anonymous, to "My Son," by Joe Williamson. Many poked fun at life on Wake; others recalled the trip out, the problems of turnover, the poor old dredge, and homesickness. In all, it was an impressive show for the hardworking construction stiffs and marines of Wake in late November 1941.[30]

Despite rising tensions in the Pacific, the men retained the kind of casual confidence expressed by one man's comment to assuage his mother's concerns: "Don't worry; Uncle will take care of us." As November waned, however, the scuttlebutt carried more talk about evacuation in the event of a war declaration "any day." Peter Hansen hoped they could wait one more month so that he could complete his contract and go home with the maximum bonus and a guarantee of future work, but he also speculated on the state of construction on Wake. "This island really is no use for anything at present, only for refueling airplanes," Hansen wrote on November 21. "They have spent a lot of money though, and could all be put out of commission by one bomb. One bomb on the little power plant would end our water supply, refrigeration, and everything else. So it would not surprise me to see a transport ship come to take us off if war is declared."[31]

ON THE BRINK

The expectation that Japan would cave in to economic and diplomatic pressures began to give way to the realization that the United States was on the very brink of war. Headlines warned the public: "War in Pacific Feared Near." Top military planners knew that U.S. forces were still weak compared to Japan, especially as construction of Pacific bases was incomplete, but many retained a contemptuous attitude toward Japan's military capabilities. Admiral Stark and General Marshall reported to the president that "war between the U.S. and Japan should be avoided while building up the defensive forces in the Far East." It was "most essential" to gain time and build up Philippine strength. If war became unavoidable, military operations should focus on holding territory and weakening Japan's economic position. The United States continued to predicate its Pacific policy on the assumption that Japan was most likely to initiate an attack on the Allies by striking Thailand, the Burma Road, or another Western colonial possession in the Far East where the thirty-five long-range B-17 Flying Fortresses already based near Manila at Clark Field, with more en route, should pose a powerful deterrent and counterattack force.[32]

In anticipation of imminent action in the Pacific Admiral Kimmel prepared to send patrol plane squadrons to Midway and Wake and requested an immediate update on facilities readiness. Water remained a chief concern as Kimmel calculated the impact of additional military personnel on Wake's sparse resources and incomplete stilling capabilities: a full patrol plane squadron comprised 382 men. If crews arrived on short notice they would find the local transportation (trucks and small boats) inadequate for the movement of men around the atoll. The limited supply, storage capacity, and efficient transfer system of aviation fuel also posed problems. While construction of avgas storage tanks at the airstrip enabled the marines to more efficiently refuel the thirsty westbound B-17s, fuel storage and transfer for seaplanes remained undeveloped pending construction of facilities on Peale. Still, the crisis demanded action. On November 10 Admiral Kimmel ordered immediate action to base twelve USN patrol planes and twelve USMC scout bombers or fighters with ground personnel on Wake.[33]

Not privy to strategic military discussions the CPNAB contractors were startled to receive an order from Captain Bruns on November 19 to reduce the number of contractors on Wake to 1,000 and cancel future employee requests in order to accommodate additional navy personnel. Midway received similar orders. At that time, there were some 1,150 civilian workers on Wake and another 200 in Honolulu awaiting transportation. In spite of the workforce reduction there was to be no corresponding reduction of work; indeed, the projects must proceed at full speed. The CPNAB Executive Committee immediately raised objections, calling the instructions "contrary to the welfare of the work," and accepted the directive under protest while they took up the matter with the contracting officer, Bureau of Yards and Docks chief Rear Admiral Moreell. The matter was still in dispute in the first week of December as more civilian contractors made their way to Wake.[34]

The vital issue of antiaircraft radar also became subject of intense scrutiny at this time. In Admiral Kimmel's "Study on Defenses" he recommended that in addition to two units already approved for (but not yet delivered to) Wake another three should be added. The extra radar befitted Wake's position on the "front lines." On November 14 Kimmel fired off a letter to Admiral Bloch demanding to know why there had been no mention of installation of radar units on Wake: one SCR-270-B and two SCR-268 fire control units were assigned to and now available for Wake and "every effort is being made for their early installation." Kimmel urged that radar installation be accomplished "as soon as practicable" with properly functioning equipment and trained crews and that he be informed when that would be possible.[35]

Meanwhile, hopes of a substantive outcome between American and Japanese diplomats in Washington D.C. had all but died. The Japanese ambassador proposed that the United States accept Japan's acquisitions in Indochina and Asia, resume trade with Japan, stop sending assistance to China, and cap American forces in the Pacific, in return for which Japan would exit Indochina after stabilizing China. The U.S. State Department floated a plan for partial agreement to this proposal among its allies. It floated like a lead balloon. On November 26 Secretary Hull presented the U.S. counterproposal to Japan, essentially saying that if Japan stopped its policy of conquest the United States would resume trade. It was the first time the Americans offered to lift the oil embargo in exchange for Japan's withdrawal from China and Indochina, but Japan did not accept the counterproposal. Negotiations ceased, and on November 27, 1941, CNO Stark sent a "war warning" to Admirals Kimmel and Hart in the Pacific that an "aggressive move by Japan is expected within the next few days." Stark speculated that likely targets included the Kra Peninsula (the narrow isthmus connecting Malaya and Thailand), Borneo, or the Philippines. He instructed Kimmel to prepare to implement war plans as outlined in WPL-46, which called for actions against the Japanese Mandates to divert enemy strength. The outposts at Midway and Wake were key components in this limited offensive strategy.[36]

The last week of November Wake welcomed the navy tug *Sonoma*, towing two full cargo barges, and the seaplane tender USS *Wright*, which arrived on November 28, carrying ground crew personnel for the incoming air squadron, other enlisted men, and several key officers, including Commander Winfield Scott Cunningham, the new commanding officer of Wake Island. By the first week of December the CPNAB work force on Wake stood at over eleven hundred. During the month of November several supervisors took vacations and seventy employees departed Wake with some having completed their contracts, others disgruntled, fired, frightened, ill, or for personal reasons. Fifty-five new employees arrived in November including an asphalt crew of about a dozen to pave the runways and a new crew of dishwashers and pot washers.[37]

November 29 delivered typically pleasant weather: "mostly clear with scattered clouds; occasional light showers; good visibility; slight northeasterly seas; maximum temperature 83." The *Wig Wag* news opened with a distillation of radio news reports regarding the Far East situation. "It seems clear that negotiations between the United States and Japan have reached their crucial stage and undoubtedly far-reaching decisions are being made. No one knows exactly what is going on in Washington. The only people who know are not talking and ordinary speculation is not very useful." Nothing definitive had come of the last-minute conference held by the president, Secretary Hull, and the Japanese diplomats. Recent press accounts confirmed the mutual incompatibility of both sides: a rupture was imminent, and the next move was up to Japan. Current speculation held that "Japan's answer may take the form of an attack on Thailand and later an attempt to break the Burma Road."[38]

Wake Island, Nov. 30, 1941
Dear Donna:
You should be here tonight. It's so beautiful it hurts. There is no breeze and the lagoon and sea are like mirrors. A few fleecy clouds and the moon almost full. The white coral looks like snow but one knows it cannot be for of course it is warm. Each full moon in turn I am amazed as is everyone by the beauty of the nights. It does something to each of us and is a common source of pleasure. It's Sunday night and outside I can hear the loudspeakers playing sacred records as I write. The current one is "In the Sweet By and By." At eight the movie will start and the theme change. They will get more customers. About 2000. Most of the people down here are avid movie-goers. It is practically the only relaxation for most of the men. A few of us go over to the Pan Air hotel occasionally and sometimes it is interesting.

I met Vincent Sheean [journalist and well-known author then on assignment for New York Herald Tribune *the other night. We had a couple drinks together and got on well as I did not mention his books nor ask him his opinion of the Japanese situation. He is a regular fellow. No high hat and just the sort that would write the books he has. A definite leaning to the left as one must be who is preoccupied with the essential brotherhood of man. I meant to take him around our project and get better acquainted but I contracted a miserable cold and couldn't do it. He told me he would be back in the spring when the shooting started which is a fair index to his opinions. The shooting seems to get nearer as time goes on. Oddly enough most of the people down here are not much worried over the possibility of war. It may be that they are resigned to it. Most of us feel it is inevitable so let it come. I for one do not feel that Japan would be so easy to conquer and I know that war with her would mean suffering and sacrifice for each of us and we seem to be readying ourselves to make it. Wake is a sort of crossroads now as are all these Clipper stops. It is much easier for anyone living east of the Axis sphere of influence to get to the U.S. this way. And most of them would like to get there.*

And all sorts of interesting people are going westward. Clipper travel is not only dull but enervating. People from the mainland find our heat oppressive. Also everyone eats too much to be comfortable. But we do have fun sometimes. Peggy Free was leaving for San Francisco the other evening and I was over to say goodbye. This takes time at Wake. Peggy was in fairly good shape when I got there and in excellent form by dinnertime which was at 9:00. After dinner we settled down to a silly dice game called "beat it you so and so." For ten cents a point. There were six of us. The fair Rebecca, a daughter of old Jerusalem who was not so fair but a clear olive. From Damascus. And a French girl from [Beirut] we called Diane. She was quite regal at first but thawed under the influence of "gin and it," a sort of reformed martini. I don't like 'em but Peggy does and it was her farewell party. Then there was Dr. Tom Barrett and Ed Jones, a Clipper captain. I won all the money but forgot to take it with me. The bar boy no doubt figures I'm the tip-pingest tippler he has served. About midnite when everyone else was long in bed, we persuaded the Chamorro boys to put on one of their ceremonial sword dances. This is something. It's a rhythmic sort of thing combining a little pure Jungle, some stately Spanish, with a dash of downbeat. As it's done with sticks, it's also noisy and everyone got up to see what was up. Mostly they were angry but soon got over it for the Chamorro boys were in dead earnest and going to town. It's done to guitar music. The Chamorros have a lot of charm and a great gentle-ness. Ever sincere. One of them sang "Marie Elena" slightly off key and then came the payoff of the evening for me. The boy got up, bowed, and said, "I will now sing a song of farewell for Mrs. Free who is leaving tomorrow, perhaps forever." We all started to smile until we looked at Peggy and saw the tears start. She was touched by this evidence of genuine affection. It was a sad song and its rendition sadder yet. Ordinarily one doesn't do this sort of thing out here for we are here today and gone tomorrow and friendship a frail and transitory affair. Each of us lives in the present alone, forgets the past and awaits the future with what equanimity he can muster . . .

Love and stuff, Yo Pap

PART III
War

THE DEFENSE OF WAKE ISLAND

— *National Archives*

CHAPTER 9

SHATTERED ILLUSIONS

THE "FIRST SHOT" PROBLEM

As negotiations ground to a halt with Japan in late November, officials at the highest levels discussed the problem of entering the war. The American public and many members of Congress knew nothing about diplomatic details or standing war plans and were still sharply divided over American war involvement. The authority to declare war lay with Congress and public support for that decision was essential. "In spite of the risk involved . . . in letting the Japanese fire the first shot," Secretary of War Stimson later testified, "we realized that in order to have the full support of the American people, it was desirable to make sure the Japanese be the ones to do this so that there should remain no doubt in anyone's mind as to who were the aggressors." Japanese troop movements and fleet disposition suggested that the first strike would be in Thailand, the Kra Peninsula, the Philippines, or Borneo. In the Far East, only an attack on the Philippines would constitute a direct strike against the United States, but the Roosevelt administration promised to support its British and Dutch friends.[1]

Once the first strike had been dealt by Japan the administration could justify U.S. entry into the war. Rainbow 5 followed the Europe-first strategy agreed upon in the spring of 1941 when Germany appeared bent on world domination. War planners anticipated that the Atlantic and Europe would continue to be the decisive theaters of war and operations in the Pacific were to facilitate that effort. Plans called for the navy to pursue a defensive strategy in the Far East and employ offensive operations only to support the defense of the Malay Barrier. That support included the actions outlined in WPL-46, which called for the navy to divert the enemy from Malaya and the East Indian archipelago by capturing possessions in the Marshalls, with Wake Island as a vital U.S. base of operations, as well as to protect the territories and shipping of associated powers and destroy enemy communications. Many in the U.S. Navy considered the Pacific Ocean the navy's preeminent theater and Japan a "worthy foe," though others, particularly in the army, maintained attitudes of Japanese inferiority and German technological superiority. War strategies had been revised with the arming of the Philippines over the past half year, but the European theater remained the priority for the Roosevelt administration.[2]

"IMMENSE STRATEGIC IMPORTANCE"

As senior ranking naval officer, Commander Cunningham took charge of the military contingents as well as the civilian population, including the contractors and Pan American employees. Major Devereux retained authority over the island's defenses. In his briefing for the assignment Admiral Bloch's chief of staff at Pearl Harbor had told Cunningham that Wake stood as an advance base of "immense strategic importance" and that rapid completion of the construction program must be his primary concern with no diversion of contractor labor or equipment for defenses. While civilian reduction orders were still under hot debate between the contractors and the navy, Cunningham issued no such directives during the first week of December and followed the stepped-up program to complete the facilities as soon as possible. Within days the commander completed his first biweekly readiness report on Wake for Pearl Harbor listing the vessels and trucks available, guns and ordnance, gasoline pumps, and radio transmitters and receivers. Cunningham estimated dates of completion for various installations and facilities reaching into 1942 and calculated fuel storage capacity.[3]

In early November Admiral Kimmel had pressured Admiral Bloch for transportation of radar units to Wake and Midway. Bloch, in turn, pressured his chief of staff, the district marine officer, and the radio material officer. Finally, on November 27 Bloch reported to Kimmel that the 4th Defense Battalion's radar equipment had arrived at Pearl: four units of SCR-270-B and twelve units of SCR-268; however, the equipment came "without spare parts and necessary accessories. Moreover, the defense battalions had only a few trained technicians and operators." A crash course was conducted to train and qualify operators to use the radar in the "anti-aircraft defenses of outlying island bases." The *Regulus*, sailing on November 29, would carry three sets to Midway, Bloch wrote, and "three SCR-268 and one SCR 270-B sets with operating personnel" for all but one of the 268 models "are being sent to Wake via the WILLIAM WARD BURROWS scheduled to sail from this port on the 28th instant." Members of the 4th Defense Battalion would relieve those of the 1st Defense Battalion on Wake as soon as crews were trained and transportation available. (The 1st Battalion had no trained radar crews.) Bloch cautioned that radar sets were being sent to Wake and Midway without spare parts and testing sets and, until the arrival of that equipment, "no assurance can be given that the sets can be maintained in operating condition." Bloch's chief of staff ordered shipment of the radar units to Wake on the *Burrows*, cautioning that "this equipment is of a classified nature and current instructions require that it be insured against observation and inspection by unauthorized persons by the posting of armed sentinels over same." Marine Gunner Edward C. Thoemmes and approximately thirty-four enlisted men would take passage on the *Burrows*. "This officer and men are the operating crew of this equipment and will be used to safeguard the equipment while en route to Wake." The *Burrows* ship log shows that Gunner Thoemmes and thirty-two marines boarded on November 28; early the following morning, dozens of navy personnel and contractors streamed aboard and the ship pulled away from Pier 31-A shortly after eight o'clock on November 29, 1941, bound for Wake Island.[4]

In keeping with the heightened pressure for completion of the construction projects, the navy stepped up efforts to expedite the flow of supplies and equipment to Wake. The tug *Arthur Foss* towed two barges as it steamed toward Wake where it was due to arrive on December 5. The *Burrows*, carrying the top-secret radar equipment and operating crews, as well as sixty navy personnel and fifty-five civilians, the makings for Christmas dinner with all the trimmings and fancy menus, a load of cement and lumber, and a cargo-laden steel barge, was scheduled to arrive shortly after the tug. At Pier 31-A a Wake-bound navy tug prepared to depart Honolulu on December 5 towing two barges, and another three loaded barges awaited transportation at the docks.[5]

A navy task force, led by the aircraft carrier *Enterprise* under the command of Admiral William F. Halsey, also steamed toward Wake during the first days of December 1941. Under high alert for Japanese attack the *Enter-*

prise carried VMF-211, a USMC squadron of twelve Grumman F4F-3 Wildcat fighters and their crews for Wake. The mission was so top-secret that the pilots were not apprised of their destination until they had landed on the carrier and Admiral Halsey issued "Battle Order Number One." En route to Wake the squadron's pilots found that their Wildcats lacked navigation equipment, direction finders, and machine guns and sights, handicaps that they and the *Enterprise* crew attempted to remedy. Navy intelligence officers, briefing the pilots on Japanese aircraft types, showed only photographs of antiquated flying boats despite the fact that Japan had been attacking China with sophisticated twin-engine bombers for several years. "If these were the aircraft with which the Japanese hoped to conquer all of Asia, then we would not have much trouble knocking them down," Lieutenant John Kinney thought at the time. Kinney recalled that the briefing "reinforced the stereotype that most Americans held of the Japanese people as short, bandy-legged men with prominent front teeth and very thick eyeglasses. We were convinced that even if the Japanese planes were mechanically adequate it would be all the pilots could do to fly them in straight lines." Admiral Halsey acknowledged that he and others were "inclined to underrate the Japs, chiefly their aviation," despite warnings from officers who had recent experience in the Far East. An Associated Press reporter in Manila quoted U.S. military personnel who derided the Japanese army as an "ill-uniformed, untrained mass of boys 15-18 with small caliber guns" who "can't shoot. Somebody gets hit about every 50000 shots."[6]

Admiral Kimmel had also dispatched a task force led by the carrier *Lexington* to carry a squadron of eighteen dive-bombers to Midway and another task force to Johnston. If war broke out while they were at sea, all were to join up with the *Enterprise* near Wake and strike into the Japanese-held Marshalls. As the *Enterprise* closed in on Wake a dozen PBY patrol bombers flew from Midway toward Wake to provide cover for the arrival of VMF-211. Off Wake's shore the U.S. submarines *Tambor* and *Triton*, which had relieved the *Narwhal* and *Dolphin* on November 25, kept a steady patrol around the strategic atoll.

NO FEARS

On Wake the increased traffic and war warnings drove the pace of the project to high speed. On December 2 navy officials ordered the contractors to move the heavy equipment from the ship channel job back to the airfield with sudden urgency for a second operational runway. As the day went by, diesel-powered machinery chewed the coral at the airfield. The dredge *Columbia* continued to grind out a low-priority barge channel in the lagoon. From one end of the atoll to the other, nearly 1,150 civilian contractors attacked dozens of projects, churned out paperwork, and kept the construction camp running. To protect this valuable military installation in the making, just over 500 military personnel manned the defenses, communications, and station operations. On the afternoon of December 3 many paused to watch as the twelve navy PBYs settled onto the turquoise water of Wake's lagoon where they formed an impressive armada. The atmosphere was charged with the electricity of vital work in the national defense, but most of the men retained a cocky confidence in American invulnerability. From the top down, the contractors had no fear of imminent, personal danger beyond a construction accident or shark bite.[7]

> *Wake Island, December 1, 1941*
> *Dear Katherine:*
> *As usual the Clippers are all messed up so I don't quite know when this will go out but will write anyway. Apparently the typhoon season is over, at least we are hoping it is, and the schedules should improve. If the war situation gets bad enough they may discontinue the planes and this would be a lonely place indeed. At that we would be no worse off than most of the Pacific Islands and they seem to get along O.K. People write much more out here than they would on the mainland. I guess it's sheer boredom. There is so little to do. . . .*
>
> *The war news is disquieting to say the least. I suppose it's always hard to reconcile ourselves to the other fellow's viewpoint as I must confess that I can't see where Japan has a leg to stand on. In the last analysis it is nothing but sheer greed on her part. If we admit her right to appropriate the other fellow's goods on the plea that the world has denied or limited her opportunities to acquire wealth, then we must grant the needy individual the same privilege to level private wealth. This is socialism or communism as you wish to call it, so we are treated to the analogous spectacle of a nation waging war through and by the principles of a social system she loudly proclaims a menace to her political security. If only her people and ours could see this clearly, war would be unthinkable. So we must accept war as a state made possible solely*

through ignorance of the people engaged in it. As Germany's social and political aims are identical with Japan's, this indictment strikes her in her most vulnerable area—her pretensions to leadership in culture. This all sounds logical to me but there must be some flaw in it for who am I to set myself against the accepted viewpoint of half the world. But I am willing to place and accept the blame for war where it really belongs—on the people themselves. If ever a people had the chance to rule themselves it was, and is, the Americans. And to me at least they are making a sad botch of the whole affair. There is not a living American who has not had the opportunity to learn the truth and what is published as the truth. It's mostly laziness that has held them back. It's so easy to read a newspaper with glaring headlines or an illustrated weekly and that is why we were a greater nation before we had those doubtful blessings. And in that happy era, people were inclined to a religious viewpoint. At least they tried to square their actions with religious precepts to some extent and questionable policy was subject to those limitations. I am not happy to admit this for my ideal would be a people, free through their own volition and not subject to either religious or political ideologies. That's Utopia and I fear we shall never reach it but the possibilities are inherent in man, so there is some hope.

All this war business has upset our program to some extent and I expect we will get greater dislocations as it grows more serious. Your imagination will have to suffice for it would serve no good end to go into any further details along this line. I had hoped all along that we could avoid this and get the job finished more quickly, but I guess we will have to accept what the gods offer.

Ted has been having some trouble. He has not confided in me but it all stems from a little laziness on his part. I think he is beginning to see the light but it's sort of a bitter pill for him to swallow. The realization that a job can only be held through his own efforts is just beginning to dawn on him and I am hoping it will have a salutary effect before it is too late. I have not, as you well know, ever been happy to have him work for me for it places me in an uncomfortable position when he gets in bad. My instincts are all to try and protect him when it is not expedient to do so. I had a long talk with Dan over all this and he at least understands. As I write this it looks as tho it all will turn out O.K.

Dan just called me to come in, that he had something to talk over with me so I'll close. I won't hear from you people for a long time as the next Clipper has not left the mainland as yet. So your next letter from me is a long ways off.

Aloha, Harry

Ted also wrote to Katherine on December 1. "Once again I take my trusty pen in hand and tax my weary brain for something to say in a letter which I know is long overdue . . . but there isn't a darn thing to write about." He reported that he was working again for Swede at the waterfront—better than for the "screwballs I've been working for"—and that he would arrange to have all of his overtime, amounting to between $700 and $1000, sent to her to invest in postal bonds. Ted directed his mother to take $25 to buy silverware or glassware for herself as a Christmas gift, and "then take $50 and take care of the rest of my shopping" for family and friends. In closing he mentioned that he must hurry as there would be a blackout drill in fifteen minutes, by now a regular occurrence.[8]

Joe McDonald typed a letter home on December 2 with similar comments about Christmas gifts, the job, and general lack of concern about the near future. Sidelined with an infected finger that required surgery, Joe anticipated a few days off. "I am sure glad you get paid whether you work or no or else I would be slightly in the hole." A recent job classification change to rodman had made no difference in McDonald's wages. "They could call me a garbageman if they would raise the pay, but the boss says no deal. He is an awful pain in the neck, you would think the raise came out of his pocket," Joe groused. He wrote about a Sigma Alpha Epsilon "fraternity meeting" one recent evening with six members in attendance, one of whom would have been Ted Olson, proudly sporting his SAE ring. Otherwise, the men did nothing but "work, eat, and sleep and that is all life out here amounts to." In the only comment relating to war danger McDonald wrote, "there are a whole flock of sailors and marines stationed here now. I guess in case Japan wants to play a little rough."[9]

Peter Hansen, now "in the twenties" in his countdown to end of contract, noted on November 29 that "the war crisis is 'grave' at this moment," but elaborated on reasons why he expected no trouble from Japan in the immediate future. "Hope they don't try some cunning tricks now." Hansen's letters were filled with endearments, bonus calculations, and plans for his imminent return, but no more sketches. He noted that "they do constantly remind us not to make any drawings of the buildings, etc., or tell anyone about the description of the work, etc. Really is ridiculous because one airplane could fly over at 20,000 and take a picture of the entire island, and we would neither hear nor see the plane." Hansen did mark the increased navy presence on the island, the submarine patrol, and the incoming pursuit planes. "Also heard that from now on there will be cruisers, destroyers, battleships and etc. always within a day's run of the island. This stuff makes us feel so much better." Wake's guns, he speculated, "couldn't sink a canoe, and a good size battleship could demolish this little island from 20 miles away," but the pursuit planes would make it hard for enemy ships to get within fifty miles, "so that's that. In all events, I am ready to evacuate any time I can do so without losing out on my contract."[10]

At the CPNAB operating base the Wake engineers finalized a large blueprint of the atoll showing progress as of December 1, 1941, based on the most up-to-date information. The drawing showed all of the facilities, installations, and excavation progress in minute detail. Three landplane runways were mapped; seaplane runways, turning basins, and channels in the lagoon were laid out and water depths marked. One legend used crosshatched markings to designate the level of progress on each excavation project and another listed each facility construction project by number and percent of completion. Additional tables accompanied the primary blueprint, detailing cargo, shipping, labor, and other facets of the operation over the previous months. Overall, the drawings showed that the Wake project was, on average, 65 percent complete at the beginning of December 1941.[11]

HARRY'S VACATION

Relentless pressure from the navy for speedy completion of construction left little room for rest, but the staff vacation rotation remained in place, perhaps more important now than earlier for keeping the key men reasonably content to stay on the job. Two assistant superintendents, Herman Echols, head of administration, and Bill Puccetti, in charge of mechanics and equipment, had just left the island for their scheduled vacations and both had plans to take the *Lurline* to the mainland on December 5. Harry Olson watched the calendar and knew that his slot was on the horizon. Dr. Tom Barrett, for months Wake's sole physician, also stood ready for a vacation. As second civilian doctor, Lawton Shank, had just completed his contract with Pan Air on Wake and signed on with CPNAB, a convenient transfer of on-island talent. Shank joined Barrett, a staff of male nurses, and dentist James Cunha to provide medical services to Wake's burgeoning civilian population. Lieutenant Kahn had arrived on the *Burrows* November 11 to serve as the military physician.

Dan Teters also craved a vacation in Honolulu with his wife, but either Teters or his field assistant, Harry Olson, had to be on site at all times. Between the project pressure and the deteriorating war situation, not to mention the uncertainty of Clipper transportation, neither man was optimistic that he would be lounging on Waikiki Beach, with or without a wife, anytime soon. When a window of opportunity suddenly opened on the afternoon of December 3 the two men argued until they came to a compromise. Harry would take the available seat on the eastbound Clipper to Honolulu the next morning, enjoy his ten days, and be back to share Christmas with his son on Wake, when Dan would take his turn for a Christmas holiday in Honolulu with his wife.

Shortly after sunrise on December 4 Harry and Dr. Barrett boarded the Pan American *China Clipper* with a passenger load that included new Soviet Ambassador Maxim Litvinov. Pete Russell and Swede Hokanson, having instructed Harry to look up their wives in Honolulu, rode the crash launch and waved them off, even though tightly-closed curtains during takeoff and landing prevented the passengers from seeing anything or anyone waving below. When a crewmember did pull the curtains after takeoff the windows revealed an endless sky and empty sea. Six years earlier to the day PAA physician Ken Kenler had departed Wake Island on the maiden voyage of the *China Clipper*. In a letter to his family written aboard the Clipper in 1935 Kenler commented that the flight "somewhat compensated the trials and difficulties experienced creating the mid Pacific bases." Harry likely shared this sentiment as he settled in for the first-class ride. Unbeknownst to the December 4 Clipper passengers the carrier *Enterprise* lay below them within a few hundred miles of Wake, having just launched the squadron of Wake-bound Wildcats. The Grumman fighters, escorted by a navy PBY, flew in formation to Wake's narrow runway, where they landed one after another in an impressive display of metal and might.[12]

The Clipper passengers settled into a comfortable time-passing routine of reading, cards, and visiting about the weather, the world, and the war. Luncheon was long and leisurely. In mid-afternoon, the Clipper abruptly dipped, catching the passengers by surprise. With a flourish, the steward announced that this was the captain's signal that they had just crossed the international date line and December 4 had become December 3. Each passenger received a personalized certificate from the "Domain of Phoebus Apollo," signed by the Clipper captain, as a token of the event. Harry tucked the document away as a keepsake.

The Clipper settled onto Midway's lagoon in the early evening and Pan American employees whisked the passengers to the dock in launches. White-uniformed Chamorros offered cigarettes; others scurried to unload the passengers' valises. Cars waited to carry all to the Pan Air hotel, a mirror image of the one on Wake. Marlyn Sheik, the general superintendent for CPNAB's Midway project, met Harry and took him for a quick ride over the operation. As on Wake, marines and other military personnel were busy setting up defensive operations while over a thousand contractors continued to work on base facilities and dredging. Harry counted eighteen scout planes at the airport facility as well as numerous patrol seaplanes in the lagoon. By all appearances Midway posed a formidable guard for Territorial Hawaii. En route to Honolulu the next morning Harry added a postscript to the December 1 letter to Katherine that he carried in his pocket:

On board the China Clipper, *Dec. 4, 1941*
This is an addition being written on the China Clipper *and we are just now passing over Laysan Island at 10,000 feet. Despite the tropic latitude it is very cold outside, 10° above. But the cabins are warm. We are 22 passengers in three compartments. Right now most everyone is sleeping. We took off in the dark at 6:00 A.M. and will land in the dark at about 6:30 P.M. We have an 11 hour forecast and 1-½ hrs. difference in time. Maxim Litvinoff, the Russian Ambassador, is stretched out sound asleep across the aisle. Madam Litvinoff, an amiable grandmotherly lady, is trying to read and talk at the same time. Just now she wanted to know if all Americans chew gum and why. I told her when I found out I would let her know. She finds much to amuse herself about the land of the free and of course they are both all smiles over the course of the war the last few days. The secretary, Anatonia Petrovna, is the one that interests me most. About 30, she is the type of revolutionary you read about. Dark, emotional, intense and more than willing to give all for the cause. I suspect she feels the same*

about Maxim, if you get what I mean. 3 interesting people. We play bridge together and here at least I am superior. I wonder, to myself of course, what quality it is that makes men great. In this case it is indefinable and must be a combination of many. I would say the outstanding ones were guile and ruthlessness. I suspect that good fortune has helped him some.

This trip came as a complete surprise. Dan is very restless since Florence left. He had a trip planned to Guam this month and we had tentatively planned a trip to Honolulu for me in January and one for him in Feb. The war situation and clipper schedules got to looking bad and I talked him out of the Guam trip. Then he decided to send me in Dec. 13. The next day I was to fly in by Navy bomber. This was called off, so we radioed George [Youmans] Wednesday at 3:30 for approval on this Clipper and got it in 40 min. So I threw my things together and here I am. I will write more later when I find out more. I am very glad to get in just now for this war business should be settled by the time I return. I had breakfast with Marlin [sic] Sheik and now have a lot of business to do for him and the Midway job as well as our own. This is the only paper on the plane and I will open your letter I had written at Wake and enclose this. I'll sure be glad to get back to civilization for a while.

Harry

The *China Clipper* landed just off Pearl City far inside Pearl Harbor on the afternoon of December 4. In the harbor battleships of the Pacific Fleet rose like a mountain chain; from each mast the Stars and Stripes snapped in the wind. After clearing customs and watching the weary Ambassador Litvinov brush aside fragrant leis and a cluster of eager reporters with equal aversion, Harry and the doctor made their way to the Moana Hotel, next door to the Royal Hawaiian on Waikiki beach. Vacation started right away for Barrett, but Harry spent the next day at the CPNAB operating base in Pearl Harbor Navy Yard going over Wake and Midway business.[13]

The base swarmed with activity: over a thousand engineers, architects, accountants, and clerks worked on a dozen major projects located on Oahu and across the Pacific. Project managers from each of the eight contracting firms now comprising CPNAB (Raymond, Turner, Hawaiian Dredging, Morrison-Knudsen, Pomeroy, Utah Construction, Bechtel, and Byrne) oversaw staff at the base and the projects in the field. By December 1941 CPNAB had completed Kaneohe and Ford Island and turned them over to the navy, but work continued at the outlying islands, with Johnston, Palmyra, and Midway nearing completion.

The massive CPNAB expansion under NOy-4173, with supplemental agreements and change orders, had added Wake, Samoa, Guam, Cavite in the Philippines, and a number of additional projects. On Oahu the Red Hill underground fuel storage, with its unprecedented design of tunnels and vertical tanks that would hold four million barrels of oil, employed thousands of men. Other CPNAB jobs on Oahu and nearby included naval air stations at Bishops Point and Ewa, the sprawling Makapala military housing development, Wahiawa radio station, and the Aiea hospital, as well as dry docks, dredging, and numerous other projects within Pearl Harbor. George Youmans managed Red Hill, Midway, and Wake for Morrison-Knudsen, and now prepared to take over leadership of the CPNAB operating committee as chairman George Ferris packed for a December vacation. Ferris and William McMenimen, chairman of the CPNAB executive committee, had first-class tickets on the passenger liner *Lurline*, scheduled to depart for the mainland on December 5. It promised to be a busy December for CPNAB in the islands.[14]

On December 5, 1941, "Boat Day" drew crowds in the thousands to Honolulu harbor and Harry Olson joined the throng. As hundreds boarded the enormous ocean liner for the voyage, hundreds of residents and well-wishers gathered on shore to see and be seen, the Royal Hawaiian Band played, hula girls danced, and the thick fragrance of flower leis mingled with cigarette smoke. Harry and Barrett bade farewell to their Wake Island cohorts, Echols and Puccetti, and others from the CPNAB group waved goodbye to Ferris and McMenimen. As the ship pulled away in a colorful blizzard of confetti streamers, canoes and speedboats followed it to the mouth of the harbor and fighters swooped overhead in a "virtual aerial circus" as pilots wagged their wings in farewell to wives. The following day, December 6, Harry joined a CPNAB gang and twenty-five thousand football fans at Honolulu stadium for the Shrine Bowl game between the University of Hawaii and the Willamette Bearcats of Oregon with a patriotic halftime show of blazing fireworks. At a party later that night Harry met Pete's wife, Eudelle Russell, and fireworks of a different sort ignited.[15]

THE FIRST SHOT

Early the next morning Harry headed out for a walk, passing through the Moana Hotel foyer where a large poster hung, featuring Honolulu's advertising slogan: "A World of Happiness in an Ocean of Peace." On the veranda, a group of Willamette ballplayers was gathering for a sightseeing tour. "We had all been out on a lovely party, gay and formal," Harry later wrote to Katherine. "It lasted until 3:30. I awoke at six, got up, bathed and ate breakfast. Afterwards I went for a walk through the grounds around the Royal Hawaiian, which adjoins the Moana. I heard all this noise, a sort of wump, wump, continuously, but put it down to practice. Finally one or two fell close and I learned what it really was."[16]

Even as Honolulu radio announcers alerted listeners that enemy planes were attacking the island, that doctors should await calls and civilians stay indoors, most Honolulu residents considered the Sunday morning activities to be yet another training exercise. At the home of George and Grace Youmans the telephone rang just after 8:30. The voice of the watchman at the operating base crackled with fear as he spoke: Pearl Harbor was under attack. "They've sunk several ships in the harbor and ships are burning where I can see them through the window of the office!" Youmans thought everyone had gone "screwy," but he decided to drive down and see for himself. A fellow Morrison-Knudsen executive later described how Youmans, with his characteristic "uniformity of temperament . . . was said to have driven his car through machine gun fire December 7 to see whether his desk on Kuahua island was being disturbed." Two days later, Youmans described the morning to Harry Morrison in a long letter:[17]

Shortly after I left the house, I could see the dense black smoke rolling up from Pearl Harbor and drifting out to sea. By then, I began to realize that this was either an enemy attack or a more than realistic staging of a test raid. As we came closer to the yard, we could see the blaze of the hangars on Hickam Field and the blazing of the sunken ships in the harbor. They had the north gate to the yard blocked from all traffic, so we went up on the hill just outside of the gate, where the housing office is located. . . . We were there only for about five minutes, when we saw about thirty planes approaching the harbor from the direction of Schofield Barracks. We all thought that they were U.S. planes, but as soon as they came within closer view, they started to drop bombs all over the place. We ran for cover but the only place we could find was a woodshed.

The planes came over us in a group, flying slowly, and some of them were not over three or four hundred feet above the ground. In fact they were so low that we could see the Japanese pilots and crews looking out of the control rooms. All of them started up their machine guns and raked the main highway and housing area with a steady stream of bullets. They then circled around and came back over us again, repeating their bombing and machine gunning. The planes then passed out to sea and out of sight. We then went into the yard to see what the real damage had been.

The principal damage of course, was to the battleships that had been moored at Ford Island. Six of them appeared to have been hit, and one had turned turtle completely, with her bottom sticking up. All of them seemed to be burning fiercely. A seventh battleship had started down the channel, and had been hit while underway, and was sinking close to the shore.[18]

Youmans described the destruction and damage to other ships in Pearl Harbor, at the dry docks, on Ford Island, and at Hickam field, where he estimated 350 lay dead and many more injured. He relayed reports of devastation at Kaneohe and Schofield Barracks, and casualties among the citizens of Honolulu. "While there is nothing official at this date, from what we have done with our forces and what I know personally, the loss on the sunk ships will be over 3,000." The CPNAB operating base quickly brought all of their resources to bear on the emergency, establishing a 24-hour watch at the office and arming the swelling tide of defense workers with tin hats as they rushed to aid the navy. The first job was to repair the water system to enable firefighting efforts throughout the afflicted harbor.[19]

The "first shot" that hit Pearl Harbor on December 7, 1941, was part of a carefully coordinated strategy. That day (December 8 on the western side of the international date line) Japanese forces also attacked multiple locations in Southeast Asia and the Pacific including Malaya, the Kra Peninsula, Singapore, Hong Kong, the Philippines, Guam, and Wake Island. The Americans and British "consistently underrated the Japanese and failed to appreciate the defiant, do-or-die mentality of its current leadership," writes historian Waldo Heinrichs. Japanese planning, organization, and willingness to take heavy risks contributed to its successes that day. Weak defenses, ineffective or obsolete weapons, poor inter-service communications, and the "rituals and routines of peace" that prevailed right up to the last moment, contributed to the shock, death, and destruction experienced by Americans that day. These and other factors reflected a persistent faith in American invulnerability and Japanese inferiority. The risk of waiting for Japan to fire the first shot was that America did not know where, when, or how it would come.[20]

"WORK STARTED AS USUAL . . ."

The contractors and most of the military personnel had enjoyed a well-deserved day off on Wake Island on December 7 (December 6 in Honolulu). A day earlier Commander Cunningham had received a message from Pearl Harbor that he could authorize destruction of confidential documents, except the current direction-finder and aircraft codes, "now or under later conditions of greater emergency." The "watered down" order, sent under deferred precedence to naval commanders in the western Pacific and Far East, belied the urgency with which the chief of naval communications security had initiated it for Wake at Pearl Harbor: Wake Island had "all the Pacific crypto systems that we have printed up to July 1942" and it would "go very hard" if they fell into Japanese hands. In an effort to bring the code books up to date naval officers had brought virtually all of the registered documents for Pacific Fleet systems with them on the USS *Wright*, and Cunningham was pleased to see how quickly the ensigns got the code books in "perfect shape" on Wake.[21]

When the wake-up whistle sounded through Camp 2 on the morning of Monday, December 8, the men rose to resume their workday routine. While the previous day off had revitalized some, it left others with hangovers from bootleg booze and too much sun. After the breakfast rush mess boys scraped leftover eggs and pancakes off plates; houseboys neatly made the beds and swept the floors of the barracks as night shift workers drifted in to catch some sleep. The westbound *Philippine Clipper* had taken off for Guam early that morning and the tug *Arthur Foss* was a day eastbound at sea, having unloaded its barges in a single day, record time for the Wake waterfront. Carpenters, steel workers, riggers, and equipment operators hopped onto trucks that carried them to job sites on Peale, Wake, or Wilkes; the camp office filled up with secretaries, clerks, bookkeepers, timekeepers, engineers, bosses, bluejackets, and a visiting government auditor. Herman Hevenor, an auditor from the Bureau of the Budget, had arrived the day before and settled in to his lodging at the naval officers' cottage for a week-long stay, and now began pulling cost-accounting records for his report.[22]

Just after daybreak an operator in the army radio van at the airstrip picked up the initial uncoded message from Hickam Field and rushed it to Major Devereux: Pearl Harbor was under attack. In short order navy communications received a priority transmission from Pearl and Pan American alerted the Wake station. Devereux immediately ordered the "call to arms" and sent a man up the fifty-foot water tower in Camp 1 to serve as lookout. Marines rushed to their positions at the gun batteries and airfield as curious civilians passed by on their way to work. Trucks delivered ammunition and marines distributed spare individual weapons to unarmed army and navy personnel and a few trustworthy civilians. The grateful recipients set to cleaning the thick cosmoline from their newly-uncrated weapons. Cunningham huddled with his officers and Dan Teters in Camp 2. In the absence of radar the lonely sentry on the water tower and four Wildcats already aloft on patrol would have to serve as Wake's early-warning system. Cunningham ordered a rotating war patrol of four fighters. The news reached the westbound Clipper and Captain John H. Hamilton turned back to Wake, dumping his fuel before landing in the lagoon. A Pan Air driver sped Hamilton to the airstrip where he and Major Putnam worked out a plan for the Clipper to lead a long-range search to the south with a fighter escort.[23]

The remainder of VMF-211 stood exposed, parked at hundred-yard intervals near the airstrip where protective revetments were still under construction. Lacking surfaced access roads for safe movement of aircraft, camouflage for facilities, and foxholes for squadron personnel, the airstrip was in a state of "something close to consternation" as pilots and mechanics scrambled to position the fighters and service and arm them for combat. With the December 6 departure of VP-22, the navy's squadron of PBYs designed for long-range searches, the twelve Grumman fighters comprised Wake's entire air force. Lacking armor, self-sealing fuel tanks, and bomb racks that matched the supply of bombs, the Wildcats needed plenty of ingenious intervention, skilled piloting, and good luck.[24]

The marines had anchored their shoreline defenses with strongpoints established at each of the three points of the atoll. Each point had a fixed seacoast battery of two five-inch guns with a battery of four three-inch antiaircraft guns nearby: Batteries B and D on Peale at Toki Point, Batteries A and E at Peacock Point on Wake's elbow, and Batteries L and F on Wilkes at Kuku Point. The five-inch guns were fully manned, but lacked spare parts. Half the three-inch guns stood idle: several lacked fire-control equipment and height finders and none had been test fired or calibrated. The eighteen .50-caliber antiaircraft machine guns of Battery H stood dispersed over the atoll in chest-deep, sandbagged emplacements with room for the gun, ammunition, and water for cooling. Four-gun platoons of .50-caliber machine guns supported each of the three-inch batteries on the points, five guns protected the airstrip, and one .50 caliber stood guard on Heel Point on the northern hump of Wake, all undermanned with half-sized crews. The thirty .30-caliber antipersonnel guns of Battery I allocated for beach defense could not possibly cover the entire periphery including lagoon and sea beaches, so the marines prepared sixty emplacements. As with the antiaircraft support, four-gun platoons stood on each point; in addition, four guns faced Wilkes channel, six were positioned near Camp 1, two covered the beach south of the airstrip, two on Heel Point, and the remaining four served as a mobile reserve. Needless to say, the antipersonnel weapons also lacked full crews. The marines doubled up on duties and officers filled multiple roles. On the morning of December 8 trucks delivered full allowances of ammunition as well as helmets and gasmasks to battery positions. Marines dug foxholes and filled sandbags at their positions while watches stood guard at the guns and fire-control instruments. Devereux specifically directed that one three-inch gun at each battery be fully manned. That was all he could spare: on December 8, 1941, the Wake Island Detachment stood at only 40 percent of the number required to man its arsenal.[25]

Civilian volunteers who had trained with the marines in the preceding weeks and others who volunteered on the spot made a critical difference in Wake's defensive capabilities: every committed and capable civilian volunteer was a welcome addition. Some two hundred civilians had participated in weapons training with the marines that fall and Teters released some that morning to report to Devereux at Camp 1 for service at battle stations. Pending further orders from Pearl, however, the civilian contractors pressed ahead at full speed on the construction projects. Throughout the morning the scuttlebutt had raced across the atoll. The sight of the returning Clipper cranked up the rumor mill and conversation buzzed among the work crews as foremen and superintendents struggled to keep the men focused on their jobs.

Pete Russell wrote in his diary on December 8, "Work as usual started but didn't end as usual." By midmorning, the news was spreading like wildfire: Japan had attacked Pearl Harbor; the war had begun.[26]

Wake churned with activity as noon approached on December 8. Food trucks carried chow from the Camp 1 mess to the gun batteries and hundreds of workers were making their way to Camp 2 for lunch. Ted Olson's crew at the waterfront broke off work and piled onto a flatbed truck for the ride to camp. A low bank of clouds hung parallel to the runway and spit a few cool drops on the men as the truck rumbled by the airstrip where dozens of marines swarmed around a cluster of Wildcats. The civilians strained to get a look at eight of the twelve recently-arrived fighters that constituted Wake's very own air force. Minutes later, as the truck rolled into Camp 2, one of the men facing backwards pointed to a formation of planes dropping out of the cloudbank over the airfield, the sound of engines muffled by the constant roar of surf. "Here comes our help!" hollered one man. Expecting B-17s, the workers turned to watch the bombers sweep in toward the airstrip and another formation approach off the tip of Wilkes. Grins lit up the faces on the truck for a moment, then melted in horror as the planes let loose a barrage of bombs over the airfield. Suddenly the sky was full of bombers, some bearing down across the lagoon toward Peale, others circling back over the airfield, and still others headed straight for Camp 2. Men poured off the truck as it careened to a stop. The ground shook with distant thumps and then popped with a fierce rain of bullets as the bombers strafed the camp and circled around for more.[27]

TARGET: WAKE ISLAND

Everywhere across the atoll men scrambled to hide: under bushes and desks, in drainpipes and ditches, against rocks and walls. In Camp 2 Swede Hokanson ran from a building and dove under an ironwood bush as the planes turned toward camp. Bullets kicked sand into his face, so he dashed for a ditch near the road between waves of gunfire. Later Swede remembered thinking as he emerged unscathed, "I don't think these yellow devils have my number." Frank B. Miller Jr., an asphalt technician who had arrived on Wake just a week and a half earlier and worked in the "concrete laboratory" had entered his barracks a few minutes before twelve. "I heard what sounded like a lot of planes, so I thought I would have a look at them. Just as I got outside and saw nine bombers flying at about one thousand feet, I heard explosions over at the airport and machine gun fire from the planes. For a few seconds, I couldn't quite figure out what was happening—then I realized that they were Japanese. I lit out from the barracks and dived under a bush with machine gun bullets buzzing all around." When a second flight bore down on him from Peale, he "made a bee line" for another bush, losing a shoe and gouging his side on the coral. "After the rain everybody seemed dazed (including myself) and didn't seem to know quite what to do. For some reason or other I didn't feel very hungry so I skipped lunch." This account marked the beginning of Frank Miller's diary; many others also wrote down the shocking events of December 8, 1941, in diaries or letters they intended to send to loved ones later.[28]

Undetected by the four Wildcats of the VMF-211 war patrol that had climbed over the cloud cover, twenty-seven twin-engine Japanese attack bombers of the Chitose Air Group from the 24th Air Flotilla, based in the Marshalls, attacked Wake in a coordinated strike that commenced just before noon and was over in a matter of minutes. One group of nine bombers dropped hundred-pound fragmentation bombs on the airfield and sprayed the area with incendiary bullets, taking out seven of the eight exposed Wildcats on the ground and inflicting terrible carnage on the crews and pilots who scrambled to get the fighters off the ground or run for cover. Two twenty-five-thousand-gallon fuel tanks and a gas truck exploded and hundreds of fifty-gallon gasoline drums blew up along the airstrip. Two formations bombed and strafed Camp 2 with devastating effect. The third division had peeled off to approach from the west over Kuku Point, hitting south Wake before banking over the lagoon, heading directly for Peale. Bombs dropped on the Pan American facilities set fire to the hotel and numerous buildings. Machine guns cut into the hull of the Clipper at its berth and navy buildings under construction, and the bombers returned for another deadly pass. The fire from the antiaircraft guns of Batteries D on Peale and E on Wake was futile; .50-caliber guns across the atoll and individual rifles aimed at the bombers in desperation. By the time the VMF-211 war patrol caught sight of smoke rising through the cloud cover it was too late to chase the attackers. From start to finish, the opening salvo on Wake Island lasted fewer than fifteen minutes. Their bombs and ammunition spent, the pilots grinned, waggled the wings of their unscathed bombers, and regrouped for the return trip south. Complacency and underestimation of Japanese capabilities that had been reinforced in the prewar months had slowed Wake's response time and allowed the enemy to escape in full force.[29]

The destruction and carnage at the airport stunned Lieutenant Kinney, one of the Wildcat pilots landing after the attack. The lack of radar and revetments, the roar of the surf drowning out the enemy's approach, and planes on the ground "like targets in a carnival shooting gallery" all contributed to the shocking destruction, but Kinney acknowledged the skill behind the attack. "The Japanese pilots began that day to disprove the stereotypes we had of them as being only mediocre aviators and so nearsighted that they could not hit their targets." On Wake, a general contempt for Japanese capabilities had lulled many into a false sense of security. Neither mediocre nor nearsighted, Japanese pilots had hit all eight Wildcats on the ground, seven of which burned beyond salvage. Tents, oxygen bottles, tools, and spare parts were destroyed; burning gasoline threw up walls of flame and thick black smoke billowed from the aboveground fuel dump. Worst of all was the human toll. Over half of the fifty-five ground crew members and six of the squadron's pilots were either grievously wounded or had died violently. Men rushed to pull the casualties from the fires and load them onto trucks for the hospital.[30]

On Peale the Pan American conflagration burned hopelessly out of control. Stunned civilian workers emerged from their hiding places, rushing to help where they could or making their way across the bridge to camp. Most of the Clipper passengers, crew, and employees had thrown themselves flat on the ground outdoors or into ditches and drainpipes, as did Captain Hamilton, who had just returned from the airfield with a reconnaissance flight plan for the Clipper. Bleeding and stunned, manager John Cooke turned to the hotel, "badly battered and one wing was already ablaze. . . . Every Pan Am Building had been hit and several were burning. Power was gone and radio was gone, all was gone. The station had been rendered useless." The attack killed ten Pan American Chamorro employees, cut to shreds or burned to death in the fires that destroyed the Pan Air complex. Scorched survivors struggled to pull the charred bodies of their friends and kin out of the inferno and gingerly placed the injured in vehicles for transport to the hospital. Dan Teters and other supervisors directed the efforts to confine the Pan Air fires and keep them from spreading to flammable materials stored nearby. Out in the lagoon the shaken dredge crew abandoned their lunch and poured off the *Columbia* onto a rescue tug that sped them to the shore of Peale where they hurried past the carnage on the hotel grounds and joined the swelling flow of contractors making their way to Camp 2.[31]

Commander Cunningham gave permission for the bullet-scarred but still airworthy *Philippine Clipper* to evacuate Pan Air passengers and American employees. Employees and volunteers gutted the plane of mail sacks, luggage, and two hundred tires intended for the Flying Tigers of the America Volunteer Group in China, and tore out the furniture to make way for a maximum passenger load. The crew booted off two Chamorro stowaways to join their fellows near the burning hotel. It was an "unfortunate time to draw the color line," Cunningham later observed. Captain Hamilton supervised the loading of passengers and a score of white employees with nothing but the clothes on their backs and the American flag that had flown over the Pan American Wake Island office. Crewmembers made last-minute offers for rides to contractors standing nearby, but all declined with casual bravado. Three non-contractor American civilians missed the flight: Pan American employee Waldo Raugust, government auditor Herman Hevenor, and Edward Clancy, a Liberty Mutual safety engineer. Across the stricken atoll men turned from their grim work to watch the overloaded Clipper make two unsuccessful runs down the lagoon before it finally lifted free on the third try and lumbered low over the steely sea, leaving Wake behind.[32]

The astonishing toll of death and destruction, injuries and damage, revealed itself as the day passed on Wake. The burst bubble of American superiority compounded the shock: no one expected the Japanese to be capable of such destructive precision and power. Hour after hour, volunteers brought the dead and wounded to the hospital in Camp 2 where the two doctors, Shank and Kahn, their assistants, and many volunteers, worked all through the day and night. Among the hospital volunteers were Frank Miller and two other recent arrivals who "were given the job of carrying all the dead men from the hospital to the icebox in the rear of the mess hall. Some of the fellows were burned to a crisp—others were mangled and torn by the shrapnel. That afternoon we put in 23 dead men," he wrote. Outside, dead fish floated on the lagoon; dead birds littered the beaches.[33]

After the initial attack many contractors stepped up to actively aid in the defense of Wake. Eighty to ninety—some veterans of the World War, some familiar with guns from hunting in the woods near home, others simply wanting to help any way they could—gathered in front of the mess hall and marines trucked them to Camp 1. Others threw bedrolls together and set out down the road on foot. Under direction of marine officers the new arrivals moved cases of ammunition from the marine storehouse and buried them in the brush; they piled cases in stacks twenty feet high and covered them with coral; they trucked three-inch shells to the batteries on the points. Those who knew their way around a gun were assigned to positions at the .30-caliber machine guns on the south beach while others took crash courses in breaking down and reassembling rifles and machine guns. Sixteen civilians stepped up to serve as an all-civilian gun crew for one of Battery D's three-inch guns under the leadership of Sergeant Walter A. Bowsher. "Within a short time they became a close knit unit able to cope with the enemy as the rest of the battery," Bowsher wrote of the civilians, more than half of whom were surveyors.[34]

Later that day, Dan Teters called a meeting in the civilian mess where he and Commander Cunningham addressed hundreds of workers, many growing angry over the navy's failure to evacuate them at the onset of war. Cunningham had sent coded messages of the Wake attack to Pearl Harbor and had received orders to conduct unrestricted warfare. However, no orders came through to cease the construction project that was suddenly even more vital to the war effort. Doing the math, the men calculated that a rescue and relief mission would take at least five days steaming at full speed from Honolulu. Dozer crews filled bomb craters on the runway and roads before dark, and the staff made plans to resume construction work on runways and the ship channel in the morning. The civilian mess geared up to feed the men outdoors.[35]

As the day waned civilian volunteers continued to augment defenses by roughing up the airfield with bulldozers and helping plant dynamite charges to preclude enemy landing. They anchored a dynamite-loaded steel barge in the access channel between Wake and Wilkes. The civilians took their dinner outside the mess hall that night and Teters passed the word that they should sleep outside of the barracks and await further orders. Men pulled mattresses out into the brush and scratched out depressions for protection. Nervous sentries patrolled the beaches and exhausted hospital staff worked through the night. It seemed as if only the dead slept that night on Wake Island.

THE NEWS: DECEMBER 7, 1941

Katherine and Donna Olson spent a lazy Sunday, sharing the newspaper in the quiet apartment in Pullman. A telephone call came through from a friend at about five in the afternoon. How were they, and did they know anything more about the Pacific? Quickly they turned on the radio; before they could hear what the announcer was saying, a telegram came to the door for Donna from another friend: "Keep your chin up, kid." Then the stunning news filled the room: the Japanese had attacked Pearl Harbor, Pacific islands, the Philippines, Hong Kong, and Shanghai. Through the night, they remained hovered over the radio and the next morning, like hundreds of other families, wrote letters. "Dear Theod," wrote Donna, "just as I was scratching December, the bulletin came over the radio that Frankie had just signed the paper making the U.S. officially at war." She told him how everyone on campus that morning "wants to know gee whiz is Ted out there?" Clutching a damp handkerchief, Katherine wrote to Harry in care of friends in Honolulu, and to Ted on Wake. "We have listened to the radio for 24 hours straight but have no definite word from Wake Island so are very anxious for your welfare," she wrote her son. "I will write more later—this is just to let you know that we are thinking of you and love you so much."[36]

In Reno, Joe McDonald's father sat down that night at 8:20 p.m. to write to his son. McDonald Sr. had been busy through the day putting out an extra of the Reno newspaper with the day's stunning news. "The A.P. carried a report, which originated in Shanghai, that the Japs had taken over Wake Island peacefully and as yet there has been no confirmation. . . . so we are much concerned." He continued with news about Nevada men already in the Pacific and more preparing to enlist, but included plenty of local gossip. Finally, at 9:30 p.m., "a dispatch just came in saying both Midway and Wake were bombed by the Japs but there were no details. Well Good Night, God Bless You and good luck. We are saying a prayer for your safety." These and other heartfelt letters never made it to Wake Island.[37]

CHAPTER 10

SHOCK WAVES

ONE FULL SPIN

As the troubled globe spun, the sun rose again on Japan, a nation electrified by its successes and a military power fully engaged in its East Asian and Pacific offensive strategies. Morning light crept across the time zones of Siberia, crested the Ural Mountains, and revealed the ravaged eastern front in the Soviet Union. It spread out over the cities and forests of occupied Europe. British bombers aimed into the sunrise to target German cities with their payloads; American sailors manned guns in convoys of ships as night gave way to gray on the Atlantic. In Washington, D.C., lights blazed in government and military offices as they had through the night, windows tightly shuttered against the rising sun.

Across the United States printing presses churned out morning newspapers with monstrous headlines, telephones delivered busy signals, and telegraphs clattered nonstop. In houses and apartments across the nation families with loved ones in the Pacific ended the long, sleepless night to resume their quest for information and reassurance. As the skies brightened over cities and towns on the West Coast nervous civil defense volunteers trained binoculars on the western horizon and naval bases stood on high alert. The carrier *Saratoga* arced out of San Diego Bay in the morning light, bristling with aircraft, including a fighter squadron of Brewster Buffalos that was destined for the defense of Wake Island. The mainland-bound *Lurline*, still many hours from San Francisco Bay, zigzagged on the rolling Pacific. No sunlight penetrated its hastily painted-over portholes, behind which huddled hundreds of frightened passengers in life jackets. As the rays of the morning sun kissed the steep green mountainsides of Oahu residents still in yesterday's clothes peeked out on quiet, flower-filled streets that belied a night of terror spent anticipating the Japanese invasion. Frantic rescue efforts continued in the burning wreckage of Pearl Harbor where men could be heard pounding on the steel plates of stricken ships.

Morning reached Midway Island on the northwestern tip of the Hawaiian chain, still smoldering from Sunday night's drive-by shelling that had caused minor damage, but left no casualties. Captain Hamilton aimed the battle-scarred Clipper into the sun on the last leg of its perilous journey from Wake to Hawaii. Underneath, a Wake-bound navy tug had reversed its course to return to Honolulu, but across the international date line the *Burrows* continued steaming toward Wake with its vital cargo. Just after 0700 on December 8 Captain Dierdorff had assembled officers and crew and read, "Hostilities have commenced. Japan has attacked Pearl Harbor." The *Burrows* continued west on a zigzag course. Farther west the sturdy tug *Arthur Foss*, hastily slathered in oil-darkened paint, plodded eastward towing two empty barges and, like other American vessels and navy ships in the dangerous Pacific waters, under strict radio silence.[1]

Hundreds of miles southwest of the tug the rising sun glinted off the sides of heavily loaded Japanese bombers lifting off a runway in the Marshall Islands and pointing north towards Wake, some six hundred miles away. As the new day dawned on Wake itself, bleary eyes scanned the clear morning sky for the dreaded enemy or friendly reinforcements. Down to three fighters, the severely crippled Wake air squadron prepared for dawn patrol and the shore batteries regrouped under full alert. CPNAB supervisors and foremen tried to organize work crews as bedraggled men emerged from the brush. Frank Miller and fellow newcomers Joseph T. McDonald of Cody, Wyoming, and Lester Winegarden of Hemet, California, rose from mattresses near the beach, ate breakfast in the open, and reported to the hospital to help. Miller noted in his diary that seven more men had died during the night and the volunteers added these bodies to the icebox morgue. Soon the sun was rising over the far western Pacific island groups and, once again, the home islands of Japan. In one full turn the world had entered a new era of human history that would be marked by the terrible necessity of numbering its world wars.[2]

The surprise attack on Pearl Harbor horrified the people of the United

States and they collectively turned toward the Pacific in shock and indigna-
tion. President Roosevelt spoke before Congress, declaring December 7 "a
date which will live in infamy," and a nearly unanimous vote promised ret-
ribution. For many Americans, the shocking attack on Pearl Harbor represented a direct attack on the resource-rich and technologically superior
United States, which reinforced American perceptions of the Japanese as
reckless and irrational.[3] Four days after the first shot, Germany and Italy
declared war on the United States. In short order, nations aligned with the
Axis or the Allies, and military strategists coordinated plans. Britain,
stretched thin as it bombed German towns, fought Rommel in North Africa,
and lost battleships in the Mediterranean, eagerly awaited the American
implementation of the Europe-first strategy. Axis troops had mowed through
continental Europe and puppet regimes governed in occupied countries, but
the German Army faltered at the outskirts of Moscow in the face of a determined Soviet counterattack and the fierce Russian winter. Still, the German
siege continued to hold Leningrad in its grip as an estimated three thousand
Soviet citizens in the city died of starvation or disease each day. In Eastern
Europe and the occupied western Soviet republics German troops and technicians methodically killed Jews and other population groups deemed unde-
sirable. Behind the screen of war the death tolls mounted into the hundreds
of thousands marked by hastily filled trenches, piles of clothing and shoes,
and the bitter smoke of incinerated flesh rising to the sky.

Capitalizing on its gains throughout the Pacific and Southeast Asia on
December 7/8, Japan continued to attack foreign-held territories before the
Americans, British, and Dutch could regroup. Strategically important and
rich in resources, these islands, ports, and regions in the Far East offered a
productive, defensive perimeter for the Japanese Empire. The Greater East
Asia Co-Prosperity Sphere, much of it taken by force, promised to feed and
fuel the Japanese military machine indefinitely. In the coming days of
December Japan quickly captured Guam with an invasion of six thousand
troops against a token defense force of five hundred, armed with nothing
heavier than .30-caliber machine guns. Japanese bombers swept over the key
Philippine island of Luzon, cutting General MacArthur's Flying Fortresses
to shreds where, despite ample warning, they sat parked on Clark Field, and
pummeling the Cavite naval base, destroying all torpedo reserves for U.S.
naval forces in the Far East. Tens of thousands of American and Philippine
troops retreated toward the Bataan Peninsula. Japanese forces invaded Burma

and Borneo and drove the British back on multiple fronts. In the face of the crushing string of Allied defeats and the bleak, black headlines, early press reports sometimes pulled out the familiar, prewar racist bravado, claiming, for example, that "Japanese firepower was so poor that soldiers on Bataan were actually fielding mortar shells with baseball mitts" and other tales of fictional heroics.[4]

PEARL HARBOR AND HONOLULU

The day after the attack on Pearl Harbor, George Youmans, Harry Olson, and others from the operating base anxiously awaited the arrival of the *Philippine Clipper* from Wake. After a quick refueling at Midway in the dark Captain Hamilton approached Oahu in the afternoon and was surprised to receive orders to land in Pearl Harbor. When the Clipper finally settled onto the smoking harbor the men were whisked away to be debriefed by navy and Pan American officials. The following morning over breakfast, John Cooke related the harrowing details of the attack on Wake and the perilous journey of the Clipper. George Youmans relayed the tale to Harry Morrison and added, "We will have more and authentic news on Wake and Midway later, but so far, what I have written is the best or rather the only information I have. The Navy is giving out *nothing* regarding any of the events of the past few days but there will be plenty to tell later on when all the facts are known. They surely caught us asleep at every point. Not a shot was fired at Wake, as the gunners were all having dinner. The same applies at many other points of attack. Dastardly as the attacks were, there will be some pertinent questions to be answered later, and the answers will be hard to make." Harry recognized an opportunity to get a personal note out to Katherine and quickly jotted a letter for Captain Hamilton to mail from the mainland.[5]

Moana Hotel, Honolulu, December 9, 1941
Dear Katherine:
A Clipper that survived the attack on Wake came in last night. The Captain said they may take off for the coast today and he will take this personally for me. We can't wire. When he left down there Ted was alright. I think he has a reasonable chance. I can't tell you what happened here except that we all are not afraid and I am confident we will come out O.K. I don't know as yet what we will do on our contracts

but don't worry. Will advise you further when I can. Don't write. I can't give you an address.

Love, Harry

CPNAB officials knew that among their remote island base projects, Wake, Guam, Cavite, and possibly Midway had been attacked by the enemy and that the other islands remained vulnerable. However, the navy kept such a tight lid on information and communication that the contractors could do little but wait. The most pressing operation remained Pearl Harbor, where the operating base, located directly across from Ford Island, stayed open around the clock to supply workers and equipment. Most office personnel had made their way to the base by Monday. "The scene was horrendous— water was burning because oil from the battleships had caught fire. They were still bringing in bodies, both dead and alive," recalled Dorothy Mitchell, who worked in the purchasing office. Clerks and typists filled wastebaskets with sand in case of fire and raced to type purchase orders for Midway, Wake, and Johnston Islands before the Japanese returned. Outside the office window they could see a destroyer headed out to sea to protect the harbor, maneuvering "back and forth like a car emerging from a tight place."[6]

Japanese bombers had hit Kaneohe and other installations on Oahu, but Pearl Harbor's terrible plight required immediate aid. The contractors operated the Red Hill mess hall continuously and brought hot meals to men working feverishly in the navy yard. The navy gave the Red Hill underground fuel storage project "No. 1 priority, after essential repairs are made of the damage in the yard," Youmans reported to Morrison. Red Hill returned to round the clock operations on December 9, with shift adjustments to fit the curfew travel prohibitions between sunset and sunrise, and Red Hill welders, compressor men, blasters, and pipe fitters also worked on emergency assignments around the navy yard.[7]

In a job assignment that they could not have imagined, the contractors excavated trenches in the Nuannu Cemetery for burials until it was full and then continued that heartrending but vital work west of the high trestle they had built for waste material from the underground tanks. Deep trenches on high ground, covered with fill from the low ground, held the bodies. "And it is a sad and terrible sight to have to do this," wrote Youmans. "Most of the bodies are burned to a crisp from the terrific heat from the burning ships. The odor is terrible and the flies are there by the millions."[8]

On navy orders the contractors had discharged all workers of Japanese ethnicity immediately following the attacks and confiscated their badges. This reduced the CPNAB workforce substantially, but was of a piece with the general fear of sabotage and spies that pervaded Honolulu. When orders came to the contractors to organize a large labor force for "special work," CPNAB offices on the mainland scrambled to find seven hundred men, primarily carpenters, to make up for the skilled Japanese workers who were now barred from the navy yard and military reservations. The loss of local Japanese labor put additional pressure on employee housing and CPNAB sped up housing and camp construction to accommodate the thousands of new employees that would be coming from the mainland over the next few weeks.

The CPNAB operation grew from eight to ten companies with the addition of Dillingham Construction and Pacific Bridge Company. Pacific Bridge, under Jack Graham, would aid in the salvage operations in the harbor. This "new work" received the highest priority behind the rescue of the few remaining surviving sailors and the heartbreaking recovery of the dead and dismembered body parts that surfaced as the days went on. The work entailed untangling and raising the damaged and flooded warships in Pearl Harbor so that tugs could move them into navy yard facilities for urgent repairs and return to service. The contractors sped up completion of Dry Dock 2, which soon began receiving ships with hull damage from the attack. The first casualty to arrive was the *Helena*, a light cruiser damaged by a torpedo. However, the navy and contractors did not move as a well-oiled machine. Time after time the navy requisitioned equipment and men only to have the civilians stand around or send them back while they tried to operate the equipment themselves, "with the usual result." George Youmans complained that the navy "ignored the contractors' requests to simply say what they wanted done and let them do it."[9]

In the first few days Harry split his time between helping out at the operating base and comforting his friends' wives in town. With increasing frequency he and Dr. Barrett joined Eudelle Russell and others at her small apartment on Uluniu Street in Waikiki where Mae and June Hokanson also stayed. Frequent visitors included the parents of Ted's best pal on Wake, Roger Smalley. The apartment was crowded, but, like others in Honolulu, they gladly traded elbowroom for group security. Under martial law Honolulu residents found their lives bound by constant blackouts, curfews, and censorship. The military and many civilians suspected "fifth columnists" among the Japanese and Japanese American residents who comprised 40 percent of the population. Fears of internal sabotage, collusion in the Japanese attacks, and an impending invasion gripped many and shattered community relations. Rumors of spying and trickery rippled through the population. One of the most popular targets was a December 5 newspaper advertisement by a silk importer for "Fashions by the Yard" that many, including Eudelle and Mrs. Smalley, suspected hid warnings of the coming Japanese raid. Harry, in daily contact with the operating base, kept the others apprised of any news from or about the men on Wake.[10]

WAKE UNDER SIEGE: DECEMBER 9–11

On Wake, the civilian workers resumed hauling mattresses and belongings from the barracks and gathered lumber and canned food for dugouts in the brush through the morning of December 9. Pilots flew in from the dawn patrol and marines and civilian volunteers manned the gun batteries. Work continued on airfield repairs and revetment construction including roofed structures to enable nighttime aircraft repair in blackout conditions. Despite the terrible human and material toll on VMF-211 the day before, air defenses remained vital to both early detection and engagement of the enemy. Lieutenant Kinney led a dedicated and talented mixed crew of military and civilian mechanics and jacks of other trades to sustain the daytime reconnaissance flights and combat air patrols for the remaining operational Wildcats. Elsewhere work continued on improvement of gun emplacements and defensive works, command posts, camouflage, foxholes and dugouts, and a secure communications network linking commands and defensive positions.

Just before noon a marine sentry on the water tower spotted a formation of bombers approaching from the east and alerted the communications network. Gunners assumed their positions and the combat air patrol rose to engage the twenty-seven bombers, quickly claiming Wake's first kill. As soon as the enemy came in range Battery E opened fire. Undeterred, the bombers struck Peacock Point, killing one marine instantly near Battery A, and swept north over Camp 2 where they unleashed their full fury. Civilian volunteers Miller and Winegarden had paused outside the hospital door, picking up water cans, when they heard the planes; McDonald was inside, talking with Dr. Shank. Suddenly, machine guns strafed the camp buildings and panicked civilians took off running across the open ground. "Winegarden ran one way and I lit out straight for the beach, diving under a bush about twenty yards from the hospital," Miller wrote. "I knew they were getting close and thought then and there that my number was up." Bombs landed on civilian barracks, navy barracks, a gas dump, the squadron storehouse, and, in one horrifying moment, the hospital in Camp 2, which was filled with casualties from the previous day. "About 40 of us began carrying out the wounded and throwing anything loose through the windows—save everything possible. In about 15 minutes it was burned to the ground." Miller looked for his friends, hoping that they had escaped somehow and would rendezvous at their place in the bushes. "They weren't there."[11]

Between the night toll and the bombing attack a dozen military personnel and fifteen civilian workers died that day including Winegarden and McDonald. Also among those killed in the hospital bombing were patients Robert Yriberry, a valued secretary to the superintendents, who had suffered shrapnel wounds in the first attack, carpenter Louis Adamson, mourned by his father who was also on Wake, and carpenter Frank Cerny, a father who left a son on Wake. "We lost quite a number of good men," Swede reflected bitterly. Fortunately the doctors and trained nurses were not among the casualties in the hospital. "Those guys know what they're shooting at and they're shooting straight," Pete Russell wrote in his diary. "Hospital terrible. . . . The toll must be around 60 by now. Moved what hospital facilities we could to magazines 10 & 13. All patients to there. Out till 3:00 A.M. Fell into a shelter with Dan and Swede." The magazines, two of four reinforced concrete structures flanking the unfinished north-south runway on the east shore of Wake and which were intended for artillery ammunition, bombs, and other high explosives and, served as make-shift hospitals for Drs. Shank and Kahn for the duration of the siege.[12]

The second attack had opened on the three-inch antiaircraft battery on Wake indicating that the Japanese had pinpointed the strong point and would return for more. Although it had been laboriously emplaced the battery was moveable and Devereux ordered its displacement several hundred yards to the west under the cover of night. Civilians worked shoulder to shoulder with marines to move the heavy guns through the night. Subsequent nights would see similar gun movements, which involved details of crane operators and hundreds of civilian sandbaggers. The following day, December 10, the expected attack arrived in late morning. Kinney's mechanics had also labored round the clock to put a fourth fighter into operation and Wake's scrappy air force rose to intercept the twenty-six Japanese bombers. Captain Hank Elrod slammed the door on two of the bombers, taking them out before they reached the atoll and thereby earning his nickname, "Hammering Hank." Below, antiaircraft batteries stood ready, including Battery E in its new position. A dummy replacement in the original position drew enemy fire, as anticipated. The bombers inflicted only light damage on Wake and Peale, but hammered Wilkes. The contractors' 125-ton dynamite dump near the new channel blew sky-high in a stunning explosion that set off ammunition and damaged guns at the nearby batteries, killing one and wounding several, and torching all of the brush on Wilkes. In San Francisco, thousands of miles to the east, *Philippine Clipper* Captain John Hamilton was telling reporters that in their initial attack the Japanese had demonstrated "an economy of action at Wake. . . . The enemy apparently knew the desired objectives and proceeded directly for them." As the days went by on Wake this continued to be proven painfully true during daily Japanese bombing raids.[13]

On December 11 the Japanese entered the second phase of their assault on Wake. While the Chitose Air Group "softened up" the atoll with three days of blistering air attacks the Wake Invasion Force made its way north from the Marshalls under the flag of Rear Admiral Sadamichi Kajioka. The task force consisted of three cruisers, six destroyers, two transports and other support. Close to five hundred men of the Special Naval Landing Force prepared for the amphibious landing. The invasion force steamed toward Wake, buffeted by heavy winds and high seas. A sharp-eyed night patrol detected the approaching surface force at about 3:00 A.M. and alerted Major Devereux.[14]

Devereux calculated that Wake stood its best chance by holding fire until the invaders were well within range of the shore guns. All battle stations stood ready in the dark. Two hours later, as dawn broke, the lead ships reached eight thousand yards south of Peacock Point, turned westward and, raising no reaction from the quiet, dark atoll, opened fire along the south shore as they maneuvered broadside. Shells hit the fuel farm at Wilkes channel setting oil tanks ablaze; the cruisers and transports closed range, firing with impunity at their prize. In dugouts across the atoll civilians roused at the noise. "About 6 a.m. shells started falling wildly all over the Island. Don't know whether it's a sea battle or an attempt to level this bunch of coral," Frank Miller wrote.

A naval ensign "next door" to the dugout gave the civilians an update. As the day brightened, Miller resumed scribbling. "Here they come," he wrote. "It's noisy again but none of the bombs seem to land very near the holes. They don't stay here very long and we're still alive and kicking."[15]

Still the Wake guns held their fire until the lead cruiser reached about 4,500 yards due south of Peacock Point. At last, Devereux gave the order for the five-inch batteries to commence firing. The shore guns and range finders had suffered damage in previous attacks, but Battery A on Peacock Point now threw off camouflage, opened fire, and hit the cruiser (the task force's flagship), which raced away, returning fire to no effect. Battery L on Wilkes fired on multiple ships in its field, including destroyers, transports, and other cruisers. One destroyer took a hit straight on, exploded, and sank with all hands. Under fire on Peale, Battery B answered another Japanese destroyer approaching from the west. With one shore gun disabled the battery nonetheless concentrated fire on the target and scored a hit, sending the destroyer smoking in retreat. By 7:00 A.M., the entire Japanese task force had turned in retreat. The flagship smoked away from Wake, visibly listing, shooting back all the while until it disappeared out of range.

The four armed and airworthy Wildcats had taken to the skies before the surface force came in range, found no enemy carrier or air cover for the invasion attempt, and now mercilessly harried the retreating task force, repeatedly returning to the airfield to refuel and rearm with hundred-pound bombs and .50-caliber ammunition. In ten sorties Wake's tiny air force bombed and strafed the retreating ships, damaging at least two more light cruisers, a transport, and a patrol boat, and thirty miles southwest of Wake sank one destroyer outright. Japanese losses in the first attempted land invasion included at least two ships sunk, four heavily damaged, and several hundred dead. Wake counted two Wildcats damaged, one irreparably in a forced landing on the south beach, some shell damage to shore batteries and installations, and four wounded personnel.

From shell-passer to sandbagger to cook, every civilian who aided the efforts on Wake that day shared in the marines' well-deserved sense of pride. Watching "the show," Swede recalled the reaction to a direct hit. "The gun crew went wild, 'We got 'em! We GOT 'EM!' they shouted just like kids after shooting their first deer." Pete, too, had a ringside seat on the running board of a pickup truck. With the victory, even the hundreds of civilians who could take credit for nothing at all joined in the celebration of collective prowess. Their victory did not erase the horrors of the past three days, but it had a cathartic effect across Wake. Commander Cunningham radioed his report to Pearl, and the news of Wake's success quickly spread. Dan Teters sent a garbled radio message to George Youmans that they were still holding out, still in possession of the island, but subject to constant attacks. They had sustained "75 casualties (this means both dead and wounded)" and requested evacuation. It was unclear at Pearl if the number included both civilians and military.[16]

The defenders did not have long to rest on their laurels: about 10:00 A.M., thirty bombers appeared from the north for their "daily milk run on Wake." The two serviceable Wildcats were aloft on combat patrol and quickly engaged the enemy, shooting two down and damaging another. The antiaircraft batteries on Peale and Wake took out another bomber and sent three smoking, but Japanese bombs pelted both islands, hitting uncomfortably close to the strongpoint on Toki Point. Devereux ordered personnel and work crews to prepare to remove Battery D from its emplacement to a position some distance to the east on Peale after dark. A large night crew assembled for the job. The displacement was complete just before dawn, the three-inch guns dug in and sandbagged in view of Peale channel, ready for whatever the new day brought.[17]

THE WAKE RESCUE PLAN

In the aftermath of the disastrous December attacks in the Pacific naval strategists were forced to redraw war plans. War had come from outside the box: the attack on Pearl Harbor sorely undermined Pacific Fleet strength. Marines, not even close to optimal numbers for the amphibious attacks outlined in war plans, were tied down defending the islands against the expected Japanese invasion. On December 9 the Joint Board altered the Rainbow 5 strategy, ordering Admiral Kimmel to eliminate offensive operations against the Marshalls and Carolines, as well as western Pacific operations in support of Commonwealth holdings. Reinforcement of the Philippines would not be possible despite the crushing blows dealt by Japanese forces there. The defenders would have to hold out as long as they could and "hamper and delay the Japanese advance" from Bataan as called for in the old War Plan Orange. (As an observer had warned back in 1898 the United States had given "hostages to fortune" by claiming such a distant colony where military sacrifices and difficulties would be inevitable.) The immediate Pacific strategy was limited to protection of the Hawaiian Islands, the West Coast, southern shipping lanes to Australia, and communications with Allies in the Far East. Wake Island alone poked well outside the Hawaiian defensive perimeter and within land-based bombing range of the Japanese mandates. Likewise, only Wake could provide the portal to future resumption of offensive naval strategy as outlined in War Plan Orange. Admiral Kimmel initiated plans to reinforce Wake, hold the island, and complete the most essential dredging and construction to make it a viable base for future operations into the Marshalls. While offensive options had slipped through his fingers with the disastrous events of the previous days, Wake might provide the opportunity to prove that the Pacific Fleet still packed a powerful punch. The problem was how to deliver it.[18]

Reinforcement of Wake required men, planes, materiel, and the wherewithal to get them there as soon as possible. Fortunately none of the three aircraft carriers stationed in the Pacific had been in Pearl Harbor at the time of the attack and all ultimately figured in Kimmel's plan to reinforce and hold Wake, which called for the carrier *Saratoga,* en route from San Diego, to form the nucleus of the task force to reinforce Wake. Task Force 14 included three heavy cruisers, nine destroyers, an oiler, and a seaplane tender converted for troop transport. Kimmel formed another task force around the *Lexington*: its mission was to divert attention from the relief force by striking south of Wake at a Japanese base in the Marshalls and if needed to provide support and cover for the *Saratoga* group. Admiral Halsey and the *Enterprise* would lead a third task force, to operate southwest of Midway during the operation to cover that flank.[19]

On December 10 two hundred marines of the 4th Defense Battalion at Pearl Harbor received orders to prepare to embark for an unnamed destination, which many guessed at once, and quickly began preparing weapons and loading equipment including radar units onto the transport USS *Tangier* for the assignment. However, the *Saratoga* was still several days east of Pearl, so the marines returned to their defensive positions in the navy yard while Kimmel's staff and Admiral Bloch fine-tuned the plan. Pearl Harbor sent a message to Wake via army radio inquiring how many planes Wake could accommodate, and Cunningham replied, "two squadrons now." The commander shared the encouraging inquiry with others on Wake.[20]

CPNAB also got wind of the operation in the planning stages. Captain Bruns told George Youmans that the navy was considering sending supply ships to Midway and Wake. Bruns asked Youmans for an estimate of the number of contractors it would take to carry on "certain items of work" and to feed the various armed forces at Wake, Midway, Johnston, and Palmyra, cautioning that they could not have very many on any of the projects. "Of course," Youmans wrote to Harry Morrison, "you realize how asinine such talk is." Youmans noted that the navy wanted complex projects completed that required coordination of numerous skills and classifications of men accomplished with a minimum number and Bruns proposed to tell the contractors how many men they would be allowed, without regard to the projects or necessities, much less the casualties that might be encountered. "It just doesn't make any sense at all to me or any of the rest of us," Youmans wrote. That same night Bruns called Youmans out to Pearl Harbor to continue the discussion, as well as other matters including work on freeing up some of the damaged ships in Pearl Harbor. With a police pass and headlights painted blue Youmans negotiated roads filled with military trucks bristling with rifles. It was "a precarious journey at best," he admitted, but nothing compared to what his flock on Wake was going through.[21]

NEWS AND RUMORS: THE FIRST WEEK OF WAR

On the mainland the December 12 newspaper headline jumped off the page: "Wake Island Holds," the first positive news that family members had heard about Wake. "The garrison on tiny Wake Island . . . has repulsed four separate enemy attacks and . . . sank one light cruiser and one destroyer by air action. . . . A resumption of the attack and a probable landing attempt is expected." At once heartening and frightening the article at least dispelled the sparse, discouraging news of the past few days. President Roosevelt himself had despaired of the remote island's fate in his speech on December 9: "The reports from Guam and Wake and Midway Islands are still confused, but we must be prepared for the announcement that all these three outposts have been seized." Newspapers carried subsequent articles with similarly disheartening statements. An Associated Press report "compiled from official and unofficial accounts" had noted the "capture of the United States island of Wake." A Reuter's dispatch from Shanghai reported that "Wake Island had been occupied by the Japanese" and that it had been "accomplished peaceably." Tokyo radio reported both Guam and Wake "under the Japanese flag." Now, finally, there came the welcome evidence that beleaguered Wake was still in American hands. Confirmation came the next day that "Valiant

Marines Hold Tiny Isles" of Wake and Midway, although "it was feared that a large number of construction workers may have been captured on the island." The families of the Wake men could do little but ride the roller coaster of emotions that such accounts produced.[22]

Katherine Olson was one of hundreds who had immediately written or called Harry Morrison and the Morrison-Knudsen offices in Boise for information following the initial attack. The next day, she received two letters in the mail, one written by Ted on Wake, and Harry's letter with the cryptic note indicating that he had taken an unexpected vacation to Honolulu. From San Francisco, Morrison replied to Katherine that he understood Olson had come to Honolulu, but was unsure if he was still there or if he had returned to Wake. Morrison sent a cablegram to George Youmans, asking him to locate Harry and "ask him to contact his wife immediately at Pullman Washington." With Washington's "refusal to give out details," Morrison apologized that he was "unable to give you prompt and reliable information concerning the welfare of your husband and son." Katherine soon received her husband's note sent via Captain Hamilton and the shot-up Clipper, and a radiogram from Honolulu early the following week: "TED STILL OK I AM WORKING HERE, HARRY OLSON" [23]

Besieged by inquiries from families anxious for the safety of the men on the islands, Harry Morrison and his staff sent many similar messages to other family members as the days went by. First word had come through from Honolulu "that damage is terrific but that the personnel of all associates are safe and sound on the island of Oahu." From California, Morrison approved a radio and press announcement issued on December 9 from the Boise CPNAB Employment office. The announcement confirmed that there had been no employee casualties on Oahu; however, "regarding Wake Island, as well as the other outlying island [sic] beyond Honolulu, no information is available as yet other than radio and press dispatches which are identical with those received by the general public."[24]

In an AP report carried by newspapers across the nation on December 14 the isolated reference to construction workers appeared as an afterthought, nor was any mention made then or later during the siege of navy and army personnel on Wake. The navy released daily official reports regarding the U.S. Marines on Wake as that dark December wore on, and the papers headlined them with such stirring assertions as "Wake Beats off Japanese Raids: Devil Dogs Continue Staunch Defense of Island." Across the nation, Americans grasping for evidence of heroism in the aftermath of the disastrous first few days of war eagerly seized the story of the brave, battered defenders of Wake. "Send Us More Japs!" the cocky Americans were said to have replied when asked what they needed. The legend was borne aloft by millions who pinned the nation's hope on the defenders of a tiny patch of American coral in the middle of the Pacific Ocean. A swell of patriotic pride rippled across the nation and Marine Corps recruiting centers signed up hundreds of new enlistees. Meanwhile the families, friends, and fellows of the men on Wake held their breath, prayed, crossed their fingers, and clung to every scrap of news that they could find. Hollywood moguls began to talk about making a motion picture.[25]

Honolulu, Dec. 13, 1941

Dear Katherine:

This is another note by special private delivery. I know you all are worried and upset by all this business but there isn't much I can do to allay your fears. As I write this Wake Island is still holding out. A message from Dan last night said they were doing O.K.: that they had some 75 casualties without giving names. Somehow I feel that Ted is O.K. Everyone is so proud of the fight the fellows have made. Dan requested evacuation so we should know more in a couple weeks. George wanted me to go back [to Wake] last night. I declined with what politeness I could muster. I look to go to work here soon. Four of us have consolidated our resources. Two girls—wives of asst. supts. down there, Tom Barrett, the doctor who came in with me, and I have moved together. At present we live at Waikiki but we are going to move to a less congested district. The girls were so frightened to death Sunday. I pray you will never have that experience. This blackout business is nuts. The evening and nights are so long. There is so much I would like to say but can't. Now. The response and attitude of the people was magnificent. We have no shelters so everyone just stood outside and watched the show. We are going to win this war but it will take some doing. So far there are no definite plans. I will write at greater length when communications are opened again. Meanwhile don't worry. We are all caught in the tide of a stream we cannot breast so we must take what is our fate without flinching.

Love, Harry

On Sunday, December 14, George Youmans received a coded message from Wake that Dan Teters would transmit important information shortly. That afternoon a navy radiogram came through with the names of fourteen civilian employees killed to date, and Youmans forwarded the list to the Boise hiring office. Censorship forbade inclusion of the source of the casualties, but he hoped that the Boise office would glean the location by matching the names to project assignments. None of the families would be contacted until the Navy Department notified the next of kin.[26]

In Reno Joe McDonald's father again sat down to write to his son on Monday, December 15:

> *We watch the news constantly and listen to the radio for a bit of news about Wake Island. . . . The heroic stand the Marines are making will go down in history and we feel sure, if God has spared you, that you are doing your share to keep our flag flying on your tiny outpost. . . . There's nothing but brief reports through the Navy to buoy our hopes and to keep our spirits alive. We know that you can take care of yourself and will survive the ordeal if anyone does but sometimes it seems hopeless. . . . May God watch over you and all the other boys on that desolate place and may Christmas dawn brightly for you and all.*

Mr. McDonald did not know that "Joseph McDonald" was on the list of casualties just received by Youmans in Honolulu.[27]

CPNAB CHALLENGES

The Base Force Salvage Organization officially began work on December 14 to coordinate the multiple tasks of immediate Pearl Harbor salvage while sparing the navy yard for the work of repairing the fleet. The mission of the salvage organization was to raise as many ships as possible off the mud and deliver them a few hundred yards for repairs. George Youmans turned Harry Olson over to this work as they awaited word of Wake. With years of experience on the Columbia River dams, as well as the past year in the trying conditions of Wake Island, Harry brought valuable skills to the new job, which he began on December 15. Youmans noted, "The work to be done by Graham is work that Olson should fit into in good shape."[28]

In their Ford Island moorings damaged warships lay two abreast with the outer ship pressing the inner against the moorings like a vise. The salvage organization first targeted the ships that could be floated, repaired, and returned to service within a few days. Divers descended through the oil scum and filth on the surface into the inky darkness. After they welded patches to the hulls, workers pumped out the water and slowly floated the ships. Early in the operation the presence of high explosives and the release of deadly gasses were constant dangers, and a thick layer of oil floated on the water. To right listing ships the men built cofferdams and then pumped air in and water out. Tugs nudged and maneuvered the damaged ships apart, then quickly guided the freed ships to dry docks: no one knew how long they would stay buoyant. Harry worked long days with the divers and welders, planned cofferdam construction, and checked in as frequently as possible at the operating base for any news from Wake or the rescue mission. On December 20, he sent a brief telegram to Katherine: "TED STILL OKAY I WILL BE NOTIFIED IMMEDIATELY IF OTHERWISE HAVE A BIG JOB HERE, HARRY OLSON. 158 ULUNIU."[29]

The status of Midway, where 1,575 CPNAB contractors remained, was also a terrible question mark during these early days of the war. Exaggerated rumors as well as "credible reports" circulated that Midway had repulsed and annihilated a Japanese landing party of seven hundred Japanese, and endured continued bombardment. Several days after the initial attack, Marlyn Sheik and others managed to send cables from Midway, but included little detail about their circumstances. As with Wake, Morrison-Knudsen had no official news to answer the relatives who besieged the Boise office for word on the Midway men. "I know you realize the danger of giving out information based on nothing but rumors and word of mouth reports," Youmans wrote to Harry Morrison. "The belief here to-day however, is that both places are still holding out, but at what cost in lives, no one knows or if they know, they [the Navy] will not give it out." In fact, Midway was shelled only once during December, on the night of December 7, with minor damage. The "Japanese landing party" turned out to be several Chinese American laundrymen who, at the time of the attack, had been asleep in the parachute loft and ran out in fear with their blankets wrapped around them. They hid behind a sheet pile wall near the beach and, during a lull in the shelling, ran on toward the boathouse. A tugboat captain in the boathouse saw them coming through the dark and lit out for camp, yelling that the "Japs had landed." While conditions deteriorated on Midway as civilians and military waited for the real thing, their counterparts on Wake dealt with the real thing every day and night.[30]

In crippled Pearl Harbor, under the tightest security, a contingent of CPNAB men helped to organize and load the *Tangier* with available materials and supplies for the rescue and relief of the civilians on Wake Island. The transport would serve as the return ride for hundreds of evacuated contractors and all of the wounded, while the remainder of civilians would stay on the atoll to provide support for the troops and repair damage. On December 15, the *Saratoga* and its escorts entered Pearl Harbor, the sight of which stunned the crews, but they remained only long enough to refuel. That day, the *Tangier* departed for a head start with a slow fleet oiler and a destroyer escort as marines on the docks waved and yelled, "Goodbye and give 'em hell!" The rest of Task Force 14 under the command of Rear Admiral Frank Jack Fletcher followed the following day. Despite the secrecy of the mission, many watched and cheered from the docks as the massive carrier, cruisers, and destroyers left Pearl midday, December 16, bound for Wake Island.[31]

WAKE UNDER SIEGE: DECEMBER 12–21

As the days dragged by on Wake the men struggled to maintain their defenses and sanity. After the first two days the contractors attempted little work on the prewar construction projects. Dan Teters met regularly with Cunningham and other officers to coordinate civilian defense assistance. Earthmoving equipment and civilian details repaired roads, built dugouts in the brush and shelters at the guns, and moved and sandbagged guns at night. They began work on a large underground hospital dugout and underground communications facility. Saturday afternoon, December 13, Teters, Cunningham, and Devereux held a mass burial for approximately forty-five military personnel and civilians who had died to date. Several other bodies had been or would be buried where they fell. The remains were carried from the large reefer box in Camp 2 and laid in a freshly dug trench, by most accounts located near the east side of the airfield close to the main road. A civilian lay minister conducted a short service that included a bugler and firing squad, and then bulldozers filled in the mass grave as the sun went down across the lagoon.[32]

While some civilian volunteers contributed steadily to the defense effort on Wake, others volunteered only when pressed, or to be in line when the chow wagon showed up. As the days went by false alarms spooked many men making it difficult for Pete Russell to field work details. The majority remained in dugouts in the brush, awaiting further bombs, orders, or the

navy's rescue, and preferably the latter. "Many good men that work hard—
some dirty slackers," Pete wrote in his diary. Sometimes there were not
enough men for a work detail; other times too many volunteered and the
extras were sent back into the brush where they "missed out on the chow."
The contractors had by now abandoned all CPNAB work, but, despite the
regular meetings between Teters and the naval officers, no effort was made
to keep the civilians in their prewar work crews to aid the defense and provide some discipline and organization.[33]

As the siege rolled on into its second week millions of flies carried dysentery through the dugouts and rats ran rampant. The civilians retrieved
canned food that they had cached in the brush as a safety measure and
deposited the rusting cans in a dedicated dugout. Meals might be "canned
beans, sardines, tuna, fruit juice, candy bars," wrote Frank Miller in his diary.
"Bring on that steak." Chet Riebel, the chief steward, tried to ensure that all
the men had access to food, and civilian cooks prepared hot meals for the
gun batteries and various stops around the atoll: chili, bread, eggs, and coffee.
Operators tended the powerhouse and water distillations plants and many
truck drivers and mechanics stayed busy. Pete, Swede, and other supervisors
organized nightly work crews and tried to check on all of the civilians after
every bombing. Some of the men washed off a week's worth of grime in the
ocean water; others stayed put in their hot holes. Days and nights blurred
into an endless stream of fear and boredom. A few civilians and soldiers
retained shortwave radios and kept a tenuous link with the outside world,
but the scuttlebutt took on a life of its own as rumors multiplied as fast as
the flies.[34]

Despite the fact that on December 10 Captain Bruns had ordered cessation of work on the project, a few days later Commander Cunningham
received a message from Pearl: "Highly desirable continue channel dredging.
Advise feasibility under present conditions with existing equipment. Give
estimated date completion." After swallowing his outrage, Cunningham
responded first with details of yet another raid, followed by extensive damage
detail and an assessment of the perilous conditions that made such work
impossible. "Principle storehouse with spare parts and construction material
burned. Machine shop blacksmith shop garage destroyed. Fifty percent heavy
digging equipment, fifty percent transportation including trucks destroyed,
eighty percent diesel oil, majority dynamite destroyed." Daytime work was
limited to six hours maximum "due heavy raids which come without warn-

ing. Have no radar . . . Morale civilian workmen in general very low." On December 17, Admiral Bloch wrote a memo to CINCPAC that, in view of damage to machinery and loss of fuel, dredging work could not continue. "Accordingly, I am giving instructions to withdraw all civilian employees there except those necessary to run the utilities, do repair work, et cetera, in all about 250." It was the uncompleted channel, however, that marked the line between Wake's viability and liability. As soon as possible, work would have to resume on this vital component in the navy's war plans.[35]

Everyone on Wake held high hopes for reinforcement and rescue, but the navy could not risk a radio transmission to inform them of the top-secret mission. As Task Force 14 steamed toward Wake, marines and sailors prepared for arrival and the probability of performing their mission under enemy fire. They drilled on deck, sharpened bayonets, studied maps of the atoll, trained on the guns, listened to lectures about radar, and went over and over disembarkation and unloading scenarios that must accomplished with the greatest speed. The mission went ahead even as Admiral Kimmel was removed as CINCPAC on December 17 for his role in the December 7 debacle. Rear Admiral William S. Pye stepped in as interim chief pending the arrival of Adm. Chester W. Nimitz from Washington where he had been serving as head of the Bureau of Navigation. The *Lexington* task force moved toward the Marshalls for a diversionary attack and the *Enterprise* task force departed Pearl on December 19 to assume a position southwest of Midway. At Wake the submarine *Tambor* had departed the "Wake patrol" to head home for repairs; now the navy dispatched the *Triton* some distance from Wake (without the knowledge of the Wake defenders) to eliminate the possibility of it accidentally firing on the friendly ships of the incoming task force.[36]

HOPES RISE

On the afternoon of December 20 a U.S. Navy PBY landed on Wake's lagoon carrying news too important to risk by radio: the task force sent to relieve, reinforce, and rescue the men would arrive within a few days. Cunningham, Devereux, Greey, and Teters received specific orders to prepare for the mission. Teters called a civilian staff meeting, announced that a ship would arrive for evacuation on the 24th, and began the process of selecting 250 men to remain on Wake to aid the defense and finish vital projects. Teters asked Pete Russell to stay on as superintendent, but, after mulling it over through the night, Pete decided "in fairness to my wife and family I think I shall decline and let Bill Ray do the job."[37]

Commander Greey received orders from Captain Bruns to cease contract work in favor of assistance to defense forces "until the situation is cleared up a little more." Bruns, writing on December 13, recommended that Greey retain 600 civilians, though the number might be further limited to 250 (as indeed it was), including skilled tradesmen, supervisors, a skeleton office staff, and camp support personnel, and evacuate the rest. The skilled trades included power plant operators, mechanics, heavy equipment and tugboat operators, and a nucleus of construction tradesmen such as welders, carpenters, electricians, and pipe fitters. Bruns anticipated that the commanding officer on Wake would require considerable defensive work including eight-foot coral embankments to protect planes at the airfield, additional magazines, completion of some air station structures and the second runway, burial of gas tanks, and enlargement of the seaplane operations area. He cautioned that they must curtail dredging work to conserve fuel, and maintain road access past the Wilkes channel site to enable vehicle access to the gun batteries at the tip of Wilkes. Bruns wrote that he was gathering such "spare parts for equipment which were on hand here ready for shipment . . . and such other supplies which we think would be useful."[38]

Rumors of the impending rescue spread rapidly across the atoll, dipping into dugouts and breaking into bunkers. By evening, as the civilian volunteers straggled into the navy bachelor officer quarters building for the night's work details, some smiles cracked the dirty, bearded faces. U.S. Army Air Force communications specialist Major Walter Bayler had orders to depart Wake the next morning on the PBY, and circulated among the hospital cots that night, taking names and messages from the wounded to wire their relatives. He also gathered official dispatches and letters hastily written by Cunningham, Devereux, and other military men and civilians, including Teters, Russell, and Hokanson. Joe McDonald, not the recreation director who had been killed on the second day, but the letter-writing surveyor who had been on Wake for nearly six months, made good on his side job as stringer for the United Press and wrote a brief dispatch on the siege to editor Frank Tremaine in Honolulu. Herman Hevenor, the government auditor who missed the Clipper on December 8, was again unable to leave Wake because the PBY lacked a spare parachute for him. He added his report for the Bureau of the Budget to Bayler's mail sack. Commander Greey wrote to

Captain Bruns with details of the damage and destruction to "practically every building and structure on the island," as well as about 90 percent of the NAS construction materials.[39]

The next morning the PBY lifted off the lagoon and the Wake men settled in to wait for the rescue fleet or the next bombing raid. Doubtless more than a few civilians placed bets on which would come first. The situation was rapidly deteriorating and although some civilians continued to man their posts or work on the new hospital and communications dugouts, others were reaching the breaking point. Winging eastward, one letter in Major Bayler's mailbag carried a message from Dan Teters to George Youmans saying that he had all of the contractors in dugouts scattered around the island, and that "the men were rendering fine service in helping with the defense of the island." Teters, too, lived in a dugout where he had two telephones and an orderly and felt "like a Mexican general." While evacuation of civilians remained entirely in the navy's hands, Teters expressed his fear that further delays might add to his "several cases of mental breakdown and shell-shock."[40]

Many of the men wrote short letters for Major Bayler to carry out. "I am overjoyed at this opportunity to drop a line to you and let you know that altho I've been hit, it is not serious and I am getting along fine," wrote one. "It has been 'Hell' for a while but I tell you that the Marines (and civilians) have been magnificent. . . . I'm thinking of you two constantly and hoping that I can join you both some time soon (I hope). Keep your chins up and do all you can at home and make it a very Merry Xmas for you and [I'm] thankful that I am alive and doing nicely. God bless you both." Others hinted at concerns and hardships on Wake under siege: "I hope they keep sending you the money every month by Golly. I'm doing a hell of a lot more than most of these civilians over here. They hide out like scaired rabbits & only come out at dark to eat." "I won't be so finicky about cleaning rabbits and chickens any more after seeing all the hell I've seen here." "I'm going to get that home for us or die trying."[41]

Just two hours after the departure of the PBY dozens of Japanese dive-bombers dropped out of the overcast sky and pummeled Wake for nearly an hour with unusually large bombs and destructive gunfire. That afternoon, "33 of our regular visitors came over and dropped their load," wrote Pete Russell. "This evacuation can come any minute." During the day the bombers hit Camps 1 and 2, the airfield, and Peale with no casualties. This day spelled the end of Wake's "pugnacious, tenacious, gallant little VMF-211" as the last two Wildcats chased down the enemy bombers with relentless fury. One barely managed to land with both pilot and plane badly shot up. The men on Wake watched the skies in vain for the other, but it never returned. The news of the loss of Wake's small but remarkably potent air force left many a man in tears, but the impending rescue and reinforcement kept hope alive. Swede, as waterfront superintendent, kept all available equipment "at the ready" for either evacuation or reinforcement. Each task would require rapid and massive movements of men and materials under extremely difficult circumstances and orders might be changed from one to the other at the last minute. Work continued on the communications dugout and supervisors honed the list of evacuees during the next day, interrupted only by a bombing raid just after noon. The hungry, weary men prepared for another long night.[42]

WITHIN REACH

Delayed by Admiral Fletcher's decision to refuel his destroyers and the onset of bad weather, the *Saratoga* task force was still several hundred miles from Wake in the early hours of December 23 when interim CINCPAC Admiral Pye received transmissions that Wake was under increasingly heavy fire. The reports of dive-bombers that could only come off aircraft carriers indicated that enemy carriers were nearby and that the task force faced certain combat if it followed through with the mission. As the hours wore on and the rescue mission pressed westward, conflicting dispatches emanated from Pearl Harbor. Early that morning Commander Cunningham radioed Pearl Harbor: "Enemy apparently landing." Hours ticked by as CINCPAC brass weighed the dilemma and Wake faced the dreaded invasion. Then Cunningham's next dispatch came through: "Enemy on island; issue in doubt." The *Saratoga* was only 425 miles off Wake, fighters poised on deck; the *Tangier* and two destroyers were set to make the run for Wake. Pye, ironically the first naval strategist to perceive Wake's potential in war plans, now made the decision to abandon it to its fate. After weighing the mounting risks to the Pacific Fleet's precious carriers Admiral Pye recalled Task Force 14 before it reached Wake. While arguably too late for relief or rescue the navy still had the opportunity to engage the enemy by "getting at naval forces with naval forces," as Admiral Kimmel had suggested back in April, and score a badly needed naval victory for the United States. Now, however, as the task force reversed its course, CINCPAC radioed Wake that there were "no friendly vessels in your area" without explicitly informing Wake that the navy had recalled the mission.[43]

As the Wake defenders fought for their lives against Japanese troops storming the shores, the sailors, aviators, and marines aboard the "friendly vessels" steaming in the opposite direction raised such opposition to the new orders that mutiny was only narrowly avoided. Eager to relieve their besieged brothers and primed for battle at Wake Island, the marines stood down only with the greatest difficulty. Rear Admiral Fletcher's own staff pleaded with him to disregard the orders and press on; at Pearl Harbor, Kimmel's staff members argued heatedly with the new CINCPAC. Admiral Pye wrote dispatches to CNO Admiral Stark in Washington reporting that enemy attackers had landed: "Wake cannot be evacuated. . . . Gallant defense of Wake has been of utmost value but hereafter Wake is a liability. In view present extensive operations I am forced to conclude that risk of one task force to attack enemy vicinity of Wake is not justifiable." Pye later wrote that "the general strategic situation took precedence, and the conservation of our naval forces became the first consideration. I ordered the retirement with extreme regret." Great bitterness attended the decision to abandon Wake, but the navy kept both the plan and the decision to abort tightly wrapped from the public eye.[44]

"JAPANESE LAND UPON WAKE: Fate of Long-Besieged Isle Is Not Known," ran the headline in bold print atop the *Honolulu Star-Bulletin*, early edition, December 23, 1941 (now December 24 on Wake). From Honolulu to Pullman, Boise to New York, San Francisco to Washington, D.C., the nation read the news with sinking heart. For families and friends of the Wake men it was the news that they had dreaded. In the apartment above Uluniu Street in Honolulu, Eudelle Russell and Mae Hokanson had just received their husbands' letters written on December 20, full of cheery bravado and sent with Major Bayler on the PBY. "Tell Harry he's missing all the fun!" joked Swede. Harry consoled the women as best he could. Rumors of the rescue mission to Wake had swept over Honolulu the previous week and, although he could have confirmed the rumors, Harry kept what he knew about the task force under his hat. There was still a chance. He did not know the status of the mission, and, as everyone else, hoped the next news would be of a heroic victory on Wake, whether it came with help or without it.[45]

THE BATTLE FOR WAKE

The first evidence that the Imperial Japanese Navy had commenced the invasion of Wake Island appeared in the form of flashing lights at sea off the north coast in the early hours of December 23. The dark night, ever-present roar of the surf, and rising squalls impeded vision and hearing. Alerted and jittery in anticipation, lookouts across the atoll detected the approaching enemy in every moving shadow and splash. Gun crews moved to their battery positions and commanders ordered patrols to watch the beaches and channels. When the attack commenced, however, it came from the south to the lee shore of Wake, as always anticipated, where the reef came closest to shore. In hundreds of rough dugouts in the brush, sleepers stirred, soon awakening to the battle upon which their lives depended.

From the dark, heaving sea, four Japanese landing craft deliberately ran onto the reef, two south of Wilkes and two off Wake, discharging hundreds of troops of the Special Naval Landing Force (SNLF). A quick flash from a searchlight on Wilkes exposed the ships, and the Wilkes defenders opened up with machine gunfire and blasts from their three-inch guns. As the first wave of enemy troops sloshed through the surf toward Wilkes they met a hail of bullets and hand grenades, but a hundred made it to shore and engaged the marines in hand-to-hand combat, pressing the defenders and their civilian volunteers back. The Japanese quickly captured Battery F and soon found and cut the telephone lines linking Wilkes with the command post on Wake. The Americans fell back and regrouped for counterattack.[46]

Meanwhile, a few hundred feet off Wake, troops slid from the other two beached landing craft into the churning surf. Their primary mission was to seize the airstrip and then make gains along the southern arm of Wake. However, the easternmost patrol boat had landed in short range of a three-inch gun that had been taken from Battery E and positioned for antiboat defense between the airstrip parking area and the south beach. Sprinting to the gun, 2nd Lt. Robert M. Hanna, another marine, and three civilians took their places, opening fire on the invaders from the three-inch gun. One shell hit a magazine on the patrol boat with the resulting explosions filling the sky with a pyrotechnic show, setting fire to the transport, and revealing the surf rapidly filling with SNLF troops. The illuminated battlefield enabled additional guns joined in the fray including a .50-caliber machine gun manned by three civilians. The burning ship also revealed the second transport run aground a few hundred yards west. Along the south beach of Wake American guns tore into the two ships and targets in the water. Bodies floated and piled up on the beach, but the Imperial Japanese Navy had ensured its success with numbers and the invaders made their beachhead.

Devereux ordered Major Putnam and the VMF-211 personnel at the airstrip to Lieutenant Hanna's aid, as well as a nine-man gun crew to truck in from one of the three-inch guns at Battery D on Peale. At the other guns on Peale the defenders, including Bowsher's all-civilian gun crew, stood ready in case the battle came to them. At the airfield Putnam directed an officer and six men to remain to guard the runway and blow it up if the Japanese broke through or attempted to use it. The loyal crew of civilian volunteers that had attached to VMF-211 earlier in the siege rebuffed Putnam's concern for their safety and joined the dozen marines heading into the brush toward Hanna's gun. The unarmed civilians shouldered ammunition for the marine's machine guns and Browning automatic rifles. As the reinforcements approached Hanna picked off a Japanese force waiting in the brush to ambush the reinforcements. Under increasing fire Putnam's marines and civilians took position in the dark, spreading out to either side of Hanna's gun.

Japanese troops broke out of their beachhead and expanded onto the airfield where they found ditches and berms for cover. They severed telephone lines laying on the ground, cutting off communications between Devereux's command post and the battle stations on Peale, Wilkes, the west end of Wake, and the airfield. The invaders fanned out, some heading east to take on Peacock Point, others laying siege to Battery E, now on the inside elbow of Wake Island near the lagoon. Other SNLF troops turned back south to surround Hanna's gun. No further reinforcements would reach the beleaguered defenders.

Dawn brought a new component to the Battle of Wake: murky gray gradually gave way to a fully lit field. In the surf just east of Camp 1 two more landing craft approached, struggling to gain purchase on the reef. Four volunteers, including a civilian veteran of World War I, grabbed grenades and made their way onto the rocky beach, not once but twice. The second effort landed at least one grenade on a landing barge with devastating effect, but could not halt the landing. Guns engaged along the shoreline and shells from distant batteries fired on the transport ships. Across the channel on Wilkes the split-up defenders managed to regroup and surprise the enemy from two directions at Battery F, killing all but two Japanese whom they took prisoner.

At Hanna's gun south of the airstrip on Wake the invaders charged Putnam's line and the Americans fought back fiercely, some falling to Japanese bullets and bayonets. Captain Elrod, the heroic Wildcat pilot, gave new meaning to his nickname "Hammering Hank" as he faced the enemy and let loose punishing sprays with his machine gun, covering the friendly lines. Gunfire, grenades, curses, and screams filled the air; Japanese casualties mounted. As the sun rose over Wake the sky filled with enemy dive-bombers strafing American gun positions. At Hanna's gun sixteen lay dead: four marines, including Captain Elrod, and twelve civilians. Most of the survivors had sustained grievous wounds, but they held the position.

By full daybreak a thousand SNLF troops swarmed over the southern arm of Wake, including Peacock Point, Japanese bombers roared overhead, and cruisers shelled the atoll. At the mined airstrip marines tried to set off the dynamite, but the generator wire to the charges had shorted. A mobile reserve of sailors, marines, and civilians fiercely held the American line between Camp 1 and the airstrip: initially pushed back to the west, the unit had counterattacked and regained the lost ground. The victorious Wilkes defenders prepared to move east toward the channel. A contingent of marines and civilians trucked in from Peale formed a line south of the command post on Wake. However, with communications severed, ammunition running out, and virtually surrounded by ships, Wake teetered on the tipping point. Commander Cunningham conferred with Major Devereux, who acknowledged the grave situation and the probability that Wilkes and the southwestern arm of Wake had fallen. Faced with this impossible situation Cunningham made the difficult decision to surrender.

CAPTURE

The Americans did not surrender Wake lightly. For the marines surrender was a bitter pill to swallow, especially so for those who had not fallen but held their ground. In the final battle of December 23 twenty-eight Americans lost their lives, half of them civilian volunteers. Ten marines from the Wake Island Detachment had fallen: one on Wake and nine in defense of Wilkes. Four members of VMF-211 who stood their ground at Hanna's gun lay dead. Twelve of the fourteen civilian dead lay at Hanna's gun: ten volunteers attached to the VMF group and two who supported Hanna's initial rush to the gun at the start of the invasion. Two additional civilians lost their lives in the battle. In contrast it is estimated that as many as five hundred Japanese troops died in the costly assault.[47]

Throughout the day the Japanese worked to gain full control of their hard-won prize. As the news of the surrender spread across Wake some marines disabled their guns and trudged away from them while others waited hours before moving out. Hundreds of civilians emerged from their dugouts and hiding places. While some of the civilian volunteers had remained at their guns, others had heeded warnings to vacate the defensive positions so as not to be associated with active combat. Many, fearing the dugouts would be targets for hand grenades, had hidden in the brush. Now men returned to their dugouts, removed some belongings, and headed toward Camp 2 where they hoped to get a meal after the long night. As they walked along the road, "a plane zoomed over very low and let go a burst of machine gun fire. We all hit the dust, thinking we were being strafed," wrote Frank Miller in his diary, "but they were evidently letting us know that they wanted us to stay put. We did." Hours earlier, during the night, Swede and a small crew had rowed out to the big tug in the lagoon to prepare it for the American landing, but gunfire had stranded them there until daylight when they returned to the dock. There they scrambled into a dugout equipped with a telephone, but found the lines dead. Weary from their ordeal they dozed off until awakened by Japanese soldiers.[48]

As the Japanese troops rounded up groups of Americans they took their valuables, forced them to strip, and marched or trucked them to a central location where many were hogtied with telephone wire. Piles of clothing lined the road, shattered eyeglasses glinted in the coral, leather wallets lay discarded like trash, and scraps of treasured letters and photographs blew away on the wind. Soldiers with machine guns and rifles and bayonets guarded and moved the groups toward the collection area near the airfield while sporadic gunfire sounded in the distance. The captors seized more stragglers as the day wore on, though a handful of civilians remained in hiding. Two men watched from a fly-infested hiding place as Japanese soldiers herded five hundred men, stripped to their shorts. "Looked like a brick wall for these men. Fred and I sat tight," wrote Logan "Scotty" Kay in his diary. A large number of men were shoved into the hospital bunker so tightly that they gasped for air. As the collection area swelled with captives, planes roared overhead, a great cluster of ships stood off shore, and two Japanese destroyers burned on the beach.[49]

Eventually, the Japanese herded all of the captured Americans onto the airstrip where they sat or knelt in rows, flanked by machine guns. "We all sat down on the coral in a tight rectangle, guarded by six machine guns and numerous soldiers," wrote Miller. "Lots of us thought we would be shot and ideas and rumors were flying thick and fast." For the first time on Wake, servicemen and civilians were mixed without regard to rank, position, or ethnicity, each man forced to face his fate in his own way. After some time, a Japanese admiral appeared, an intense argument ensued among the officers, and soon the machine gunners were ordered to stand down. The prisoners listened to a proclamation announcing the capture of Wake by the Japanese Empire, followed by the decision to spare the lives of the prisoners. Eventually the Japanese soldiers released the captives from their bonds and the unclothed were allowed to scavenge a piece or two of clothing from the random piles tossed out of trucks.[50]

The first two days of captivity were brutal. Packed "like sardines" into an underground hangar for hours during the first night, the Americans could neither sit nor lie down, and many fainted or vomited. Back outside the next day they baked until they blistered on the coral airstrip, then shivered through rain squalls the next evening (Christmas Eve), some carving shallow depressions in the ground for a bit of protection. The wounded lay exposed to the elements as well, protected only by odds and ends of canvas that Pete and others had obtained. Doctors were denied access to their instruments and medicines. Dysentery victims multiplied. When the captives received their first sustenance in many hours, a crust of dry bread and a gulp of gasoline-tainted water, they devoured it "like wolves."[51]

December 25 dawned on newly-named Otorishima, Japanese for "Bird Island," formerly known as Wake Island. " 'Merry Christmas' the cry could be heard thruout the whole gang. Pretty hard to completely dampen the spirits of free men," Pete wrote in his diary. Late that afternoon the prisoners marched three miles to Camp 2 under heavy guard. Now separated into military and civilian groups the captives moved into the remnants of the barracks. The Japanese had separated out ten officers, including Cunningham and Devereux, and civilians Herman Hevenor and Dan Teters, the first day and placed them in the two cottages still standing on Heel Point. Christmas dinner for the officers consisted of crackers and evaporated milk; for the hundreds in the dark barracks of Camp 2 it was bread and jam. The elaborate holiday feast destined for the CPNAB mess hall, from burr gherkins to demitasse, sat in Honolulu, having completed a long round trip on the *Burrows*.[52]

Honolulu T.H., Dec. 29, 1941
Dear Katherine:
I have waited long to write this letter in the hope that I would have something definite to say about Ted. But to date it is still uncertain. As you well know the boys at Wake surrendered on the 23rd. Since that time we have had no word except that the girls each got letters from their husbands dated the 20th. How the letters got here I do not know but they had been censored. Ted was alive and well at that time and cheerful. Roger Smalley and he were together as they have been all along. I have a lot of hope that they all will come through O.K. They were not belligerents and if the Japs stick to international law the fellows will be treated better than prisoners of war. They have a tough pull ahead of them but if they use their heads they will make it. I know there is not much comfort in all this for you, but this is war and it will avail you nothing to quarrel with what fate has given us. Here we are all in the same boat and we make every effort to be as gay and cheerful as the fellows down there were when they last wrote. They were living in a dugout and bombs were falling, but they said they were well and almost happy. So that's the way we try to be. You may be sure that Ted will never be bored again. He will always have something to talk about. The girls haven't given up hope yet and look for them all to come in the next few days. I don't see how it could happen though, so am resigned. . . .

I have no plans for the future. I don't know how long this will last and what the authorities propose to do on the work out here. Dr. Barrett left for the mainland to join the service. So I have a small harem on my hands. The girls are thinking of going back but are not sure as yet. I hate to see them go for they make it very comfortable for me. I work long hours as does everyone and if you don't have someone to do for you, it is difficult to get along with the restrictions we live under. We had a nice Xmas. Each of us got gifts for the other and I fared very well. We were all pretty low Xmas Eve as that was the day we got the word definitely, but we rallied and got over it.

I have tried to tell you what I know and how I live within the limits of the censorship. If there is any change I will wire you. My best to Donna and chin up to you both.

Harry

Did you get my letters I sent Dec. 7 and 10? I lost—left—my trunk with all my books, two suits, all my underwear, pyjamas, Dad's watch, union card, addresses, etc. How do the people feel about the war over there? Are they united and willing to back us up out here? We are not afraid.

CHAPTER 11

FEAR ITSELF

<hr />

THE OUTLYING ISLANDS

AMERICANS FACED THE NEW YEAR OF 1942 WITH AN UNFAMILIAR UNEASE. The sudden and precipitous descent into war and the string of Japanese victories in the Pacific produced a haze of fear that thickened to the west. West Coast cities cowered behind blacked-out windows; Honolulu shuddered under air raid sirens. Pearl Harbor rebuilt with a fury to avenge the death, destruction, and humiliation of the disastrous attack of December 7 and to carry the fight to Japan's door. At the CPNAB operating base in Pearl Harbor work continued around the clock, but one of the most difficult jobs was to count the missing men. Swallowed up in the yawning maw of the Japanese war machine were at least 1,200 American contractors: 1,145 on Wake, 71 on Guam, 37 at Cavite Navy Yard, about eight miles southwest of Manila, and an unknown number of others still on the outlying islands. Fears for the American workers and servicemen in the Pacific gripped their families and friends as they and the nation faced a new year at war.

The western-most CPNAB projects were at Guam, sponsored by J. H. Pomeroy Company, and Cavite, sponsored by the W. A. Bechtel Company, both under construction for less than a year. The contractors had only sent key men from the mainland for these projects as Admiral Ben Moreell had authorized the hiring of local workers. Long supply lines and time-consuming delays hampered progress at the vulnerable, far-western sites. Japanese bombers targeted the fledgling Guam construction project in Apra Harbor on December 8 where a small garrison put up token resistance. One panicked CPNAB worker died at the end of a Japanese bayonet. The Japanese held the captured Americans on Guam until late December and then shipped them to Kobe in the home islands where they interned the prisoners in several camps and private homes.[1]

In the Philippines the navy had added two projects in Manila Bay to Contract NOy 4173: Cavite Naval Air Station at Sangley Point and the Naval Ammunition Depot at Mariveles on the Bataan Peninsula. From late summer 1941 the U.S. Army had been fortifying the Philippines with long-range B-17 bombers and additional troops, conveying a sense of security to Americans in the islands. However, despite knowledge of the Japanese attack on Pearl Harbor, military forces in the Philippines were unprepared when the Japanese unleashed their Formosa-based bombers on Clark Field. On December 8 all of General MacArthur's B-17s sat on the ground and half of them were destroyed in short order. On December 10 the Japanese turned against the incomplete navy installations on Cavite where four of the thirty-seven American contractors died. Most of the remaining American contractors retreated with the American/Filipino military forces to Bataan and Corregidor. In early January a small group that included George Colley of Bechtel, the Cavite project manager, escaped in an attempt to reach Australia in a small boat, but they were soon captured and interned.[2]

The CPNAB projects on Johnston, Palmyra, American Samoa, and Midway remained under the American flag in late December, but the navy kept a tight lid on information relating to them, even to CPNAB officials. Upon receiving the shocking news of Pearl Harbor all of the island outposts manned their defenses, waited, and watched the seas and skies for enemy attack. Johnston Island, with 462 civilian contractors and a detachment of the Marine Corps's 1st Defense Battalion, was shelled on December 15 and several times during the following week. Forewarned and well prepared they suffered only minor damage and minimal casualties, but many feared worse to come. The *Burrows,* en route to Wake when war broke out, had received orders to divert to Johnston where it arrived on the day of the attack. Loaded with 77 Johnston contractors, the *Burrows* managed to escape damage and departed that evening, arriving in Honolulu on December 20. Palmyra, with 351 civilians and also defended by a detachment of marines, took one bombardment that targeted the contractors' dredge. The Palmyra contractors scrambled to build bomb shelters and morale declined as fears rose. The navy evacuated 112 civilians who arrived in Honolulu on January 3; the remaining contractor personnel stayed behind to finish runways and defense installations on the island.³

With the coordinated Japanese attacks in the Pacific the CPNAB operation on American Samoa immediately instituted nightly patrols. The navy yard project at Pago Pago employed about thirteen hundred civilians, most of them local men. Strategically located on the southern Pacific line of communication between the United States and Australia, Samoa offered a tempting target for the Japanese, but they did not attack until mid-January when a Japanese submarine shelled the island. The navy quickly evacuated a number of civilians, but subsequent sporadic shelling resulted in only minimal damage. With the successful reinforcement of Samoa by marines from the *Yorktown*-based task force on January 23, 1942, CPNAB considered Samoa alone of the outlying projects safe enough for continued contractor operations and supplied it directly from Alameda.⁴

On Midway the December days had crept by as more than sixteen hundred CPNAB workers, Pan American staff, and cable station workers monitored the news of Wake's heroic defense. Rumors flew about the Wake rescue mission and the men watched and waited, expecting the Japanese to return to Midway at any time. Major Bayler, who had flown from Wake to Midway on December 21, gave his eyewitness account of the Wake siege to eager listeners. Midway's military defenses included marines from the 6th Defense Battalion, two air squadrons, and a naval detachment. Captain C. T. Simard, USN, served as island commander. The Wake and Midway CPNAB projects had long been linked by their physical challenges, common Morrison-Knudsen sponsorship, good-natured rivalry, and often mirror-image operations, and there was every reason to expect they the Japanese would target both of these valuable projects. Although unmolested since the initial shelling by homeward-bound Japanese warships on the night of December 7, Midway had no way of knowing that the next attack was not lurking just over the horizon. Civilian morale, ever a problem at Midway, plummeted. An entry in the Midway Naval Air Station diary noted the "almost daily commitment" of civilians to the "local hoosegow" for "suspicious or demoralizing attitude, statements, or actions." Many contractors had scattered into the brush and stole food while others carried the burden of responsibility, just as at Wake. However, on Midway civilian supervision also broke down and the men divided into opposing camps, making a bad situation worse.⁵

Because of the navy's tight control of information in December 1941,

Americans assumed that Midway was subject to frequent attacks during the first weeks of war. Daily communiqués from the navy reported that "Wake and Midway continue to resist" and papers across the nation passed the word on to the public. With little to resist but each other, the men on Midway festered. A week into the war Marlyn Sheik announced that the navy intended to remove a "considerable number" of contractors to make room for additional military personnel. Sheik requested men to report to their supervisors by December 20 if they volunteered to remain to assist the defenders and eventually complete contract work. If volunteer numbers were insufficient, Sheik noted, he would select additional men and expect them to cooperate. A thousand miles west, Japanese bombs had likely destroyed the "multigraph" machine that churned out the *Wake Wig Wag,* but Midway continued to produce the *Gooney Gazette.* Its weekly whimsy considerably muted by war, the *Gazette* dated December 23, 1941, opened with a special report: "The Japanese have landed at last at Wake Island at a cost known only to themselves." Midway received the first reports of the fall of Wake from a Melbourne, Australia, radio broadcast on the morning of December 23 (December 24 in Melbourne and on Wake), followed by KGEI reports from San Francisco throughout the day. (KGEI was a high-frequency, short-wave radio established by General Electric in 1939. KGEI was the *only* radio station at that time on which news from the mainland United States could be heard in the Pacific.) The fate of their compatriots struck new fears into the Midway men as their bloodshot eyes scanned the horizon.[6]

For the men of Midway the horizon produced friends, not foes. After another sleepless night, they cheered as the USS *Tangier* and its escorts steamed up to the island to evacuate civilians. The squadron of Brewster Buffalos intended for the reinforcement of Wake took off from the carrier *Saratoga* and the planes landed, one after another, on Midway's runway. The Midway civilians soon learned that they were not the "first choice" evacuees for Task Force 14, but that mattered little to the hundreds who gladly boarded the transport. One observer dismissed them as "the scum of the West Coast." On December 31, the *Tangier* and its escorts reentered Pearl Harbor carrying just over 800 Midway evacuees. About 775 civilian contractors remained on Midway, most of whom were later evacuated by ship on February 1, 1942.[7]

The return of the *Tangier* without a single man from Wake dashed hopes that anyone had escaped the invasion, but the Midway rescue and confirmation of only a single attack and minimal damage was good news, if there was any to be found in these dark days. As for Wake, it was as if a black curtain had descended over the island. "They are either prisoners or have been murdered, which is the only word for it I can think of," George Youmans wrote from Honolulu. "I can't help but feel that a slip was made in this instance, as there was here and elsewhere on December 7th. But no amount of explanations or future knowledge will bring back the boys that have lost their lives in a brave attempt to do their part when they were caught like rats in a trap." Also unknown was the fate of the CPNAB men on now Japanese-occupied Guam and those at Cavite who still held out as the Philippines continued to struggle against the Japanese onslaught.[8]

GHOST WORDS

In the first days of war hundreds of Wake families received airmail letters, sent from Wake just days earlier, as well as cards and packages sent by ships' mail over recent weeks. These tangible links with their loved ones brought fresh tears and fears to the surface. Here were cheery greetings, "nothing-new" letters, little shell trinkets, and latest countdowns to the end of the contracts, now suddenly not worth the risk at all. On December 8 in Pullman, Washington, a mailman delivered two letters to Katherine, one from her husband, the other from her son, both headed "December 1, 1941, Wake Island." Dozens of Wake men sent "Xmas cards" drawn up by one of the fellows and run off on the multigraph machine. The cards featured a fish jumping from the blue waves under a palm tree and a drawing of Wake Island, surrounding the sentiment "A Merry Xmas and a Lucky '1942'." A favorite printed postcard depicted a cartoon drawing of a Wake worker snoozing in his bunk, dreaming of a cozy fireplace at "Home Sweet Home." Joe McDonald's parents received his last letter, which was dated December 2. Ironically it began, with "Nothing really important has happened since the last letter. Life really seems sorta futile when you don't do anything but work, eat, and sleep and that is all life out here amounts to." The men had mailed gifts and cards home on the USS *Wright*, which pulled away from Wake November 30, and airmail letters on the Clipper that carried Harry Olson to Midway and Hawaii on December 4. Peter Hansen sent one by the Clipper and then used his new Underwood portable typewriter (purchased for $15 from another worker) to write a quick note to his "darling family" the evening of December 4 for a navy bomber to carry out. "We are at last out of the twenties and in the teens and it won't be long now," Hansen wrote, counting, as always, the exact numbers of days gone and remaining, 273 and 19 respectively, on his contract. "I want to know who is the most anxious to see me. This is very important so don't fail to tell me."[9]

Fourteen families received dreaded letters by registered mail just after Christmas. Based on the December 14 communication from Wake to Pearl Harbor and relayed to Washington, Admiral Moreell composed letters informing families of the death of their son or husband. "Your natural grief at your loss should be assuaged by the knowledge that he died to protect our freedom and that his death will not be in vain." While the sudden outbreak of war dealt such a blow to thousands of families of military men, the sorrow was compounded by utter shock for the families of civilians cut down on Wake. In Reno, Nevada, a letter came to the parents of Joe McDonald. In Twin Falls, Idaho, Mrs. Louis Adamson had just received a package sent by her husband on December 2 from Wake with "four shell necklaces, a party bag and a jewel box made from a cocoanut shell . . . fashioned by the 'men in coveralls' in their spare time," when the letter came. Her father-in-law was still on Wake, status unknown. Letters came to the parents of Fritz Schaefer and a dozen other families elsewhere. These letters confirmed the worst fears for these families. Local newspapers carried the stories and obituaries and the families held funerals in the coming days for the men whose lives had been so tragically cut short. No one knew that the list from Wake contained errors; no one knew how many names were yet to come.[10]

BEHIND THE CURTAIN OF WAR

Of the 523 military personnel and 1,193 civilians on Wake at the start of the siege (the civilians comprising 1,145 CPNAB contractors, 46 Pan American employees, and the visiting government auditor and safety engineer), 92 had died, including 48 military personnel, 34 contractors, and 10 Pan American employees. Exact numbers remained unclear in the aftermath of surrender, and several men remained missing. The two American doctors and their assistants continued to care for the wounded and sick, despite having little in the way of medical supplies. The Japanese had barely enough medicines and supplies for their own casualties and provided none to the Americans. Of the Japanese invasion force, hundreds lay dead, dying, or wounded. The Japanese piled their dead like cordwood and burned them; on Wake Island, just south of the runway, marines were permitted to bury sixteen American bodies with their possessions in a shallow grave near Hanna's gun where they had fallen.[11]

In what remained of the barracks in Camp 2, the civilian prisoners of war struggled to find bedding and space to sleep, the former in short supply as the men had dragged many mattresses into the brush for the dugouts during the siege. As many as 150 men now stuffed into barracks wings built to house 40. They doubled up on beds, crowded onto porches, curled up on box springs covered by straw mats, or tried to sleep on the floor until they could scrounge up something better. Weakened and dispirited from the ordeal of surrender, the lack of food, and declining hopes the men struggled to adjust to their new circumstances. A few barracks were completely demolished and the others had sustained damage from direct hits or strafing. Broken glass lay everywhere, and the rooms had obviously been ransacked, but the men at least had roofs over their heads, albeit leaky ones.

Many of the men had taken their valuables to dugouts early in the siege, but the Japanese had quickly stripped the barracks of any remaining possessions (as they did watches, rings, and wallets from the men themselves) before allowing the men back inside. Portable electronics such as radios and razors, tools, typewriters, and other items of value were seized by Japanese troops who were astonished by the technological plethora on the remote island. Hastily labeled "Property of His Imperial Majesty," American electronics and valuables piled up for shipment home to Japan. Initially assuming that the camp was the base for the marine garrison the Japanese troops scorned the "extravagance and hedonism" of American Leathernecks and were shocked by the posters of scantily clad pin-up girls that plastered the walls of what were in fact civilian barracks. As Shigeyoshi Ozeki, the landing party's doctor, later recalled, officers ordered the posters removed immediately, although some Japanese troops managed to liberate many of the pin-ups, which they found "most invigorating." A number of seized electronics and valuables also "disappeared" over the coming weeks, some of them grabbed by visiting Japanese war correspondents who returned home with an item or two to sell on the black market.[12]

For the captives their first real meal appeared at dinner on December 26: a bowl of stew followed the next day by hot creamed tuna, then mush for breakfast, signaling the resumption of camp kitchen activity. Chet Riebel, whose steady food service through the siege brought high praise from many, gave Pete Russell an apron to enable him to move around more freely. "Seems to be a magic 'open sesame' to have an apron on!" Pete and Riebel personally delivered the hot stew meal to Dan Teters and the officers housed with him. After two days the Japanese stopped such visits, as well as any communication between the cottages.[13]

In Camp 2 the warm food raised spirits. It rapidly became apparent that the route to more food was through volunteer work details for the Japanese, a wrenching dilemma for many who craved extra rations, but detested the notion of working for the enemy. Frank Miller, the asphalt technician who was just marking the end of his first month on Wake, found that a work detail also afforded Americans the chance to get out to their dugouts to retrieve their belongings and canned food caches in the brush. While many recovered everything that they could carry in the seconds allotted to their searches, except what had already been discovered by the Japanese, and stashed the extra food in the barracks to augment their meager diet, others focused on finding tangible items of personal value. Dr. Ozeki was in the company of one American who dug up a small trunk and brushed the sand off, opening it with such excitement that Ozeki thought it must contain jewelry or gold. The man threw aside canned food, clothing, magazines, and cigarettes until "he sighed in relief as he pulled a woman's photograph out, pressing it to his lips," and walked back toward camp. For many, the tangible connections to family, like the photos of Pete Hansen's wife and three little children that had been tucked in his cigarette case for months, were their most prized and irreplaceable possessions.[14]

TO WORK OR NOT TO WORK

The first prisoner work details began with surrender as some were ordered to bury the dead, dig latrines, or move ammunition at the shore guns. Once the Japanese had secured the occupation and moved the prisoners into housing they increased the work details. In the early days language differences, misinterpreted gestures, misunderstood intentions, and impatient guards interfered with the work. While a number of the Japanese could speak a little English, there was but one official translator, an officer by the name of Katsumi. Irritated guards employed face slapping as the most common punishment for insubordination, but they could not always detect disobedience in their midst. Pete Russell's attempts to organize the Americans met with little success, but he and others did prepare lists of the prisoners' names, ages, hometowns, and trades for their captors. Each prisoner received a wooden tag to carry at all times bearing his name, barracks number, and trade. As the days went by overall treatment improved. More specific work orders included repairs to bombed buildings, roads, and the airfield, and unloading Japanese barges at the waterfront. The Japanese commandeered some civilians to work on fortifications and defenses against the expected American attack.[15]

From the beginning the American prisoners found creative ways to sabotage the work. Ordered to clean American guns, the marines polished the outsides, but poured saltwater or sand inside. Workers cleverly rendered their tools unusable. One worker took an opportunity to encircle a new Japanese gun emplacement with bright white coral, giving it the effect of a bull's-eye for any friendly bomber overhead. If the day did not offer an opportunity for direct sabotage the men could work slowly and sloppily, and still net extra food for lunch and possibly some booty from the brush. "Goldbricking," once decried as disreputable, now became honorable behavior.[16]

By the end of the first week a four-strand barbed wire fence, five feet high, encircled the barracks. The civilian prisoners received a list of rules and a daily schedule with meal times and two roll calls during the day. Each barracks appointed a supervisor to assume responsibility and convey all communications to Japanese sentries or officers. Guards permitted the civilians to converse only with other men in the civilian barracks and not with the American servicemen who were housed in separate barracks. No one was allowed outside the "confine compound" without Japanese orders or instructions with offenders "liable to be shot"; disobedient behavior or violation of rules would result in severe punishment. Inside the compound the prisoners languished with little to do and too much nervous tension. Guards patrolled the perimeter day and night, and forbade the prisoners to smoke during nightly blackouts. Arguments raged over trifles and "selfish attitudes" ran rampant; millions of flies endemic to Wake drove everyone crazy. Some men found diversion in constructive activities such as patching up their quarters and catching rainwater to shower and wash clothes. Others read books for hours on end or played cards to pass the time. Utterly cut off from news of the outside world, scuttlebutt went into overdrive: "rumors, rumors, rumors that is all we hear."[17]

For Dan Teters, Herman Hevenor, and the U.S. Navy and Marine Corps officers sequestered away from camp in the two cottages on Heel Point the days dragged by. During the first days they swept out broken glass and fallen plaster and ate what canned food and crackers they could find until meals started coming from the mess. Rats came in through the broken windows at night. A civilian clerk, John Rogge of Idaho, was assigned to one of the cottages where he served as "janitor and handyman" and secretary to Cunningham. Japanese soldiers kept both houses under constant guard and after two days allowed the men no further contact with the other cottage or any of the barracks. Teters and the officers endured repeated interrogation sessions over the coming days; in between, they read or played cards. Several of the cottage guards spoke a little English and some interacted freely with the Americans and disregarded blackout restrictions. Devereux, Cunningham, and those who knew about the U.S. Navy's rescue and reinforcement task force, still expected its arrival at any time and "dreamed [it] would come to our aid." Indeed, in all American quarters on Wake, hopes and rumors of an imminent rescue persisted for days. However, when American eyes scanned the horizon, they saw only more Japanese ships and planes. Soon, only scuttlebutt sustained the hope of rescue.[18]

HONOLULU, JANUARY 1942

"Remember Gallant Wake!" "Remember Pearl Harbor!" Little boxes bearing these exhortations peppered the daily Honolulu papers during the early months of war. Harry Olson, working on the Pearl Harbor salvage operation, drove home every evening in a 1942 Hudson assigned to him to the comfortable, furnished house near Waikiki Beach that he and the Wake wives rented. Like everyone else in Honolulu, when darkness fell they drew the blackout curtains and stayed in, ears tuned for any noise that might mark another attack or the dreaded invasion. Each man, woman, and child was issued a gas mask and ordered to carry it at all times. In the rental house on Royal Hawaiian Avenue and other dwellings in Honolulu hopes turned from rescue of the Wake men to their repatriation, and life settled into a restrictive routine marked by fear of the unknown.

The adrenalin-fueled panic and shock of the first days of war had tempered into a deep unease that manifested itself in emotional, physical, and social malaise. Sporadic bombs and gunfire kept nerves on edge. A pall of racist suspicion hung over Honolulu during the early weeks of war. Many among the non-Japanese population were certain that dastardly deeds had or would be accomplished by their Japanese American neighbors, most of whom were horrified at the Japanese attack and shamed by their neighbors' suspicions. As the weeks went by no one produced evidence of any espionage or sabotage by Japanese residents, but military wives and others evacuated to the mainland spread the rumors of Japanese fifth columnists where they took on a new life with dire consequences for the West Coast population. Prewar palliatives of Japanese military inferiority began to give way to an agonizing fear of the "Japanese superman," a potent enemy who had America locked in his sights. Yet in the early weeks of war most Americans remained confident that their military would quickly rise to meet this challenge and make short order of the Pacific campaign.[19]

In the offices of the CPNAB operating base in Pearl Harbor executives and staff adjusted to the changing demands of wartime. Quietly, many, including Harry Olson and George Youmans, blamed the navy for failing to get the Wake men out in time. In January C. P. Schoeller, the chief engineer of the Wake project, prepared a lengthy report of the progress made on the Wake project until the Japanese attack abruptly curtailed it, including detailed instances of navy delays, indecisions, and altered priorities that had occurred over the past year. Schoeller completed his fifty-six page Wake report on January 15, 1942. CPNAB continued operating, although mail delays, tied-up telephone lines, and censorship impeded mainland communications. The navy reevaluated all of the CPNAB projects in light of the emergency and ordered outlying projects on islands still in U.S. hands wrapped up. Supplied directly from Alameda, only Samoa would continue. Workers and supervisors poured into Oahu from the closing projects as the operating committee decided how to sort it all out. The Red Hill underground fuel storage project and the salvage of damaged ships in Pearl Harbor remained high priorities, but the contractors' portion of the salvage work diminished as the Bureau of Ships took over the operation. Harry Morrison wrote Youmans that he should "make it plain" to Harry Olson that they considered him "part of our organization," and that he would have a job with M-K when the salvage work ended. While deeply concerned for family and friends on Wake, the men also lamented the fate of the Wake project itself, once a shining star in the CPNAB constellation. "We build and others destroy," Youmans observed wryly.[20]

415 Royal Hawaiian, Jan. 7, 1942
Dear Katherine:
A month has gone by since all the excitement started and life goes on on a more or less even plane. Of course you know from the newscasts

that we are under martial law which is necessary for many reasons. Some other precautions are fast becoming so much a part of our daily life that we accept them as a matter of course. We all work long hours and are gone from home most of the daylight time. As you can see by the address, we have moved. We have a lovely apartment too, quite the nicest I have ever seen. The girls are very good to me and I have never lived so well. So I can't really say the war has done me any harm.

There is no further word from Ted or any of the fellows at Wake. The last message only said that the Japs were landing and as far as I can learn there has been nothing since. Everyone I talk to is of the opinion that the Japs will treat the fellows well and it is just a matter of waiting until they return. I suppose you have shed many tears over this and you can well imagine how we all feel here sometimes. But we are resolved that we will act as tho the fellows were still down there working and act as near normal as we can. We have a rule that when any of us gets to feeling too bad that they are allotted 15 minutes in the bathroom and they must come out smiling. Some of the smiles are not so hot, but we all try hard and get by pretty good.

You know it is only a miracle that I am not down there with them. It all started as a joke. Dan wanted to go to Guam but I talked him out of that. Then he wanted to come to Hono. but I insisted he couldn't go until I had gone first. We had planned on Jan. 10 for me and Feb. 1 for him. But he got anxious to come in and as there was a Clipper in we radioed to Hono. for an O.K. and got it. That was the last Clipper from the Orient so you can see how narrowly I missed all that mess. Now whenever I feel like growling, I just think how darn lucky I am and resolve to be thankful.

I don't know if you have received any of my letters or radiograms. I got the letter you sent c/o Belle but that is all. You may write me here as I expect to be here for some time. Don't expect to hear from me as often as in the past for the mails are overtaxed and there is really nothing to write of any interest that would pass the censor.

As I expected, the people I work for now do not pay any allotments so I will enclose my check in its place. I have opened an account here.

Tell Donna I will write her one of these days and I must write Jim. Please don't worry about Ted or I for we will come out of this O.K.

Harry

THE *NITTA MARU*

On Wake the scuttlebutt had sustained the rumors of navy rescue for a few days after capture, but new rumors of repatriation or removal eclipsed that now-remote possibility. We're being moved later today! We'll be taken away before January 20! Leaving soon on two Portuguese ships for Canada! At last the scuttlebutt bore fruit: the first exodus of prisoners from Wake occurred in mid-January. A few days earlier the men were directed to turn in lists of personal belongings that identified items now in their possession and those that had been lost, as well as an estimated value for each. Frank Miller itemized everything from a watch, slide rule, and diving mask, to all manner of clothing (including six neckties) and fifty books. He listed all of his possessions as lost, save two pairs of shoes, four pair underwear, and his glasses. The next day the Japanese ordered all of the civilians to pack and assemble near the mess hall. The *Nitta Maru*, a converted passenger liner, loomed offshore.[21]

Under the sudden orders, the prisoners rushed to pack up their meager belongings. Men tied cuffs of spare trousers and shirtsleeves to stuff in extra items before marching to the mess hall under guard. There Japanese soldiers separated the crowd of well over 1,000 men into two groups: the smaller group of about 360 included Pete, Swede and other key men, equipment operators, various tradesmen, including carpenter Pete Hansen and asphalt technician Frank Miller, and Dr. Shank. The twenty wounded marines would also remain on Wake until they had healed sufficiently for travel. The larger group would leave the island the following day for points unknown. A few negotiated last-minute identity switches, some of which enabled family members to stay together. Scuttlebutt raged through the day and far into that night when the men returned to the barracks to wait. Where will they take us? What will become of us? Who will have it better, those who stay or those who go? The next day, January 12, 1942, in a blizzard of confusion, the men remaining on Wake managed to bid their friends farewell before the guards herded them into the mess hall. Japanese guards then began to line up the larger group, count them off, and load them onto trucks. (A total of 367 civilians, including 2 Pan Air employees, remained on Wake following the departure of the Japanese transport ship from the atoll.)[22]

Pete Russell and Swede Hokanson, the latter weak from a bout of dysentery, circulated among the men to say their goodbyes. The civilians, whether departing or remaining, expected to be in line for exchange and repatriation and back home drinking beer and kissing girls before long. Harry Olson, the lucky SOB, would buy the first round. Ted Olson and his friend Roger Smalley boarded a truck for the waterfront where they and hundreds of others were loaded onto lighters and carried out to the massive hull of the *Nitta Maru*. They timed their leaps from the lurching barge to the open hatch on the ship. Barely inside, Japanese sailors caught the men roughly, sprayed them with an unknown substance, and pushed them into a gauntlet of more sailors who rained blows on the prisoners with clubs. Most were stripped of their carefully packed bundles. Pushed down into the dark bowels of the ship, men scrambled to find their friends and a space to claim. A list of regulations strictly forbade talking, moving about, and other actions and attitudes. It was little comfort that the "Navy of the Great Japanese Empire will not try to punish you all with death."[23]

Packed flesh to flesh on the steel decking with four metal buckets in the corners for toilets, the prisoners received a dipper of gruel, a small dried fish, and a little water for sustenance each day. They were quiet, miserable, and filthy. Not long into the voyage, they began to shiver in their light tropical clothing. Ted noted that they must be going north and he tried to remember the features on the globe in the sunny fraternity house a year ago. Growing weaker by the day the men turned inward, trying to block out the horrors around them, clenching their teeth, holding their bowels, vomiting as the ship lurched. Once a guard hauled a man up, tied ropes to his wrists, and strung him from the rafters, beating him with a heavy club: some thought they recognized John Polak, the office manager and pioneer party member. The *Nitta Maru* plowed on.[24]

JAPANESE PROPAGANDA

The first indications that some of the Wake men were alive brought a flood of relief to family members back home. Reports of shortwave broadcasts from Tokyo announcing the arrival of Wake captives in Japan left many family members with mixed emotions of joy and fear. The *Nitta Maru* arrived in Yokohama with 1,235 prisoners of war from Wake Island. "Showing little signs of ordeal except overgrown beards and soiled uniforms, the men all indicated they were more worried about their families back home than about themselves," newspapers reported, naming Commander Cunningham and Nathan Daniel Teters, "civilian in charge of 1050 defense employees on the island," among the arrivals.[25]

During their two-day stay in Yokohama the Japanese gave several prisoners opportunities to send personal messages to their families over the radio: shortwave radio sets across the United States picked up the transmissions. Not at liberty to speak freely the prisoners took different tacks to convey their conditions and reassure their loved ones. In a message addressed to his wife Dan Teters said, "I am being well treated by the Japanese and everything is going along as well as could be expected." George Essaff, a camp foreman on Wake, described the trip to Japan aboard a "fine ship" on which "we were bedded nicely . . . with plenty of warm blankets." Lieutenant John Kinney, one of the USMC aviators, and the navy physician, a reporter noted, sounded tired and spoke slowly, in measured phrases. Hudson Sutherland, a driller foreman from Portland, said "So far we have been treated fine, I think." The majority of prisoners remained in their dank dungeon below decks during the stay in Yokohama and knew nothing of events transpiring topside.[26]

In addition to the radio transmissions the Japanese produced a visual record. Photographers demanded and cajoled smiles from select prisoners and the cameras flashed. Later, the photographs of the Yokohama "press conference," as well as an aerial image of Wake taken during the siege and photographs of later radio broadcasts in prison camp, appeared in the Japanese propaganda magazine *Freedom*, published in English by the Japanese at Shanghai. The large, glossy magazine gave a positive spin to internment of U.S. subjects from Wake and Guam, and may have been intended for use in future negotiations for prisoner exchanges. Copies of *Freedom* were distributed and shared in the POW camps and some of the photographs found their way to the American press, appearing in U.S. newspapers in the fall of 1942.[27]

In one issue of *Freedom* featuring the Wake prisoners the magazine referred to their hazardous voyage, and stated that "hundreds were sea-sick but when they first sighted peaceful Japan with no trace of war consternation, they shouted, 'here we come Japan!' This group was far more rowdy and boisterous than the Guam batch for they sang and danced, happy to find a new haven." There was, of course, no singing and dancing in the hellish holds of the *Nitta Maru*. Nor did *Freedom* magazine mention the five prisoners, two marines and three sailors, who were hauled out of the holds not far out of Yokohama and beheaded before the assembled crew, their bodies mutilated and thrown overboard to avenge Japanese losses in invasion of Wake.[28]

The Japanese press went to great lengths to create a body of propaganda to support the benevolent Japanese treatment of prisoners of war. JOAK, "Japan's foremost radio station," sent crews into the POW camps in the spring of 1942 to plumb the "wealth of human interest which must lie hidden under the bearded exteriors of the inmates." In addition to the Yokohama broadcasts, technicians now recorded more stories and messages "for keeps in sound tracks inscribed deeply on black discs" and sent them off to Tokyo for broadcast over JOAK's powerful shortwave radio. In what became a familiar refrain prisoners reassured their families not to worry; they were fine. However, *Freedom* took pains to drive its point home: "The shame the men have borne in their hearts for their pitiful resistance against a power the world once claimed would have no showing against the military might of untried America, rankled less through Japanese kindness. JOAK's opportunity to these men brought them nearer to home . . . where they would like to be." The writer elaborated on the beneficence and kindness of Japan, despite "mendacious propaganda" from the West that persisted in claiming the opposite. Photographs showed internees lounging around the Zentsuji camp on the island of Shikoku, Japan, "situated among hills and fragrant pine woods" and "more like a summer resort than a place of confinement."[29]

THE PACIFIC WAR: JANUARY–FEBRUARY 1942

The Pacific Fleet, under the command of Admiral Nimitz from December 31, 1941, had two primary defensive objectives early in the war: to protect Hawaii and to maintain the southern Pacific communication route to Australia and New Zealand. Japanese forces moved quickly and with astonishing success in the western Pacific, and pressed toward the critical southern route and the southwestern seas near Australia. As for Wake Island, the U.S. Navy was not yet equipped or able to deploy a full amphibious assault to retake the island, much less to mount an assault on any Japanese territories. By January 1942, however, the first of many photographic reconnaissance missions dispatched from Oahu had flown high over Wake, gathering data for maps and future operations against the Gilbert and Marshall Islands. American resolve was high, but resources were stretched thin in the Pacific. After the initial shock that the Japanese had initiated the Pacific war without following long-held American war plan expectations, the U.S. Navy had to adapt its strategy to a new Pacific dynamic that in the early months of 1942 clearly favored the enemy. When the Japanese captured Rabaul, just off

New Guinea, the navy seized an opportunity to mount diversionary, carrier-based raids against outer Japanese bases including the Marshalls and Wake.[30]

Admiral William Halsey's *Enterprise*-based task force accomplished the first successful raid on Wake Island on the morning of February 24, 1942. Cruisers and destroyers bombarded the atoll outside the range of Wake's shore batteries, hitting several buildings. Dozens of bombers and fighters off the *Enterprise* followed the bombardment with an aerial attack. Pilots picked their targets carefully, aware that there "probably were still some of their countrymen captive on Wake." The attack destroyed three Japanese flying boats in the lagoon and damaged or destroyed several small boats, hangars, shore batteries, fuel dumps, and the ill-fated dredge *Columbia*. One American dive-bomber and crew were lost in the raid. As for diversion, the American raid did not lure Japanese forces away from aggressive action in the southwestern seas as hoped. Japan did not seem to mind the attacks "any more than a dog minds a flea," as one officer remarked.[31]

The Japanese garrison and the American POWs who remained on Wake "minded" the February attack considerably more. While the departure of the bulk of prisoners on the *Nitta Maru* had resulted in fewer restrictions and more living space and food on Wake, the prisoners yearned for a sign of Uncle Sam. The Americans began construction of a large prisoner dugout north of the barracks in mid-January. As the Japanese stalled over constructions materials, it took ten days to build the bomb shelter. Fortified with twelve-by-twelve timbers, the shelter was large enough for all three hundred-plus POWs remaining on Wake. Some reflected with bitterness that their own navy had deferred construction of such a shelter until it was too late.

The day the dugout was finished, January 31, Pete wrote, "I hope we never have cause to use it yet in the same breath I hope our forces re-take the island." Frank Miller also marked the day: "Now when Uncle Sam comes we'll have a nice cozy hole to dive into. . . . Anyway, there's nothing we can do here to hurry or hinder his coming." The dugout had hosted many test runs during the first three weeks of February as the jittery Japanese raised alarm after false alarm. On the morning of February 24 Pete Russell had just taken his first few mouthfuls of breakfast when he heard the air raid siren and all of the prisoners ran for the dugout. The bombardment from the task force drove the prisoners in and out of their shelter throughout the day; they found the American raid at once welcome and fearsome.[32]

The day after the raid, Pete wrote that he "awoke early and peacefully and disappointedly. Disappointed because of the peaceful awakening. I was sure that 'Sammy' would return in force and [do] that which we have been praying he would do. No such luck." In the lagoon, the dredge had taken two direct hits and the wood deck caught fire. Some may have argued it was a fitting end for the expensive behemoth that never measured up on Wake, but others had lived on the dredge and nursed it as well as cursed it. Claude Howes, one of the *Columbia*'s original crew, noted that the Japanese took a detail of men out to the dredge to fight the fire. Of greater interest to all on Wake was the appearance two days later of a pair of American survivors from the downed dive-bomber. The Japanese hauled them in from Wilkes where they had landed in a rubber boat the night of the attack, interrogated them, and threw them in the jail until March 3 when they were taken off the island.[33]

The Japanese garrison on Wake frequently went on high alert throughout the spring of 1942 and scuttlebutt flourished on both sides of the barbed wire. A civilian POW, who carried food to the jailed American fliers and talked with them briefly, delivered a welcome glimpse of the outside to the other POWs. The *Enterprise* had brought the raid to Wake to find out "what the Japs have," Tommy reported, and the navy does "know that we're on the island." The crowning tidbit—that things were "going along all right for the allies"—invigorated the Wake scuttlebutt. While the Japanese occasionally passed on accurate news, such as the successful U.S. raid on Marcus Island March 4, the prisoners felt utterly closed off from the great sweep of war across the world.[34]

Far to the west Japanese forces broke through the beleaguered defenses on the Bataan peninsula and fierce fighting continued as weeks turned to months. President Roosevelt ordered General MacArthur to leave the Philippines for Australia where he was appointed as the supreme commander of the Southwest Pacific Area. The British lost Malaya, Singapore, and Rangoon to the relentless Japanese. Half a world away Soviet defenses and counterattacks reversed some German gains. In North Africa the British suffered setback after setback against Rommel's war machine. The headlines of American newspapers blared bad news week after week, and the nation labored under the very real fear that the Allies might well lose this world war. In fact, things were not "going along all right for the Allies."

THE UNKNOWN

Unofficial Tokyo reports in January announced the arrival of the *Nitta Maru* at Yokohama and described the Wake group of 1,235 as including 30 officers, 423 non-commissioned officers and enlisted naval personnel, and 782 civilians. Except for a handful of families who could confirm their relative's identity by radio broadcast, photograph, or news account, no one knew exactly who was and who was not in this prisoner group, where they were going, or what had become of the others. Several hundred Wake contractors were unaccounted for, even given the rough estimate of Wake civilians at the time of capture. After word of the fourteen contractor deaths early in the siege the navy had given no further information on civilian casualties on Wake. The navy's silence frustrated Harry Morrison: "This indicates the extremes to which the country is going to suppress information which can be of no use to anyone except to the families of the men." Major Walter Bayler, who left Wake on December 21, had submitted a confidential report estimating 80 civilian dead and 250 wounded, but without confirmed identities, there was nothing to be gained by sharing those figures.[35]

For one family a remarkable glimmer of hope emerged in late February; sadly, it came at the expense of another family. Young Joe McDonald's bereaved father, the editor of the *Nevada State Journal*, doggedly pursued information relating to the death of his son by writing to Admiral Moreell and corresponding with Patrick A. McCarran, the senator from Nevada and a close friend of the family. Out of the blue an astonishing letter arrived in late February 1942 from Frank Tremaine of the United Press in Honolulu. Tremaine explained that he had just received a dispatch written by Joe McDonald on Wake during December, but held by the navy for two months. Joe's dispatch described "11 bombings and one shelling since the beginning of the war," and the assertion that "since the third day of the war, no damage has been done and no casualties have been suffered." The details revealed that Joe had written the dispatch on December 20 and sent it to Honolulu on the PBY that returned to Pearl Harbor with Major Bayler. This date was nearly a week after Dan Teters had transmitted the list of early casualties including McDonald's name to Pearl Harbor on December 14. The navy had forwarded the list to Admiral Moreell in Washington, who had written letters of notification and condolence to the families. If Joe had in fact written that dispatch, he could not have been among those killed the week before. In a strange twist of fate, there were two men named Joe McDonald who had volunteered at the hospital when it was bombed on the second day of the siege, and it was the newly-arrived recreation director from Wyoming, Joseph T. McDonald, friend of Frank Miller, who perished. Joseph F. McDonald, Jr. of Nevada remained alive, at least as of December 20.[36]

Family members were desperate to find out what had happened to their husbands and sons. Where were they? Were they dead or alive? Telephone calls, cables, and letters to all possible authorities netted the same basic reply: we do not know. Early in 1942 several family members organized the Pacific Island Workers' Association (PIWA) in Boise in order to communicate with family members of the civilian prisoners and address the immediate problems of information and relief. One of the PIWA's first letters to members, dated February 12, 1942, copied a telegram from the International Red Cross. Japan had not ratified the Geneva Prisoner of War Convention of July 27, 1929 (also called the International Red Cross Agreement at this time), but the Japanese Red Cross stated, "We are carrying on relief war prisoners civilian internees according spirit Geneva Convention 1929 and with authorization government we have organized . . . relief services for war prisoners civilian internees for their relief through intermediary International Red Cross." The PIWA letter urged members to submit their Red Cross forms to the committee as soon as possible and added that progress was being made for legislation for the relief of prisoners' dependents.[37]

Outside of Idaho family members working alone or with others in their region followed other avenues of contact with their congressional representatives and various government and military agencies. In February, from the family home in Portland, Katherine Olson initiated contact with all of the Oregon congressmen, as did dozens of other Oregon families. By March word came that the State Department had begun negotiating with the Japanese through the Swiss government for prisoner exchanges and the release of American civilians.[38]

Secretary of State Hull delegated the matter to the provost marshal general of the U.S. Army, and Prisoners of War and Civilian Internees information bureaus were established. As soon as the Japanese government provided official lists of prisoners and internees to the International Red Cross the War Department would notify family members. The Department of State, wrote Hull, was "deeply concerned over the plight of Americans who are now in enemy-occupied territory." The "absence of any . . . pertinent international agreement to which both the United States and Japan are parties" barred him from being able to offer any assurances regarding the possibility of prisoner exchange or early return. Through the Swiss intermediary the U.S. government announced that it intended to observe the Geneva Prisoners of War Convention of July 27, 1929 to "any civilian enemy aliens that may be interned," and hoped that "enemy governments"—meaning Japan—would reciprocate. The Japanese signified that they would cooperate and were "prepared to carry on relief work with the internees in accordance with the Geneva Convention. This covers both civilian internees and war prisoners." At this time, on February 19, 1942, President Roosevelt issued Executive Order 9066, authorizing the initial removal of 112 thousand Japanese Americans from the West Coast for reasons of "military necessity."[39]

Letters and cables flowed between government and Red Cross officials and the families as they awaited official notification. Norman H. Davis, chairman of the American Red Cross, reported that they had received general information that prisoners taken from Wake and Guam were in Japan and that a delegate of the International Red Cross Committee was free to visit them, though Japan had not yet submitted a list of names. The American Red Cross stood ready to "rush relief supplies" and to establish lines of communication between prisoners and their families, and supplied local Red Cross chapters with instructions and forms for families to submit inquiries. The Olsons, like hundreds of American families that spring, waited anxiously each day for the telephone to ring, for the mail to come, for a knock at the door.[40]

A LEGAL CONUNDRUM

A host of complex legal problems attended the capture of hundreds of civilian workers from the Pacific islands. While the thousands of military POWs came under the umbrella of their respective military organizations the civilians were in legal limbo. Japan chose to regard the construction workers as prisoners of war instead of civilian internees and rebuffed all military, public, and private efforts to have them repatriated. As employees of private contractors they were protected by workmen's compensation laws, but the contractors were not obligated to continue paying wages and salaries as the workers' individual contracts had been "breached by a third party."

CPNAB allotment checks had been issued for hours worked on Wake in November, but in the chaos following the attacks censors held up the mail. Near the end of December Harry Morrison discovered that the mix-up had resulted in families not receiving their allotments. "If this is true, someone should take it on their soul and conscience for the damage done to the dozens of people with their little children at Christmas time who have been deprived of the benefit of these pay checks," he wrote to George Youmans. "In several instances where we have been able to develop the situation, we have taken care of these people with our own funds." Morrison hoped for the prompt restoration of the allotments to the families "even though they cannot have the benefit of communication with their loved ones." The delayed November pay allotments arrived in the second week of January, but a long struggle had just begun.[41]

The difficulty of determining precisely who was and was not on the island on December 8, 1941, compounded the problem. With the continuous turnover of employees before the war, the abruptly severed communications with the outlying islands when war began, and the clamp-down on communications between Hawaii and the mainland it took weeks to come up with a reliable list of the missing men. Working in late December with the most recent Alameda employee list for Wake showing 1,163 employees as of November 1, 1941, Harry Morrison used a green pencil to check off and circle the names from the "Navy Fatality List" and a red pencil to mark those who left Wake prior to the attack. The process continued as letters and telegrams poured in, revised lists were compiled from Alameda records, evacuees from the other outlying islands were counted, and representatives of the Liberty Mutual Life Insurance Company fanned out across the country to confirm information with families.[42]

The cost-plus-fixed-fee contract arrangement with the navy did not allow for continuation of wages in these circumstances, but the plight of dependents raised an ethical dilemma. Hundreds of wives and children depended on the allotments provided by the civilian contractors. As of December 8, 1941, the 1,145 Wake contractors included approximately 680 single men, 380 married men, 45 who were separated or divorced, and another 40 whose marital status was unknown. Given the relatively low wage-earning power of women and the prevalence of alimony in divorce cases, at least four hundred of the Wake contractors were responsible for all or the significant portion of the income of their families. For most of the dependent families of the men who had taken the risky Pacific defense jobs in the Depression years of 1940 and 1941 there were few safety nets or sources of credit: they were utterly dependent on the allotments.[43]

The navy not only had no legal responsibility for their welfare or wages, but also was "expressly prohibited" from compensating the families of the civilian POWs by the laws governing military expenditures. However, in this unprecedented crisis Admiral Moreell and CPNAB executives urged the navy to authorize full payment of wages for all of December. The Longshoreman's Act provided for federal payments of insurance funds to dependents at pre-scribed monthly rates based on earnings and number of dependents as well as death compensation, but it was unclear how and when such disbursement would commence. The Liberty Mutual Insurance Company immediately began investigations into each civilian worker's family. Pending the results of the investigation the navy directed CPNAB to pay $100 to each family for the month of January 1942 and later authorized the same for the month of February.[44]

Katherine Olson received a letter accompanying the January check stat-ing that the $100 payment was a "voluntary contribution, authorized by the Navy" and had been made to the closest relative according to employee records. If the recipient was not in fact "the person the employee himself would designate," CPNAB requested that the money be returned for redi-rection. Many of the single men's families received only the January payment and not the second $100. In cases where no family was located neither pay-ment was made, nor were any of these funds held for the prisoners upon their return. Katherine's letter also explained that despite newspaper reports of captured Wake employees in Japan there was still no official report of their location. CPNAB would continue to make "every effort to determine their whereabouts and welfare, and eventually to return them to the Mainland." In the meantime family members should contact local chapters of the Amer-ican Red Cross, the agency working to establish communication with the prisoners.[45]

During February President Roosevelt established a $5 million "Civilian War Relief Fund" for dependents of civilians missing due to enemy action. The fund was administered by the Social Security Board and payments com-menced in March 1942. The Old Age Pension Plan of the Social Security Act formed the basis for regulations and rates, but made for a flimsy safety net: a wife received $45 per month and $15 per child, up to three children. Peter Hansen's wife received the maximum of $85 per month for the fam-ily—less than half the monthly allotment of $190 that the carpenter had been able to send home during his time on Wake. A parent more than 50 percent dependent on the employee received $30; if both parents qualified they received $45 per month. Any further public assistance would require congressional authorization.[46]

Congress passed a law for higher rates of payment for missing military and civilian workers in early March 1942, raising hopes among the families of the CPNAB civilian prisoners. During congressional debate David I. Walsh, Democratic senator from Massachusetts and Chairman of the Naval Affairs Committee, confirmed that the bill would cover the CPNAB employees. However, after PL 490, known as the "Walsh Bill," was signed March 7, 1942, it was found that while the bill did cover full pay for military prisoners and missing civilians on the payroll of the United States it *did not* cover the civilians employed by contractors to the government.[47]

THE PRISONERS OF WAR

For the Americans who remained on Wake the days blurred into a tedious repetition of work details and long hours of reading to pass the time. The prisoners noted the comings and goings of Japanese ships and planes, and their hopes rose and fell with continued air raid alerts and alarms. Pete Russell wore a blue armband to signify his superintendent status, but he was a prisoner like the others, and every day "was as tiresome and monotonous as all the rest." Such work as the men did was sporadic and desultory. Pete wearily kept up his diary and found and copied into it a list of the civilians who had died during the siege and battle. He showed the Japanese where the scattered burial sites lay and marked the graves, visited with Dr. Shank most every evening, and started working on a Japanese vocabulary. During March he often took some of the Japanese officers and others out on the reef to fish and catch lobsters. On March 18 Pete noted that it was six months from the date he had gone to Hawaii in September, and "today was my day to go on vacation and join my darling in Honolulu." For Frank Miller, who had arrived on Wake in late November, March 1 was a red-letter day: "A new month! I'm started on my $30 bonus! Ha!"[48]

The POWs may have complained that the long days on Wake were monotonous, but then an air raid would jolt them out of their complacency, or a member of the "walking dead" would emerge from the brush. Lloyd McKeehan was brought in on January 20, nearly a month after the capture of the island. On March 10 two bedraggled Americans, Scotty Kay and Fred Stevens, long given up for dead, came out of hiding. The Japanese slapped the two men into the brig immediately, releasing them after a week when it became apparent that they were not shot-down pilots but construction workers who, against all odds, had succeeded in hiding out for over seventy days. Moving frequently and narrowly escaping exposure, the two middle-aged men had lived off food stashed during the siege until they grew too weak to continue. Kay kept a diary of their ordeal, which had been buried, dug up, and reburied many times. Pete scratched their names off his list of dead civilians.[49]

In late January the *Nitta Maru* had arrived at its destination on the Japanese-held coast of China near Shanghai and on shaky legs the prisoners were marched to a camp at Woosung. Far from the summer resort depicted in Japanese propaganda, the "Shanghai War Prisoners Camp" was the bleak and barren destination of most of the Wake captives. The thin, tropical clothing on their backs gave the prisoners no protection from the cold. Surrounded by two electric fences, the camp was comprised of seven old wooden barracks formerly used by the Japanese army, several other buildings and gravel roads, and an open field. Each large barracks building was 210 feet long and 50 feet wide and housed about 230 prisoners, separated into sections of 36 men each. There were no pine woods, fragrant or otherwise, in the vicinity.

By February 1, 1942, there were fifteen hundred prisoners at the Shanghai War Prisoners Camp at Woosung, including survivors of the USS *Wake* and the HMS *Peterel*, both of which were Yangtze River gunboats, North China Marines captured at Tientsin and Peking, and the military and civilian prisoners from Wake Island. Bare boards on raised platforms with thin, cotton blankets—four to a man—served as their beds; cold winter winds blew in the broken glass panes. Meager rations of rice and a kind of stew formed the basis of their diet, and tea five times a day was the only potable liquid. Enlisted men and civilians soon started to work at leveling a field for the Japanese to use as a parade ground, repairing roads, and, later, gardening and raising chickens for the Japanese. Upon their arrival in late January the men from Wake had received some additional clothing and shoes, but continued to suffer from the cold and poor medical treatment. Common punishments included face slapping and beatings, and the Japanese guards employed group punishment for individual offences as "object lessons." For the first few months the Japanese barred the Red Cross from visiting or providing supplies, and prisoners received no outside correspondence.[50]

In March 1942 five of the prisoners in the Woosung camp, including Commander Cunningham and Dan Teters, hatched an escape plan. After two weeks of secret preparations they crept out of the barracks on the night of March 11, 1942, evaded the sentry patrolling the gravel road, and made their way to the electric fence. Earlier, Japanese guards had made a show of dragging a dead dog from under the fence to prove that it was lethally charged. while the escapees were not completely convinced, they took pains to avoid contact with the wires as they dug under them. Once safely on the other side, they wound their way through the Yangtze delta country, trying to locate bridges across the canals and to avoid "night soil" fertilizer deposits.[51]

Near dawn, they took refuge with a Chinese farmer, but that afternoon Chinese troops surrounded their hideout, marched them to a nearby village, and turned them over to the Japanese. After a surprisingly light interrogation by the Kempeitai, the Japanese military police, and a couple of days in the Woosung jail their captors returned them to the Woosung prison camp where they were ordered to show their escape plan and route to the humiliated camp commandant. Guards paraded the chained escapees in front of the other prisoners who, "brought out supposedly to see how hopeless it was to try to escape, wore secret smiles."[52]

Later, the escapees were taken to Shanghai, tried, and sentenced. Despite Dan Teters's attempts to claim the right of repatriation as a civilian, the Japanese ruled that his active participation in Wake's defense made him ineligible. Teters received a sentence of two years imprisonment; Cunningham and the two other military officers were sentenced to ten years each, and the young Chinese interpreter who had accompanied them got one year. In the Woosung camp, the vicarious thrill of their fellow prisoners' near-escape faded for the men as the days rolled by.[53]

CHAPTER 12

HOPE

***

THE SEABEES

"For my part, with Wake as a horrible example," George Youmans wrote in December 1941 when the fall of Wake was still a raw wound, "we do not feel justified in asking our men to remain on these isolated locations, when proper protection cannot be guaranteed or furnished. If they volunteer, that is something different, but as most of our supervisory staff want to return from the islands, any volunteers should be inducted into the armed service, so they would avoid being shot or executed in case of capture, if the islands were captured by the enemy. As civilians bearing arms, they would be liable to execution if captured. If on military rolls, they would be treated as prisoners of war. (Maybe.)"[1]

Early in the prewar CPNAB construction program, Admiral Moreell had recognized the problems of using civilian contractors on remote projects. Distance and time increased discontent among the workers. Most civilian laborers knew nothing of military organization or discipline, and they risked only their job and pay if they decided to quit. By the fall of 1941, when Admiral Kimmel was relying on the "instinct for self-preservation" among civilian construction workers on the outlying Pacific islands, Moreell was already working on an alternate plan. Recognizing that the new Pacific bases might become targets for enemy attack, Moreell conceived of a separate construction organization within the navy to augment or supplant the civilian workforce. He first focused on Iceland, however, where civilian labor had deteriorated to an alarming level in the fall of 1941. He received authorization in October to form five companies (just under five hundred men) to be trained in Rhode Island as a naval construction unit. They never made it to Iceland. With the events of December 1941 the companies were deployed to the South Pacific. Given the shocking attacks in the Pacific and the fall of Wake, Guam, and Cavite it was clear that the special circumstances of conducting the Pacific war required new tactics. The construction component was vital to establishing and extending the reach of American naval forces in the Pacific.[2]

On December 28, 1941, the U.S. Navy officially launched its new force: the construction battalions, soon known as CBs, or seabees. As Admiral Moreell later reflected the terrible experiences on Wake and elsewhere in the Pacific during December 1941 had revealed that "it was neither fair to the individuals concerned, nor in the interest of over-all military efficiency, to call upon civilian workers, untrained in combat duties and in measures of self-protection, to work under enemy fire." Moreell was careful to acknowledge those civilian workers who had "contributed outstanding services" in the defense of the Pacific islands in the early days of the war, but "they themselves will admit that had they been trained in combat duty, they could have accomplished even more in support of our own military operations."[3]

The navy called for volunteers and a hundred thousand men stepped forward over the first few months of 1942. Many of them were the same experienced tradesmen who had been civilian defense workers. The average age of a seabee was thirty-one, which was a full decade older than the average enlisted man in the regular service. Skilled in their trades and already temperamented to fight, the new boots needed only to be taught how to "salute, shoot, and rig a hammock." The navy commissioned qualified civilian engineers and started seabee enlisted men at higher pay rates than sailors in the regular service. Seabees received training in combat duties and procedures to effect quick, emergency repairs of damage done by the enemy, all the while fulfilling their primary mission: to build bases, harbors, airfields, and other land-based support for the navy in what were now war zones. During World War II, more than 325 thousand men and 8 thousand officers of the Civil Engineer Corps served in the navy's construction battalions.[4]

CPNAB IN WARTIME

During the navy's transition to construction battalions the civilian contractors wrapped up some of their Pacific-island projects while expanding and adding to others on Oahu. The navy had deferred or abandoned most of the contracted work on the remote Pacific islands still in U.S. possession and taken over all previous services provided by the contractors, including supply and subsistence, purchasing, forwarding, and transportation. Where a few civilian contractors remained on the outlying islands, their work was restricted to defense-related projects. Hundreds of workers left Midway, Johnston, and Palmyra and came to Honolulu where some continued to work for the contractors and others headed for the mainland to work or join the armed forces.

On Oahu CPNAB's work continued on high-priority projects at Pearl Harbor: the underground fuel storage tanks at Red Hill and two dry docks in the navy yard. Thousands of civilian contractors worked on projects at Ford Island, Barbers Point, and Kaneohe, additional dredging in Pearl Harbor, construction of Aiea Hospital, and the giant Makapala housing project. New CPNAB projects called for underground tunneling and storage of heavy explosives at Waipahu and for a top-secret, "superpower" radio transmitter high on a cliff on Maui. By the end of May 1942 CPNAB counted 18,095 employees on the payroll with an additional 142 naval personnel "on board." Red Hill, still under Morrison-Knudsen sponsorship, employed 3,384, by far the most on any single CPNAB project. New hires continued to flow in from the mainland and few disgruntled quitters swam home against the stream now that it was wartime.[5]

With the navy also pouring sailors, technicians, and equipment into Pearl Harbor for the salvage operation, relatively few CPNAB men worked on that effort in the harbor, but their contribution was significant in the early months of war. Jack Graham of Pacific Bridge Company, Harry Olson, and other skilled civilians worked long hours to right and raise the damaged ships that the navy could repair for speedy return to service in the Pacific. However, the navy continued to stall on covering the salvage work by contract and, in fact, considered the civilian contribution to be "not of a major nature" to warrant one. The *California* proved to be their most challenging job. In late February the contractors began construction of a full cofferdam around the stricken battleship and it floated free on March 30. As the water receded, hospital personnel stood by with canvas bags into which they floated badly decomposed corpses and body parts. An unexplained explosion on the *California* a week later blew a patch off, but after quick repairs navy tugs finally managed to nudge the ship into dry dock on April 9.[6]

While George Youmans continued to guide Morrison-Knudsen's vital work on the Red Hill project and other CPNAB business in Hawaii, Harry Morrison expanded the company's involvement in defense work and war industry on the mainland in early 1942, especially in shipbuilding contracts. Morrison continued to respond personally to repeated inquiries from Wake family members as well as families of the missing men from Guam and Cavite. Where the navy had confirmed deaths he extended his deepest sympathy, and he steadfastly stayed the course with all who sought information on their missing loved ones. A new company magazine, *The Em Kayan*, made its debut in March 1942 and often featured articles and updates on the CPNAB men. The magazine conveyed confidence and optimism as it covered Morrison-Knudsen's many construction projects and hard-working, fun-loving employees, and the positive attitude carried over to the plight of the Pacific men as well.

The pilot issue of *The Em Kayan* included an editorial from the January 1942 issue of *Pacific Builder and Engineer* that spoke of the CPNAB workers in glowing terms. "The good construction man is a rugged individualist with well formed opinions as to such matters as independence, self-reliance, and taking any lip from a Jap. It would be difficult to imagine those crews on isolated Wake and Guam stopping to weigh their chances for success or waiting for the Navy to come to their rescue. We wager that history will tell a dramatic story of the role these construction crews played as reinforcements to the Marines in the heroic defense of Guam and Wake—a role that will inspire fellow members of the fraternity to grimly speed revenge by expediting the enormous program of war construction that now lies immediately ahead."[7]

The company magazine also carried a story entitled "Thunder over the Islands" that included eyewitness accounts of the Japanese attacks on Palmyra and American Samoa. The article offered a short history of Wake and an overview of the Morrison trip to Wake between October 15 and November 5, 1941, during which they had enjoyed visiting with the Boise boys, but narrowly missed a typhoon: "The yellow typhoon had more expert and sinister direction." The article included several poems written by Wake men in November when "the spell of the South Seas, the perfumed breezes and the moon magic of the blue Pacific broke down the hard and crusty shell of Wake Island workers in an all-out poetry blitzkrieg." Subsequent issues of the company magazine kept the CPNAB story alive, even though details remained sketchy. With few facts and little new information, the editor relied on occasional flights of hyperbole regarding the "indomitable courage" of the CPNAB army. Stock photographs and drawings of palm-laced tropical islands and bare-breasted native women illustrated articles about the Pacific island contractors. *The Em Kayan* also noted the key role played by the CPNAB hiring office in Boise, sponsored by the company, and featured M-K employees involved in the organization.[8]

On April 13, 1942, the CPNAB Executive Committee held a special meeting and passed a unanimous resolution establishing a $300 thousand fund to assist the dependent families of the missing workers. Harry Morrison took the job of directing the fund and setting up the charitable foundation, selecting Tom Hoskot of Morrison-Knudsen to serve as the secretary-treasurer. The Boise-based Pacific Island Workers Association became the nucleus for the new Pacific Island Employees Foundation (PIEF), its officers administering the charitable fund at its incorporation June 1, 1942.

TO THE MAINLAND

In Honolulu, sporadic shelling of the islands by Japanese submarines and heart-stopping air raids, as well as the presence of a large Japanese American population that many still suspected of sabotage, justified the continuation of martial law. The charming city suffocated under restrictions including rigid blackouts and curfews, strict censorship, business closures, rationing, and long lines for everything. Authorities had ordered residents to build bomb shelters and wear gas masks, lei-makers wove camouflage nets instead of flowers, and soldiers slathered public buildings in dark paint and erected miles of barbed wire along the beaches. Many schools were closed and converted to military use; others operated with little attention to actual academics. At Robert Louis Stevenson School seventh-grader June Hokanson, Swede's daughter, joined her classmates digging trenches in the schoolyard and drilling endlessly with their gasmasks. In town residents found lines long and supplies short. Officials urged and then ordered nonessential civilians who were not permanent residents to leave for the mainland.[9]

The great ocean liners continued to ply the Pacific route between the West Coast and Honolulu along with many navy ships and troop transports in well-armed convoys. However, blacked-out windows, stomach-churning zigzag maneuvers, and constant, mandatory use of life jackets sharply curtailed the glamour of the ocean voyage. Overhead, Pan American Clippers shuttled back and forth on their abridged transpacific route between San Francisco and Hawaii, carrying high-ranking officers and government officials. Ships disgorged thousands of fresh troops and defense workers in Honolulu. Wounded military personnel, tourists, navy and army families, and families of defense workers, in that order of priority, boarded for the return trips to the mainland. In the early, chaotic weeks of the war the navy's organization of evacuation left much to be desired and ships departed only partially filled. "You never saw such a mess in your life," wrote George Youmans to Harry Morrison, but over time the process became much more efficient.[10]

The wives of the Wake Island supervisors who had stayed on in Honolulu also prepared to depart. Hopes for rescue or quick repatriation of the Wake men had dwindled and they had long since shelved plans for welcome-home celebrations. During the many weeks since December 7 Harry Olson had lived with his friends' wives and grown close to "the girls," Mae and June Hokanson, and Pete Russell's wife, Eudelle. In the spring the Hokansons took passage on an aging Dutch ship loaded with wounded troops and navy families for the perilous ten-day trip to the West Coast. Their ship and other transports were part of an enormous convoy that reached as far as the eye could see and included damaged naval ships heading back for repairs all guarded by U.S. Navy destroyers. Several weeks later Harry Olson and Eudelle Russell closed up the rental house on Royal Hawaiian Avenue that they had shared alone since the others departed. Eudelle boarded an eastbound ship and made her way to Salem, Oregon, where her daughter and other family members lived. With his part in the Pearl Harbor salvage work completed and no other reason to remain, Harry accepted a job with Morrison-Knudsen on a navy contract project in Pocatello, Idaho, and boarded a ship to San Francisco with a contingent of CPNAB men who had been released from the Midway project. As his ocean liner pulled away from Honolulu there were no white-clad crowds waving aloha, no bands playing, no fragrant leis or confetti, no native boys diving for tossed coins.[11]

In the early months of war Katherine Olson devoted herself to the task of locating Ted and preparing the Portland house for her husband's return. Harry's letters from Honolulu had dwindled to a near stop and only an occasional, cryptic telegram apprised her of his whereabouts and plans. When he finally returned it was only to leave right away for the Pocatello job where he was to be general construction superintendent on a $20 million Morrison-Knudsen contract with the navy for a gun relining plant. It was a "rush job" with no provisions for family residence, Harry explained, dispelling any thoughts Katherine might have about joining him. Within a few weeks Eudelle Russell joined Harry as his secretarial assistant and they took up residence in a Pocatello hotel.

In April copies of a cable dated March 18 from the International Red Cross in Geneva to the U.S. Department of State surfaced and local Red Cross chapters sent it to POW families, raising hopes among many families. A Red Cross representative had visited the Zentsuji POW camp and offered a detailed description of location, facilities, food, work, and the fact that 374 prisoners were currently interred there, including "20 from Wake." The report conveyed a positive overall assessment of Japan's "model" POW camp: adequate meals, recreation, hygienic facilities, and pay for work. The Red Cross advised families to try sending letters via their agency, addressing the envelope with the words "Believed to have been taken prisoner by Japan on the Island of Wake." Katherine Olson's congressman sent the translated cable and assured her that he would contact her immediately upon receipt of any definite information including prisoner names and locations from the "State, War, and Navy Departments."[12]

THE PRISONERS

For the 387 American prisoners still on Wake Island that spring life revolved around food, tobacco, work, and the constant ebb and flow of scuttlebutt that kept hopes alive. Air raids occasionally shattered the grinding tedium of captivity. Each man handled the experience in his own way; some handled it better than others. "It is my firm belief that the U.S. forces will not come in here unless they need the island," Pete Russell wrote in his diary on April 1, 1942, "and from all appearances, they do not." Yet he too clung to the hope that their ordeal would soon end. Pete, like others, made sure to include careful observations of Japanese ship and aircraft traffic in his diary. Persistent rumors had Uncle Sam just over the horizon, coming to the rescue. "Nothing different today," Pete wrote on May 14, 1942, "except the scuttlebutt is getting so thick it is hard to wade out." The men bet often and heavily, fifty dollars here and ninety dollars there, on whether they would leave Wake by the end of this week, by the end of this month, by the end of next month. Pete generally won, betting against the sooner option, whatever it was.[13]

By April, the American food storage was running out and prisoners began receiving Japanese rations, which consisted of rice-based meals, fish, rabbit, and tea, augmented by the occasional wild bird egg. Beer and sake could be had by trade. Dysentery and other illnesses continued to plague the camp and at night the barracks were "thick with rats." Every few weeks the Japanese celebrated some national holiday with games and special meals displacing work for a day or half-day. For many Americans the highlight of the week was tobacco day when they were given a pack or two of cigarettes or some tobacco that they could roll. Occasionally their captors doled out toiletries. A Japanese language contest was held for the prisoners in late April with a toothbrush and tooth powder as prizes for the ten men who knew the most words. Ships came in nearly daily with provisions, equipment, "Jap engineers" by the hundreds, and one brought an acting troop: rumor had it that "47 whores" were part of the entertainment. The Americans had to content themselves with games, books, and visiting. Those who had relatives or hometown friends in the group could ameliorate their loneliness by reminiscing about good old days. Pete's cousin Donald Rohan "stopped by for a talk and we fished several streams around home for an hour or so."[14]

The Japanese organized work schedules and each morning trucks packed tight with prisoners left the compound for points around the atoll. However, the organization was loose and the actual labor was even looser. For many the day's work consisted of hiding out, sitting around, whiling away hours reading, or leaning on a shovel and assuming the "WPA pose." The Americans had little incentive to labor with gusto for their captors and apparently received scant punishment for the generally slow pace. Punishment was, however, constant and harsh for the imported Korean and Chinese workers, whom the Americans referred to as "coolies." Still, many Americans worked at repairs, remodeling, and new construction and the Japanese pushed for completion and partial paving of all three runways at the airfield. Plans included construction of a marine railway and a 120-foot bridge to arc fifty feet over the barge channel between Wake and Wilkes, but these languished in the layout stage. Prisoners also labored on Japanese defenses, including tank traps, trenches, and a network of concrete pillboxes, magazines, command posts, and bomb shelters. Heavy equipment operators trained Japanese counterparts who took over some of the American machinery. Every such change, every arrival of a big ship, and every significant movement of planes fueled the prisoners' scuttlebutt of their impending departure.[15]

Swede Hokanson was one of a number for whom a work slow-down was just not enough. These men continued to look for every possible opportunity to actively sabotage the work. On their own or with others they perpetrated trickery at the docks, manipulated materials orders, cleverly concealed structural flaws in the Japanese dugouts and gun emplacements, incapacitated the dredge, hoisted damaged Japanese boats and planes and "accidentally" damaged them more: as the weeks passed they grew ever more adept at their deceptions. Most of the sabotage slipped by unnoticed, but occasionally the Japanese detected something amiss, and meted out punishment if they caught the culprit.[16]

On April 26 morning roll call revealed that two men were missing. Elmer Mackie and Donald Sullivan, two dredge hands, had made their escape by whaleboat, their absence well covered by others. A few other prisoners had been in on the carefully laid plan: Mackie and Sullivan had squirreled away food, water, a sail, a small engine, and a hundred gallons of gas. They had a compass but no sextant, and it was said that neither of the men knew much navigation. On May 5 a proclamation was read to the assembled prisoners that the two Americans had been captured at sea and executed and that henceforth rules would be more rigid on Wake. The Japanese interpreter Katsumi privately told some of the men that they heard via radio that the men were captured at Truk in the Marshalls, taken aboard a warship, and shot. The prisoners doubted this, and preferred to imagine the two had made what many dreamed of: a successful escape from "Otorishima."[17]

One prisoner suffered the ultimate punishment on Wake. Julius "Babe" Hofmeister, a roofer in his midthirties with a weakness for booze and an aversion to forced labor, drank his way through all the alcohol he could find during the siege and early months of captivity. He had been repeatedly warned, punished, given the "water cure," and even jailed with another prisoner and starved for several days in mid-April with little discernible effect. On May 8 Babe was arrested for sneaking outside the compound in the night, breaking into the Japanese canteen, and getting drunk again. This was the last straw: Babe was summarily tried and sentenced to die. Pete Russell, Swede Hokanson, and the other supervisors and foremen were forced to witness the execution of Hofmeister, who knelt before a ditch where he was beheaded on May 10, 1942. The following day the Japanese took the twenty wounded American servicemen, now sufficiently recuperated for transport, aboard the *Asama Maru* for prison camps in Japan.[18]

By the end of April, the first names of some of the men in the Woosung (Shanghai) POW camp began to trickle out via the Red Cross. Joe McDon-

ald's father immediately wrote to Commander Cunningham at the Shanghai camp in care of the Red Cross in Geneva. He explained the mix-up in
the death notification and inquired if Cunningham knew the whereabouts
of his son, Joe, "a husky youngster." By then, Cunningham, as well as Dan
Teters and the three other Woosung escapees were languishing in solitary
confinement at the Kiang-wan Military Prison outside of Shanghai awaiting
sentencing for their conviction, curiously, as deserters of the Japanese
army.[19]

THE NEWS: APRIL–MAY 1942

On April 9, 1942, Bataan surrendered to the Japanese. While several thousand soldiers retreated to the stronghold of Corregidor, the Japanese took
thirty-five thousand American and Filipino defenders prisoner and forced
many of them on the torturous Bataan Death March. By mid-April the
British defense of oil fields in central Burma collapsed under relentless Japanese pressure. The April 18 Doolittle raid against Tokyo and other Japanese
cities gave Americans a rare occasion to cheer, but by the end of the month
Japan had swept into central Burma, established a key foothold in the
Solomons, and stood poised to break through to Australia.

The Battle of Coral Sea in the first week of May, waged almost entirely
by carrier aircraft, gave the Japanese another victory, but their heavy losses
stalled the momentum they had maintained since December 7. The Americans lost the carrier *Lexington* and two other ships, and the carrier *Yorktown*
was damaged in the battle. On May 7 the last holdout in the Philippines
fell and the Japanese took sixteen thousand defenders prisoner at Corregidor.
As predicted by many naval strategists over the decades the Philippines could
not ultimately hold out against Japan. Despite the five-month stand by
American and Filipino defenders, their sacrifices carried little strategic value:
American and Allied forces were nowhere near the neighborhood.[20]

In Europe, Soviet troops bore the brunt of the Axis onslaught as Germany conscripted soldiers from its partner countries and poured a "surge"
force of more than half a million men against the eastern front. By mid-May
Germany was finally victorious in the Crimea, with horrific casualties on
both sides, but continued to meet fierce Soviet resistance to the east. Meanwhile, beleaguered British forces were losing ground in North Africa against
Rommel's army. The grim headlines followed day after week after month.
As new draftees swelled the ranks of U.S. forces and Allied military leaders

planned new strategies for Europe, an unanticipated opportunity presented itself in the Pacific at Midway atoll.

WAKE ISLAND, SUMMER 1942

In late May the American prisoners on Wake Island began to note unusual Japanese movements that suggested preparations for a great battle. Increasing numbers of bombers and ships arrived at the atoll, and on May 30 the Japanese commandant questioned a number of the Americans about Midway, lighting a new streak of scuttlebutt among the prisoners. Groups of Japanese bombers began to fly in and out daily and a flotilla of ships departed to the northeast on June 2. Frank Miller and others who worked at the airfield had to walk to and from camp as transportation had been curtailed to conserve gas. By June 7 the men counted over thirty bombers on Wake. "I think the heavy concentration is for the purpose of attacking our fleet if it gets close enough," Pete Russell wrote. The next day both Pete and Frank noted the departure of the bombers, arrival of nineteen more, and considerable ship activity offshore. "Japanese say a big sea battle taking place between here and Midway."[21]

By late May U.S. naval intelligence had intercepted Japanese messages regarding an impending attack on Midway preceded by diversionary strikes in the Aleutian Islands. Naval commanders anticipated that the Japanese would launch an air attack from carriers and initiated regular B-17 patrol flights from Midway, but the possibility of a night strike by enemy landplanes launched from Wake Island concerned them. In fact, two land-based bombers from Wake did maul U.S. patrol planes in the days leading up to the battle. This suggested that if American strategy included an attack on Wake, the "proper time . . . was just at sunset, as only then could these planes be caught on the ground." The focus for both sides, however, remained on Midway. Forewarned and prepared, Admiral Chester Nimitz led the U.S. Navy into battle at Midway on June 4, 1942. In fierce fighting, Japan lost four aircraft carriers and a heavy cruiser, as well as 332 planes. The U.S. lost the carrier *Yorktown*, a destroyer, and 147 planes, but still held Midway at the end of the battle. On the night of June 6 Major General Clarence L. Tinker led a fresh group of army B-24 Liberators armed with 500-pound bombs off Midway into an overcast sky in order to attack Wake and eliminate the enemy bomber base there. They never found the atoll and Tinker's plane was lost at sea. Meanwhile the Japanese forces retreated to Wake Island, hoping to lure the American task force into range for attack, but the Americans did not take the bait.[22]

By June 10 word rippled through the Wake camp that the U.S. Navy had badly beaten the Japanese at Midway. Dozens of bombers and ships returned to Wake, looking to Swede Hokanson like a "pack of dogs after a fight," and the island went on high alert in anticipation that American forces would chase the enemy down and liberate Wake. Japanese pilots rotated through patrols and practiced skirmishes (judged "not so hot" by prisoners watching the show), air raid warnings shrieked, but there was no sign of the American navy. Within a few days the Japanese bombers all took off for the Marshalls.[23]

The attempt to capture Midway confirmed American speculation that Japan's intentions were to use Wake as a forward base for offensive action eastward toward Midway and Hawaii. Wake had provided both a point of origin and staging base for the bombing attack against Midway. In addition, Wake provided a base for aerial reconnaissance of American shipping and naval task force operations, communications facilities to transmit the information to higher command, and, potentially, bombers with which to attack American sea lanes to the Southwest Pacific. The failure at Midway did not end Wake's effectiveness in Japan's Pacific strategy: the future remained wide open in mid-1942. In U.S. strategy, Japanese-occupied Wake posed a threat that would have to be neutralized, but was "never regarded as an objective of major importance."[24]

On June 23 the Wake prisoners glumly marked six months as Japanese prisoners. "God grant we do not have to be here another like period," wrote Pete Russell. "Seems more like six years but, then, it could have been infinitely worse," Miller wrote in his diary. "It's probably only a matter of time until we all get back home, but I do wish there were some way of speeding the passage of the darned thing, or at least some way of knowing how much longer we still have to put in." The Midway battle gave everyone on Wake the jitters, but soon the hot, sultry weather gave way to rains so heavy that they that rivaled the anticipated air attacks. By June 24 Pete had ceased to mark the comings and goings of enemy craft, but noted that Wake had collected a record-breaking 400 thousand gallons of rainwater on that day alone, for a total of 647thousand gallons since June 15. On June 28 showers of a different sort fell over Wake, reawakening the heart-pounding combination of fear and hope in the prisoners. As a barrage of American bombs dropped over the atoll in the dark the prisoners scrambled into clothes and dodged blasts of coral as they ran for the dugout. Some fell on the coral as others trampled over them; one man suffered two broken toes. Pete dove into the dugout just as the Japanese antiaircraft guns opened up. Wake stayed on nervous alert for a number of days, presumably with an attendant rash of hasty bets among prisoners on how soon the invasion and rescue would come, and four prisoner barracks instituted their own night watches with pairs of men taking one-hour slots. The patrols allowed all to sleep better with the assurance that they would have better warning the next time.[25]

While Dr. Shank dealt with individual injuries and illnesses among the prisoners and Dr. Cunha filled cavities and pulled teeth, the Japanese monitored the general health of the prisoner population. In early July, they responded to general weight loss, lethargy, and colds among the men by ordering physical exams, typhus shots, dysentery medication, and vitamin supplements. The prisoners enjoyed increased rations: "meatballs, catsup, mashed potatoes, and gravy" on July 8. The new regimen, however, could not save carpenter William Miles, who died of septicemia July 15 and was buried by the common grave near the airfield. Lloyd McKeehan, the "28-day wonder" who had surrendered after nearly a month in hiding, survived an appendix operation. As the summer weeks wore on ships arrived nearly daily with supplies, cement, and equipment, as well as regular deliveries of food, primarily rice. The men increasingly found their rice and barley "garnished with nice succulent gray worms" or swallowed flies with a mouthful of dinner in the field, but retained fair general health except for colds, dysentery, and in September a run of jaundice through the camp.[26]

Work details continued, ranging from mundane jobs to specific military projects such as construction of concrete gun emplacements. Heavy equipment operators stayed busy on roads, trenches, the airfield, and building sites. Frank Miller welcomed one assignment to "repairing chairs for the Nips" in the old movie screen shed on August 3 and 4. "Spent more time sitting on the work than working on the sit (a good example of the retrogressed brand of humor prevalent on Wake)," he wrote in his diary. Increasingly in August and September the Japanese assigned details to work on pillbox positions at strategic points around the island. The gun nests were constructed with thick concrete walls and roof and three openings for machine guns. Tradesmen including carpenters and steel workers remained in crews for the work assignments, but others might find themselves assigned to any of a number of jobs, even crating empty beer bottles for shipment back to Japan. Often the men hid out in the barracks or brush to escape notice, and thus work. So many men whiled away the time reading that the Japanese forbade taking books out of camp and held the books in an office, dolling out batches of a hundred at a time, which the men had to check out individually, as if in a library. "Time still drags heavy," Pete Russell wrote in the diary where his entries grew increasingly brief and terse as he marked the passage of time. By September accusations of prisoner sabotage increased and guards brandished pistols and lead pipes to threaten suspected saboteurs.[27]

CONFIRMATION

A number of families began to receive the long-awaited confirmation of the location of their loved ones in early summer. In mid-June Katherine Olson received the news that Ted was alive and interned by Japan at Shanghai. A swelling stream of mail confirmed the news as the days went by: the War Department Office of the Provost Marshall, Navy Bureau of Yards and Docks, Red Cross, and the Pacific Island Employees Foundation in Boise. Oregon Congressman James Mott wrote to Katherine, "I rejoice with you in the knowledge that your son is a prisoner and not a casualty." The families of Roger Smalley, Joe McDonald, and hundreds of others were receiving similar barrages of telegrams and mail with the welcome news. There were no such notices for Eudelle Russell, Mae Hokanson, Peter Hansen's wife, Frank Miller's folks, or for over three hundred other families waiting for word on their missing men, who were, unbeknownst to them, still on Wake Island.[28]

Appended to the official notices were directions for sending mail to the internees and instructions to discuss only personal matters as the Japanese government would censor all letters before delivery. Family members, eager to reach out to their men at last, scrupulously followed instructions for addressing the envelopes. Two weeks later the War Department Office of Supply advised the families that they might also send postage-free parcel by a Red Cross ship sailing in mid-August. The War Department mailing suggested items such as cigarettes, toothbrushes, and underwear, and included explicit instructions regarding restrictions, size and weight limits, and specific wording for the addressee.[29]

Like Katherine, many other parents, wives, girlfriends, and relatives wrote letters right away. Virtually all obeyed the content control guidelines although some occasionally passed on news of good old "Uncle Sammy's" travels that escaped the censors. Joe McDonald's parents wasted no time writing to their son. "It seems like life is starting all over again, now that we can actually write to you and with the hope that you may eventually get it." From Honolulu, Roger Smalley's mother wrote with "oceans of love . . . We are so anxious to hear from you and hope and pray that you are safe and that you will be back with us soon again right away." Mrs. Smalley also mentioned that "June and Mae Hokanson went back to New Mexico. Tell Ted and Sweed hello from us," she wrote."[30]

On July 15, 1942, the War Department officially confirmed the names of 156 of the nearly 800 Americans captured on Wake and interned at Shanghai, opening the floodgates to more and more names. Newspapers and radio stations released names of local men reported as prisoners of war. The Portland papers printed the names of some of the Oregon men, their home addresses, and next of kin. The twenty-three names included Ted Olson, and listed Katherine Olson and the Moore Street address in Portland. However, it was not long before the names trickled to a stop, leaving hundreds of families to wait, hoping for the best and fearing the worst. No one had yet received a letter from a POW himself.[31]

However, the prisoners had been allowed to write their first letters from Woosung as early as late May. Some of the letters from Shanghai War Prisoners' Camp made it through censors and long sea voyages sooner than others did. John Polak, Wake's office manager, obtained permission from the Japanese authorities to write to Harry Morrison informing him of the large number of Wake employees interned at Shanghai, "all in good health and well treated," and requesting that Morrison pursue repatriation for them through American authorities if he had not already done so. If such efforts had failed, Polak wrote, "It is urgently requested that financial relief be forwarded to us via official channels now open. Also please advise if the employees' monthly allotments are being continued. This is a matter of great concern to us." As the prisoners' letters started to appear, many echoed Polak's interest in repatriation and concerns about continuing wages.[32]

In a letter written to his congressman Daniel C. Hall described daily life in the prison camp including meals, light work, and evening games. Still the approximately 770 Wake civilians found it harder to adjust to prison life than the marines who were generally younger and had the benefit of military training and discipline. Hall implored his senator to use his influence for their repatriation and, in the meantime, to help set up a fund through the contractors and official channels "whereby we could be self-supporting in an atmosphere more to the liking of a civilian."[33]

Ted Olson's carefully written letter, like most, was tied up by the censors for months:

> *Dear Mother and Family,*
> *I hope this letter finds you all well and happy. I don't know if you received my radio message or not, so I'll tell you now that I'm well and getting along fine.*
>
> *A couple other fellows and I are raising chickens for the Japanese. It is interesting work and helps to pass the time away.*
>
> *I would like to know if my pay is still going on or not. If none is coming home, would you please contact Alameda and find out what the situation is. Write and let me know. My address is at the bottom of this letter.*
>
> *Let Dee Dee know that I'm all right and give her my address. Tell her I'll write as soon as I can. We are allowed to write one letter per month.*
>
> *I don't know when I'll be home but hope that it will be sometime in the near future. Don't worry about me. Give everyone my love.*
> *Love, Ted Olson*
> *Shanghai War-prisoner's Camp*
> *Japanese Field Post Office 106, Shanghai, Central China, Barracks 5*

Repatriation remained a running theme throughout the early months of war in the scuttlebutt on Wake, the drafty barracks of Woosung, and in homes and offices across the nation. Most expected that Japan would send the civilian prisoners home, possibly in some form of exchange with Japanese civilians in the United States. Congressmen, War Department officials, and Red Cross representatives continued to press for an exchange. The early letters to and from the Shanghai War Prisoners' Camp at Woosung in the summer of 1942 convey optimism that such a solution was not only possible, but also probable.

The key complication that stood in the way of repatriation was that

Japan was not bound by Geneva protocol, although it had signaled its intention to negotiate "in the spirit of the Geneva Conventions." Authorities carefully monitored the signals from Japan and kept hopes alive with cautious optimism. Those familiar with the Geneva Conventions knew that certain sections specifically defined civilian militias and volunteer groups (Article 4.1.2) and that if the Wake civilians did not fall under those definitions Japan should not consider them prisoners of war.[34]

Early in 1942 the U.S. State Department chartered the *Gripsholm* as an exchange and repatriation vessel under the protection of the Red Cross. It departed New York on the first voyage for this purpose on June 18, 1942, with over a thousand Japanese deportees and family members. The ship stopped in Rio de Janeiro to pick up several hundred more Japanese nationals, and arrived in Mozambique in late July 1942. There the *Gripsholm* met the *Asama Maru* and *Conte Verde*, which together carried about 1,500 Allied civilians from Japan, Shanghai, Indochina, and the Philippines, many of them in appalling physical and mental condition from their ordeals. At least one Wake family had received notification that repatriation might be imminent: the War Department notified the mother of Jack E. Ward that a "J. Ward" was on the list of those who were to depart Shanghai on the *Conte Verde* and advised her to "watch the daily paper for details" on the exchange ship arrival. However, neither Jack Ward nor any of the hundreds of other civilian prisoners in the Shanghai War Prisoners' Camp were among the repatriated passengers. After the *Gripsholm*'s return to New York on August 25, 1942, returnees shared news of POW conditions under the Japanese, although none pertained directly to the Woosung camp. Japan eventually classified the captured Wake, Guam, and Cavite civilian workers as prisoners of war rather than civilian internees, dashing hopes for their repatriation during the war.[35]

Financial matters remained a chief concern. The prisoners assumed their contracted allotments were still being sent to the mainland on their behalf, which was not the case. In fact, dependents were then receiving only the small monthly checks allotted by the Social Security Administration pending further legislation. The newly incorporated Pacific Island Employees Foundation, which had been set up by Harry Morrison in the spring and funded with $300 thousand from the CPNAB companies, identified needy dependents and began to augment the Social Security payments with charitable relief funds on both regular and special needs bases. In addition to providing relief for dependents, the PIEF began to issue monthly newsletters with updates on information regarding the status and location of the missing men, a matter of vital importance to all.[36]

The men who had been on Wake for some time and whose jobs qualified for overtime had accumulated a substantial sum held by the navy on deposit in Honolulu at the time of the Japanese attack. This was the "Unpaid Wages, Overtime, and Bonus Account." Early in 1942 the funds were transferred to the mainland where they remained under navy control and could only be accessed by court order. Few dependents went through the process to apply for appointment as trustees in order to obtain the funds. The Social Security payments remained woefully insufficient for dependent families. Clearly, there was a pressing need for legislation to compensate the civilian contractors and their hard-pressed dependents. California union leader C. J. Haggerty lobbied in Washington on behalf of the newly-formed "Women of Wake" organization, led by Mary Ward of Los Angeles. In the summer of 1942 it was apparent that the support of the American Federation of Labor, as well as military and government agencies, gave a bill the best chance of passage.[37]

INTERNMENT OF JAPANESE AMERICANS

In contrast to the captured Wake Island civilians, who were considered prisoners of war by Japan, the United States government used the term "civilian evacuees" for the Japanese Americans who were rounded up early in 1942. The government repatriated hundreds of Japanese nationals, including diplomats, businessmen, and journalists, as well as family members who accompanied them, on the exchange ships. However, the Western Defense Command recommended to the secretary of war the physical removal of some 112 thousand West Coast Japanese Americans to inland "relocation centers" based on the likelihood of sabotage. Lieutenant General John L. DeWitt, head of the Western Defense Command, declared that the "Japanese race is an enemy race" and, despite Americanization, "the racial strains are undiluted. A Jap's a Jap," DeWitt pronounced more than once. "The very fact that no sabotage has taken place to date," he wrote, "is a disturbing and confirming indication that such action will be taken." In the early 1942 atmosphere of fear the War Department approved DeWitt's recommendations on the basis of military necessity. Relocation of the Japanese Americans, two-thirds of whom were American citizens, received endorsement all the way up the chain of command. The War Relocation Authority (WRA) was created by executive order on March 18, 1942, to identify inland areas suitable for "relocation centers." The exclusion area comprised all or parts of the West Coast states between Canada and Mexico. The WRA chose remote, rural locations for ten centers that were built in short order in Idaho, Wyoming, Colorado, Utah, California, Arizona, and Arkansas.[38]

Domestic defense, argued the government, justified internment of Japanese American citizens. Motivated in part by the imported Hawaiian hysteria that conjured up fifth-columnists and saboteurs behind every palm tree in the early weeks of the war, the sweeping legislation was designed to preclude any such action on the mainland. With imminent, wholesale movement of tens of thousands of Japanese Americans from the West Coast to inland regions, the government quickly chose contractors to build the relocation centers. In Idaho, the job of rapid camp construction was made to order for Boise's Morrison-Knudsen Company. The fact that a large percentage of the CPNAB civilian POWs held by Japan were local men hired through the M-K-affiliated office gave pause to some: building internment camps in Idaho might end up being detrimental to the civilian POWs in Japan, especially if the Japanese Americans were mistreated. However, the argument for moral equivalency did not deter Morrison-Knudsen from taking on two relocation camp contracts in early summer of 1942: a $3.5 million contract for Minidoka in south-central Idaho and another for Tule Lake in northern California. Under intense pressure from the WRA, the contractors threw up spare, Spartan structures in record time for immediate occupancy. Each relocation center had thirty to forty residential blocks with military-style barracks, mess halls, latrines, and laundry. The self-contained camps included schools, post offices, hospitals, and warehouses inside barbed-wire enclosures with guard towers.

Morrison-Knudsen's *Em Kayan* magazine made scant mention of the company's participation in the construction of Japanese internment camps in the inland western states. However, a brief article printed in July 1942 entitled "Keep 'Em Together" celebrated the completion of California's Tulelake Japanese Evacuee Reception Center, a project of 1,439 buildings, utilities, and roads, built "on an assembly line plan" with remarkable rapidity. The company completed a modern hospital, the writer boasted, in fifteen days. The mess hall, started on a Saturday, had four thousand internees sitting down "to the best mess in all of California" the following Tuesday. Morrison-Knudsen's partner in the Tule Lake project was Ford J. Twaits Company. The *Em Kayan* made no reference to the camp's purpose and neither this nor any subsequent issue mentioned the company's construction of the Minidoka internment camp in M-K's home state of Idaho.

"WAKE ISLAND," THE MOVIE

On August 11, 1942, Paramount Pictures released America's first World War II combat film, *Wake Island*, and it showed to packed audiences in movie theaters across the nation. Conceived in December 1941, before the siege of Wake was even over, the screenplay went through numerous revisions to end up with a dramatic, quasi-historical plot and went into production early in 1942. With technical advisors from the U.S. Marine Corps and civilian contractors, producers kept the script under tight guard to protect "extremely confidential" information. Location shots were filmed at Salton Sea, California, where a four-thousand-foot clay runway was constructed for the war film. Just a mile away contractors worked feverishly to convert a seaplane base for navy use in the real war. Two thousand Filipino actors portrayed the Japanese invaders since all West Coast Japanese American actors had by then been "relocated." The movie took many liberties with historical accuracy and a contemporary critic derided the "carelessness, conventionality, lack of imagination, lack of insight into faces, minds, motions," but the movie delivered a patriotic punch. *Wake Island* received nominations for four Academy Awards, winning one for Best Director. Audiences walked away from the theaters with mistaken assumptions that the civilians had refused to cooperate with the marines and that all of the Americans had been annihilated in a Pacific Alamo, but infused with a patriotic glow that translated into thousands of marine enlistments and spurred war bond sales across the nation.[39]

Among the Wake veterans who had left the island prior to the Japanese attack, many viewed the motion picture and press coverage with dismay. Herman Echols, the assistant superintendent of administration on Wake who, like Harry Olson, had departed for vacation just days before the war began, wrote a scathing letter to the editor of the *Saturday Evening Post*, with a carbon copy to Harry Morrison. Echols described "the agony" of sitting through a special preview of the picture, "into which, for no good reason apparent to me, a feud between the civilian personnel and Marine personnel on Wake prior to December 7, 1941 was injected," and proceeded to rebut many aspects of the film that disparaged the civilian efforts and accomplishments. "I would not detract a bit from the splendid work of the Marines and other armed forces at Wake or elsewhere, but I know there is an equally interesting and dramatic story in the life and work of these particular civilians who were on Wake Island, who volunteered and were training along with the Marines on anti-aircraft and other defense equipment, who are now dispersed God knows where, and who continue to be ignored or mis-represented in official circles."[40]

THE PACIFIC WAR

By July 1942 Japan's Greater East Asia Co-Prosperity Sphere stretched from the Japanese home islands north to encompass Attu and Kiska in the Aleutians, south around the Gilberts, west into the Solomons, including Guadalcanal, and over most of New Guinea. The line of conquests continued up around the Dutch East Indies including Borneo, Sumatra, and Malaya, and north into Indochina and Burma. It pressed into India before circling back toward the east, skirting the Chinese coastal areas, bulging into north China and Manchuria, and crossed over Korea to complete the circle. Inside the sphere were the Bonins, Formosa, the Philippines, Carolines, Marianas, Marshalls, and Wake Island. However, safely outside the sphere sat Midway Island, where U.S. forces had halted Japan's expansion in the June battle. Japanese long-range submarines still penetrated far across the Pacific that summer, occasionally lobbing shells at the Hawaiian Islands, and even approached the continental West Coast. A Japanese submarine hit a lighthouse on Vancouver Island in British Columbia and, more seriously but also without damage, shelled Fort Stevens, near Astoria, Oregon.

The United States took the offensive for the first time with the August 7 invasion of Guadalcanal and began what promised to be a long battle with heavy losses on both sides for control of the Solomons. The seabees made their debut at Guadalcanal where the 1st Marine Division had established a toehold. Armed with one rifle for every two men, the eleven hundred seabees of the 6th Naval Construction Battalion repaired and completed a runway under fire and dashed out to fill craters and lay new steel planking between strafing attacks. The first real test of the seabee model—trained, armed, and disciplined construction workers in uniform—was a success.[41]

As the seabees trained and prepared to take over many of the projects and types of work originally envisioned for CPNAB, Admiral Moreell made a special effort to acknowledge the contribution of the civilian contractors. On June 19, 1942, he issued an official letter of commendation for CPNAB's overall work in the Pacific and reviewed the unprecedented growth and accomplishments of the consortium. Organized in the late summer of 1939 for $15 million of work over three years, CPNAB had taken on additional and expanded projects totaling about $250 million, of which the contractors had completed $160 million in less than three years. The contractors had achieved this under great difficulties and challenges, especially with the loss of personnel in the Philippines, Guam, and Wake. Moreell expressed his deep personal appreciation to all engaged in this tremendous undertaking. Their great sacrifices, he wrote, were justified only by the great prize at stake, one worth fighting for: "democracy . . . to pass on to our children and our children's children for all time." In the summer of 1942 over 18 thousand CPNAB employees still toiled on the "front lines of war" doing work that Moreell declared was "the most important activity being carried out."[42]

Allied offensive action increased in the Pacific and Asia as U.S. forces hit Japanese holdings in the Aleutians, raided Makin Island in the Gilberts, and reinforced the Australian defense of Port Moresby, Papua New Guinea. Britain went on the offensive in Burma and Chinese troops began to gain on Japanese forces in China. However, Wake Island, once so important in naval strategy, now fell far down the list of priorities, and the navy did not attempt to regain the atoll. Warships and bombers often used it for target practice en route to the battle zones in the western Pacific.

The grand sweep of war had brushed the controversial matter of its origins aside. On a brief visit to the mainland in the spring of 1942 George Youmans had noted that "evidently, the whole affair is being 'soft-pedaled' as much as possible by the Administration and the War and Navy Departments." The Roberts report and "setting Admiral Kimmel and General Short down" was not the answer to it, he argued. "If the House and Senate do not instigate an investigation of the whole reason and cause of our lack of preparedness, they are certainly negligent in their duties to the taxpayers. There is plenty of evidence available, if they really want to get it, showing how the appropriations have been wasted and defense facilities delayed by inefficient management of those in authority, all the way down from the President. Our files at Pearl Harbor are full of such data, if we were asked to produce it."[43]

CHAPTER 13

ATTRITION

<hr/>

THE SEPTEMBER EXODUS

ON WAKE ISLAND LITTLE CHANGE MARKED THE TURN FROM SUMMER to fall in 1942. The American prisoners, working at a fraction of their prewar speed, had managed to lay out a new airport parking area, completed the diagonal runway, and built hangars and pillboxes for their captors. A bout of jaundice had run through the camp; food and tempers were short. Despite the constant scuttlebutt predicting departure and ample warning signs that it was imminent the news in late September took them by surprise: the majority of them would leave Wake shortly. The Japanese made out a list of about 100 Americans to remain on Wake to continue working; the rest would be shipped to prison camps in Japan. Orders came for the larger group of 265 to pack their belongings. Pete Russell, Frank Miller, and others tucked diaries into secret pockets that they had sewn earlier; many like Peter Hansen scrambled to find places to hide precious photographs and letters. Some of the men negotiated last-minute switches. When the Myers father and son saw they were to be separated, the crane operators said that they did not care whether they stayed or went as long as they could be together. Joe Mittendorff, another crane oiler, would stay in young Leroy's stead. Doctors Shank and Cunha would stay to care for the remaining prisoners on Wake. No one knew if it would be better to stay or to go, but everyone had an opinion on it.[1]

The time came for departure. Goodbyes were hard on many who had forged deep friendships in the ten months of shared imprisonment on Wake.

Now the men climbed into trucks for the last ride to the waterfront and waved farewell to their friends. What was left of Camp 2 disappeared behind them. The trucks rumbled past concrete pillboxes that the prisoners had worked on steadily for their captors since early August. Somewhere in the distance lay the graves of their fallen compatriots. At the waterfront the *Tachibana Maru*, a combination freighter-tanker, loomed off shore.

As the men got out of the trucks and assembled, guards examined their baggage. Swede Hokanson later told a story that he had left his jacket on the derrick barge and asked a guard for permission to go get it. On the barge, he climbed down the ladder for one last "good deed" on Wake: taking up a crowbar, Swede punched through a soft plank on the bottom until the water came gushing in. He climbed out of the hold, dropped the crowbar over the side, picked up his jacket and the cane that he used now, and returned to the dock. The prisoners lined up and awaited their turns for transport to the Japanese ship. As the boats and barges carried them out the channel they turned for a last look at Wake. They could all agree that it had not turned out to be quite what they had bargained for. From the shore a few men waved, their faces growing indistinct with distance.[2]

Chance, more than choice, determined who would survive the next three years. The voyage of the *Tachibana Maru*, similar in its horrors to that of the *Nitta Maru*, brought 265 additional American civilian prisoners to Japan. On October 11, 1942, the ship docked at Yokohama where the Japanese separated five men, including Pete Russell, and sent them to Ofuna prison camp. Pete's prison transfers indicate a track shared by only a few of the Wake group. In December 1942, he was moved to Yokohama where the prisoners worked in the Mitsubishi shipyard. On December 21, 1942, Pete was issued a card to write his first note home. Within a month, he fell gravely ill with beriberi. From September 1943 to November 1944 Pete remained in a Tokyo hospital camp. When he received his first box from home on January 9, 1944, he found Eudelle's return addresses of Pocatello and Spokane puzzling. Soon letters began to come from family and friends. "I've read them all a dozen times but the one from my darling's I read & re-read all day long." Eudelle's letters did not reveal that she was living with Harry Olson.[3]

Swede Hokanson and the majority of the Wake prisoners from the September exodus traveled by train three days south to Sasebo and another thirty miles to an airfield and dam site. The camp, later designated Fukuoka 18-

B, or "Camp 18," was unknown to the outside world until its inmates were identified late in 1944, and little came out about it after the war. During their internment the POWs built Soto Dam for their captors, slaving away under horrific conditions and ruthless guards. There was no comfort of letters in or out for these prisoners. "Their treatment under the Jap Navy was cruel and barbarous and many died from pneumonia brought on by malnutrition and exposure," wrote Tom Hoskot in a report to Harry Morrison shortly after the war ended.[4]

Frank Miller, the young asphalt technician who had arrived on Wake just days before the Japanese attack and whose wartime diary revealed much about conditions on Wake up to September 29, 1942, resumed writing in his diary on a "snowy and cold and muddy" February 8, 1943. All diaries and receipt books had been confiscated for inspection, which may explain a large gap of the previous several months. Miller's entries contain sparse information about his work details: "Cement today and the toughest one yet. Carried a longhaul with not nearly enough men in the carrying line. . . . Mess detail for me today. Had no food given to me while washing dishes, but I did find a few cigarette butts. . . . Worked in the rain across the canyon today and spent most of the time shivering." His few terse entries, with an occasional characteristic flash of dark humor, described beatings, grueling work, a starvation diet, the deaths and burials of fellow prisoners, and his weakening condition. His final entry, dated February 22, 1943, opened with the death of his friend, Bill Lindquist, the tenth death since their arrival three months earlier. A long list of foods followed: "peanut butter & honey peanut butter & maple syrup . . . fried red cabbage, butter . . . onions & break eggs on top—turn . . . Divinity candy—shop across from Paramount . . . Soup—baby limas cooked till mushy with diced bacon." Franklin B. Miller, Jr. died on April 27, 1943, aged 29, one of fifty-three Wake POWs to die at Camp 18.[5]

Others kept diaries at the notorious Camp 18. Oscar Lent's small book is evidence that the gambling drive remained alive even in the worst conditions: "Bridge—A $5 cake or $5 worth of French Pastry—out of this camp by July 1, 1943 . . . Red—I say the average height of draftees in this war is 5'8". He says 5'7". 1 lb. of Van Dine's chocolate cherries." Full pages were dedicated to ongoing bets with individuals, evens and odds, the prizes ranging from sweet delicacies to bottles of booze (specific to brand and size), ten dollars on a case and lighter set or pen and pencil set, gallons of "assorted fountain syrups." Lent's diary also includes the last will and testament of Clinton Stone, signed by witnesses, and contains many of the men's names and addresses, as well as cryptic notations in the margins indicating deaths. Always hungry, the prisoners took small comfort in talking about and writing down favorite foods: Lent listed a long string of foods in which he underlined several, perhaps his favorites, including applesauce cake, huckleberry pie, roast chicken and dressing, fried apples, and fried sweet potatoes. Few diaries contained deep thoughts, but on a page shared with the brandy and rum proportions of a proper Tom and Jerry, he wrote, "I know I am here. I know I had nothing to do with my coming, and I shall have but little, if anything, to do with my going; therefore I will not worry, because worries are of no avail."[6]

The Japanese closed Camp 18 in April 1944 and moved the survivors to Fukuoka 1-B, with slightly better conditions. Still, Wake Islanders struggled to stay alive. Peter W. Hansen, the letter-writing carpenter who had counted each day left on his contract on Wake as he yearned for his beloved wife and three children, died on March 21, 1945, aged 44, after the move to Camp 1. Prison camp records listed "natural causes," but, after more than three years as a prisoner and no contact with his family, Hansen surely died with a broken heart.[7]

WOOSUNG AND BEYOND

At the Woosung POW camp in September 1942 Ted Olson found his name on a short list of prisoners to be transferred to Japan. The camp buzzed with scuttlebutt and many considered this first exodus of Woosung prisoners to be the start of a prisoner exchange and repatriation. However, the list of seventy men, all but one Wake civilians, appeared to be trade-specific with thirty skilled carpenters and a like number of steel workers including Ted slated for the move. The men packed their chipped rice cups, ragged chow bags, and such meager belongings as they had acquired in nine months at Woosung. They scribbled their friends' names and addresses on scraps of paper, promised to contact family members when they made it home, and threatened to show up on each other's doorstep to collect bets, virtually all of which now involved copious amounts of delicious food. The seventy prisoners said their last goodbyes and trudged out through the big gates of the prison camp.

At the docks the group boarded a waiting ship where guards immediately put them belowdecks. After the ship made its way out of the Yangtze River the guards allowed the men to come out on deck where they watched the sea gradually turn from yellow to deep blue. For several days the men lounged in comparative freedom on deck, watching mist-shrouded islands pass by. Locked below at night some talked of taking over the ship, but no one knew what they would do then. Finally the ship entered the main islands of Japan and docked in Moji Bay on the northern side of the island of Kyushu. Throngs of Japanese citizens lined the streets of Kokura, taunting the prisoners as they marched by, some throwing sticks and rocks at them from an overpass. Japanese guards clubbed those in the crowd who approached too close. When they entered the sprawling steel town of Yawata the prisoners knew that they would not be going home any time soon.[8]

Ted Olson's group of seventy, followed in November 1942 by another, similar-sized contingent, of which fewer than half were Wake civilians, were initially interned in an existing prison camp known as Yahata until later renamed Fukuoka 3-B. That "camp" was, in fact, an old three-story hospital on a hill, which the prisoners nicknamed the Castle, or Citadel. Most of the American and other Allied prisoners worked as slave laborers in the Yawata Steel Works. The carpenters in Ted's group had little carpentry to do: they performed whatever tasks ordered by their captors, including the onerous work of unloading iron from ship holds. Ted drove rivets in the steel mill day after day, jumping in a crouched position from one steel plate to the next. On December 15, 1943, the Japanese closed the Citadel and moved the prisoners thirty miles north to a camp near Moji Bay and the Kokura Arsenal and city. Now the prisoners rode the train every day to and from the Yawata steel mills. There is no evidence that the prisoners of Fukuoka 3 received letters or parcels from home, but after a year's internment, they were allowed to send a few brief, typed postcards. On the night of June 15, 1944, American B-29s Superfortresses bombed the Yawata plant. Despite the target value of bombing the largest steel works in the Japanese Empire, the area's poor radar characteristics allowed it to escape further raids during the major fire-bombing campaign conducted by the U.S. Twentieth Air Force against Japanese cities. While some prisoners were transferred out as the war proceeded, many, including Ted, remained at Fukuoka 3 for the duration of the war. Nine deaths among the Wake civilians are recorded from this camp.[9]

The largest group of Wake prisoners, both military and civilian, including Roger Smalley and Joe McDonald, stayed in Woosung until that camp

closed in December 1942. At that time, all 1,500 prisoners were marched
about ten miles to Kiangwan, which also carried the designation of Shanghai War Prisoners Camp. While still subject to forced labor and difficult
conditions the prisoners in Kiangwan had access to more frequent communications with home, received packages, experienced a greater variety of
occupations and pastimes, and had the camaraderie of friends and, some
cases, family, to help them endure the first years of imprisonment. Two
groups totaling about 520 men were culled from Kiangwan in August 1943:
400 were sent to Osaka 13B (Tsumori) and the other group went to Tokyo
5D (Kawasaki) POW camp for steel mill labor. Another half dozen Wake
men were hand-picked for their public relations skills and sent to Tokyo to
work in some connection with Japan Radio Broadcasting. The remainder
languished in Kiangwan until the camp closed in May 1945, when they
were herded into train cars for the start of their long trip to Japan and dispersal into the harsh camps of the home islands for the duration of the war.
In just over three years Shanghai War Prisoners Camp had claimed ten
Wake civilians, five at Woosung and five at Kiangwan.[10]

THE HOME FRONT

In homes across the nation, families of the Wake men followed the war news
and waited for any word from or about their loved ones captured in the
Pacific. While still pursuing the Europe-first policy the United States commanded sufficient resources to push back against the Japanese, initially in
the South Pacific. The Battle of Midway had turned the tide and demonstrated the power of carrier-borne forces. With construction assistance from
the seabees, the Marine Corps initiated amphibious operations in the Solomons. By 1943 and 1944 carrier-based forces were advancing into the Central Pacific against the Japanese mandates in the Gilberts, Marshalls, and
Marianas as America sought bases from which to launch raids on Japan's
homeland.

In the fall of 1942 Katherine Olson read the Portland daily papers and
listened to war news on the radio as she continued to focus her efforts on
her missing son. The letter that he had written from Woosung in the spring
finally reached her in October and she promptly forwarded a copy to the
Pacific Island Employees Foundation. The PIEF included snippets of the
early POW letters in their December 1942 newsletter to construct a mosaic
of the prisoner experience for family members. Meanwhile Katherine care-

fully followed Red Cross instructions to send mail and parcels to Ted at Shanghai War Prisoners Camp, unaware that he had long since been moved to the camp in Japan. She wrote her letters, read her papers, and marched to her volunteer job at the Aircraft Warning System call center in Portland as her personal life crumbled around her: Harry, ensconced with Eudelle in Pocatello, Idaho, had filed for divorce, which was finalized in December 1942. The elder Olson son, Jim, enlisted in the army and went to fight in Europe, and Donna left college to remain in Portland. Donna, however, often visited her father and became well acquainted with Eudelle and her daughter, Bethene. Katherine found work with United Airlines at the Portland Airport, her first job outside the home.

When the contractors completed the Pocatello Naval Gun Plant in record time and turned it over to the navy, the government issued an official commendation to Harry Olson and the other key men for service beyond the call of duty. He and Eudelle moved to Spokane, Washington, in 1943 and brought Donna from Portland to live with them. Harry soon took a job at the top-secret Hanford, Washington, compound where he helped to design cooling tanks for the production of the atomic bomb. He continued to work for Morrison-Knudsen on other assignments during the war.

M-K and the other CPNAB contractors went their separate ways as the war progressed. CPNAB's contracts eventually wound down in the Pacific. Proud recipients of the first Army-Navy "E" award in October 1942, an honor that was renewed the following year, CPNAB finally closed its operating base in Hawaii in December 1943. The organization built the seabee base at Port Hueneme, California, and continued to operate a procurement division for the navy through the war. George Youmans returned to the Morrison-Knudsen Company in Boise where he received accolades for his dedicated service as M-K's point man in CPNAB. While awaiting final figures, the contractors calculated that by the end of 1942, work done under contracts NOy-3550 and 4173 amounted to $240,227,665. The government paid the contractors a fee of $8,056,750; the net after non-recoverable expenses and before taxes and company overhead, was just under $7 million. Morrison-Knudsen's share of the fee was $1,070,305.[11]

Ongoing efforts to secure compensation for the CPNAB prisoners of war resulted in Public Law 784, effective January 1, 1943. Payment of wages and credits, based on those used in the Longshoremen's and Harbor Workers' Compensation Act, were made retroactive to January 1942 and continued until the date of the employee's return. The U.S. Employees Compensation Commission (USECC) administered the Treasury Department payments of wages and allotments to dependents. At $108.33 per month and with higher allotments to dependents, the compensation exceeded the previous Social Security-administered funds, but still fell far short of the earning levels the men had reached in 1941.[12]

Lobbyists and others, including Wake wife Mary Ward and, working separately, CPNAB's Lee Warren and Florence Teters, continued to pressure Congress until they achieved passage of an amendment in December 1943 that raised credits to the full wages paid to civilian employees of the government in the "same or most similar occupation in the area nearest." While it was impossible to find a direct counterpart to the remote Pacific island jobs and the contractors had not been directly employed by the government, Public Law 216 allowed for adjustments to arrive at pay levels comparable to those received by most of the contractors before they were taken prisoner. Dependents could draw up to seventy percent of the monthly payments. The government paid a benefit of $7,500 upon notification of death, and disability benefits would address wartime injuries upon the return of the men. The new pay rates were effective January 1, 1944, and not retroactive.[13]

OCCUPIED WAKE

The Japanese occupation on Wake Island enjoyed its most productive year in 1942. Despite the failure to take Midway, this easternmost outpost of the Japanese sphere in the Pacific remained well supplied with food and fuel and virtually unmolested by the Allies. Maximum effort was expended to sustain and maintain air operations on the atoll. During 1942 the Japanese completed the three-runway layout initiated by the contractors before the war utilizing the existing east-west runway and building out the north-south and diagonal runways, which were finished to 1,680 and 4,870 feet respectively. The occupiers extended the contractors' crushed coral road system to include secondary and connecting roads to various facilities and defensive works, totaling some 22 miles. An extensive communications network built with underground telephone cables and overhead wires linked the three islands. They expanded barracks, water distillation facilities, and power plants to service a future garrison of as many as 4,000 men. The departure of 265 American POWs in September 1942 reduced the labor force for projects, but much of the base construction work had been accomplished by then.

For continued labor 98 Americans remained as well as a considerable number of Chinese and Korean workers.[14]

As during the American period, water supplies proved the key component upon which size of the garrison depended. The Japanese supplemented water distillation units with rainwater catchment systems and brackish wells and built storage facilities around the atoll. Short of a deluge of rain, water supplies did not exceed more than a few days' requirements. When RAdm. Shigematsu Sakaibara took command of Wake in December 1942 the atoll's garrison comprised twenty-seven hundred Japanese personnel. At its peak in January 1944, the garrison numbered approximately thirty-seven hundred.[15]

By December 1942 ten land-based navy bombers stationed on Wake conducted patrols toward Midway to the northeast and provided some reconnaissance on American shipping, but little attention was given to defensive air strength until the spring of 1943 at which time a fifteen-plane squadron of fighters arrived from Truk. The fighter squadrons provided both patrol and protection, evidence of a growing awareness of the need for defense of the outpost. In early 1943 Wake's air strength reached its peak when both bomber and fighter squadrons were rotating in and out at three-week intervals, with as many as sixty planes and 250 crew on Wake at a time. Seaplane runways and facilities languished, unused except for occasional visitors. The land-based naval air forces operated independently of the island commander, a division of command that would complicate responses when Wake eventually came into American sights.[16]

The United States initiated offensive operations in 1943, but never targeted Wake for recapture. The atoll was more of a sideline operation: at most, "strikes against it were diversionary and protective in nature;" at least, they were harassment or target practice. From mid-1943 U.S. Army Air Force bombardment squadrons of B-24 Liberators, mostly from Midway, began regular strikes against Wake. The first recorded strike occurred on July 7, 1943, when eight Midway-based B-24s bombed the atoll; thereafter, such strikes occurred with some frequency. In addition a number of navy shore-based and carrier-based squadrons attacked Wake, as well as surface ships en route to other destinations.[17]

At the start of the Gilbert Islands campaign the United States subjected Wake Island to the most intensive bombardment of the war on October 6–7, 1943. Robert Sherrod, a war correspondent aboard one of the carriers observed cruisers, destroyers, and other carriers stretching for miles to the horizon, and calculated that the concentration of explosives on Wake amounted to two hundred tons per square mile, the heaviest attack to date. The primary purpose of the attack, according to Sherrod, was to "find out whether the Japanese Navy dared to come out and flight" for this possession, twice as far from the United States mainland as Tokyo: that is what made this "deliberate, devastating attack a slap in the face of Japan." Riding in the back seat of a Douglas dive-bomber in the third strike of the first day as the planes circled the island, allowing the warships to bring their big guns in range, Sherrod marveled at the limitless, clear blue sky filling with planes lifting off from the various carriers. "The sky was not black with planes, but it was a respectable gray," an exhilarating sight to the writer who had witnessed the struggle to field ten fighters at a time against Rabaul and Port Moresby in the early months of war. Now above Wake he watched as the warships opened up, their first salvos splashing into the lagoon or offshore as they found their range, and then striking land with what looked like "sharp pinpricks of fire, like little electric bulbs being flashed." Now the bombers took their turn. Shivering in the thin air at 14,500 feet, Sherrod braced as his pilot warned, "Hold your hat. Here we go," and nosed the bomber into a steep dive. At 2,000 feet he dropped his thousand-bound bomb on a sand-covered oil tank and pulled out at "considerably less than 1,000 feet." The burning oil tank sent flames up 200 feet, one of two dozen fires burning across the atoll as the bombers pulled out of range for the warships to resume their assault. They were only half way through the first day: the second day "tore Wake to pieces," leaving little left to target. One captain shook his head, saying, "I suppose that there are a lot of Japs who wish they had never seen Wake Island."[18]

In the two-day attack Task Force 14 struck Wake with carrier-based aircraft flying 510 sorties and dropping 340 tons of bombs. Fleet units blasted Wake's shore installations and other facilities with a total of 3,198 rounds of five- and eight-inch projectiles. The devastating attack destroyed 90 percent of the buildings on Wake, erasing virtually all of the Japanese progress to date, as well as the base construction initiated by the Americans in 1941. Direct hits struck hangars, repair shops, power plants, water distilling facilities, barracks, and all manner of other structures, including a large steel-frame building on Heel Point, originally intended as the Bachelor Officer Quarters building for the U.S. Navy, wiping out an enormous stockpile of food storage. None of the Japanese bombers or fighters on Wake survived the attack: the bombers, including reinforcements that had arrived during the attack, were either taken out in the air or destroyed on the ground; the fifteen to twenty resident fighters rose to intercept the attackers and not one returned. Three to four hundred men died in the attacks, including eighty Korean workers who had taken refuge under an old Pan Air building. The fate of the remaining American POWs on Wake would be determined by the Japanese command's reaction to this devastating attack.[19]

THE POWS IN JAPAN

As the months turned into years the prisoners from Wake Island in Japanese POW camps festered. Each man had to draw on his own physical and emotional resources to face the ordeal, and some managed better than others. Location, camp conditions, access to mail and Red Cross packages, and labor varied from camp to camp: good luck and bad fell without discrimination on the prisoners. The Wake Islanders reached deep inside themselves for the strength and stamina to endure forced labor, corporal punishment, torture, dire living conditions, poor or non-existent medical care, and near-starvation rations. Military prisoners had the advantages of training and organization by unit and rank, as well as the certainty that their nation stood behind them. Civilian prisoners had the advantages of friends and relatives in the group; on average, more maturity; and practical skill sets. Occasionally the prisoners benefitted from compassionate captors or the kindness of local folk who passed them food at great danger to themselves. Occasionally they suffered under the abject cruelty of brutal guards who took pleasure in inflicting pain or the hatred of war-ravaged crowds who pelted them with rocks as they passed by. A great deal of time passed somewhere in between.

In his book *Victory in Defeat: The Wake Island Defenders in Captivity* historian Gregory Urwin argues that a number of factors contributed to the comparatively high survival rate of the Wake Islanders as prisoners of war. First, the healthy physical labor, ample food, the ban on alcohol, and controlled conditions that sustained them as they built and fortified the base put them in "prime physical shape" when war came to Wake. Second, the campaign for Wake was relatively short at sixteen days with minimal but adequate nutrition and sanitation throughout. Fewer than one hundred died and the wounded received prompt medical care. The Japanese treated their new prisoners decently, allowing them to move back into Camp 2 and eat from the American mess hall. Despite the horrors they experienced on the voyage on the *Nitta Maru* the majority of prisoners entered the first prison camps in relative physical strength. Finally, they were fortunate to land in two nearly "model" internment camps, Zentsuji and Shanghai War Prisoners Camp at Woosung, later transferred to Kiangwan. Unit cohesion and buddy systems enhanced the Wake Islanders' chance of survival. In contrast, many of their future fellow prisoners would emerge from the three-month-long defense of the Bataan Peninsula emaciated and diseased, and if they survived the infamous Bataan Death March, were thrown into the horrors of Camp O'Donnell. Some 18 thousand American military died before they ever reached the holds of the unmarked "hell ships" going to Japan. Those who made it through the gauntlet straggled into Japan's POW camps in worse shape than those already there. Most of the Wake Islanders, by contrast, had had luck on their side.[20]

As the Allies bore down hard on Japan in 1944 and 1945 the increasing desperation of the Japanese was reflected in worsening conditions for their prisoners of war. An order issued by the Japanese War Ministry dated August 1, 1944, called for the execution of all Allied prisoners "at such time as the situation became urgent and it be extremely important . . . to annihilate them all, and not to leave any traces." During the last year of the war thousands more Allied prisoners were shipped from the squalid POW camps in the Philippines to Japan. By now American submarines and bombers were targeting Japanese shipping. In a terrible irony, 5,089 prisoners perished in the hell ships between September and December 1944 when U.S. naval forces torpedoed and sank four of the enemy POW transports. Twelve CPNAB contractors, who had worked on the Cavite project and had remained interned in the Philippines until October 1944, died when their ship was sunk in the South China Sea.[21]

In May 1945 the Japanese vacated the Kiangwan POW camp and loaded train cars with 950 prisoners, including the Wake POWs: their destination was Japan. From Nanking they travelled to Fengtai where they encamped for about a month and then resumed their journey through North China, Manchuria, and Korea. A handful of men managed to escape into China during the transfer. Wake civilians Bill Taylor and William "Jack" Hernandez pried open a window and leaped from the moving freight train in the dark of night. Although Hernandez broke his leg in the fall and could not continue, Taylor made his escape. So too did a group of four marines, including

Lieutenants Kinney and McAlister of Wake Island. The remainder arrived in Fusan, Korea in June 1945 and were split into three groups and ferried to the southern tip of Honshu for dispersal among the POW camps of Japan. For those who ended up in Japan and those already interned there, the last months of war were brutal. The Japanese shuffled and transferred prisoners from camp to camp and cut already-sparse rations. The cruelty of the guards rose as the dregs of the social order were called in to replace soldiers sent out to die for the Emperor.[22]

On the home front, censor-stamped POW letters and postcards, many months old, trickled in, giving hope to families that their loved ones were still alive. No prisoner, however, could write home about his travel plans. As American forces came within range of Japan and news accounts filled with the costly island campaigns and bombing raids on Japanese cities, families dealt with mixed emotions, hoping for decisive victory, yet fearing for the fate of the prisoners.

In February 1944, Morrison-Knudsen's company magazine, *The Em Kayan,* printed the "M-K Roll Call of PNAB," and called on families of the POWs to submit photographs of the Wake, Guam, and Cavite men. Beginning with the April 1944 issue and continuing through January 1945 the magazine reprinted sets of photographs and lists of names. All told, *The Em Kayan* printed 797 photographs, about 740 of which were Wake men. Some four hundred families either did not receive the request for photographs or did not have a photo to send. In 1945 the photographs were incorporated in the same ten groups as they had appeared in the magazine installments into a CPNAB publication prepared by *Em Kayan* editor Paul Nations and PIEF secretary Tom Hoskot to be printed and distributed upon the return of the men. The blue-covered book, *A Report to Returned CPNAB Prisoner of War Heroes and Their Dependents*, contains a detailed description of steps taken to achieve financial compensation and relief for dependent families through the government and of the work done by the Pacific Island Employees Foundation, Inc., to provide financial assistance and information to the families of the POWs during the war. The faces looking out of eighteen pages of prewar photographs first published in the company magazine and later in the "blue book" offered comfort to the civilian families that their men were not forgotten.

In 1944 the principals of the CPNAB companies also commissioned a book project. Initiated by eastern companies Turner and Raymond, and with the blessings of Admiral Moreell, the contractors lined up a New York publisher and selected David O. Woodbury, an author and journalist for *Collier's Magazine*, to write a full-length account of the Pacific Naval Air Bases construction program. All agreed to provide Woodbury with interviews and records to expedite the process and Woodbury, his research assistant, and two artists flew into action. Preparation for the story, which included action-packed tales of the M-K-sponsored projects Midway, Wake, and the Red Hill Underground Fuel Storage, which remained top-secret during the war, required considerable background information from Morrison-Knudsen Company. In September 1944 Harry Olson was chosen as "the man to write the story of Wake, particularly as regards operations in the field. As we see it, Harry," wrote Paul Nations, the *Em Kayan* editor, "it will be up to us at this end to tell our own story of our jobs, inasmuch as the final product will be prepared in the east." Harry, then a superintendent on the Inyokern, California, naval base construction project for M-K, wrote a five-page summary of the Wake operation, and it was forwarded to Woodbury along with articles written by Marlyn Sheik on Midway, J. V. Otter of the Boise hiring office, and others. Woodbury utilized additional sources, including USS *William Ward Burrows* Captain Ross Dierdorff's "Pioneer Party" article to write the Wake chapters. No one yet knew the full story of Wake Island.[23]

WAKE IN THE PACIFIC STRATEGY

After the devastating carrier-based attack on Wake in October 1943 during the Gilbert Islands campaign, the atoll found itself squeezed in an American vise from which there was no escape. The destruction of the vast majority of above-ground buildings and facilities drove the Japanese to build numerous living quarters and storage facilities in underground units dispersed across the atoll. The Americans subjected Wake to an unrelenting campaign of attrition with regular bombing raids and an increasingly effective blockade that prevented Japanese reinforcement and resupply.

During the Marshall Islands campaign from December 1943 to May 1944, carrier-based aircraft and fleet units and army and navy land-based bombers conducted sustained attacks against Wake. In the six-month period nearly a thousand sorties were flown over Wake: 1,079 tons of bombs and 7,092 rounds of five- and six-inch shells fell on the atoll, over half the total tonnage dropped on Wake during the entire war. Generally the Americans "followed current tactical orders and doctrine for the type of aircraft and unit involved" for aerial attacks, which were initiated by strafing fighters and followed up with a combination of high-altitude heavy bomber strikes and various smaller carrier-based formations, including low-flying fighters as well as dive-bombing and glide-bombing from optimal angles. Lacking fighters for interception after the October 1943 strike, Japanese defensive measures were limited to antiaircraft artillery fire, which was hampered by lack of radar fire control as well as American utilization of altitude, cloud cover, sun position, and coordination of attacks. Starting with the fall of Kwajalein, Wake's chief source of supply, in February 1944, by the middle of 1944 the American air and naval blockade effectively neutralized Wake and subsequent bombing was conducted for target practice and harassment.[24]

As Japan's sphere of control shrank and the Wake garrison found itself cut off from its line of supply, the enlisted men lived, starved, and died in underground huts along the shores of Peale. The torpedoed and subsequently bombed wreckage of the *Suwa Maru* listed in the surf on the south side of Wake where the Japanese supply ship had run aground with one of the last shiploads of supplies in the summer of 1943. From January 1944 only five submarines managed to evade the blockade to bring in small amounts of food and ammunition. When Admiral Halsey intercepted the *Takasago Maru*, a Japanese hospital ship carrying malnourished Japanese soldiers away from Wake in July 1945 he was angered by orders to let the ship proceed to Japan. "For three years we had been blockading the by-passed Jap islands in an attempt to force their surrender," Halsey wrote. Evacuation of nearly a thousand starving enemy soldiers meant that "Wake's scanty provisions would last that much longer." The evacuation provided little relief for the Japanese garrison.[25]

WAR'S END

Having weighed the costs of an amphibious invasion of Japan's home islands, President Truman decided to employ the Manhattan Project's atomic bombs in August 1945 to end the war. After considerable debate the target committee had selected four locations for the single-strike attacks, including two alternates in case of adverse conditions. The targets Hiroshima, Kokura, Nagasaki, and Niigata were chosen for maximum destructive potential and the presence of significant war manufacturing facilities. They had purposely been spared the most destructive firebombing during the preceding months. The designated number-two target, Kokura Arsenal and City, also stood near

Japan's largest steel manufacturing facilities: the Yawata mills where the prisoners of Fukuoka 3-B, including Ted Olson, toiled. On August 6 the *Enola Gay* released "Little Boy," a uranium-235 atomic bomb, over Hiroshima with devastating effect, but without the anticipated surrender of Japan. On August 8 the Soviet Union declared war on Japan. That day a B-29 bombed the Yawata Steel Works. The following day *Bockscar*, another B-29, carrying a powerful plutonium bomb, headed for Kokura, but hazy smoke covered the target area and a reserve fuel pump failed, restricting range. The crew diverted to the alternate target, Nagasaki, where it dropped the bomb nicknamed "Fat Boy" on the city. Japan surrendered on August 15, 1945.[26]

Guards fled the Japanese prison camps and the prisoners rejoiced. As the days went by, American bombers flew over the camps dropping heavy crates of food, cigarettes, and clothing to the men. Many sickened from gorging on foods that they had craved so long. Others traveled to nearby towns and ports, reveling in their newfound freedom of movement. Over the coming weeks the U.S. military officially liberated the camps and processed the ex-POWs for the long return home. It could not come soon enough and for many the wait in Okinawa, the Philippines, Guam, and Honolulu for "stabilization," hospitalization, or transport was nearly unbearable.

Swede Hokanson and the remnants of the September 1942 Wake exodus group boarded a train and arrived two days later at Nagasaki Harbor where the "smell of decaying bodies . . . permeated everything." Military aircraft carried able-bodied prisoners to Manila, while the sick and injured, including Hokanson, remained aboard a hospital ship in the radiation-saturated harbor for ten days. Eventually Swede, like thousands of other ex-prisoners, stood at the railing of a ship entering San Francisco Bay. Officials at the docks gave the returnees instructions to make contact with the nearest CPNAB branch offices, detention and disability claim forms, information on "temporary relief," including housing, food, and clothing for the estimated five to ten day processing period, as well as the welcome news that in a few days a USECC contact would deliver a check for $1083.30 and other information relating to compensation. The small blue information booklet concluded with a warning to "be careful of your money en route home. Sharpers are crooking many returnees out of their money. Knockout drops in a drink are a favorite stunt." Some heeded the recommendation to check in to a hospital for examination as soon as possible; some made a beeline for bars and brothels; others headed straight home.[27]

Pete Russell had left his diaries with another prisoner upon his discharge from the Tokyo hospital in November 1944 when the Japanese sent him to POW camp Tokyo 1B at Yokohama for work in the shipyards. Near the end of the war an American bomber targeted his shipyard and his legs and arms were burned badly from the fire. A month after the Japanese surrender, American forces liberated Pete's camp and put him on a hospital ship to Guam. Pete's son Peter, now stationed as a signalman on the torpedo-damaged USS *Pennsylvania* in Apra Harbor, signaled the incoming hospital ship to inquire, as he always did, if it had any POWs from Japan aboard. In a remarkable story of persistence, faith, and luck, Peter and his father were reunited in the harbor at Guam.[28]

By the time Pete Russell and Swede Hokanson returned to the mainland, bad news awaited both of them. Mae informed Swede that she had fallen in love with a contractor from Midway whom she had met in Honolulu and she wanted a divorce. Eudelle Russell had continued to write and send packages to Pete in Japan without divulging her changed circumstances. Eudelle met Pete in San Francisco, confronted him with letters written by past girlfriends and forwarded to her during the war, and told him about Harry and their plans to marry once she obtained a divorce. Harry met Pete in Portland behind closed doors. Harry and Eudelle married in November 1945. Pete soon remarried his first wife, who was the mother of their children.

Katherine traveled to San Francisco that fall to meet her returning son. When Ted did not appear at the appointed time at the Hotel St. Francis, Katherine sent a panicked telegram to Portland and received a quick response: "Try Roger Smalley in Alameda," cabled Ted's brother, Jim. While she was out, Ted left a note: "Be right back. Gone to get something to eat!" Finally, mother and son were reunited and made their way back home to Portland. Family and friends waited at the train station to greet them. Donna remembers her brother stepping off the train, grinning broadly from a slightly greasy, bloated face, his feet clad in odd, light slippers, and snapping his fingers to the latest music blaring from a small radio. Home at last.

THE LIBERATION OF WAKE ISLAND

Led by RAdm. Shigematsu Sakaibara the Japanese garrison on Wake formally surrendered on September 4, 1945, just offshore of Wake aboard the USS *Levy*. Brigadier General L. H. M. Sanderson (USMC) accepted the surrender and in a flag-raising ceremony on Wake that afternoon turned the island over to Commander William Masek of the U.S. Navy. The marines, including Col. Walter Bayler, who was the last American to leave Wake freely in December 1941 and now the first to set foot back on the atoll, and several war correspondents and photographers took the first look at structures and conditions on Wake under the Japanese. The Americans found most of the Japanese garrison of just under 1,250 men to be in severely debilitated condition—although officers, by contrast, appeared well-fed—and distributed rations and medical supplies.[29]

Concrete steps led from the pier toward a white frame building flanked by circular steps, built during the Japanese occupation as a mess hall, but used now as a command post with ammunition stacked inside. Scattered remnants of Camp 1 stood beyond the waterfront: the water tower built under Harry Olson's direction and used as an observation tower during the 1941 siege, remained standing, though "now staggering on three rusty legs." Two wooden sticks across a tank trap marked all that was left of the old Camp 1 administration building. Colonel Bayler noted considerable change in the very face of the island: the Japanese had brought sand and coral in to bolster their defenses. At the airstrip near the old underground hangar stood three wrecked Japanese planes; across the field in the brush lay the remains of several VMF-211's Grumman Wildcats from, which had so gallantly defended Wake in 1941. Rusty remnants of American machinery littered the landscape in almost any direction and there was little left of Camp 2, the once-thriving contractors' town. All that remained of the Bachelor Officer Quarters under construction in December 1941 were "a few toilet bowls staring bleakly into the Pacific sky."[30]

When asked if there were any Americans buried on the island the Japanese affirmed that there were two common graves, one holding the remains of eighty, and the other with an unknown number. Large crosses marked the rock-mounded graves; one also carried a marker that read "WILL MILES DIED JULY 15, 1942." The Japanese did not know who Miles was, but one explained that "he was the most important, so we placed his name on top of the grave," an honor that the old carpenter might have appreciated. The graves showed signs of very recent attention: newly trimmed bushes and posts, still tacky with fresh paint, surrounded the burial area.[31]

On September 28, 1945, the Marshalls-Gilberts-New Britain Party arrived on Wake to conduct the U.S. Strategic Bombing Survey. Field investigations and interviews of Japanese officers were held over five days and revealed the extent and impact of the U.S. bombing campaign on Wake during the Japanese occupation. Destructive as the air and naval attacks had been Admiral Sakaibara attributed only 10 percent of the garrison's difficulties to them, but 90 percent to the effects of the blockade, which ended regular surface communication in February 1944. The last supply ship to reach Wake arrived in January 1944. Thereafter submarines became the sole source of supply, arriving every four to six weeks with small stores until late June 1945, after which the atoll was completely isolated. Lack of food and medicines had the most debilitating effect on the population. Fish, birds and eggs, and rats augmented the enlisted men's diets while they maintained the strength for the hunt—in a single day, 40,000 rats were killed for a feast—but there were no reports of cannibalism on Wake as there were from other islands. The debilitation of the men directly affected their work: by January 1945 they could barely sustain two hours a day and in the closing months were incapable of any work at all.[32]

On October 9, 1945, Captain Earl A. Junghans arrived to assume command and oversee construction of a new American naval air base. He toured Wake with Sakaibara and his officers and later wrote up the notes on his observations. Remarkably, the "spindly bridge of steel frame and wooden planks" still stood between Wake and Peale Island. Most exposed installations had been destroyed during intense U.S. bombardment during the war, though Swede's seaplane ramp still remained. Japanese gun batteries and pillboxes stood futile guard on Peacock Point and other positions around the atoll. Everything else, including barracks and storage, had been moved underground or partially dug-in with a camouflage of coral sand and morning glory vines. Sakaibara's command post, an imposing, concrete-roofed, three-story building that also served as dormitory for the officers and communications center, stood overlain with sand and vines near the bridge to Peale.[33]

From the Japanese garrison's height of several thousand troops, Captain Junghans estimated that more than thirteen hundred died of disease and starvation and another six hundred fell as battle casualties. (The Strategic Bombing Survey based its counts of seven to eight hundred battle casualties and fifteen hundred malnutrition deaths on Japanese officers' estimates during September interviews.) In a diary found and translated by Junghans's interpreter a Japanese soldier known only as Watanabe graphically described the relentless bombing and descent into starvation during 1944 and 1945.

As the Japanese command cut rations to thin rice gruel and occasional crackers, the men scrounged for supplemental food: roasted rat, fish killed by bombs dropped in the lagoon or their own dynamite, "octopus vines," leaves, "grass dumplings." Dozens were thrown in jail for trying to steal food, some even tortured and starved to death in punishment. A submarine occasionally penetrated the blockade to bring in supplies, but the food was soon gone or sequestered for officers. Watanabe's last entry is dated March 17, 1945. He died of malnutrition before the surrender. During the weeks after the surrender U.S. forces removed the sorry remainder of enlisted men from the island, having found them to be too weak for work parties and some even "too far gone to be resuscitated" with American C and K rations.[34]

With the liberation of the last POW camps in Japan the Americans knew that in September 1942 nearly one hundred of the Wake contractors had remained on the atoll and were still unaccounted for. Numerous official inquiries to the Japanese government during 1943 had received no response. When questioned by Captain Junghans the Japanese officers on Wake told nearly identical stories: at the time of the devastating US carrier-based attack on October 6 and 7, 1943, half the prisoners died in a direct hit on their bomb shelter. The remaining prisoners killed a guard, stole rifles, and made a stand, but all died in the ensuing fight; their remains lay buried in the two gravesites near Peacock Point. The Strategic Bombing Survey interviewers got the same story.[35]

On the mainland, with the help of the returning ex-POWs officials struggled to piece the scenario together. The men who had survived the notorious Camp 18, and were the last to see the ninety-eight alive in September 1942, confirmed that the men had remained on Wake and that they had a six-month supply of American food left on the island at that time. Junghans, ordered to detain Sakaibara and a dozen officers on Wake, sought answers from the silent graves and correspondence from the mainland. Responding to a November letter sent by Mrs. Caroline L. Ward inquiring about her son, Allen A. Cavanagh, Junghans responded that he greatly regretted that he was unable to give her good news about her son, but hoped that "your son will at last turn up safe and sound. He repeated the story told him by the Japanese officers, cautioning that it was "only information obtained from an unreliable source." Junghans confirmed that no Americans were found on the island when it was retaken. Three graves had been identified which, "the Japanese claim, contain all the American civilian bodies as follows: one grave is marked with the name Will Miles; a second (unmarked) contains 42 bodies; the third (unmarked) 83 bodies. None have been identified to date, nor has the number of bodies been verified." Junghans requested that the "contractor from Idaho" (meaning Morrison-Knudsen) be contacted to provide further information. Dan Teters wrote to Junghans in December, confirming the mass burial of 42 in December 1941 and several other burials of battle casualties elsewhere. "We know of 109 reported deaths on Wake," Tom Hoskot wrote to Harry Morrison, "so if disinterment locates the remains of more white men than 109, then the balance must be from these men." The third grave on Wake suggested that "the mystery of the missing ninety-eight men is near solution." The question remained: how did they die?[36]

In November 1945 the sixteen Japanese officers were taken to Kwajalein for the War Crimes Trials. Two men committed suicide en route and another while in prison. At Kwajalein, the true story came out. One of the American prisoners had been beheaded in July 1943 for stealing food. Three months later, during the attack of October 6 and 7, 1943, the American prisoners had in fact escaped injury in their shelters. Commander Sakaibara expected an invasion to follow and, fearing that prisoners might escape to aid the invaders, ordered their execution en masse. Japanese guards marched the prisoners in three groups to the northwestern-most beach of Wake, blindfolded them and tied their hands behind their backs, and lined them up facing the ocean. At the order the guards opened fire until all lay dead. The bodies were hastily buried in a tank trap nearby, but soon disinterred for a body count: one American was missing. The man remained at large for a week, but was caught on October 15. Sakaibara personally beheaded him on Peale; his blood washed out on the rising tide. Only an inscription on a coral rock on Wilkes Island, etched by an unknown American prisoner, or prisoners, before the massacre—"98 U.S. PW 5-10-43"—remained to mark their presence. The Japanese had reburied the jumbled bones of the murdered men in a common grave prior to surrender.[37]

The ninety-eight included men of many skills and trades: carpenters, plumbers, electricians, steel workers, mechanics, heavy equipment operators, cooks, and medical personnel. They ranged in age from twenty-two to fifty-five, half were single, half married, and some had young children at home. Many of the families did not learn what happened to their loved ones for years. At the trial in Kwajalein a few scraps of evidence were presented to the court. One was a pair of trousers labeled "H. L. Hettick," the name of a CPNAB scraper operator; another was a sheet of metal with a penciled inscription: "July 23, 1942," followed by the figures 7 and 8 superimposed, "months a captive, Floyd Forsberg, 1210 N. Wilton Road, Hollywood, California." Admiral Sakaibara was executed for his crime on June 18, 1947. The graves on Wake were opened in 1946 in an attempt to identify individuals, but what lay inside was a "mixed collection of bones forever incapable of being separated." The remains of seventy-two skeletons were reinterred with the other war dead in the Wake Cemetery. In 1947 and 1948 U.S. Army graves registration units exhumed the graves and removed the remains to Oahu where they were later interred with honors in the National Memorial Cemetery of the Pacific in the Punchbowl above Honolulu. Decades later a beachcomber found an old metal bracelet on Peale with the hand-carved inscription, "R.A. Andre Pendleton, Oregon USA, Prisoner Wake Isle, 12/23/42." The bracelet bearing the name of the replacement captain of the dredge, rests in the Wake museum among hundreds of pieces of rusted metal, shell casings, broken glass and pottery shards: all that remains of CPNAB Project 14 and its gallant, but futile defense.[38]

In all, 250 of Wake's 1,145 civilian contractors died by the end of the war. They included 34 men who were killed during the siege and battle in December 1941, 4 deaths on or near Wake in early 1942, 114 who perished in POW camps in Japan or China, and the 98 who were massacred on Wake in 1943. In addition to the CPNAB civilians, 12 of 45 Pan American employees died, 10 in the initial attack on December 8, 1941, and 2 in POW camps. Of 524 military personnel, a total of 74 died, including 48 in battle on Wake and 26 in POW camps: the story of their valiant defense of Wake Island against all odds stands tall in the heritage of the United States Marine Corps. As officers and enlisted military personnel, they had well-defined responsibilities during their service, knew the risks of combat, and retained specific rights after the war. The Wake civilians had none of the above: their situation was unprecedented and unanticipated in spite of the clear signs of war on the horizon in December 1941. The civilian contractors, including the CPNAB companies and their employees, took risks to work on the outlying island contract by choice, banking on the financial rewards. The prevailing national hubris, however, distorted honest calculations of risk in the Pacific for military and civilians alike.[39]

The Wake civilians' story offers a valuable window on the "why" of the war in the Pacific, a question that was drowned out by the war itself and the national memory of the "greatest generation" that fought it. The strategic challenges and harsh realities of forty-four months of war in the Pacific erased many of the biases and inefficiencies that had hampered America's prewar preparation. In the end the technological might and inventiveness of the U.S. military and American industry did bring victory over Japan. However, the appalling toll of internment and death among Allied and U.S. servicemen and civilians in the Pacific, most of whom were captured in the early months of war, remains evidence of a complacency that lingered too long. The United States had acquired its far-flung possessions and spheres of interest in Asia and the Pacific at the end of the nineteenth century with relative ease, but it failed to secure them in the changing world of the early twentieth and to recognize and respect the forces at work in the neighborhood. The price too many Americans paid rests in Punchbowl Cemetery in the rows of graves and lists of names of the missing.

In late October 1945 the 85th Naval Construction Battalion arrived at Wake to commence construction of a new American naval base. The seabees' ships rocked offshore as lighters and barges ferried the men and their supplies and equipment into Wilkes channel to the waterfront unloading area. The ring of hammers, the roar of heavy machinery, and shouts of American construction workers filled the air of Wake again as the surf crashed against the reef, rats sniffed out new opportunities, hermit crabs skittered along the beach, and thousands of birds soared overhead.

APPENDIX I

POSTWAR WAKE ISLAND

THE UNITED STATES NAVY RETAINED FORMAL JURISDICTION OVER THE atoll until 1962, but with postwar demobilization placed Wake into caretaker status in 1947. At that time the navy delegated administration to the Department of Commerce, and the Civil Aeronautics Administration (Federal Aviation Administration from 1958) maintained air operations on Wake from 1947 to 1972. In 1962 Executive Order 11048 transferred authority from the U.S. Navy to the Department of the Interior. When the FAA ceased operations there in 1972 the U.S. Air Force took over as user and steward of the site. During the decades since World War II many government agencies and commercial enterprises obtained land use permits, often overlapping and creating some confusion among participants and observers as to who had the superior authority.

Wake's postwar vitality has always been based on airfield operations. The CAA/FAA paved and extended the east-west runway during its tenure and Pan American Airways and Transocean Airlines maintained stations and facilities on Wake. Military aircraft and transpacific commercial airliners regularly stopped over on Wake. During the 1950s, 60s and 70s, Wake hummed with activity with as many as a thousand residents at a time stationed by the FAA, air force, coast guard, commercial airlines, and the American civilian contractor, which also employed a large contingent of Filipino employees. The atoll's downtown area, always anchored on northwest Wake Island where the CPNAB contractors had built Camp 2 in 1941, offered movie theaters, a bowling alley, barber shop, several bars (including the well-loved watering hole, Drifter's Reef, built in 1949 and repeatedly restored after storm damage), and a bank. An AM radio station played the latest music, and golfers could tee off on the local course. Employees brought their families to Wake and for perhaps the only time in its history the sound of children's laughter rose over the ever-present roar of the surf. They went to school, played on the beach, and swam in the lagoon; many stayed in touch long afterwards, connected by the unique experiences of their youth.

The atoll also served as a major refueling stop for military aircraft during the Korean War (1950–53) and the Vietnam War (1964–73). Many a veteran recalls ferrying aircraft through Wake or landing there on a crowded transport plane. In 1975, as victorious North Vietnam initiated the reunification of Vietnam, the United States State Department sponsored the evacuation and relocation of Vietnamese refugees in Operation New Life. Over several months thousands of refugees landed on Wake in transit, temporarily expanding the population by many times and straining resources. For many of the displaced Vietnamese, especially women and children, the quiet, isolated atoll offered a moment of respite and peace.

With some regularity, though not enough to predict the next one, typhoons, strong storms, and storm surges have hit Wake, causing widespread damage and destruction on the low-lying atoll. Full strength typhoons struck Wake in 1952, 1967, and 1981. In 2006 Typhoon Ioke hit Wake as a category 5 storm: damage from Ioke is still visible and some facilities were not rebuilt. In advance of Ioke, Wake's entire population was evacuated by air to Hawaii. Storm surges such as the ones in December 2008 also cause considerable damage with as much as several feet of water washing into ground floor barracks and other buildings. Wake is watchful when tsunami warnings occur, but the underlying topography of the atoll lacks the land mass to allow a destructive tidal wave to build.

Storms, surges, and the relentless surf have buried and uncovered countless layers on the seaward beaches of Wake, both hiding and revealing evidence of the atoll's troubled history. When ordnance or human bones occasionally surface the finder alerts the authorities for investigation and controlled removal. The Joint POW-MIA Accounting Command (JPAC), dispatches teams of forensic anthropologists and photographers to collect skeletal remains and study them in their central laboratory at JPAC headquarters, Joint Base Pearl Harbor-Hickam. In the spring of 2011 the discovery of human remains on the north beach of Wake Island, which were in danger of being washed out to sea, prompted an intensive JPAC investigation. Authorities have reason to expect that the remains relate to the massacre of the ninety-eight contractors in October 1943. As of this writing JPAC is seeking family members of the men who died on Wake to provide mitochondrial DNA samples for possible matches and identification of the remains.

Under USAF administration for several decades by the 15th Air Base Wing, headquartered at Hickam Air Force Base on Oahu, control of Wake passed to the 611th Air Support Group, Joint Base Elmendorf-Richardson, Alaska, in the fall of 2010. Stationed on the atoll, Detachment 1 of the 611th oversees operations and Chugach Federal Solutions, Inc., maintains facilities and operations under the current Base Operations Support Services contract. In 2012 approximately one hundred men and women (far more of the former, the majority of whom are Thai workers employed by Chugach) reside on Wake. The population swells with recurring missions of the U.S. Army's Strategic Missile Defense Command, which administered Wake from 1994 to 2001. Frequently host to military aircraft in transit and in-flight refueling units, Wake's airfield still provides a reliable toehold in the Central Pacific, although it is closed to commercial traffic.

Since Wake Island received National Historic Landmark status in 1985, items dating to the prewar and World War II periods have been protected as historic artifacts. Commitment to historic preservation and cultural resource management has ebbed and flowed over the years, but current efforts are encouraging. Residents and beachcombers have donated hundreds of artifacts as well as postwar memorabilia that are displayed in the Wake Island Museum and cases in the base operations building. In 2008 a full museum inventory and catalog was completed and artifacts continue to be found and added to the collection. Across the road and facing the sea to the east stand four memorials commemorating the sacrifices in the war. Constructed, emplaced, and dedicated over the years by World War II Wake survivors, the memorials ensure that the men who lost their lives and those whose lives were forever changed by Wake Island are not forgotten. The Japanese dedicated their shrine in the late 1950s and a few hundred yards south the stark white memorial of the United States Marine Corps rose in 1966. In 1967 a non-denominational chapel was erected nearby. Two other memorials now complete "memorial row," evenly spaced between the Japanese and U.S.

Marine Corps memorials: a simple engraved block is dedicated to the Gua-manian employees of Pan American Airways who were killed or captured and a large, granite memorial emplaced in 1988 commemorates the sacrifices of the civilian contractors. A second Japanese memorial stands at the curve in the road opposite Heel Point, the location of the mass burial site of over a thousand of their wartime dead whose remains were repatriated in the 1970s. The civilian contractors also placed a stone bearing the names of the ninety-eight near the POW rock on Wilkes.

National Historic Landmark status protects structures from the World War II era, many of which are falling to ruin, inundated by storm surges and the relentlessly creeping morning glory vine. A few structures, however, remain in good shape. Just steps away from memorial row stand three CPNAB-constructed concrete bunkers on the east shore of Wake that were originally intended as high explosives magazines, but used as command posts and hospitals during the siege in December 1941. A tilting jumble of con-crete situated just off the main road in downtown Wake serves as a constant reminder of the Japanese occupation: a sign announces that this crumbling ruin was Admiral Sakaibara's command post. The indestructible fortress withstood unrelenting American bombing raids in the war, but seventy years of time and tide have taken their toll. Close by stands the approach to the wooden bridge built by the contractors to Peale. The bridge that withstood the war was replaced after storm damage a decade later; that wooden bridge burned in 2003 and only stunted piers remain poking out of Peale channel.

Around the elbow of Wake several sets of stone and concrete revetments stand in sturdy silence south of the runway. Rebuilt or constructed in full by the Japanese to protect their landplanes, the handsome revetments reflect the confidence of the first year of the occupation when they had the time (and laborers) to select coral boulders and set them in an artistic herringbone pattern in concrete. Across the causeway linking Wake to Wilkes the POW rock stands by the lagoon as a sturdy, silent witness to the ninety-eight. A restricted gravel road—Wilkes stands in the final approach path for the 10,000-foot runway—leads through dense brush hiding elaborate stone net-works of Japanese defenses. At the site of the never-completed ship channel a narrow strip of ground that is dry at low tide allows passage to the rest of the island, most of which is occupied by nesting birds. On Kuku Point a large, sand-filled Japanese pillbox sits tilted on the west-facing beach where the sea moves it from time to time. On deserted Peale, a mile distant across the lagoon, an enormous, rusty, eight-inch gun brought in by the Japanese points toward the empty Pacific. Swede Hokanson's seaplane ramp still offers a gentle slope up from the turquoise lagoon to a vast concrete parking area where tufts of grass poke through the seams and hermit crabs skitter on the edges. Nearby a few broken legs of the Pan American pier stand in the coral rubble. A chipped concrete block bears an etched date: "Apr 16 1936." The legs that once supported the ramp that carried well-dressed Clipper passengers to the Pan Air Hotel quickly disappear into the jungle wall. Peale is now deserted, approachable only by water.

The lack of arable soil and fresh water have mitigated Wake's usefulness to humans through most of history, but out on the reef, the result is a pristine and healthy coral bed, well-populated by colorful marine life. Visibility stretches as far as the eye can see. Evidence of maritime mishaps appear at the moorage area including two heavy anchors and anchor chains that snake along parallel to Wilkes and the ghostly remains of the sunken *J.C. Stoner* off Wilkes channel. Little remains of the *Suwa Maru*, the Japanese supply ship that grounded on the reef in 1943, farther east off the south shore. Weaving through coral outcroppings, sharks, eels, rays, and brightly colored fish are at home on their "perch"; at seventy feet the reef ends abruptly, and the "gigantic toadstool on a slender stem" that witnessed so much history in so little time gives way to the deep blue depths of the Pacific.

APPENDIX II

CIVILIAN CONTRACTORS: THE QUICK AND THE DEAD

AFTER THE EX-POWS RETURNED TO THE MAINLAND IN THE FALL OF 1945 they dispersed far and wide. Many came home grievously sick or disabled from their horrific experience—one died on a hospital ship before reaching shore at San Francisco—and spent many months in recuperation; an unknown number died within a few years of their liberation. A core group of survivors, however, immediately began to organize an association in order to keep track of their fellows and to lobby for further compensation and disability coverage. They held their first reunion in Boise in December 1945, and took the name "Workers of Wake," retaining the momentum built during the war by the "Women of Wake" and its chief champion Mary Ward, who became the first president of the new group. Early on the Workers of Wake included their fellow ex-CPNAB survivors of Guam and Cavite in the organization.

In the first decade after the war the survivors pursued lawsuits and legislation relating to their internment. A class action lawsuit brought against five of the CPNAB companies was dismissed and the 1951 treaty with Japan ended any attempt to pursue compensation from that quarter. The survivors received additional compensation for their years of internment in the War Claims Acts of 1948 and 1952 and amendments to other legislation. In the 1950s the group entered a period of deep division and reorganized as the "Survivors of Wake, Guam, and Cavite," at the end of the decade. The survivors focused on achieving veterans' status, which was finally awarded in

1981, providing those who applied with recognition, medals, and veterans' benefits including medical coverage. In the late 1980s a number of survivors and their families joined group trips to Wake Island. The survivors' group officially disbanded in 2004, but the "Wake Family" still holds an annual reunion in Boise and never forgets those who paid the ultimate price.

250 CPNAB EMPLOYEES DECEASED IN WAR[1]

34 Died in Siege and Battle of Wake Island, December 1941:

Adamson, Louis A.
Bond, Gordon C.
Bryan, Robert L.
Bucy, Eddie L.
Calkins, Clarence C.
Cerny, Frank J.
Corten, Paul
Gay, Paul J., Jr.
Gibbons, George F.
Gossman, Paul A.
Graham, Milo S.
Hall, John E.
Higdon, Ralph
Hoskin, Chester D.
Jones, Rex Dean
Krueger, Reinhard W.
Lemke, Myron A.
Lilly, David E.

McDonald, Joseph T.
McGallister, William
 (aka Charters, Carl
 "William")
McKinley, Jack F.
Miller, Don K.
Peterson, Hurschel L.
Ray, Clyde W.
Reeves, Forrest W., Jr.
Reiger, Gregory C.
Ritter, Commodore P.
Slafer, Edward W.
Sorensen, John P.
Stevenson, Clinton L.
Winegarden, Lester W.
Woodward, George L.
Yeager, Harry
Yriberry, Robert L.

4 Died on or near Wake, 1942:

Hofmeister, Julius M.
Miles, William

Mackie, Elmer E.
Sullivan, Donald L.

98 Massacred on Wake, October 1943:

Abbott, Cyrus W., Jr.
Allen, Horace L.
Anderson, Norman A.
Andre, Roland A.
Anvick, Allen E.
Baasch, Carl A.
Bellanger, George C.
Bowcutt, Don R.
Boyce, Dolphia M.
Cantry, Charles A.
Carlson, Stanley A.
Cavanagh, Allen A.
Chambers, David S.
Chard, Donley D.
Church, Carleton G.
Cormier, Louis M.
Cox, Karl L.
Cummings, David E.
Cunha, James A.
Davis, Joseph R.
Dean, George W.
Dobyns, Harold L.
Dogger, Martin H.
Dreyer, Henry M.
Dunn, Joseph M.
Fenex, Jack A.
Flint, Howard A.
Fontes, Glen B.
Forsberg, Floyd F.
Francis, Dale G.
French, Albert P.
Froberger, Lawrence G.
Gerdin, William P.

Gibbs, Charles A.
Goembel, Clarence R.
Haight, Ralph E.
Haines, William H.
Hansen, Vernon L.
Harris, George
Harvey, Wilbur C.
Hastie, Frank
Hettick, Howard L.
Hochstein, Ernest A.
Jensen, George A.
Jones, Alfred A.
Keeler, Ora K.
Kelly, Martin T.
Kennedy, Thomas F.
Kidwell, Charles A.
Kroeger, Woodrow W.
Light, Rolland E.
Ling, Henry C.
Lythgoe, Gene
Marshall, Irving E.
Martin, John
McDaniel, James B.
McInnes, Thomas L.
Migacz, Frank
Migacz, Melvin
Miller, Irwin E.
Mitchell, Howard H.
Mitchell, Wayne E.
Mittendorf, Joseph F.
Mueller, Carl W.
Myers, Richard B.
Olmstead, Clifford A.

Pease, Gordon H.
Pratt, Archie H.
Preston, Donald W.
Rankin, Morton B.
Ray, William H., Jr.
Reynolds, William H.
Robbins, Sheldon G.
Schemel, Charles M.
Schottler, Herman
Shank, Lawton E.
Shepherd, Orbin R.
Sherman, Glenwood H.
Shriner, Gould H.
Sigman, Russell J.
Simpers, William T.
Smith, Charles E.
St. John, Francis C.
Stone, Willis C.
Streblow, Alvin L.
Stringer, Wesley W.
Susee, Arthur J.
Tart, Lacy F.
Thompson, Glenn H.
Tucker, Earl E.
Vancil, Vernon
VanValkenburg,
    Ralph W.
Vent, Glen
Villines, Charles M.
Williamson, Frank E.
Wilper, Redmond J.
Woods, Charles
Yuen, Harry T.K.

114 Died in Japanese POW camps:

Anderson, Eric W.
Bailey, George E.
Berger, Irving N.
Bowers, Frank B.
Brown, Edward J.
Bukacek, Lad
Campbell, Claude L.
Carr, Louis
Christy, Arthur W.
Clelan, John L.
Cooper, Robert P.
Corak, John
Davis, Lee R.
Davis, Kenneth C.
Dillon, George O.
Dixon, Theron B.
Donovan, Harry W.
Driscoll, Leo P.
Dyer, Fredrick E.
Easter, George C.
Eliassen, John H.
Esmay, Wayne E.
Ewing, James F.
Farstvedt, Knut
Follett, Frank F.
Franklin, Mark B.
Gammans, John W.
Garrison, John R.
Gehman, Ralph A.
Goodpasture,
  Dexter D.
Goodwin, Ralph H.
Gottlieb, Henry
Greve, Louis
Grim, William B.
Hance, Loren H.
Hansen, Peter W.
Hanson, Fred A.

Hardisty, Herbert A.
Hart, Irving W. Jr.
Helander, Charles O.
Hensel, Theodore F., Sr.
Hewson, Albert A.
Hill, Norman L.
Hornyak, John M.
Howard, Ray L.
Huntley, John W.
Jimison, Harold E.
Johnson, Edwin W.
Johnson, Harold L.
Judd, Clayton F.
Kapihe, Robert
Kelley, Sidney D.
Kelly, Fred W.
Kelly, Samuel D.
Kelso, Orval A.
Kent, Lloyd R.
Keyser, George E.
Knox, Elbert H.
Larson, Julius L.
Lawson, William S.
Leahey, Larry M.
Lendewig, Lloyd T.
Lindquist, William O.
Loveless, Phillip V.
Manson, William R.
McCulley, Charles E.
McEvers, Ralph
McKeehan, Lloyd S.
Meyer, Lester T.
Miller, Charles M.
Miller, Silas W.
Miller, Frank B., Jr.
Moe, Charles A.
Moon, Clarence L.
Murdock, William I.

Nead, Ralph E.
Nelson, Edward A.
Newhoff, Benjamin H.
Nicks, Quinton D.
Niklaus, John F.
Nygard, Andrew
O'Neal, John H.
O'Neill, Joseph C.
Pawlofske, Richard P.
Peterson, Hjalmar M.
Pfost, Orlie E.
Proteau, Lawrence H.
Proteau, George F.
Puccetti, Elmer
Reed, Harry E.
Reid, Russell
Rensberg, Harold O.
Riddle, Lonnie B.
Rienks, Donald H.
Riffel, John H.
Robbins, Paul J.
Robertson, Charles B.
Robertson, Dale O.
Selleseth, Oscar A.
Smith, Abner J.
Staten, Mark E.
Stone, Clinton M.
Sweet, Harry V.
Thomas, Owen G.
Truy, Joseph D.
Villa, Edward E.
Walker, George M.
Wilkin, Robert S.
Williams, Joseph V.
Williams, Donald M.
Worley, William J.
Yeramian, Vahran J.
Zeh, Fred

NOTES

ABBREVIATIONS USED IN NOTES:

IDS: *Idaho Daily Statesman*, Boise, ID
ISHS: Idaho State Historical Society Public Archives and Research Library, Boise, ID
JMFC: Joseph F. McDonald, Jr. Family Collection
JPAC: Joint POW-MIA Accounting Command
MKR: Morrison-Knudsen Company Records
NAPR: National Archives Pacific Region, San Francisco, CA
OFC: Olson Family Collection
PHFC: Peter W. Hansen Family Collection
RG 5:   Geographical Files, Record Group 5, U.S. Navy Seabees Museum (SMPH maintains its own RG classification system which is separate from the National Archives system)
RG 12:   Bureau of Yards and Docks, Record Group 12, U.S. Navy Seabees Museum
RG 24:   Records of the Bureau of Naval Personnel, Record Group 24, National Archives
RG 80:   General Records of the Department of the Navy 1798–1947, Record Group 80, National Archives
RG 181:   Records of Naval Districts and Shore Establishments, Record Group 181, National Archives
SMPH: U.S. Navy Seabees Museum, Pt. Hueneme, California

INTRODUCTION

1. *Building the Navy's Bases*, 2:121; "The Earth Movers III," *Fortune*, October 1943: 144. (Parts I–III, *Fortune*, August–October 1943, privately rebound), McClary-Morrison Collection, Boise, Idaho; *The Em Kayan*, March 1944: 18. $332 million in 1943 is equivalent to about $4.43 billion in 2012. CPNAB also acted as

the navy's general purchasing agent during the first two years of the war, and procurement drove the actual contract totals to over $692 million by the end of 1943.

2. Woodbury, *Builders for Battle*, 242.
3. Prange, *Verdict of History*, 30; Dower, *War Without Mercy*, 98, 108–110.
4. E. S. Miller, *War Plan Orange*, 241–45.

CHAPTER 1: ONE BIG OCEAN

1. Dierdorff, "Pioneer Party," 501; "Technical Report and Progress History Contracts NOy-3550 and NOy-4173, Pacific Naval Air Bases and Aviation Facilities," A-489-91, NOy-3550, Section XI: "Wake," Folder 1, Box 3, Sub-series A: NOy Contracts, Series IV: Contracts, Bureau of Yards and Docks, RG 12, SMPH (hereafter cited as "Technical Report").
2. "Technical Report," A-491; George L. Youmans to Harry W. Morrison, October 20, 1940, File C-24-2, Box 116673, MKR. (All citations hereafter to MKR will be to Box 116673 unless otherwise noted.)
3. Primary sources use "Contractors Pacific Naval Air Bases" without additional punctuation and use the acronyms CPNAB and PNAB interchangeably. CPNAB will be used herein.
4. "Technical Report," A-485.
5. G. L. Youmans to H. W. Morrison, August 16, 1940, October 20, 1940, File C-24-2, MKR.
6. "Contract Information" Bulletin No. 5, January 6, 1941, Tab 12: "Wake Island," File C-24-16; Chief BuDocks to OinC 4173 (Rear Admiral Ben Moreell, Chief of the Navy's Bureau of Yards and Docks, to Captain Henry Bruns, Officer in Charge of contract NOy-4173), August 12, 1940, File C-24-16; Youmans to Morrison, August 16, 1940, File C-24-2, MKR.
7. Bonny, *Morrison-Knudsen Company*, 18–20; Wolf, *Big Dams*, 30; "The Earth Movers I," *Fortune*, August 1943:99. The "Six Companies" actually numbered eight: during the 1930s the group included Morrison-Knudsen Co. of Boise;; Utah Construction Co. of Ogden; MacDonald & Kahn, Inc. of San Francisco; J. F. Shea Co., Inc. of Los Angeles; Pacific Bridge Co. of Portland; and a joint venture of H. J. Kaiser Co. of Oakland, W. A. Bechtel Co. of San Francisco, and Warren Brothers Paving. By 1941 Warren Brothers was no longer a member and General Construction Co. of Seattle had joined the partnership.
8. Wolf, *Big Dams*, 131–32.
9. *Spokesman Review*, October 13, 1940; Katherine Olson to Donna Olson, [October 1940], OFC.
10. Hokanson, *Man Called Swede*, 107–10; Swede Hokanson interview with Bill Kauffman, photocopy of transcript in author's possession, *Those Who Also Served*, Aviator Pictures, 2002.

11. *Spokesman Review*, October 7, 15, 17, 1940; Sperber, *Murrow*, 179.
12. *Spokesman Review*, October 3, 13, 23, 1940.
13. LaFeber, *Clash*, 60–61; Ferrell, *American Diplomacy*, 40–48.
14. Ferrell, 105–06; Hamm, *America's New Possessions*, 110–11, 123–26.
15. Ferrell, 57–60, 69, 107; LaFeber, *Clash*, 88–92.
16. E. S. Miller, *War Plan Orange*, 16–22, 25, 33–34; LaFeber, 135.
17. E. S. Miller, *War Plan Orange*, 35–37; Lundstrom, *First South Pacific Campaign*, 13; S. E. Morison, *Rising Sun in the Pacific*, 27–29.
18. Hamm, *America's New Possessions*, 157–59; Homer C. Votaw, "Wake Island," 2–3, mimeographed transcription, OFC (source: U.S. Naval Institute *Proceedings*, January 1941: 52–55).
19. Captain E. A. Junghans, USN, "Wake Island, 1568–1946," 3, MS 748, Box 1, Fol. 4, John Rogge Papers, ISHS.
20. E. H. Bryan, Jr., extracts from "Field Notebook," 1923, F7, Eg 60, "Wake Island (1)," 14ND HQ, Commandant's Office, Classified Correspondence 1912–41, RG 181, NAPR; E. S. Miller, *War Plan Orange*, 238–39.
21. Iriye, *Power and Culture*, 3–6; Divine, *Reluctant Belligerent*, 4–5, 43; Ferrell, *American Diplomacy*, 181–85.
22. Iriye, 16–17; S. E. Morison, *Rising Sun*, 30; E. S. Miller, *War Plan Orange*, 26; Spector, *Eagle Against the Sun*, 20–21.
23. Ferrell, *American Diplomacy*, 187–89; Schlesinger and Bruns, *Congress Investigates*, 4:2738, 2767; Divine, *Reluctant Belligerent*, 9–13.
24. Divine, 43–48; S. E. Morison, *Rising Sun*, 42–43, 58–60; Ferrell, 189–90.
25. Ferrell, 191–92.

CHAPTER 2: OPPORTUNITY KNOCKS

1. Daley, *American Saga*, 135–37, 141; E. S. Miller, *War Plan Orange*, 173; CNO to CO USS *Nitro*, November 13, 1934, and accompanying documents, Eg 60, "Wake Island (1)," Box 42, 14ND HQ, Commandant's Office, Classified Correspondence 1912–1941, RG 181, NAPR.
2. S. E. Morison, *Rising Sun*, 33; E. S. Miller, *War Plan Orange*, 239; Executive Order 6935 in General Order No. 66, Navy Dept., Washington DC, May 13, 1935; Pan American Airways permit, March 12, 1935, in "Wake Island, Aviation Landing," Wake Island, General Information, Geographical Files, RG 5, SMPH.
3. Lt. C. W. Porter, "Report on Pan American Airways 1935 Pacific Expedition and Information in regard to the Islands of Midway and Wake," Sections 1–4, October 30, 1935; Chief of the Bureau of Yards and Docks to Lt. Carl W. Porter, March 21, 1935, Eg12-1, Box 41, 14ND HQ, Commandant's Office, Classified Correspondence 1912–1941, RG 181, NAPR.
4. Grooch, *Skyway to Asia*, 89–95; Daley, *American Saga*, 157–58.
5. Grooch, 96–97, 103–10, 157–58; Daley, 159–64; Krupnick, *Pan American's*

Pioneers, 22–31, 35–36 (includes photographs from scrapbook of Myron L. Kenler, physician on Wake during 1935).

6. W. B. Miller, "Flying the Pacific," 693–96.

7. Lt. J. G. Johnson to CNO, January 10, 1935, Eg 60, RG 181, NAPR.

8. Porter, "Report," Section 1: 27–28, 32, 37, 247; Section 2: 13, "Wake Island" map, Eg 12-1, RG 181, NAPR.

9. E. S. Miller, *War Plan Orange*, 240; Cressman, *Magnificent Fight*, 10–11; Urwin, *Facing Fearful Odds*, 45–46; "Wake Island," letters and memoranda, Document No. 84, House of Representatives, 75th Congress, 1st Sess., Wake Island, General Information, Geographical Files, RG 5, SMPH; Spector, *Eagle Against the Sun*, 57–58.

10. *Building the Navy's Bases*, 1:26.

11. *Building the Navy's Bases*, 1:27; Woodbury, *Builders for Battle*, 40–41.

12. *Building the Navy's Bases*, 1:28–29; Woodbury, 51–55; Urwin, *Facing Fearful Odds*, 56–58; B. Moreell to Rear Admiral A. T. Church, August 1, 1939, Wake Island, General Information, Geographical Files, RG 5, SMPH.

13. CINCPAC to CNO, "Study of Defenses and Installations at Outlying Pacific Bases," October 21, 1941, 1–2, RG 80, NA (photocopy in author's possession, courtesy G. J. W. Urwin); Col. Harry K. Pickett and Capt. Alfred R. Pefley, "The Defenses of Wake," with Plans and Estimates for the Installation and Maintenance of the Defense Detachment, U.S. Marine Corps, 10 October 1939; 14ND HQ, Commandant's Office, RG 181, NAPR.

14. *Building the Navy's Bases*, 1:77–80.

15. Woodbury, *Builders for Battle*, 62–65; Wolf, *Big Dams*, 127; "The Earth Movers II," *Fortune*, September 1943: 144.

16. "Contracts NOy-3550 and NOy-4173: Pacific Naval Air Base Contractors," [January 1943], 8–9, File C-24-16, MKR (hereafter cited as "Contracts: PNAB"); *Building the Navy's Bases*, 2:121.

17. Schlesinger and Bruns, *Congress Investigates*, 4:3118; "Contracts: PNAB," 10–11, MKR; B. Moreell to Captain Arthur C. Davis, November 23, 1940, Wake Island, General Information, Geographical Files, RG5, SMPH. With the new contract, CPNAB executives recalculated their partnership to 25% for each of the 3 original partners, 15% for M-K, and 10% for Pomeroy. H. W. Morrison to G. L. Youmans, August 24, 1940, and other correspondence in File C-24-11, MKR, reveals that Morrison reluctantly agreed to syndicate M-K's share of the CPNAB contract with Six Companies members upon their request, giving M-K only 30% of the 15%, or about 5% of the contract (capital contributions and fee share). See also Ch. 6, note 13.

18. "Contracts: PNAB," 1–6, File C-24-16; G. L. Youmans to H. W. Morrison, May 2, 1942, File C-24-2, MKR.

19. Harry Olson to Katherine, November 7, 1940, OFC.

20. "Contracts: PNAB," 2, MKR.
21. Wolf, *Big Dams*, 133–34; Woodbury, *Builders for Battle*, 135–37.

CHAPTER 3: HONOLULU HOTBED

1. Allen, *Hawaii's War Years*, 82–83.
2. "Contracts: PNAB," 5–6, 21–22, File C-24-16, MKR.
3. "Contracts: PNAB," 2–5; G. L. Youmans to H. W. Morrison, March 2, 1942, File C-24-2, MKR.
4. Prange, *At Dawn We Slept*, 66.
5. *Em Kayan*, September 1960, 13, 19; G. L. Youmans to H. W. Morrison, November 17, 1940, File C-24-2; H. B. Olson, [Wake Report, October 3, 1944] (hereafter cited as "Olson Report"), File C-24-1A, MKR.
6. "Technical Report," A-468-70, SMPH; "Olson Report," MKR.
7. Confidential photographs of Wake and Guam, H. W. Butzine, Envelope 17, Box 5, Commandant's Outlying Islands Photographic Records 1935–41, 14ND HQ, Commandant's Office, RG 181, NAPR; G. L. Youmans to H. W. Morrison, August 16, 1940, March 2, 1942, File C-24-2, MKR.
8. "Schoeller Report," 5, 7, 10; G. L. Youmans to H. W. Morrison, November 20, 1940, File C-24-2, MKR. In contrast to frequent documentation in civilian records of navy delays in providing and approving plans throughout 1940 and 1941, the navy's "Technical Report," A-492-93, asserts "plans were available as needed" and "There were no delays in receipt of Navy approvals."
9. Youmans to Morrison, November 17, 1940; Woodbury, *Builders for Battle*, 120–22.
10. Harry to Katherine, November 17, November 24, and December 11, 1940, OFC.
11. Allen, *Hawaii's War Years*, 83–84, H. W. Morrison to W. V. McMenimen, November 26, 1940, File C-24-2, MKR.
12. Allen, *Hawaii's War Years*, 250.
13. Harry to Katherine, November 24, 1940.
14. Allen, *Hawaii's War Years*, 256–58; Morrison to McMenimen, November 26, 1940; *Hawaii Sentinel*, December 19, 1940, copy located in File C-24-2, MKR.
15. Harry to Katherine, December 9, 1940.
16. Dierdorff, "Pioneer Party," 501; M. B. Sheik, "Midway Islands," [September 1944], File C-24-1A, MKR.
17. Pickett and Pefley, "The Defenses of Wake," Part 1, 3–4, 14ND HQ, Commandant's Office, RG 181, NAPR.
18. Wake blueprint, proposed layout: October 17, 1940, File 2E; "Contract Information" Bulletin No. 5, January 6, 1941, Tab 12: Wake, File C-24-16, MKR.
19. Harry to Katherine, December 11, 1940.
20. Ibid.

21. *Idaho Daily Statesman* (hereafter cited as *IDS*), December 8, 10, 1940.
22. Divine, *Reluctant Belligerent*, 86; Iriye, *Power and Culture*, 20.
23. *IDS*, December 7, 11, and 12, 1940; Goralski, *Almanac*, 141–42.
24. Dower, *War Without Mercy*, 98.
25. Grooch, *Skyway to Asia*, 40–43, 61–62, 99.
26. Daley, *American Saga*, 160.
27. Harry to Katherine, December 25, 1940.

CHAPTER 4: PIONEER PARTY
1. "Olson Report," File C-24-1A, MKR; Dierdorff, "Pioneer Party," 501–02; "War Diary of Leal Henderson Russell 1940–1945," 1, transcription and copyright by Stephanie Russell Persson, 1987, used with permission (hereafter cited as "Russell Diary"); "Ship's log of the USS *William Ward Burrows* (AP6), 26 December–," RG 24, NA, ms notes by G. J. W. Urwin, copy in author's possession (hereafter cited as Urwin, "*Burrows* Log"), December 26, 1940; "Technical Report," A-486-87, SMPH.
2. Dierdorff, "Pioneer Party," 502.
3. "Russell Diary," 1–3.
4. Harry to Katherine, January 1, 1941, OFC.
5. Dierdorff, "Pioneer Party," 503.
6. Harry to Katherine, January 1, 1941; Dierdorff, "Pioneer Party," 503; Urwin, "*Burrows* Log," January 1, 1941.
7. Dierdorff, "Pioneer Party," 503; "Russell Diary,"3.
8. Dierdorff, "Pioneer Party," 503–04; "Russell Diary," 4; Urwin, "*Burrows* Log," January 8–9, 1941.
9. George L. Youmans to Harry W. Morrison, January 11, 1941, File C-24-2, MKR.
10. Harry to Katherine, January 10, 1941.
11. Dierdorff, "Pioneer Party," 505.
12. Harry to Katherine, January 18, 1941.
13. "Russell Diary," 5.
14. "Schoeller Report," 1–7; Harry W. Morrison to W. V. McMenimen, October 21, 1941, File 2E, MKR. Contract NOy-4173 covered the Wake project; a supplement to contract NOy-3550 authorized an additional $15,000 for surveys on Wake. Subsequent change orders and supplements for Wake raised the contractors' estimated expenditures to $26,500,000 by October 1941.
15. "Russell Diary," i, 9.
16. Ferrell, *American Diplomacy*, 192–93.
17. *IDS*, January 9, 10, 15, 1941.
18. *IDS*, February 20, 26, 1941, March 14, 1941.
19. S. E. Morison, *Two-Ocean War*, 38–39; *IDS*, January 9, 1941, February 6, 1941.
20. Schlesinger and Bruns, *Congress Investigates*, 4:3118–19, 3128, 3141.

21. *IDS*, January 23, 1941, March 2 and 30, 1941.

22. "Russell Diary," 11.

23. Harry to Donna, February 7, 1941.

24. Sheik, "Midway Islands," File C-24-1A, MKR.

25. "Russell Diary," 12.

26. "Schoeller Report," 7–9.

27. Dierdorff, "Pioneer Party," 508; Woodbury, 147–48.

28. J. V. Otter, "History of PNAB Work," September 26, 1944, and Sheik, "Midway Islands," File C-24-1A, MKR; Urwin, "*Burrows* Log," January 29–February 2, 1941; Woodbury, *Builders for Battle*, 162–63.

29. Harry to Ted, February 27, 1941.

30. Kaucher, *Wings over Wake*, 41, 45, 91. See 35–48 and 80–147 for Kaucher's experiences on Wake.

31. Harry to Katherine, January 18, 1941, March 5, 1941.

CHAPTER 5: SECOND GEAR

1. Urwin, "*Burrows* Log," March 2–18, 1941; "Russell Diary," 19–20.

2. Urwin, "*Burrows* Log," March 24–26, 1941; Harry to Katherine, March 23, 1941, OFC; Peter Hansen to family, March 24, 1941, August 19, 1941, Peter W. Hansen Family Collection (hereafter cited as PHFC), used with permission of Mary Anne Collins, Houston, Texas.

3. Harry to Katherine, March 23, 1941, Harry to Donna, May 4, 1941.

4. Peter Hansen to family, March 11, 1941, March 24, 1941, PHFC.

5. G. L. Youmans to H. W. Morrison, March 15, 1941, File C-24-2, MKR; Harry to Katherine, March 23, 1941. Wives of CPNAB general superintendents on Midway, Guam, and Samoa also lived on location.

6. *IDS*, March 9, 1941.

7. J. V. Otter, "Report on Employment Office: Boise Idaho," November 24, 1941, File C-24-1A, MKR.

8. J. V. Otter to B. J. Weis, September 26, 1944, File C-24-1A, MKR.

9. *IDS*, March 9, 26, 27, 1941; Otter to Weis, September 26, 1944.

10. Harry to Katherine, March 29, 1941.

11. *IDS*, April 16, 1941, quotes *New York Post*.

12. Harry to Katherine, April 30, 1941.

13. "Russell Diary," 23, 26, 28–30.

14. Harry to Katherine, May 13, 1941.

15. "Russell Diary," 21–22; G. L. Youmans to H. W. Morrison, June 20, 1941, File C-24-2, MKR.

16. "Russell Diary," 23–24.

17. "Ship's log of the USS *Regulus* (AK14), 1 January–31 December 1941," RG 24, NA, ms notes by G. J. W. Urwin, copy in author's possession (hereafter cited as

Urwin, *"Regulus* Log"), April 12, 1941; Harry to Katherine, May 13, 1941.

18. Harry to Katherine, April 12, 1941, June 14, 1941.

19. Urwin, *"Regulus* Log," April 13–20, 1941; "Russell Diary," 26–27; Harry to Katherine, April 12, 1941, May 13, 1941.

20. *IDS*, April 10, 1941; Harry to Katherine, April 30, 1941; Charlie Appelhanz, "Hell in the Pacific," 243–44, privately printed, copyright 2001.

21. G. L. Youmans to H. W. Morrison, July 11, 1941, quoting letter to Dan Teters, June 30, 1941, File C-24-2, MKR; Harry to Donna, May 4, 1941.

22. *IDS*, May 21, 1941; Employment contract, Charles E. Smith, MS 738, Box 2, Fol. 12, Survivors of Wake, Guam, and Cavite Papers, ISHS; "Final Report PIEF, June 1, 1946," 8–13, File C-24-20-4, Pacific Island Employees Foundation Records, Box 116657, MKR.

23. Harry to Donna, April 11, 1941, Harry to Katherine, May 13, 1941.

24. Harry to Donna, April 11, 1941.

25. "Executive Order 8802, Prohibition of Discrimination in the Defense Industry, June 25, 1941," http://docs.fdrlibrary.marist.edu/od8802t.html; Harry to Katherine, June 8, 1941.

26. H. W. Morrison to G. L. Youmans, April 21, 1941, File C-24-2, MKR.

27. Harry to Katherine, March 29, 1941, April 3, 1941.

28. Peter Hansen to family, April 29, 1941, PHFC.

29. Harry to Katherine, April 24, 1941, May 13, 1941, June 8, 1941.

30. Harry to Donna, May 4, 1941; "Second Consolidated Bomber from America," *The Mercury* (Hobart, Tas.), April 17, 1941, http://trove.nla.gov.au/ndp/del/article/25857007.

31. Harry to Katherine, April 24, 1941; *Wake Wig Wag*, July 15, 1941, MS 351, Fol. 3, Raymond Forsythe Papers, ISHS.

32. Harry to Katherine, April 3, 1941; S. E. Morison, *Two-Ocean War*, 33–36.

33. E. S. Miller, *War Plan Orange*, 264–65; Urwin, *Facing Fearful Odds*, 113–14.

34. Iriye, *Power and Culture*, 13; Frank, *Downfall*, 22–23; *IDS*, March 7, 1941.

35. E. S. Miller, *War Plan Orange*, 217, 245–46; Prange, *At Dawn We Slept*, 65; Heinrichs, *Threshold of War*, 130–31.

36. Urwin, *Facing Fearful Odds*, 63; Pickett and Pefley, "The Defenses of Wake," Parts 1–7, 14ND HQ, Commandant's Office, RG 181, NAPR; E. S. Miller, *War Plan Orange*, 242.

37. Beard, *Appearances and Realities*, 424–27; S. E. Morison, *Rising Sun*, 56–57, 225–27; Heinl, "Defense of Wake," 2.

38. CINCPAC, "Study on Defenses and Installations at Outlying Pacific Bases," 2–5, RG 80, NA; Cressman, *Magnificent Fight*, 24–25.

39. "Russell Diary," 34–36.

40. "Address of the President Delivered by Radio from the White House, May 27, 1941, http://www.mhric.org/fdr/chat17.html; *IDS*, May 27–28, 1941.

41. Peter Hansen to family, May 8, 1941, May 22, 1941, June 7, 1941, PHFC.
42. Peter Hansen to family, May 22, 1941; Hansen to Bud, June 10, 1941, PHFC.
43. Urwin, "*Regulus* Log," May 12–29, 1941; "Russell Diary," 35–36.
44. Harry to Katherine, April 24, 1941, Harry to Donna, June 14, 1941.
45. "Testimony of Claude Davis Howes," http://home.comcast.net/~winjerd/ Howes.htm; Harry to Katherine, June 8, 1941.
46. "Technical Report," A-495-96, SMPH; "Schoeller Report," 41-42, MKR; Harry to Katherine, June 8, 1941.
47. "Schoeller Report," 40–43; G. L. Youmans to H. W. Morrison, June 20, 1941, File C-24-2, "Wake Island General Island Layout OB Drawing No. 80-W-1, R-4, revised June 14, 1941, File 2E, MKR.
48. Peter Hansen to family, May 12, 1941, June 21, 1941, PHFC.
49. Allen, *Hawaii's War Years*, 432.
50. Harry to Katherine, June 21, 1941.

CHAPTER 6: HIGH CENTER

1. *IDS*, April 10, 1941.
2. Jack Hoskins to folks, June 20, 1941, Hoskins to Dorothy, October 1941, John R. Hoskins Collection, used with permission of Artys Hoskins, Spokane, WA.
3. Joe McDonald to folks, June 10, 1941, Joseph F. McDonald, Jr. Family Collection, used with permission of Joseph F. McDonald III, Idaho Falls, ID (hereafter cited as JMFC).
4. Ted to Mother, May 26, 1941, OFC.
5. Ted to Mother, May 26, 1941, Ted to Mother and Sis, June 5, 1941.
6. Jack Hoskins to Dorothy, October 1941, Hoskins Collection; Joe McDonald to folks, June 11, 1941, June 15, 1941, JMFC.
7. Harry to Katherine, June 8, 1941.
8. Ted to Mother, July 1, 1941; Joe McDonald to folks, June 21, 1941, JMFC.
9. Ted to Donna, [July 1941].
10. Urwin, "*Regulus* Log," June 23–29, 1941; Ted to Mother, July 1, 1941.
11. Darwin Meiners letter dated July 8, 1941, quoted in *Astorian-Budget*, Astoria, Oregon, and *Daily Evergreen*, Pullman, Washington, n.d., OFC; Ted to Mother, July 1, 1941; Harry to Katherine, July 2, 1941; Joe McDonald to folks, July 1, 1941, JMFC; Urwin, "*Regulus* Log," June 29–July 4, 1941.
12. Harry to Katherine, July 2, 1941.
13. "Contracts: PNAB," 11–15, File C-24-16, MKR; "The Earth Movers III," *Fortune*, October 1943: 144. Two of the new CPNAB partners, Utah and Bechtel, were "Six Companies" members, which further complicated M-K's syndicated investment in CPNAB (see Ch. 2, note 17).
14. "Russell Diary," 44; Harry to Katherine, July 2, 1941; Peter Hansen to family, July 27, 1941, PHFC.

15. "Schoeller Report," 11–12, MKR; COM14 to Com Base Force, July 17, 1941, NA39, "Wake, April 2, 1941–February 3, 1943," 14ND HQ General Correspondence 1935–1942, RG 181, NAPR.

16. Koistinen, *Arsenal of World War II*, 141–42.

17. "Russell Diary," 43–44.

18. G. L. Youmans to H. W. Morrison, July 11, 1941, File C-24-2, MKR; "Technical Report," A-495-96, SMPH; Harry to Katherine, July 5, 1941; "Testimony of Claude Howes," http://home.comcast.net/~winjerd/Howes.htm.

19. "Schoeller Report," 38–41.

20. "Schoeller Report," 41–44; G. L. Youmans to H. W. Morrison, June 26, 1941, File C-24-2; H. W. Morrison to N. D. Teters, July 16, 1941, File C-24-16, MKR; Commander Patrol Wing 2 to COM14, June 18, 1941, NA39, RG 181, NAPR.

21. "Schoeller Report," 44–45; G. L. Youmans to H. W. Morrison, September 21, 1941, File C-24-2, MKR; E. J. Wilson, "Lament of the Dredge Columbia," Poetry Supplement [November 1941], McClary-Morrison Collection. The U.S. Navy's "Technical Report," A-495-99, makes no mention of channel plan changes, blames dredge breakdowns and weather for all delays, and states in error that the dredge worked on widening the pilot channel to three hundred feet—an ill-conceived plan that the contractors persuaded the navy to abandon. The navy's report asserts that "the work at Wake Island proceeded very much as originally contemplated," with only the addition of a one-division submarine base in October. The report does not mention the ship channel that the contractors finally received approval to begin cutting through Wilkes in the fall of 1941, and which became the project of highest priority for the navy.

22. Harry to Katherine, July 2, 1941.

23. Youmans to Morrison, July 11, 1941, and July 12, 1941, File C-24-2, MKR.

24. Iriye, *Power and Culture*, 26–29.

25. Goralski, *World War II Almanac*, 168–69; Schlesinger and Bruns, 5:3278; Iriye, 20, 28; Kimmel, *Admiral Kimmel's Story*, 34–35.

26. Iriye, 29; E. S. Miller, *War Plan Orange*, 60–62; "The Philippine Independence Act (Tydings-McDuffie Law)," http://www.philippine-history.org/tydings-mcduffie-law.htm.

27. G. L. Youmans to H. W. Morrison, June 20, 1941, MKR; Joe McDonald to folks, August 9, 1941, JMFC; Peter Hansen to family, July 18, 1941, PHFC.

28. Ted to Donna, [July 1941].

29. Peter Hansen to family, July 22, 1941, PHFC; Jack Hoskins to Dorothy, October 1941, Hoskins Collection.

30. Daley, *American Saga*, 177; Woodbury, *Builders for Battle*, 164.

31. Joe McDonald to folks, July 12, 1941, July 19, 1941, JMFC; Peter Hansen to family, July 5, 1941, PHFC.

32. Joe McDonald to folks, July 19, 1941, JMFC.
33. Joe McDonald to folks, July 6, 1941; Jack Hoskins to Dorothy, October, 1941, Hoskins memoir and artifacts in Hoskins Collection.
34. Peter Hansen to family, July 22, 1941, July 27, 1941, PHFC.
35. H. W. Morrison to W. V. McMenimen, October 21, 1941, File 2E; "Schoeller Report," 47–49, MKR.
36. Urwin, "*Burrows* Log," August 2–4, 1941; Orval Kelso quoted in Emmett, ID newspaper article, n.d., courtesy Barry Kelso, Boise, ID; Peter Hansen to family, July 27, 1941, PHFC.
37. G. L. Youmans to H. W. Morrison, August 10, 1941, File C-24-2, MKR; "Russell Diary," 50.
38. RoinC to N. D. Teters, August 6, 1941, quoted in "Schoeller Report," 45.
39. "Schoeller Report," 24–26; COM14 to ChBuNav, August 22, 1941, and enclosure "Facilities at Wake," NA39, RG 181, NAPR.
40. G. L. Youmans to H. W. Morrison, August 14, 1941, File C-24-2, MKR.
41. Joe McDonald to folks, August 15 [1941], JMFC; "Russell Diary,"51–52.
42. Harry to Donna, August 17, 1941.

CHAPTER 7: BAITING THE HOOK
1. Urwin, "*Regulus* Log," August 19–22, 1941; Urwin, *Facing Fearful Odds*, 115, 117.
2. Harry to Donna, August 17, 1941, OFC.
3. Admiral Bloch to Major Hohn, August 27, 1941, NA39, RG 181, NAPR.
4. Ted to Mother, August 26, 1941, OFC.
5. Darwin Meiners letter dated September 19, 1941 quoted in *Astorian-Budget*, January 12, 1942, OFC; Joe McDonald to folks, August 22, 1941, JMFC; Peter Hansen to family, August 19, 1941, PHFC.
6. Joe McDonald to folks, August 22, 1941, September 12, 1941, September 14, 1941, JMFC.
7. "Russell Diary," 55; *IDS*, September 28, 1941; Peter Hansen to family, August 30, 1941, PHFC; Harry to Katherine, September 1, 1941.
8. Kimmel, *Admiral Kimmel's Story*, 13, 21; Urwin, *Facing Fearful Odds*, 110–11; Heinl, *Defense of Wake*, 10.
9. Kimmel letter dated September 12, 1941, quoted in Urwin, *Facing Fearful Odds*, 115–16.
10. CINCPAC, "Study on Defenses," 2–3.
11. CINCPAC, "Study on Defenses," 6–7, 11, and COM14 to CINCPAC, October 17, 1941 (copy included in "Study on Defenses").
12. Bloch to Hohn, August 27, 1941; Prange, *Verdict of History*, 520–21.
13. CINCPAC, "Study on Defenses," 27–29.
14. Layton, *"And I Was There,"* 170–71; Heinrichs, *Threshold of War*, 144, 195;

Dower, *War Without Mercy*, 108; Frank, *Downfall*, 48; Spector, *Eagle Against the Sun*, 74–75.

15. H. W. Morrison to W. V. McMenimen, October 21, 1941, File 2E, MKR; Devereux, *Story of Wake*, 27; Heinl, *Defense of Wake*, 7; "Russell Diary," 57.
16. Harry to Katherine, September 11, 1941.
17. Kimmel, *Admiral Kimmel's Story*, 14; G. L. Youmans to H. W. Morrison, September 21, 1941, File C-24-2, MKR.
18. "Fireside Chat 18: On the *Greer* Incident, September 11, 1941," http://millercenter.org/scripps/archive/speeches/detail/3323; *IDS*, August 23, 1941, September 12, 1941.
19. Ferrell, *American Diplomacy*, 200.
20. Kimmel, *Admiral Kimmel's Story*, 40; Prange, *At Dawn We Slept*, 289–90.
21. Morrison to McMenimen, October 21, 1941; "Schoeller Report," 46–47; E. S. Miller, *War Plan Orange*, 291.
22. W. V. McMenimen to Executive Committee, September 22, 1941 and Youmans to Morrison, September 21, 1941, File C-24-2, MKR.
23. Chester Ratekin to "Bright Eyes," October 8, 1941, courtesy Larry Weirather, Vancouver, WA.
24. Hokanson, *Man Called Swede*, 115–21; *IDS*, September 28, 1941; Joe McDonald to folks, July 12, 1941, August 22, 1941, JMFC.
25. Harry to Katherine, October 13, 1941.
26. Harry to Katherine, September 11, 1941.
27. "Technical Report," A-496-98, SMPH; Youmans to Morrison, September 21, 1941.
28. "Schoeller Report," 51–53; G. L. Youmans to H. W. Morrison, November 20, 1941, File C-24-2, MKR. "Technical Report," A-494, states that Wake submarine base plans largely followed Midway plans, "revised to adapt them to local conditions. Such changes and revisions as were made were of a minor nature. . . . No complaints were recorded."
29. "Schoeller Report," 25–27.
30. Ibid, 24.
31. Morrison to McMenimen, October 21, 1941.
32. Youmans to Morrison, September 21, 1941; W. V. McMenimen to H. W. Morrison, September 22, 1941, File C-24-2; "Wake Island September 1941," File C-24-2A, MKR. In September 1941, the Wake payroll totaled $235,673.88, including overtime, bonus amounts, and staff salaries. Average wage was calculated at $.9599 per hour and camp operation costs at $1.491 per man-day. Staff and engineering overhead costs of $20,530.42 represented 8.71% of payroll.
33. "Russell Diary," 54, 58–59; Hokanson, *Man Called Swede*, 121–22.
34. A. Morrison, *Those were the Days*, 263–64. *The Em Kayan* originally published Morrison's diary account of the trip in issues February 1946 and April 1946.

Dates are "give or take a day" in both the book and the magazine issues.

35. Seattle newspaper article, n.d., quotes a visiting friend's description of the Teters cottage, copies in John R. Hoskins Collection and OFC.

36. Joe McDonald to folks, July 12, 1941, JMFC.

37. A. Morrison, *Those were the Days*, 266–67; *Wake Wig Wag*, October 16, 1941, McClary-Morrison Collection, Boise, Idaho; Peter Hansen to family, October 15, 1941, PHFC.

38. A. Morrison, *Those were the Days*, 266–70.

39. Morrison to McMenimen, October 21, 1941; "Minutes for Meeting No. 10, Wake Island," November 1, 1941, 10–11, File C-24-2A, MKR.

40. "Russell Diary," 61; Mae Dukes and June Hohner conversations with author.

41. A. Morrison, *Those were the Days*, 267; H. W. Morrison to N. D. Teters, November 5, 1941, File C-24-2A, MKR.

42. Joe McDonald to folks, October 6–24, 1941, November 3, 1941, JMFC; Peter Hansen to family, October 26, 1941, PHFC.

43. Peter Hansen to family, September 24, 1941, October 19, 1941, PHFC.

44. Chet Ratekin to "Bright Eyes, October 8, 1941; Urwin, "*Regulus* Log," October 1, 1941.

45. Peter Hansen to family, October 5–15, 1941, PHFC; Dierdorff, "Pioneer Party," 508.

46. Joe McDonald to folks, September 26, 1941, JMFC; Peter Hansen to family, September 24, 1941, PHFC.

CHAPTER 8: RUSH HOUR

1. "Ship's log of the USS *Curtiss* (AV-4), 14 October–November 1941," RG 24 NA, ms notes by G. J. W. Urwin, copy in author's possession (hereafter cited as Urwin, "*Curtiss* Log"), October 14–29, 1941.

2. A. Morrison, *Those Were the Days*, 268–69; Joe McDonald to folks, October 24, 1941, JMFC.

3. Joe McDonald to folks, November 3, 1941, JMFC; Cressman, *Magnificent Fight*, 45–47.

4. "Report of Ships Arriving at Wake Island Between 21 October and 31 October 1941," A. S. Walton to Major Devereux, December 1, 1941, NA39, RG 181, NAPR.

5. Joe McDonald to folks, October 24, 1941, JMFC; *Wake Wig Wag*, October 26, 1941, MS 351, Fol. 3, Raymond Forsythe Papers, ISHS; Richards comment on navy routing slip, November 24, 1941, NA39, RG 181, NAPR.

6. *Wake Wig Wag*, October 26, 1941.

7. A. Morrison, *Those Were the Days*, 271.

8. "Russell Diary," 61–62; A. Morrison, *Those Were the Days*, 272–73.

9. "Russell Diary," 62–63; Urwin, "*Curtiss* Log," October 30–November 1, 1941.

10. *Wake Wig Wag*, November 1, 1941, McClary-Morrison Collection.

11. *Wake Wig Wag*, November 1, 1941; Lloyd Nelson quoted in "Little Wig Wag," October 2002 and conversations with author, 2008; N. D. Teters to C. P. Schoeller, October 31, 1941, File 2E, MKR. Teters also confided his opinion of the new RoinC: "Greey is a horse's ass of the first water."

12. A. Morrison, *Those were the Days*, 274–75; G. L. Youmans to H. W. Morrison, November 20, 1941, File C-24-2, MKR.

13. *IDS*, November 11, 1941.

14. Peter Hansen to family, October 17, 1941, PHFC; *Wake Wig Wag*, October 26, 1941, November 1, 1941.

15. *IDS*, October 18, 1941, November 9, 1941; Divine, *Reluctant Belligerent*, 155; Heinrichs, *Threshold of War*, 205.

16. Clare Boothe, "Destiny Crosses the Dateline," *Life*, November 1941: 98–109.

17. "Schoeller Report," 53–55; Youmans to Morrison, November 20, 1941.

18. Youmans to Morrison, November 20, 1941.

19. "Schoeller Report," 50.

20. Col. Harry K. Pickett to COM-14, October 22, 1941; Captain Bruns to District Marine Officer, October 10, 1941, NA39, RG 181, NAPR.

21. CINCPAC, "Study on Defenses," 31–32, 41; COM-14 to CINCPAC, October 17, 1941 (copy included in "Study on Defenses"), RG 80, National Archives.

22. H. W. Morrison to W. V. McMenimen, October 21, 1941, File C-24-5, MKR.

23. "Minutes of Meeting No. 10," Wake Island, November 1, 1941, File C-24-2A; Morrison to McMenimen, October 21, 1941, MKR; "Wake Island Alphabetical List of Employees as of November 1, 1941," Pacific Island Employees Foundation (hereafter cited as PIEF), Box 116657, MKR.

24. *Wake Wig Wag*, November 6, 1941, McClary-Morrison Collection; *Wake Wig Wag*, November 9, 1941, photocopy in author's possession.

25. Peter Hansen to family, November 10, 1941, PHFC.

26. Urwin, "*Burrows* Log," November 11, 1941; "Russell Diary," 65; Peter Hansen to family, November 10, 1941, PHFC.

27. Peter Hansen to family, November 19, 1941, PHFC.

28. Joe McDonald to folks, November 20, 1941, newspaper clippings, JMFC; *IDS*, November 29, 1941.

29. *Wake Wig Wag*, October 8, 1941, photocopy in author's possession; *IDS*, November 29, 1941.

30. "Poetry Supplement," McClary-Morrison Collection; *Em-Kayan*, March 1942, 14.

31. Clint Haakonstad transcript, OH 996, ISHS; Peter Hansen to family, November 21, 1941, PHFC.

32. Dower, *War Without Mercy*, 108–09; Beard, *Appearances and Realities*, 447–49.

33. Major Devereux to COM-14, November 4, 1941; ComPatWingTwo to COM-

14, November 7, 1941; CINCPAC to ComAcPatW2, November 10, 1941, NA39, RG 181, NAPR.

34. "Schoeller Report," 5–6; OinC to Executive Committee, November 19, 1941; Executive Committee to OinC, December 1, 1941; W. V. McMenimen to Admiral Moreell, radiogram dated December 3, 1941; G. L. Youmans to H. W. Morrison, December 5, 1941, File C-24-2, MKR.

35. CINCPAC, "Study on Defenses," 16; CINCPAC to COM-14, November 14, 1941, NA39, RG 181, NAPR.

36. S. E. Morison, *Rising Sun*, 75–78; Divine, *Reluctant Belligerent*, 157–59; Kimmel, *Admiral Kimmel's Story*, 43; Schlesinger and Bruns, *Congress Investigates*, 5:3278, 3285, 3287.

37. Cunningham and Sims, *Wake Island Command*, 23–28; "Alphabetical List of Employees as of November 1, 1941," date-stamped December 28, 1941, PIEF, Box 116657, MKR.

38. *Wake Wig Wag*, November 29, 1941, McClary-Morrison Collection.

CHAPTER 9: SHATTERED ILLUSIONS

1. Beard, *Appearances and Realities*, 519, Schlesinger and Bruns, *Congress Investigates*, 5:3291-92; Divine, *Reluctant Belligerent*, 159–163; Kimmel, *Admiral Kimmel's Story*, 43; Heinrichs, *Threshold of War*, 215–16.

2. Kimmel, *Admiral Kimmel's Story*, 23–24; Frank, *Downfall*, 22–23.

3. Cunningham and Sims, *Wake Island Command*, 21–23; Cunningham to COM14, December 4, 1941, NA39, RG 181, NAPR.

4. CINCPAC to COM14, November 14, 1941; Routing slip No. 4380, November 15, 1941; COM14 to District Marine Officer, November 19, 1941; COM14 to CINCPAC, November 27, 1941; COM14 to Commanding Officer, USS *Burrows*, November 25, 1941; NA39, RG 181, NAPR; Urwin, "*Burrows* Log," November 28–29, 1941, RG 24, National Archives. These documents indicate that radar units and operating crews were indeed en route to Wake before the Japanese attacked, a fact that counters previous assertions by historians and other writers that radar was never sent to Wake.

5. Urwin, "*Burrows* Log," November 28–29, 1941; "Schoeller Report," 12, MKR.

6. Halsey and Bryan, *Admiral Halsey's Story*, 70–76; Kinney and McCaffrey, *Wake Island Pilot*, 46–49; Toland, *Rising Sun*, I:308–09.

7. "Schoeller Report," 49.

8. Ted to Mother, December 1, 1941, OFC. Blackout drills had been conducted since early November, according to orders by Major Devereux dated November 6, 1941, and printed in *Wake Wig Wag*, November 9, 1941. "Technical Report," A-505, SMPH, states in error that "there is no evidence that air-raid or blackout drills were conducted prior to the unexpected assault."

9. Joe McDonald to folks, December 2, 1941, JMFC.

10. Peter Hansen to family, November 28, 1941, PHFC.
11. "Progress as of December 1, 1941," map and accompanying documents, File 2E, MKR.
12. "Russell Diary," 69; Krupnick, *Pan American's Pioneers*, 41; Urwin, *Facing Fearful Odds*, 175–76.
13. Clarke, *Pearl Harbor Ghosts*, 38–39.
14. G. L. Youmans to H. W. Morrison, December 5, 1941, File C-24-2, MKR.
15. "SS *Lurline* Souvenir Passenger List," December 5, 1941, http://www.helianthus-productions.com/passenger.html; Clarke, *Pearl Harbor Ghosts*, 3–11, 44; *New York Times*, December 11, 1941.
16. Clarke, 35, 184; Harry to Katherine, December 29, 1941, OFC.
17. G. L. Youmans to H. W. Morrison, December 10, 1941, File C-24-2, MKR; *Em Kayan*, February 1944: 9.
18. Youmans to Morrison, December 10, 1941.
19. Ibid.
20. Heinrichs, *Threshold of War*, 219; Spector, *Eagle Against the Sun*, 96–98.
21. Toland, *Infamy*, 297–98; Prange, *At Dawn We Slept*, 465; Goralski, *Almanac*, 185; Cunningham and Sims, *Wake Island Command*, 50.
22. "The Justine Foss: Tug's wartime tragedy recalled by Drew Foss," http://home.att.net/~AIRBOY/foss1.html accessed June 10, 2008; G. L. Youmans to H. W. Morrison, December 31, 1941, File C-24-2, MKR.
23. Heinl, *Defense of Wake*, 13; Cunningham and Sims, *Wake Island Command*, 52–56; Devereux, *Story of Wake*, 42–47; Kinney and McCaffrey, *Wake Island Pilot*, 55–56.
24. Heinl, *Defense of Wake*, 11, 13–15; Urwin, *Facing Fearful Odds*, 183.
25. Wake had a total of 524 military personnel: marines numbered 449, including medics and personnel of VMF-211. The 1st Defense Battalion numbered 15 officers and 373 men (by USMC standards, Wake's batteries required 43 officers and 939 men). In addition, 68 navy and 6 army personnel maintained non-combat functions on the atoll; one unlucky sailor from the submarine *Triton* lay in sick bay. Heinl, *Defense of Wake*, 10–11, 14; Urwin, *Facing Fearful Odds*, 140–41, 183, 213–15.
26. Urwin, *Facing Fearful Odds*, 276; "Russell Diary," 70.
27. Urwin, *Facing Fearful Odds*, 254.
28. Hokanson, *Man Called Swede*, 124–25; Frank B. Miller, Jr., "Diary," December 8 [1941], transcription and copyright by James Bair, Ansonia, CT, used with permission (hereafter cited as "Miller Diary." Note: diary entries do not include year; hereafter all citations to December dates are 1941.)
29. Heinl, *Defense of Wake*, 14–15; Urwin, *Facing Fearful Odds*, 244–45, 251, 257; Youmans to Morrison, December 10, 1941 (account based on Pan American eyewitnesses); Lee W. Wilcox Diary, 3–4, transcribed by Mary-Anne Collins,

PHFC. Detailed descriptions in Devereux, *Story of Wake*, 51–53; Urwin, Ch. XVII in *Facing Fearful Odds*; Cressman, Ch. 4 in *Magnificent Fight*; and all memoirs from personal perspectives.

30. Kinney and McCaffrey, *Wake Island Pilot*, 57–59; Urwin, *Facing Fearful Odds*, 262–63.

31. Youmans to Morrison, December 10, 1941; Krupnick, *Pan American's Pioneers*, 431–32; "Testimony of Claude Davis Howes," December 8, 1941. "Guamanian [*sic*] on Wake Island," Veterans Affairs Office, Office of the Governor, Gov't of Guam, September 26, 1985, MS 738, Box 2, Fol. 11, Survivors of Wake, Guam, and Cavite Papers, ISHS, provides details on the forty-five PAA Chamorro employees. The ten who died on December 8 included a cook, two mess men, and several carpenters, mechanics, laborers, and stock clerks.

32. Daley, *American Saga*, 317–18, 508 (Daley fails to account for the Chamorro employees left on Wake); Cunningham and Sims, *Wake Island Command*, 63; Krupnick, *Pan American's Pioneers*, 436. The presence of Edward S. Clancy on Wake has not previously been acknowledged. H. W. Morrison to A. F. Noll, April 6, 1942, File C-24-1, MKR, includes a March 31 report from Noll, VP of Liberty Mutual Insurance Company, referring to Liberty Mutual's "full-time safety engineer employed for Midway and Wake, headquartered at Midway but on Wake at the time of capture;" Urwin, *Victory in Defeat*, 254, mentions Clancy's role as a civilian leader in Kiangwan POW camp; Joe Goicoechea conversation with author, December 7, 2010, confirms Clancy's presence during siege, capture, and internment.

33. "Miller Diary," December 8; "Russell Diary," 70.

34. Urwin, *Facing Fearful Odds*, 277–78, 287; Bowsher statement and roster of volunteer gun crew, December 15, 1979, Survivors of Wake, Guam, and Cavite binder, courtesy Alice Ingham, Boise, ID.

35. Cunningham and Sims, *Wake Island Command*, 65–66.

36. Donna to "Theod" and Mother to Ted, December 8, 1941, OFC.

37. Mother and Dad to Joe, December 7, 1941, JMFC.

CHAPTER 10: SHOCK WAVES

1. Daley, *American Saga*, 319–20; G. L. Youmans to H. W. Morrison, December 10, 1914, File C-24-2, MKR; Urwin, "*Burrows* Log," December 8–9, 1941. *Arthur Foss* log at http://home.att.net/~AIRBOY/foss1.html accessed June 10, 2008. The tug took twenty-two days to reach Honolulu from Wake, during which its whereabouts were unknown to Pearl Harbor.

2. "Miller Diary," December 9.

3. Dower, *War Without Mercy*, 111.

4. Goralski, *Almanac*, 188–91; S. E. Morison, *Two-Ocean War*, 80–82; Andrews, "Defense of Wake," 6.

5. Youmans to Morrison, December 10, 1941.
6. Dorothy Mitchell Urwin quoted at www.ronpenndorf.com/scrmblfeb7.html, accessed June 25, 2007, and in telephone conversation with author, May 19, 2008.
7. Youmans to Morrison, December 10, 1941.
8. Ibid.
9. Madsen, *Resurrection*, 38–43; Youmans to Morrison, December 10, 1941.
10. *Honolulu Star Bulletin*, December 5, 1941, clipping of original "Fabrics" advertisement in Scrapbook 1, Roger Smalley Collection in author's possession, courtesy of Arlene Smalley, Surprise, AZ; Allen, *Hawaii's War Years*, 55–56; Clarke, *Pearl Harbor Ghosts*, 48–50.
11. Urwin, *Facing Fearful Odds*, 288–89; "Miller Diary," December 9.
12. "Final Report, Pacific Island Employees Foundation," June 1, 1946, 15–20 (Wake CPNAB casualty list), File C-24-20-4, PIEF, Box 116657, MKR; PIEF Bulletin dated December 1, 1942, OFC; Hokanson, *Man Called Swede*, 128; "Russell Diary," 70.
13. Cunningham and Sims, *Wake Island Command*, 76–77, 80, 82; Heinl, *Defense of Wake*, 19; "Miller Diary," December 10; Hamilton quoted in *New York Times*, December 11, 1941. Battery E was moved again on the night of December 10 to a position north of the runway near the lagoon.
14. Urwin, *Victory in Defeat*, 14.
15. "Miller Diary," December 11. Details of the invasion attempt from Heinl, *Defense of Wake*, 23–28; Urwin, *Victory in Defeat*, 14–15. For further detail, see Urwin, *Facing Fearful Odds*, Ch. XX ; Cressman, *Magnificent Fight*, Ch. 5 ; Devereux, *Story of Wake*, 80–96; Cunningham and Sims, *Wake Island Command*, 85–95.
16. Hokanson, *Man Called Swede*, 131; "Russell Diary," 71; G. L. Youmans to H. W. Morrison, December 15, 1941, File C-24-2, Box 116673, MKR.
17. Heinl, *Defense of Wake*, 29.
18. Lundstrom, *First South Pacific Campaign*, 15; Ferrell, *American Democracy*, 40.
19. Graybar, "American Pacific Strategy," 138–42; Heinl, *Defense of Wake*, 20–21; Halsey and Bryan, *Admiral Halsey's Story*, 83–84; and Lundstrom, 16–17.
20. Heinl, "We're Headed for Wake," 35–38; "Russell Diary," 71.
21. G. L. Youmans to H. W. Morrison, December 19, 1941, File C-24-2, MKR.
22. Spokane, WA, *Spokesman Review*, December 9–15, 1941; FDR speech at http://millercenter.org/scripps/archive/speeches/detail/3325.
23. H. W. Morrison to Katherine, December 12, 1941 and H. W. Morrison to G. L. Youmans, cable dated December 12, 1941, OFC; Harry to Katherine, December 15, 1941.
24. B. J. Weis to H. W. Morrison, telegram dated December 8, 1941, CPNAB press release dated December 9, 1941, File C-24-1, MKR.
25. *Spokesman Review*, December 15, 1941; *Time*, December 15, 1941, December

22, 1941. On "Send more Japs," see Cunningham and Sims, *Wake Island Command*, 108–10, 145; Devereux, *Story of Wake*, 114–15, and Andrews, "Defense of Wake," 7.

26. Wake to Pearl, radiogram via Naval Communications, December 14, 1941, File 2E; Youmans to Morrison, December 15, 1941, MKR.

27. Dad and Mother to Joe, December 15, 1941, JMFC.

28. Youmans to Morrison, December 15, 1941; Madsen, *Resurrection*, 38.

29. Salvage detail in Madsen, *Resurrection*, Ch. 3; Allen, Hawaii's War Years, 104; *Building the Navy's Bases*, 2:129–30.

30. Youmans to Morrison, December 10, 1941 and December 31, 1941; Marlyn Sheik cable dated December 14, 1941, File C-24-2, MKR.

31. Youmans to Morrison, December 31, 1941; Madsen, *Resurrection*, 47–48; Heinl, "We're Headed for Wake," 36–37.

32. Discrepancies abound in the date, location, and number of remains interred in the mass burial. Most sources concur that the ceremony occurred December 11, and state that as many as eighty bodies were laid to rest, but at least two contemporary diarists affirm the burial on December 13: "Russell Diary," 71; "Miller Diary," December 15. The inflated death count must be corrected for more accurate accounting of casualties and postwar disinterment, though exact figures remain unknown. By December 13 the remains of ten deceased PAA civilians, approximately eighteen CPNAB, and approximately twenty-six military may have already been stored. Postwar disinterment of the grave accounts for approximately forty-two remains in the grave. See also Cunningham and Sims, *Wake Island Command*, 101–14 on events.

33. "Russell Diary," 71; "Miller Diary," December 17.

34. "Miller Diary," December 12–19; "Russell Diary," 71–73.

35. "Schoeller Report," 3, 6; Admiral Bloch to CINC, December 17, 1941, NA39, RG 181, NAPR; Cunningham and Sims, *Wake Island Command*, 104–05; Urwin, *Facing Fearful Odds*, 378–79.

36. S. E. Morison, *Rising Sun*, 241; Layton, *"And I Was There,"* 338–39; Heinl, "We're Headed for Wake," 37–38.

37. "Russell Diary," 73; Cunningham and Sims, *Wake Island Command*, 113–14.

38. Captain Bruns to Commander Greey, December 13, 1941, NA39, RG 181, NAPR; Cunningham and Sims, *Wake Island Command*, 113–14; Cressman, *Magnificent Fight*, 164–66. Unknown if Bruns-Greey letter accompanied the orders delivered on December 20 or if it was on a ship in the task force. Sources differ on orders.

39. "Russell Diary," 73; Hokanson, *Man Called Swede*, 134; Bayler and Carnes, *Last Man Off Wake*, 134–36; Cunningham and Sims, *Wake Island Command*, 114–15; Devereux, *Story of Wake*, 135–36; McDonald article and February 1942 documents in JMFC; Cressman, *Magnificent Fight*, 171–72.

40. Youmans to Morrison, December 31, 1941. (Woodbury, *Builders for Battle*, 323–24, quotes the letter from Teters to "George", but mistakes the recipient as George Ferris, the CPNAB Operating Committee chairman, instead of George Youmans, to whom it was sent.)

41. "Ben to Dot and Helen," December 20, 1941, and additional letters quoted in "Women of Wake," *Graphic Picture Newsmagazine*, October 1942: 6.

42. Prange, *At Dawn We Slept*, 576–77; "Russell Diary," 73; Junghans, "Wake Island," 12; Hokanson, *Man Called Swede*, 139–40; "Miller Diary," December 21–22.

43. Many sources examine the recall of the task force: see S. E. Morison, *Rising Sun*, 243–52; Layton, *"And I Was There,"* 340–41, 344–46; Halsey and Bryan, *Admiral Halsey's Story*, 84; Heinl, *Defense of Wake*, 37–39, Graybar, "American Pacific Strategy," 142–50; and Prange, *Miracle at Midway*, 5–6, 97. Cressman, 224, quotes CINCPAC War Plans Officer C. H. "Soc" McMorris admitting that "we had no more idea 'n a billygoat what Japanese forces were close to Wake."

44. S. E. Morison, *Rising Sun*, 253–54; Urwin, *Facing Fearful Odds*, 518.

45. Harry to Katherine, radiogram dated December 20, 1941; Harry to Katherine, December 29, 1941; Mae Dukes conversations with author.

46. Detail for this section on the Battle for Wake derived from Heinl, *Defense of Wake*, 40–59; Urwin, *Facing Fearful Odds*, 445–529; Urwin, *Victory in Defeat*, 17–20; Cressman, *Magnificent Fight*, 192–226; Cressman, *Magnificent Fight: Marines*, 23–32; Cohen, *Enemy on Island*, 41–45. See also Cunningham and Sims, *Wake Island Command*, 124–37; Devereux, *Story of Wake*, 147–95.

47. Urwin, *Facing Fearful Odds*, 526; Cressman, *Magnificent Fight*, 211, Records of the Pacific Island Employees Foundation, Box 116657, MKR. After the war Cunningham and Devereux cited approximately 250 civilians who had actively contributed to the defense of Wake. Lawton Shank was awarded the Navy Cross and Cunningham recommended 24 civilians for the Bronze Star Medal and 179 (including 6 Pan American employees) for the Medal of Freedom. Devereux listed 57 civilians who served with the marine detachment, some of whom received the Bronze Star Medal. Captain Winfield S. Cunningham, USN, to Secretary of the Navy (Board of Decorations and Medals), 2 May 1946, three letters of recommendation for Navy Cross and Bronze Star Medal awards and citations, photocopies in author's possession, courtesy Gregory Urwin; Cunningham to Secretary of the Navy, 3 May 1946, recommendations for the Medal of Freedom and supporting documents, photocopies in author's possession, courtesy Gina Nichols, U.S. Navy Seabee Museum; Col. James P. S. Devereux, USMC, to the Board of Awards, Navy Department, 13 September 1946, "Recognition of services of certain civilians," photocopy in author's possession, courtesy Leilani Magnino.

48. "Russell Diary," 74; "Miller Diary," December 23; Hokanson, *Man Called Swede*, 140–41.

49. Kay diary quoted in Weller, *First into Nagasaki*, 152. All memoirs recount the capture and experiences of the first days as POWs from personal perspectives.
50. "Miller Diary," December 23; Suey "Eddie" Lee interview with Lana Lee, April 10, 2009, transcription in author's possession, used with permission of Lana Lee, San Francisco, CA.
51. "Miller Diary," December 23–24; "Russell Diary," 74.
52. *Freedom* Magazine, [1942], copy in author's possession, courtesy Leilani Magnino, Petersham, MA; "Russell Diary," 74; "Miller Diary," December 25; Devereux, *Story of Wake*, 201–04; Souvenir Christmas Menu in MS 748, Box 1, John Rogge Papers, ISHS.

CHAPTER 11: FEAR ITSELF
1. Tom Hoskot to B. J. Weis, September 1, 1944, File C-24-1A, MKR.
2. Hoskot to Weis, September 1, 1944; "Progress Report No. 7, October 1, 1941, CPNAB Philippines," File C-24-1, MKR; Woodbury, *Builders for Battle*, 327–29.
3. Woodbury, 330–36; Huie, *Can Do*, 68; January 1942 lists of evacuees, File C-24-17, PIEF, Box 116657, MKR.
4. *Em Kayan*, March 1942: 12–14, S. E. Morison, *Rising Sun*, 259.
5. Bayler and Carnes, *Last Man off Wake*, 149–50; Sheik, "Midway Islands," File C-24-1A; G. L. Youmans to H. W. Morrison, December 31, 1941, File C-24-2, MKR; S. E. Morison, *Coral Sea*, 73–74.
6. Midway "Special Notice" and *Gooney Gazette*, December 23, 1941, MS 749, Box 1, Fol. 10, John Rogge Papers, ISHS; Sheik, "Midway Islands," MKR.
7. Youmans to Morrison, December 31, 1941; S. E. Morison, *Coral Sea*, 73–74.
8. Youmans to Morrison, December 25 and 31, 1941; Sheik, "Midway Islands;" Woodbury, *Builders for Battle*, 371–73; S. E. Morison, *Rising Sun*, 258; Midway damage detail in "Investigation of South Sea Islands," films from 6th Defense Battalion Fleet Marine Force, Midway, January 1, 1942, Envelope 18, No. 5, Box 5, 14ND Commandant's Outlying Islands, Photographic Records 1935–1941, RG 181, NAPR. Sources differ on Midway casualties. Shelling damaged or destroyed a seaplane hangar and PB4, a laundry building, radio transmission building, and a powerhouse where a shell exploded. The majority of Midway contractors evacuated in late December and on February 1, 1942, with only a few remaining for emergency work.
9. T. Bailey Lee to H. W. Morrison, McClary-Morrison Collection; Krupnick, *Pan American's Pioneers*, 426; Peter Hansen to family, November 28 and December 4, 1941, PHFC; Joe McDonald to folks, December 1, 1941, JMFC.
10. *IDS*, December 27, 1941; Admiral Moreell to Mrs. J. F. McDonald, December 24, 1941, and newspaper article, "His Heritage," December 30, 1941, JMFC.
11. Discrepancies in statistics abound in accounts. The author derived accurate civil-

ian figures from comparison of numerous primary records, and uses military figures provided by G. J. W. Urwin in 2010. Grave of 16 Wake defenders in Junghans, "Wake's POWs," 48.

12. Urwin, *Facing Fearful Odds*, 541–42; Ozeki, "Wake Island In Sight," two accounts, translated by Daniel King, edited by G. J. W. Urwin, at http://astro.temple.edu/~gurwin/ffoozeki.htm, 9, 15.

13. "Russell Diary," 75.

14. "Miller Diary," December 27–28; Ozeki, "Wake Island In Sight," 9, 17.

15. "Russell Diary," 74–76; "Miller Diary, January 10 [1942] (Note: diary entries do not include year; hereafter all citations to January through September are 1942); "Copy of Report Received from Frank R. Mace of Four Lakes, Wash. Facts Relative to the Defense and Capture of Wake," December 26–January 12, attachment to letter from Tom Hoskot to H. W. Morrison, October 25, 1945, File C-24-1, MKR.

16. Devereux, *Story of Wake*, 208–09; Magnino, *Jim's Journey*, 74.

17. "Russell Diary," 75–76; "Miller Diary," December 29–30.

18. Cunningham and Sims, *Wake Island Command*, 142–46; Devereux, *Story of Wake*, 201–03, 207–10.

19. Fuchs, *Hawaii Pono*, 301–05; Clarke, *Pearl Harbor Ghosts*, 164–69; Dower, *War Without Mercy*, 110–17.

20. Youmans to Morrison, December 25 and 31, 1941; Morrison to Youmans, December 31, 1941.

21. "Miller Diary," January 10–11, list following April 24 entry.

22. "Russell Diary," 77–78.

23. "Japanese Naval Regulations for Prisoners of War," MS 748, Box 1, John Rogge Papers, ISHS. Many memoirs describe the horrific voyage that followed.

24. Astarita, *Sketches*, 12–14; Magnino, *Jim's Journey*, 85–86; Ted Olson conversations with author.

25. *Portland Oregonian*, [January 18, 1942], OFC.

26. L. Burkhalter to H. W. Morrison, January 21, 1942, File C-24-17, Box 116657, MKR; undated newspaper clippings, Hoskins Collection and Smalley Collection.

27. Cunningham and Sims, *Wake Island Command*, 153–55; *Freedom*, n.d., MS 748, Box 1, Fol. 12, John Rogge Papers, ISHS; Magnino, *Jim's Journey*, 114–18; *St. Petersburg Times*, September 12, 1942; Cohen, *Enemy on Island*, 60–62.

28. *Freedom*, Rogge Papers, ISHS; Urwin, *Victory in Defeat*, 92–95; Cunningham and Sims, 156–60, includes postwar testimony of the onboard execution.

29. *Freedom*, Rogge Papers, ISHS. A caption in the article refers to 1,300 Wake men interned in this camp, although only about 30 Wake military POWs and Herman Hevenor were interned there.

30. S. E. Morison, *Rising Sun*, 257–61; Allen, *Hawaii's War Years*, 208; Lundstrom,

First South Pacific Campaign, 28–31; Halsey and Bryan, *Admiral Halsey's Story*, 84–85; Miller, *War Plan Orange*, 333.

31. Halsey and Bryan, 98–99; Karig and Kelley, *Battle Report*, 272–79; "USS Enterprise CV-6: Bombing Squadron Six Action Report—24 February 1942," http://www.cv6.org/ship/logs/action19420224-vb6.htm; Lundstrom, 34; S. E. Morison, *Rising Sun*, 268.

32. "Russell Diary," 79, 81–82, 87; "Miller Diary," January 31.

33. "Russell Diary," 87–88; "Miller Diary," February 24–26; Howes, "Testimony," February 24–26.

34. "Miller Diary," February 27; "Russell Diary," 87.

35. Morrison to Youmans, December 31, 1941. In addition to Bayler, other key sources carry exaggerated civilian fatality estimates: Cunningham and Sims, 140 (about 80 dead), and Heinl, *Defense of Wake*, Appendix III (70 dead); many secondary accounts cite those numbers. A total of 44 civilians, including 34 CPNAB and 10 PAA, are confirmed as having died during the siege and battle on Wake.

36. Frank Tremaine to Joseph McDonald, February 20, 1942, copy of Wake press release and correspondence in JMFC. Fritz Schafer was also mistakenly reported killed in the December radiogram; the family received an official letter and held a funeral in Boise. The Schafer error may have been due to the mistaken identity of Edward Slafer, a deceased office clerk. Two others who had died were not reported (Corton and Hall), and another was listed in error (Dogger), although he died later on Wake.

37. J. W. Crowe, Pacific Island Workers Association, to Member, February 12, 1942, OFC.

38. Various correspondences to Katherine Olson, OFC.

39. Cordell Hull to James Mott, February 19, 1942, appended to Mott to Olson, February 23, 1941, OFC.

40. Norman Davis to Rufus Holman, February 14, 1942, appended to Holman to Olson, February 20, 1942, OFC.

41. Morrison to Youmans, December 31, 1941; J. V. Otter to H. W. Morrison, January 14, 1942, File C-24-17, Box 116657, MKR.

42. "Wake Island Alphabetical List of Employees as of November 1, 1941," 1–20, date-stamped December 29, 1941, annotated; B. J. Weis to J. V. Otter, January 2, 1942; Otter to Morrison, January 14, 1942, March 7, 1942; and J. C. Waters to H. B. Colbert, Liberty Mutual, February 21, 1942, File C-24-17, PIEF, Box 116657, MKR.

43. "Final Report PIEF June 1, 1946," File C-24-20-4, PIEF, Box 116657, MKR; "Survivors of Wake, Guam, and Cavite" roster, courtesy Alice Ingham, Boise, ID.

44. *Report to Returned CPNAB Prisoner of War Heroes and their Dependents*, 11–12 (hereafter cited as *Report to POWs)*; Youmans to Morrison, December 31, 1941;

"Final Report PIEF." The August 1941 Defense Base Act covered workers on military bases outside the U.S., though not war zones; the Longshore Harbor Workers Compensation Act of December 1942 included war hazards, but in the workplace only, not POW camps or occupied territory.

45. CPNAB to Dependents of Wake Island Employees, February 2, 1942, OFC; "Final Report PIEF," 21–51, lists all wartime compensation paid to individuals.

46. *Report to POWs*, 12–13; American Red Cross to Bernice Hansen, May 13, 1942 and PIEF to Hansen, June 23, 1942, PHFC.

47. Report to POWs, 14.

48. "Russell Diary," 82, 88–92; "Miller Diary," March 1.

49. "Russell Diary," 79, 82 (list), 89; Weller, *First into Nagasaki*, 152–73.

50. "Report on American Prisoners of War Interned by the Japanese in Japan," Office of the Provost Marshall General, 19 November, 1945, in "The Japanese Story," American Ex-POW National Medical Research Committee, Packet #10, located in MS 748, Box 1, Fol. 11, John Rogge Papers, ISHS.

51. Cunningham and Sims, *Wake Island Command*, 173–82.

52. Ibid, 183–87.

53. Ibid, 191–97.

CHAPTER 12: HOPE

1. G. L. Youmans to H. W. Morrison, December 31, 1941, File C-24-2, MKR.

2. *Time,* April 19, 1943 and January 3, 1944; Huie, *Can Do*, 66, 81.

3. Moreell forward in Huie, 9.

4. Huie, 25–26, 83–84; *Building the Navy's Bases*, 1:133–35.

5. CPNAB Operating Committee to Executive Committee, "Progress Report May 1942," MKR; Woodbury, *Builders for Battle*, 342–43, 349.

6. Madsen, *Resurrection*, 140–42, 160–72.

7. *Em Kayan*, March 1942: 7.

8. *Em Kayan,* March 1942: 12–14, and issues April–June 1942.

9. Dye, *Hawai'i Chronicles III*, 39–40, 49–51; Allen, *Hawaii's War Years*, 121–24; June Hohner conversations with author.

10. Youmans to Morrison, December 31, 1941.

11. Mae Dukes, June Hohner, and Bethene Schlicker, in separate conversations with author.

12. James Mott to Katherine Olson, April 22, 1942, including translated Japanese cable, OFC.

13. "Russell Diary," 92, 98.

14. "Russell Diary," 92–95, 100; "Miller Diary," March 14, April 1–30.

15. "Russell Diary" and "Miller Diary," numerous entries; Junghans, "Wake Island," 17–18.

16. Hokanson, *Man Called Swede*, 152–57, 160–62; Tom Hoskot to H. W. Morri-

son, November 29, 1945, PIEF, Box 116657, MKR.

17. "Russell Diary," 95–96; "Miller Diary," April 26, May 5; Hoskot to Morrison, November 29, 1945; Junghans, "Wake Island," 18.

18. "Russell Diary," 97; "Miller Diary," May 8, 10; Hokanson, *Man Called Swede*, 157–58.

19. Joe McDonald [Sr.] to Cunningham, April 30, 1942, JMFC; Cunningham and Sims, *Wake Island Command*, 194–95.

20. E. S. Miller, *War Plan Orange*, 63.

21. "Russell Diary," 100–01; "Miller Diary," May 30, June 10.

22. Prange, *Miracle at Midway*, 133–34, 160–62, 355–57; S. E. Morison, *Coral Sea*, 151–52.

23. Hokanson, *Man Called Swede*, 164.

24. "Reduction of Wake," 5–6, 11.

25. "Russell Diary," 102–03; "Miller Diary," June 23, June 28–July 1.

26. "Miller Diary," July–September; "Russell Diary," 104–06.

27. "Miller Diary," August–September; "Russell Diary," 105–06; Hokanson, *Man Called Swede*, 169–70.

28. June 1942 correspondence in OFC, JMFC.

29. July 1942 correspondence in OFC.

30. Dad and Mother to Joe, June 18, 1942, JMFC; Mother and Father to Roger, June 6, 1942, Roger Smalley Collection.

31. Undated newspaper clippings, OFC.

32. John Polak to H. W. Morrison, June 1, 1942, File C-24-17, PIEF, Box 116657, MKR.

33. Hall letter in Appelhanz, "Hell in the Pacific," 255.

34. W. M. Pierce to Katherine Olson, February 13, 1942, and C. D. Pennebaker to Katherine, June 13, 1942, OFC.

35. "*Drottningholm* and *Gripsholm*: The Exchange and Repatriation Voyages During WWII," http://www.salship.se/mercy.asp; H. F. Bresee to Mrs. J.C. [E.C.] Ward, June 23, 1942, PIEF, Box 116657, MKR.

36. *Report to POWs*, 14; J. V. Otter to H. W. Morrison, March 7, 1942, File C-24-17, and "Final Report PIEF June 1, 1946," PIEF, Box 116657, MKR.

37. *Report to POWs*, 15, 19; "Women of Wake," *Graphic Picture Newsmagazine*, October 1942: 3–6.

38. Goralski, *Almanac*, 191; Dower, *War Without Mercy*, 80–81; Rostow, "Our Worst Wartime Mistake," *Harpers Magazine,* September 1945: 195–96.

39. Dick, *Star-Spangled Screen*, 125–27; "The New Pictures," *Time*, September 14, 1942; Urwin, *Facing Fearful Odds*, 11–12; Suid, *Guts and Glory*, 39–40; Cohen, *Enemy on Island*, 96–97.

40. H. E. Echols to the Editor (cc: H. W. Morrison), April 6, 1943, PIEF, Box 116657, MKR.

344 • NOTES TO PAGES 285-298

41. Huie, *Can Do*, 39–42.
42. Moreell, letter of commendation, June 19, 1942, and H. W. Morrison acknowledgement, July 13, 1942, File C-24-1, MKR.
43. G. L. Youmans to H. W. Morrison [partial letter, n.d., located in sequence between January 8 and March 18, 1942], File C-24-2, MKR.

CHAPTER 13: ATTRITION

1. "Russell Diary," 106–07, 187–90 (lists of 265 names of men who departed and 98 who remained on Wake); "Miller Diary," September 25–29; Leroy Myers interview with Bill Kauffman, *Those Who Also Served*, Aviator Pictures, 2002.
2. Hokanson, *Man Called Swede*, 171–72.
3. "Russell Diary," 131, 136.
4. "Fukuoka 18-B Sasebo," http://www.mansell.com/pow_resources/camplists/fukuoka/fuku_18_sasebo/fuk_18_sasebo_main.html; T. S. Hoskot to H. W. Morrison, November 29, 1945, PIEF, Box 116657, MKR.
5. "Miller Diary," February 8–22 [1943], "Final Report of PIEF June 1, 1946," File C-24-20-4, PIEF, Box 116657, MKR. Additional detail on Camp 18 conditions and deaths can be found in the diaries and accounts of Claude D. Howes, Oscar C. Lent, Otto H. Luleich, Lee W. Wilcox, and the taped memoir of Leroy Myers.
6. "Oscar Claude Lent Diary," copy in author's possession courtesy Gregory Urwin.
7. C. R. Middleton, USECC, to Bernice Hansen, October 30, 1945, PHFC.
8. Burton, *Traveling*, 81–83.
9. Burton, *Traveling*, 83–84; Urwin, *Victory in Defeat*, 322–25; Holmes, *Unjust Enrichment*, 72–73; "Fukuoka #3," http://www.mansell.com/pow_resources/camplists/fukuoka/fuku_3_tobata/fuku_3_main.htm, Frank, *Downfall*, 50, 277.
10. Urwin, *Victory in Defeat*, 250–51, 275–81.
11. "Contracts: PNAB," 24–25, 34–36, File C-24-16, Box 116673, MKR; *Em Kayan*, February and March 1944; M-K Annual Reports, Box 134094, MKR.
12. *Report to POWs*, 15–17.
13. *Report to POWs*, 17–19; *Em Kayan*, March 1944:18; Earl English to CPNAB executives, March 13, 1944, File C-24-11, Box 116673, MKR.
14. "Reduction of Wake," 6–8.
15. Ibid, 7, 10.
16. Ibid, 9–10.
17. Ibid, 11.
18. Sherrod, "Hold Your Hat Here We Go," *Life*, October 25, 1943, 27–29.
19. "Reduction of Wake," 11, 13–15.
20. Urwin, *Victory in Defeat*, 334–340. Urwin calculates death rates in captivity at 21.9 percent for the Wake contractors and 5.4 percent for Wake's captured mil-

itary personnel, compared to an overall death rate of 38.4 percent for American POWs in the Pacific.

21. Holmes, *Unjust Enrichment*, 122–26; Frank, *Downfall*, 160–61; "Final Report PIEF," 14–15.

22. Taylor, "A Move and a Chance for Escape," Ch. 14, in *Rescued by Mao*; Kinney and McCaffrey, "Escape," Ch. 8, in *Wake Island Pilot*; Urwin, *Victory in Defeat*, 277–87.

23. Various correspondence and reports in File C-24-1A, Box 116673, MKR.

24. "Reduction of Wake," 11–12.

25. Halsey and Bryan, *Admiral Halsey's Story*, 257–58; Junghans, "Wake's POWs," 44–46.

26. Frank, *Downfall*, 150–51, 262, 284; Thomas and Witts, *Enola Gay*, 275–76; Toland, *Rising Sun*, 2:988, 991.

27. Hokanson, *Man Called Swede*, 233–35; "Final Report PIEF," Box 116657; "Instructions to Returning POWs," MS 748, Box 1, Fol. 10, John Rogge Papers, ISHS.

28. Addendum to "Russell Diary," courtesy of Peter G. Russell, Ogden, UT

29. Harwell, "The Wake Story," 22–24; Junghans, "Wake's POWs," 44–45.

30. Harwell, 24–26.

31. Ibid, 26.

32. "Reduction of Wake," 18–21. The species known as Wake Island Rail, a small, conspicuous, flightless bird, became extinct during the occupation: Olson, "The Extinct Wake Island Rail," 684–85.

33. Junghans, "Wake's POWs," 44–46.

34. Junghans, "Wake Island," 22–23, and appended document, "Life on Wake Island—From a Japanese Diary," aka the "Watanabe Diary," MS 748, John Rogge Papers, ISHS.

35. Junghans, "Wake Island," 23; Junghans, "Wake's POWs," 49–50; "Reduction of Wake," 14, 21, 52.

36. E. A. Junghans to C. L. Ward, November 17, 1945; T. S. Hoskot to H. W. Morrison, November 29, 1945; N. D. Teters to E. A. Junghans, December 11, 1945, PIEF, Box 116657, MKR.

37. Junghans, "Wake Island," 23–24; Junghans, "Wake's POWs," 49–51; "6 Japs Hanged," *Navy News*, Guam Edition, Vol. 3, No. 171, June 20, 1947, photocopy in author's possession, courtesy Herb Brown.

38. "Final Report PIEF;" "Rear Admiral Shigematsu Sakaibara, Imperial Japanese Navy, et all, Trial by Military Commission in the Marshall Islands," partial transcript, 28–30, copy courtesy of Floyd Forsberg, Big Timber, MT; Junghans, "Wake Island," 24; Andre bracelet found by Barbara Bowen; Wake Island; Wake Island Museum artifact inventory and photographs, courtesy Kurt Schweigert, Golden, CO.

39. See Appendix II, note 1, for sources for final casualty statistics. In addition, "Guamanian [*sic*] on Wake Island," Veterans Affairs Office, Government of Guam, MS 738, Box 2, Fol. 11, Survivors of Wake, Guam, and Cavite Papers, ISHS; various correspondence with G. J. W. Urwin.

APPENDIX II

1. Survivors of Wake, Guam, and Cavite Papers, MS 738, ISHS, Boise, ID, and additional records courtesy Alice Ingham, Boise, ID; Pacific Island Employees Foundation records, Box 116657, MKR, URS Corp., Boise, ID; A Report to Returned CPNAB Prisoner of War Heroes and their Dependents, 1945 (contains errors); "War Diary of Leal Henderson Russell 1940–1945;" Records of Group Burial 4568 GB#71, National Memorial Cemetery of the Pacific and memorial plaque, July 1953, Honolulu, HI (Gibbons, Higdon, and Miles interred in separate graves in NMCP; McGallister is listed by legal name of Charters); Joint POW-MIA Accounting Command records, JBPHH, HI; Wake Island civilian memorial plaque, Wake Island; Center For Research: Allied POWs under the Japanese: POW camp records used with permission of the late Roger Mansell, http://www.mansell.com/pow-index.html, Palo Alto, CA.

WORKS CITED

<hr>

(Note: this is not a comprehensive Wake Island bibliography; there are many additional primary and secondary accounts.)

PERSONAL PAPERS, MANUSCRIPTS, AND DATABASES:

Appelhanz, Charles, "Hell in the Pacific: American Civilian Workers, Wake Island, and Japanese Internment." Copyright 2001, privately printed, Topeka, KS.

"Center for Research: Allied POWs under the Japanese," Roger Mansell, Director, Palo Alto, CA. http://www.mansell.com/pow-index.html.

Hansen, Peter W., Collection, including letters and documents, in possession of Mary-Anne Collins, Houston, TX.

Hoskins, John R., Collection, including letters, documents, artifacts, and memoir, in possession of Artys Hoskins, Spokane, WA.

Junghans, E. A., "Wake Island 1568–1946," in John Rogge Papers, MS 748, Idaho State Historical Society, Boise, ID.

McDonald, Joseph F., Jr., Collection, including letters and documents, in possession of Joseph F. McDonald III, Idaho Falls, ID.

Miller, Frank B., Jr., Diary, copyright 2006 by James Bair, Ansonia, CT.

Russell, Leal H., Diary, copyright 1987 by Stephanie Russell Persson, Littleton, CO.

Smalley, Roger H., Collection, including letters and scrapbooks, in author's possession, courtesy of Arlene Smalley, Surprise, AZ.

Urwin, Gregory J. W., Ship Log notes, RG 24, copy in author's possession.

COLLECTIONS IN PRIVATE AND PUBLIC DEPOSITORIES:

Morrison-Knudsen Company Records, Boxes 116673, 116657, 164094, and *Em Kayan* Collection, URS Corp., Boise, ID.

Raymond Forsythe Papers, MS 351, Idaho State Historical Society Public Archives and Research Library, Boise, ID.

John D. Rogge Papers, MS 748, Idaho State Historical Society Public Archives and Research Library, Boise, ID.

Survivors of Wake, Guam, and Cavite Papers, MS 738, Idaho State Historical Society Public Archives and Research Library, Boise, ID.

Records of the Bureau of Yards and Docks: Contracts, NOy Contracts, RG 12.

Geographical Files: Wake Island, General Information, RG 5, U.S. Navy Seabees Museum, Port Hueneme, CA.

Records of the Bureau of Naval Personnel: Logs of U.S. Naval Ships and Stations, 1801–1946, RG 24, National Archives, Washington DC.

General Records of the Department of the Navy, 1798–1947: Records of the Secretary of the Navy, RG 80, National Archives, Washington DC.

Records of Naval Districts and Shore Establishments: 14th Naval District Headquarters (Pearl Harbor, HI), Commandant's Office, Classified Correspondence, 1912–1941 (Declassified NND 803006); General Correspondence (formerly classified) 1935–1942 (Declassified NND 868167 and 868128); Marine Corps Plans for Defense of Various Islands (formerly classified) 1939–1941 (Declassified NND 868169); Progress Photographs, Outlying Islands 1935–1942 (Declassified NND 868130), RG 181, National Archives and Records Administration – Pacific Region (San Francisco).

BOOKS, ARTICLES, AND FILM:

Allen, Gwenfread. *Hawaii's War Years, 1941–1945*. 1950. Reprint, Kailua, HI: Pacific Monograph, 1999.

Andrews, Peter, "The Defense of Wake." *American Heritage*, July/August 1987, 65–80. Reprint: http://www.americanheritage.com/content/defense-wake.

Astarita, Joseph, *Sketches of POW Life*. New York: Rollo Press, 1947.

Bayler, Walter L. J. and Cecil Carnes. *Last Man off Wake Island*. Indianapolis: The Bobbs-Merrill Co., 1943.

Beard, Charles A. *Appearances and Realities: President Roosevelt and the Coming of the War, 1941*. 1948. Reprint, New Brunswick: Transaction Publishers, 2003.

Bonny, J. B. *Morrison-Knudsen Company, Inc.: Fifty Years of Construction Progress*. New
York: Newcomen Society of North America, 1962.

Boothe, Clare. "Destiny Crosses the Dateline." *Life*, November 3, 1941, 98–109.

Building the Navy's Bases during World War II: History of the Bureau of Yards and Docks and the Civil Engineering Corps 1940–1946. 2 vols. Washington DC: U.S. Government Printing Office, 1947. http://www.ibiblio.net/hyperwar/USN/Building_Bases/index.html.

Burton, John H. *Traveling Life's Twisting Trails*. New York: Vantage Press, 1965.

Clarke, Thurston. *Pearl Harbor Ghosts: The Legacy of December 7, 1941*. New York: The Ballantine Publishing Group, 2001.

Cohen, Stan. *Enemy on Island, Issue in Doubt: The Capture of Wake Island*. Missoula: Pictorial Histories Publishing Co., 1983.

Cressman, Robert J. *"A Magnificent Fight:" The Battle for Wake Island*. Annapolis: Naval Institute Press, 1995.

_____. *A Magnificent Fight: Marines in the Battle for Wake Island*. Marines in World War II Commemorative Series. Washington DC: Marine Corps Historical Center, 1992.

Cunningham, W. Scott with Lydel Sims. *Wake Island Command*. Boston: Little, Brown, and Co., 1961.

Daley, Robert. *An American Saga: Juan Trippe and his Pan American Empire*. New York: Random House, 1980.

Devereux, James P.S. *The Story of Wake Island*. 1947. Reprint, Nashville: The Battery Press, 1997.

Dick, Bernard F. *The Star-Spangled Screen: The American World War II Film*. Lexington: University Press of Kentucky, 1985.

Dierdorff, Ross A. "Pioneer Party—Wake Island." United States Naval Institute *Proceedings* 69 (April 1943): 499–508.

Divine, Robert A. *The Reluctant Belligerent: American Entry into World War II*, 2nd Ed. New York: John Wiley & Sons, Inc., 1979.

Dower, John W. *War Without Mercy: Race and Power in the Pacific War*. New York: Pantheon Books, 1986.

Dye, Bob, ed. *Hawai'i Chronicles III: World War Two in Hawaii, from the pages of Paradise of the Pacific*. Honolulu: University of Hawaii Press, 2000.

"The Earth Movers I – III." *Fortune* (August, September, October 1943).

Ferrell, Robert H. *American Diplomacy: The Twentieth Century*. New York: W.W. Norton & Co., Inc., 1988.

Frank, Richard B. *Downfall: The End of the Imperial Japanese Empire*. New York: Random House, 1999.

Fuchs, Lawrence H. *Hawaii Pono: A Social History*. New York: Harcourt Brace Jovanovich, 1961.

Goralski, Robert. *World War II Almanac 1931–1945: A Political and Military Record*. New York: Bonanza Books, 1981.

Graybar, Lloyd J. "American Pacific Strategy After Pearl Harbor: The Relief of Wake Island." *Prologue: The Journal of the National Archives* 12 (Fall 1980): 134–150.

Grooch, William S. *Skyway to Asia*. New York: Longmans, Green and Co., 1937.

Halsey, William F. and J. Bryan III. *Admiral Halsey's Story*. New York: McGraw Hill, 1947.

Hamm, Margherita Arlina. *America's New Possessions and Spheres of Interest*. London: F.T. Neely, 1899.

Harwell, Ernie. "The Wake Story." *Leatherneck*, November 1945, 22–26.

Heinl, R. D. *"The Defense of Wake: Marines in World War II Historical Monograph."*

1947. Reprint, http://www.ibiblio.org/hyperwar/USMC/USMC-M-Wake.html.

Heinl, Robert Debs, Jr. "We're Headed for Wake." *Marine Corps Gazette*, June 1946, 35–38.

Heinrichs, Waldo. *Threshold of War: Franklin D. Roosevelt and the American Entry into World War II.* New York: Oxford University Press, 1988.

Hokanson, Walter N. *The Man Called Swede.* 1st Books Library, 2003.

Holmes, Linda Goetz. *Unjust Enrichment: How Japan's Companies Built Postwar Fortunes Using American POWs.* Mechanicsburg, PA: Stackpole Books, 2001.

Huie, William Bradford. *Can Do: The Story of the Seabees.* New York: E.P. Dutton & Co., 1944.

Iriye, Akira. *Power and Culture: The Japanese-American War, 1941–1945.* Cambridge: Harvard University Press, 1981.

Junghans, Earl A. "Wake's POWs." United States Naval Institute *Proceedings*, February 1983, 43–50.

Karig, Walter and Welbourn Kelley. *Battle Report: Pearl Harbor to Coral Sea.* New York: Farrar & Rinehart, 1944.

Kaucher, Dorothy. *Wings over Wake.* San Francisco: John Howell, 1947.

Kimmel, Husband E. *Admiral Kimmel's Story.* Chicago: Henry Regnery Co., 1955.

Kinney, John F. with James M. McCaffrey. *Wake Island Pilot: A World War II Memoir.* Washington DC: Potomac Books, Inc., 2005.

Koistinen, Paul A. C. *Arsenal of World War II: The Political Economy of American Warfare, 1940–1945.* Lawrence KS: University Press of Kansas, 2004.

Krupnick, Jon E. *Pan American's Pacific Pioneers: The Rest of the Story.* Missoula: Pictorial Histories Publishing Co., 2000.

LaFeber, Walter. *The Clash: U.S.—Japanese Relations Throughout History.* New York: W. W. Norton & Co., 1997.

Layton, Edwin T. *"And I Was There:" Pearl Harbor and Midway—Breaking the Secrets.* New York: William Morrow and Co., Inc., 1985.

Lundstrom, John B. *The First South Pacific Campaign: Pacific Fleet Strategy December1941–June 1942.* Annapolis: Naval Institute Press, 1976.

Madsen, Daniel. *Resurrection: Salvaging the Battle Fleet at Pearl Harbor.* Annapolis: Naval Institute Press, 2003.

Magnino, Leilani Allen. *Jim's Journey: A Wake Island Civilian POW's Story.* Central Point, OR: Hellgate Press, 2001.

McPoil, William D. "The Development and Defense of Wake Island 1934–1941." *Prologue: The Journal of the National Archives* 23 (Winter 1991): 360–66.

Miller, Edward S. *War Plan Orange: the U.S. Strategy to Defeat Japan, 1897–1945.* Annapolis: Naval Institute Press, 1991.

Miller, William Burke. "Flying the Pacific." *National Geographic* 79 (December 1936): 665–707.

Morison, Samuel Eliot. *History of United States Naval Operations in World War II.*

Vol. 4, Coral Sea, Midway and Submarine Actions, May 1942–August 1942. 1948. Reprint, Boston: Little, Brown, and Co., 1988.

_____. *History of United States Naval Operations in World War II*. Vol. 3, The Rising Sun in the Pacific: 1931–April 1942. 1948. Reprint, Boston: Little, Brown, and Co., 1988.

_____. *The Two-Ocean War: A Short History of the United States Navy in the Second World War*. Boston: Little, Brown, and Co., 1963.

Morrison, Ann. *Those Were the Days.* Boise, ID: The Em-Kayan Press, 1951.

Olsen, Storrs Storrs L. and Mark J. Rauzon, "The Extinct Wake Island Rail *Gallirallus Wakensis*: A Comprehensive Species Account based on Museum Specimens and Archival Records," *The Wilson Journal of Ornithology* 123, no. 4 (2011): 663–922.

Prange, Gordon W. *At Dawn We Slept: The Untold Story of Pearl Harbor*. New York: Penguin Books, 1982.

_____. *Miracle at Midway*. Edited by Donald M. Goldstein and Katherine V. Dillon. New York: McGraw Hill Book Co., 1982.

_____. *Pearl Harbor: The Verdict of History*. Edited by Donald M. Goldstein and Katherine V. Dillon. New York: McGraw Hill Book Co., 1986.

A Report to Returned CPNAB Prisoner of War Heroes and their Dependents. Boise ID: Pacific Island Employees Foundation, Inc., 1945.

Rostow, Eugene V. "Our Worst Wartime Mistake." *Harpers Magazine*, September 1, 1945, 193–201.

Schlesinger, Arthur M. and Roger Bruns. *Congress Investigates, 1792–1974*. Vol. 4 and Vol. 5. New York: Chelsea House, 1975.

Sherrod, Robert. "Hold Your Hat Here We Go." *Life*, October 25, 1943, 27–29.

Spector, Ronald H. *Eagle Against the Sun: The American War with Japan*. New York: Vintage Books, 1985.

Spennemann, Dirk H. R., ed. "To Hell and Back: Wake During and After WWII." http://marshall.csu.edu.au/Marshalls/Marshalls_History.html#USA.

Sperber, A. M. *Murrow: His Life and Times*. New York: Freundlich Books, 1986.

Suid, Lawrence H. *Guts and Glory: The Making of the American Military Image in Film*. Lexington, KY: University Press of Kentucky, 2002

Taylor, William. *Rescued by Mao: World War II, Wake Island, and My Remarkable Escape to Freedom Across Mainland China*. Sandy, UT: Silverleaf Press, 2007.

Thomas, Gordon and Max Morgan Witts. *Enola Gay*. New York: Stein and Day, 1977.

Those Who Also Served: The Civilian Construction Men of Wake Island. DVD. Produced
and written by William F. Kauffman. Aviator Pictures, 2002.

Toland, John. *Infamy: Pearl Harbor and its Aftermath*. Garden City, NY: Doubleday, 1982.

_____. *The Rising Sun: The Decline and Fall of the Japanese Empire, 1936–1945.* 2 vols. New York: Random House, 1970.

The United States Strategic Bombing Survey. *The Reduction of Wake Island.* Naval Analysis Division, Marshalls-Gilberts-New Britain Party. Washington DC: U.S. Government Printing Office, 1946. Reprint: http://www.scribd.com/doc/70239773/USSBS-Report-74-The-Reduction-of-Wake-Island.

Urwin, Gregory J. W. *Facing Fearful Odds: The Siege of Wake Island.* Lincoln, NE: University of Nebraska Press, 1997.

_____. *Victory In Defeat: The Wake Island Defenders in Captivity, 1941–1945.* Annapolis: Naval Institute Press, 2010.

Votaw, Homer C. "Wake Island." United States Naval Institute *Proceedings* 67 (January 1941): 52–55.

Weller, George M. *First into Nagasaki: The Censored Eyewitness Dispatches on Post-Atomic Japan and its Prisoners of War.* New York: Three Rivers Press, 2006.

Wolf, Donald E. *Big Dams and Other Dreams: The Six Companies Story.* Norman, OK: University of Oklahoma Press, 1996.

"Women of Wake." *Graphic Picture Newsmagazine*, October 1942, 3–6.

Woodbury, David O. *Builders for Battle: How the Pacific Naval Bases were Constructed.* New York: E.P. Dutton & Co., 1946.

INDEX

ABC-1 Staff Agreement, 96–97
Adamson, Louis, 215, 244
Alameda Naval Air Station, CPNAB and, 35
Andre, Roland A., 156
Army-Navy "E" award, 293
Arthur Foss (tugboat), 114, 170, 187, 199, 209
Asama Maru (Japan), 273, 281
Atlantic Charter/Conference, 122
atomic bomb, 301–302
Australia, 142, 158, 219, 240, 241, 254, 256, 274, 286
Axis. *See individual countries*

B-17s, Flying Fortresses, 1, 121, 129, 141–143, 162, 163, 177
B-24s, Liberators, 163, 275, 295
B-29s, Superfortresses, 291, 302
Balchen, Bernt, 95
Barbers Point, 267
Barrett, Thomas, 90–92, 180, 192–193, 195–196, 213, 222, 237
Base Force Salvage Organization, 223–224
Bataan Death March, 274, 298
Bayler, Walter L. J., 228, 229, 231, 241, 257, 304
Bellinger, Patrick N. L., 116
Bennington (USS), 20
Bishop's Point, 40

Bloch, Claude C.: channel and, 116; Cunningham and, 186; dredging work and, 227; evacuation of women and, 158; Hawaii and, 139; Kimmel and, 178; marines and, 136; public works and, 41; radar and, 186–187; submarine base and, 146; supplies and, 130; transportation and, 114; Wake's role and, 99; war plans and, 140–141, 219
Bockscar (B-29), 302
Boise, ID, 83–84, 129, 154–155, 165, 175, 221, 224, 268, 315. *See also* CPNAB employment office, Boise, ID; Morrison-Knudsen Company; Pacific Island Workers' Association (PIWA)
bomb shelters, 149, 240, 255, 269, 272, 306
Bonamy, Jack, 71, 76
Bonneville Dam, 13, 45, 50, 61, 85, 157
Boothe, Claire, 168
Bowsher, Walter A., 206
Brewster Buffalos, 208, 242
Britain, 14, 49, 63–64, 96, 102, 106, 121, 128, 210, 286. *See also* London
Brown, Herb, 126
Bruns, Henry: arrival on Wake of, 133; defense plans and, 228; dredging work and, 226; magazines and, 149; on Midway, 69; order from, 177; reports to, 229; role of, 41–42; ship channel